Methuen's Manuals of Psychology

(Founder editor C.A. Mace 1946-68)
General Editor H.J. Butcher

Readings in Human Memory

Also by John M. Gardiner, in collaboration with Zofia Kaminska:
First Experiments in Psychology (in Essential
Psychology: General editor, Peter Herriot)

Readings in
Human Memory

John M. Gardiner

METHUEN & CO LTD
11 New Fetter Lane
London EC4P 4EE

First published in 1976
By Methuen & Co Ltd
11 New Fetter Lane, London EC4P 4EE
Printed in Canada
By Web Offset Publications
Don Mills, Ontario

Editorial matter
©John M. Gardiner 1976

ISBN 0 416 79210 3 (hardback)
ISBN 0 416 79220 0 (paperback)

Contents

Acknowledgements

For permission to reprint the readings in this book, the editor and publishers thank the following sources:

Reading 1	American Psychological Association and Nancy C. Waugh
Reading 2	Academic Press, Richard C. Atkinson and Richard M. Shiffrin
Reading 3	Academic Press and Murray Glanzer
Reading 4	Academic Press and Fergus I.M. Craik
Reading 5	American Psychological Association and Walter Kintsch
Reading 6	Academic Press and Harvey G. Shulman
Reading 7	American Psychological Association and Dewey Rundus
Reading 8	American Psychological Association and Michael I. Posner
Reading 9	American Psychological Association and Neal E.A. Kroll
Reading 10	American Psychological Association and Delos D. Wickens
Reading 11	American Psychological Association and Moshe Anisfeld
Reading 12	American Psychological Association and James J. Jenkins
Reading 13	American Psychological Association and Endel Tulving
Reading 14	American Psychological Association and Norman J. Slamecka
Reading 15	Academic Press and Endel Tulving
Reading 16	Academic Press and Endel Tulving
Reading 17	American Psychological Association and Michael J.A. Howe
Reading 18	Academic Press and John D. Bransford
Reading 19	Academic Press and Allan M. Collins
Reading 20	American Psychological Association and Benson Schaeffer
Reading 21	Academic Press and Roger Brown

General introduction

The study of memory processes has undergone a profound transformation during the last ten to fifteen years. During this time, we have witnessed the partial replacement of one general theoretical structure by another. At present, there is no single accepted view which spans the entire field. We are, perhaps, in the midst of what Kuhn (1970) has termed a paradigm shift. This shift is due largely to the wholesale importation of information-processing concepts from the field of computer science. Traditional associationism, with its stimulus—response orientation, no longer dominates the study of memory processes.

This transformation manifests itself in several ways. It is reflected in the increasing usage of the term 'memory' itself, rather than the more traditional label 'verbal learning'. It is reflected in the terminology and language employed in the journals. Twenty years ago words such as storage, buffer, code, capacity, search, and retrieval would have conveyed little to the student of memory processes. The journals then were crowded with terms such as acquisition, retention, interference, and response competition. However, more is involved than the simple exchange of one set of verbal labels for another. In essence, what has changed is the ideational framework, or set of orienting attitudes, which govern the direction and flavour of research in the area.

Thus questions and problems which seem of central relevance to the traditional associationist may have little or no relevance to the information-processing theorist. New questions, new problems, take their place. Hence the adoption of the information-processing view of memory has led to the discovery of a wide variety of previously unknown phenomena, to the introduction of a new range of experimental techniques, and to a considerable broadening in the scope of what appear to be the relevant and important theoretical issues.

It would be misleading to imply, however, that the more traditional associationist approach has undergone anything like a total eclipse. As Tulving and Madigan (1970) point out in their trenchant review, the two 'sub-cultures' coexist side by side. Nor should it be imagined that the 'conflict' between the two approaches is of the kind which permits any empirical or theoretical resolution of their differences. While there may well be areas in which some 'dialogue' between the two can be useful, essentially the differences are a matter of strategy, reflecting considerations as to which general approach is likely to be of greater heuristic value in furthering our understanding of memory processes.

This set of readings is concerned exclusively with the fruits of the information-processing approach. The readings have been grouped, somewhat arbitrarily, under three major headings: two-store models of memory; dimensions of encoding; organization and semantic memory. The rationale behind this division is the notion that these sections reflect some of the most important 'growth areas' of research in human memory during the last ten or so years. Separate introductions are provided for each of the three parts, and it is hoped that the articles selected will prove a useful basis for seminars and tutorial teaching, as well as for private study. To this end, the articles within each section are, in many cases, grouped in twos or threes centring around fairly closely related topics. In all but one case (Atkinson and Shiffrin, 1968) the articles are reprinted here in their entirety, as published originally by the authors.

This book is intended also to be a companion volume to Peter Herriot's *Attributes of Memory* (1974). The main purpose of Herriot's text is to provide second and third year undergraduate students with an up-to-date account of those recent developments in memory research which stem from the information-processing approach. The present volume permits the student to consult, without the necessity of conducting his own 'search' through the journals, a selection of the original sources which Herriot discussed in his text. Broadly speaking, while Herriot's account focuses mainly on the study of coding processes, the readings give greater weight to two-store models of memory. Herriot discusses the readings in Part 1 in chapters 1 and 7; those in Part 2 in chapters 2, 3, and 4; those in Part 3 in chapters 5 and 6.

Readings in Human Memory was initiated by Peter Herriot and I am grateful to him for his advice and encouragement throughout the preparation of the book. I am indebted also to Grant McIntyre for smoothing the path to publication, and to Mary Keane for secretarial assistance. Finally, I thank those whose co-operation made this book possible: the authors and original publishers of the articles reproduced here.

References

ATKINSON, R.C. and SHIFFRIN, R.M. (1968). Human memory: A proposed system and its control processes. In K.W. Spence and J.T. Spence (eds.) *The Psychology of Learning and Motivation* 2 New York: Academic Press.

HERRIOT, P. (1974) *Attributes of Memory* London: Methuen.

KUHN, T.S. (1970) *The Structure of Scientific Revolutions* (2nd ed.) Chicago: University Press.

TULVING, E. and MADIGAN, S.A. (1970) Memory and verbal learning. *Annual Review of Psychology* 21: 437-84.

JOHN M. GARDINER
1974

PART 1

Two-store models of memory

Introduction

A major focus of research in human memory during the last ten or so years has been the construction of models of memory based largely on an analogy with computer information processing. Central to such models is the division of memory into several stages of processing, or separate 'stores'. Following sensory registration, two such stores have been commonly distinguished, the short-term store, or primary memory, and the long-term store, or secondary memory. It is important to note that these terms refer to theoretical constructs and not to the time at which memory is tested. Thus short-term memory performance may reflect the operation of both short and long-term memory stores.

Within this framework, research has been concentrated on defining the retention characteristics of each store, the format or code in which information is held in each store, and how information is transferred from one store to another. One of the first full descriptions of memory processing which drew heavily on the computer analogy, and which distinguished between sensory, short-term, and long-term stages in the memory system, was put forward by Broadbent (1958). Since then there has been a spate of broadly similar models, the essential characteristics of which were well described by Murdock (1967) as the 'modal' model. Among the best known and most influential of two-store models are those of Waugh and Norman (Reading 1) and Atkinson and Shiffrin (Reading 2).

The two-store or dichotomous view of memory processing has not gone without its general critics. Melton (1963), Murdock (1972), and Tulving (1968) are among those who have argued that the available evidence is equally compatible with a unitary view of memory. The adequacy of the evidence adduced in support of the two-store position has also been challenged in recent critiques by Craik and Lockhart (1972) and Wickelgren (1973).

Three of the strongest lines of evidence which favour the two-store position come from studies of serial position effects in free recall, studies of acoustic and semantic coding, and certain clinical data which show a clearly dichotomous breakdown in memory performance. These lines of evidence are reviewed in chapter 7 of Herriot's *Attributes of Memory* (1974).

The papers by Glanzer and Cunitz (Reading 3) and Craik (Reading 4) are both concerned with serial position effects in free recall. In free recall it has been widely accepted that the last few items in the list are retrieved from the short-term store and that the earlier items in the list are retrieved from the long-term store. This conclusion follows from evidence which indicates that a number of variables, such as presentation rate, time of test, and word frequency, have differential effects on the serial position curve.

Glanzer and Cunitz, for example, found that if recall is delayed by following list presentation with a rehearsal preventing task, then the superior recall of the last few items in the list—the recency effect—was eliminated. Recall of earlier items in the list was not affected. Even more dramatically, Craik found that if an unexpected final recall test followed a series of immediate free recall trials, recency items, though best recalled on the immediate test, were recalled least well subsequently. While such evidence provides compelling support for the two-store position, it is also possible to account for these results without invoking the postulate of two storage mechanisms. Jaccoby and Barz (1972), for example, argue that an interpretation in terms of the different encoding strategies adopted by subjects in order to meet the task requirements may be more appropriate.

Earlier studies by Conrad (1964) and Baddeley (1966 a; 1966 b) strongly suggested that whereas in the long-term store information is coded semantically, the short-term store utilized a phonemic form of coding. The paper by Kintsch and Buschke (Reading 5) exploits the Waugh-Norman probe procedure to show that secondary memory was impaired by semantic similarity, whereas primary memory was impaired by acoustic similarity. Kintsch and Buschke followed earlier similar studies by examining confusion errors following either semantic or acoustic similarity. Unlike Shulman's paradigm (Reading 6), the task does not require a particular form of encoding. Shulman's results suggest that the short-term store may utilize semantic coding if by so doing performance in the task is optimized. Further evidence has recently accumulated which suggests that the short-term store may hold a variety of codes (e.g. Glanzer, Koppenaal, and Nelson, 1972) and coding differences no longer seem to be valid grounds for distinguishing short-term and long-term stores.

The final paper in this section, by Rundus, reports a series of studies on rehearsal processes in free recall. The notion of rehearsal as the process whereby items in short-term store are transferred into long-term store is common to all two-store formulations. Rundus's data show clearly that subjects do not rehearse in a simple mechanical fashion. While earlier models (e.g. Waugh and Norman) focused on the 'amount' of rehearsal, there is now good evidence that neither the length of time an item stays in the short-term store, nor the number of times an item is repeated, determine how well it will be registered in secondary memory (e.g. Craik and Watkins, 1973). The focus now is on type of rehearsal, rather than amount, and on the encoding strategies which subjects utilize in meeting various task requirements.

Within the two-store position, perhaps the most general trend over the last few years has been an increasing emphasis on 'process' rather than 'structural' aspects of the modal model. This reflects a shift away from interest in the basic limitations of the memory system towards it capabilities, in terms of the strategies which subjects utilize in a typical memory task. The kinds of task which have been used in the laboratory in themselves may lead to an overestimate of structural limitations and an underestimate of potential capability, in terms of coding strategy. A danger in box models is that we may tend to think of the model in too literal a fashion. We may tend to think that subjects can only process to-be-remembered material through the 'box sequence'. Evidence which suggests that information may be entered directly into the long-term store, without passing through the short-term store, has been presented by Shallice and Warrington (1970). Current views of the short-term store emphasize control processes rather more than structural limitations, and identify the short-term store with the information to which the subject is currently attending. Such information may include information retrieved from the long-term store, and may be held in a variety of codes, depending on task constraints and task requirements.

References

BADDELEY, A.D. (1966 a) The influence of acoustic and semantic similarity on long-term memory for word sequences. *Quarterly Journal of Experimental Psychology* **18**: 302-9.

BADDELEY, A.D. (1966 b) Short-term memory for word sequences as a function of acoustic, semantic and formal similarity. *Quarterly Journal of Experimental Psychology* **18**: 362-5.

BROADBENT, D.E. (1958) *Perception and Communication* London: Pergamon Press.

CONRAD, R. (1964) Acoustic confusions in immediate memory. *British Journal of Psychology* **55**: 75-84.

CRAIK, F.I.M. and LOCKHART, R.S. (1972) Levels of processing: A framework for memory research. *Journal of Verbal Learning and Verbal Behavior* **11**: 671-84.

CRAIK, F.I.M. and WATKINS, M.J. (1973) The role of rehearsal in short-term memory. *Journal of Verbal Learning and Verbal Behavior* **12**: 599-607.

GLANZER, M., KOPPENAAL, L., and NELSON, R. (1972) Effects of relations between words on short-term storage and long-term storage. *Journal of Verbal Learning and Verbal Behavior* **11**: 403-6.

JACCOBY, L.A. and BARZ, W.H. (1972) Rehearsal and transfer to LTM. *Journal of Verbal Learning and Verbal Behavior* **11**: 561-5.

MELTON, A.W. (1963) Implications of short-term memory for a general theory of memory. *Journal of Verbal Learning and Verbal Behavior* **2**: 1-21.

MURDOCK, B.B. (1967) Recent developments in short-term memory. *British Journal of Psychology* **58**: 421-33.

MURDOCK, B.B. (1972) Short-term memory. In G.H. Bower. (ed.) *The Psychology of Learning and Motivation* **5** New York: Academic Press.

SHALLICE, T., and WARRINGTON, E.K. (1970) Independent functioning of verbal memory stores: A neurophysiological study. *Quarterly Journal of Experimental Psychology* **22**: 261-73.

TULVING, E. (1968) Theoretical issues in free recall. In T.R. Dixon and D.L. Horton (eds.) *Verbal Behavior and General Behavior Theory* Englewood Cliffs, N.J.: Prentice-Hall.

WICKELGREN, W.A. (1973) The long and the short of memory. *Psychological Bulletin* **80**: 425-38.

N.C. Waugh and D.A. Norman

Primary memory

Reprinted from *Psychological Review* (1965)
72 (2):89-104.

A model for short-term memory is described and evaluated. A variety of experimental data are shown to be consistent with the following statements. (a) Unrehearsed verbal stimuli tend to be quickly forgotten because they are interfered with by later items in a series and not because their traces decay in time. (b) Rehearsal may transfer an item from a very limited primary memory store to a larger and more stable secondary store. (c) A recently perceived item may be retained in both stores at the same time. The properties of these 2 independent memory systems can be separated by experimental and analytical methods.

It is a well-established fact that the longest series of unrelated digits, letters, or words that a person can recall verbatim after one presentation seldom exceeds 10 items. It is also true, however, that one can nearly always recall the most recent item in a series, no matter how long the series—but only if this item may be recalled immediately, or if it may be rehearsed during the interval between its presentation and recall. Otherwise it is very likely to be lost. If we may assume that attending to a current item precludes reviewing a prior one, we can say that the span of immediate memory must be limited in large part by our inability to rehease, and hence retain, the early items in a sequence while attempting to store the later ones. Our limited memory span would then be but one manifestation of our general inability to think about two things at the same time.

Why should an unrehearsed item in a list be forgotten so swiftly? Is its physiological trace in some sense written over by the traces of the items that follow it? Or does this trace simply decay within a brief interval, regardless of how that interval is filled? Tradition, in the guise of interference theory, favors the first explanation (McGeoch, 1932; Postman, 1961), although some psychologists now think that new memory traces must fade autonomously in time (Brown, 1958; Conrad, 1957; Hebb, 1949). Until now, no one has reported any data which clearly contradict either of these ideas. In fact, when we first considered the problem of the instability of recent memory traces, we thought it entirely possible that both decay and interference operate over brief retention intervals to produce forgetting, and we therefore designed an experiment to weigh their respective effects.

The results of this experiment were unexpectedly straightforward—and seemingly inconsistent with certain other existing data on immediate retention. We have been able, however, to formulate a simple quantitative model which relates our results to those reported by other investigators. What began as an attempt to evaluate two very general hypotheses about the forgetting of recent events has therefore resulted in a specific theory of short-term memory.

We shall describe our experiment in Section I below. A major portion of this paper, Section II, will be concerned with the description and application of our model. In Section III we shall discuss this model in relation to the general question of whether short- and long-term retention represent distinguishably different psychological processes.

I. Probe-Digit Experiment

Our experiment was designed to measure the recall of a minimally rehearsed verbal item as a joint function of the number of seconds and the number of other items following its presentation. The general procedure was as follows. Lists of 16 single digits were prepared with the aid of a standard table of random numbers, under the constraint that no digit should appear more than twice in a row. The last digit in every list was one that had occurred exactly once before, in Position 3, 5, 7, 9, 10, 11, 12, 13, or 14. On its second appearance, this "probe-digit" was a cue for the recall of the digit that had followed it initially.

The lists were recorded on two magnetic tapes; they were read in a monotone voice by a male speaker at a constant rate of either one or four digits per second. Each of the nine possible probe-digit positions was tested 10 times. The two tapes accordingly contained 90 test lists (plus 8 practice lists) apiece, all read at the same rate. The last digit in every list, the probe-digit, was accompanied by a high-frequency tone to aid the subject in detecting the end of the list. The position of the initial presentation of the probe varied randomly from list to list on each of the two tapes.

The subject's task was to write down the digit that had followed the probe digit in the list, guessing if he did not know. Since the probe-digit was unique in Positions 1 through 15, there was only one possible correct answer on any trial. Every subject listened to the list through earphones for a total of 12 experimental sessions, 6 with each tape, alternating between fast and slow lists. The first session under each condition and the first eight lists listened to in each session were considered to be practice and, unknown to the subject, were not scored.

The subjects received explicit instructions to control rehearsal by "thinking only of the last digit you have heard and never of any of the earlier ones." These instructions were repeated before the second session, and occasional reminders were given throughout the course of the experiment. Thus, the subjects were to rehearse every item during the interitem interval immediately following it. Our instructions were not designed to eliminate the rehearsal of single items as such, but rather to eliminate the rehearsal of *groups* of digits. The experiment actually tested the retention of a digit pair, the probe-digit and its successor. The retention of this pair should be independent of the interitem interval, if the instructions to avoid grouping were followed faithfully. We hoped, in effect, to test the retention of unrehearsed pairs of digits under two rates of presentation.

The subjects were four Harvard undergraduates, three males and one female.

The responses were scored and analyzed to yield a serial position curve for each rate of presentation, relating the relative frequency of an item's correct recall to its distance from the end of the list. A comparison of the two functions allows us to assess the relative effects of decay and interference on short-term forgetting, according to the following line of reasoning. Consider the recall of Item i from the end of the line. If the list was read at the rate of one item per second, then i items would have intervened, and i seconds would have elapsed between the time the subject heard the item and the time he attempted to recall it. (We count the second appearance of the probe-digit as an intervening event.) If the items were read at the rate of four per second, on the other hand, then only $i/4$, rather than i, seconds would have elapsed between the occurrence of Item i and the subject's attempt to recall it. A total of i other items would, of course, still have intervened between these two events. Therefore, if the probability of recalling Item i from the end of a slow list were identical with the probability of recalling Item $4i$ from a fast list, we could conclude that recent memory traces decay in time, independently of one another. Conversely, if the probability of recalling Item i were invariant with rate of presentation, we could conclude that rapid forgetting is caused primarily by retroactive interference.

The results of the experiment are shown in Figure 1. The scores for the individual subjects are presented in Figures 1A and 1B. The pooled data, corrected for guessing, are shown in Figure 1C.[1] Each point in Figures 1A and 1B is based on 50 observations; each point in Figure 1C, on 200. It is evident that there are consistent differences among subjects, but little interaction between subjects and serial positions. Furthermore, although there appears to be a slight interaction between relative frequency of recall, or $R(i)$, and rate of presentation, it is clear that the effect of rate is relatively small compared to the effect of serial position. The main source of forgetting in our experiment was interference.

The differences between the two sets of points shown in Figure 1C are not statistically reliable, according to an analysis of variance performed on the number of items recalled by each subject at each value of i under the two rates of presentation ($F < 1$ for the mean square between rates tested against the interaction between subjects and rates). This conclusion is

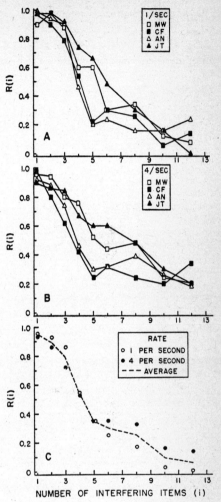

Fig. 1. Results of the probe-digit experiment. (Figures 1A and 1B represent retention functions for individual subjects under two rates of presentation; in Figure 1C these data have been pooled.)

borne out by the results of nine Kolmogorov-Smirnov two-sample tests, one for each value of i, performed on the distributions of number of items recalled per subject per session under the two rates of presentation. We have therefore fitted the points shown in Figure 1C with a function that represents the probability of recalling

---

[1] The response set—the 10 digits—was known to the subjects, and they knew that the probe would not be the same as the test digit. Thus the probability of correctly guessing the answer, g, was 1/9. A standard normalizing technique was used to eliminate the effects of guessing from the data, namely, $p(\text{recall}) = [p(\text{correct}) - g]/(1 - g)$.

Item i from the end of a series, estimated across rates of presentation. This function decreases monotonically with i, attaining a value of about .07 at $i = 12$.

II. MODEL FOR PRIMARY MEMORY

When we compared the foregoing results with the typical outcome of the first trial in a standard list-learning experiment, we found ourselves facing two dilemmas. In the first place, it often happens that an item in a long list is recalled after 10 or 20, or even more, items have followed it. But in our experiment, probability of recall was effectively zero for the eleventh item in from the end of a list. In the second place, various investigators have shown that probability of recall increases with presentation time (see Posner, 1963), yet in our experiment this probability, for all practical purposes, was independent of the rate at which the digits were read.

In seeking for a way to account for these discrepancies, it occurred to us that one difference between our experiment and previous ones in this area is that we instructed our subjects not to think about any item in a list once the next had been presented. This instruction to avoid rehearsal is, to be sure, rather unorthodox, although not completely without precedent (Underwood & Keppel, 1962). In order to minimize rehearsal, many experimenters try to keep the subject so busy that he does not have time to rehearse; but we think it highly likely that a well-motivated subject who is trying to learn a list will rehearse unless specifically enjoined from doing so. The typical subject's account of how he learns a list (Bugelski, 1962; Clark, Lansford, & Dallenbach, 1960) bears us out on this point. In fact, it is probably very difficult *not* to rehearse material that one is trying to memorize.

We shall assume here that rehearsal simply denotes the recall of a verbal item—either immediate or delayed, silent or overt, deliberate or involuntary. The initial perception of a stimulus probably must also qualify as a rehearsal. Obviously a very conspicuous item or one that relates easily to what we have already learned can be retained with a minimum of conscious effort. We assume that relatively homogeneous or unfamiliar material must, on the other hand, be deliberately rehearsed if it is to be retained. Actually, we shall not be concerned here with the exact role of rehearsal in the memorization process. We are simply noting that, in the usual verbal-learning experiment, the likelihood that an item in a homogeneous list will be recalled tends to increase with the amount of time available for its rehearsal. The probe-digit experiment has shown, conversely, that material which is not rehearsed is rapidly lost, regardless of the rate at which it is presented. It is as though rehearsal transferred a recently perceived verbal item from one memory store of very limited capacity to another more commodious store from which it can be retrieved at a much later time.

We shall follow James (1890) in using the terms *primary* and *secondary memory* (PM and SM) to denote the two stores. James defined these terms introspectively: an event in PM has never left consciousness and is part of the psychological present, while an event recalled from SM has been absent from consciousness and belongs to the psychological past. PM is a faithful record of events just perceived; SM is full of gaps and distortions. James believed that PM extends over a fixed period of time. We propose instead that it encompasses a certain number of events regardless of the time they take to occur. Our goal is to distinguish operationally between PM and SM on the basis of the model that we shall now describe.

Consider the general scheme illustrated in Figure 2. Every verbal item that is attended to enters PM. As we have seen, the capacity of this system is sharply limited. New items displace old ones; displaced items are permanently lost. When an item is rehearsed, however, it remains in PM, and it may enter into SM. We should like to assume, for the sake of simplicity, that the probability of its entering SM is independent of its position in a series and of the time at which it is rehearsed. Thus, it would not matter whether the item was rehearsed immediately on entering PM or several seconds later: as long as it was in PM, it would make the transition into SM with fixed probability. (Our PM is similar to Broadbent's, 1958, *P* system. One difference between our two systems is that ours relates rehearsal to longer term storage, whereas his does not.)

Finally, we shall assume that response-produced interference has the same effect on an item in PM as does stimulus-produced interference. That is, the probability that an item in PM will be recalled depends upon (*a*) how many new items have been perceived plus (*b*) how many old ones have been recalled between its presentation and attempted recall. Thus, if an item appears in Position *n* from the end of a list and the subject attempts to recall it after recalling *m* other items, it is as if the item had appeared in position $i = n + m$ in the list, and recall was attempted at the end of the list. This assumption is rather strong, but recent studies by Murdock (1963) and by Tulving and

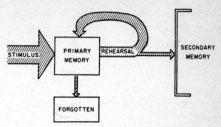

Fig. 2. The primary and secondary memory system. (All verbal items enter PM, where they are either rehearsed or forgotten. Rehearsed items may enter SM.)

Arbuckle (1963) have, in fact, failed to reveal any consistent differences between stimulus- and response-induced interference in the retention of paired associates. It may not be unreasonable to suppose, therefore, that the two sources of interference exert equivalent effects on free and serial recall.

According to our hypothesis, then, the probability of recalling an item which has been followed by *i* subsequent items is given by the probability that it is in PM, in SM, or in both. Assuming that these probabilities combine independently,

$$R(i) = P(i) + S(i) - P(i)S(i) \quad [1]$$

where $R(i)$ is the probability that Item *i* will be recalled, $P(i)$ is the probability that it is in PM, and $S(i)$ the probability that it is in SM. The probability that this item is in PM is then given by

$$P(i) = [R(i) - S(i)]/[1 - S(i)]. \quad [2]$$

We assume that $P(i)$ is a monotonic decreasing function of *i* and that

$$\lim_{i \to \infty} P(i) = 0.$$

We should like specifically to test the hypothesis that $P(i)$ is independent of the value of $S(i)$ and, in fact, varies with *i* in the manner of the probe-digit data. (This hypothesis is stated more formally in the Appendix.) In order to do so, we need data on verbal retention that meet the following requirements.

1. They should come from an experimental situation where at least some of the items are retrieved from PM.

2. The subject should have been allowed to rehearse, so that $S(i) > 0$.

3. The value of $S(i)$ should preferably be constant and independent of i.

4. The experimental lists should be long enough to let us estimate $S(i)$ for $i > 12$.

5. We should know the location of a given item in the stimulus list (n) and in the recall list (m), so as to be able to estimate the total number of interfering items $(i = n + m)$.

The free-recall experiment is well suited to our purposes. Subjects can (and usually do) recall the last few items in a list right away, and the middle portion of the serial position curve (after the first three and before the last seven items) is effectively flat, thereby providing a convenient estimate of $S(i)$ (Deese & Kaufman, 1957; Murdock, 1962; Waugh, 1962).

Testing our hypothesis against data collected in a free-recall experiment therefore involves the following steps:

1. First, we estimate $S(i)$ from the average proportion of items recalled from the middle of a long list.

2. We then estimate $P(i)$ for each of the last seven items in the list by Equation 2.

3. We plot this estimate against $n + m = i$ and compare the resulting function with that shown in Figure 1.

Fortunately, we did not have to perform a free-recall experiment especially for this purpose: several such studies have been carried out and reported

in sufficient detail to enable us to test our hypothesis against their results. We have chosen to analyze four sets of data collected by three different investigators: Deese and Kaufman (1957), Murdock (1962), and two as yet unpublished experiments conducted by Waugh. The two principal variables that affect $S(i)$ in free recall appear to be length of list (the amount of material that is to be retained) and presentation time (the amount of time available for the rehearsal of a given item). Manipulating these variables results in orderly changes in the value of $S(i)$, so that our estimates range from .08 to .45 across the four experiments.

1. In Deese and Kaufman's study, the subjects listened to lists of 32 unrelated English words read at a rate of one per second, and began recalling them immediately after the last had been spoken. Deese and Kaufman have presented a serial position curve based on these data and have also reported the relation between an item's serial position in recall and its position in the original list. We can thereby estimate i for each item in their lists, letting an item's average position in recall be our estimator of the amount of response interference (m).[2] We estimated $S(i)$ by the proportion of items recalled after the first three and before the last seven serial positions in the original list.[3] (This

[2] It is not really correct to use the average of the serial positions in recall as an estimate of $m + 1$: the total effect of response interference should depend on the variance of this distribution as well as on its mean or median. It is the only alternative open to us, however, since our correction for asymptote must be applied to the average proportion of items retained, estimated across serial position in recall.

[3] In estimating $S(i)$, we ignored the recall of the first three items on a list because

same general procedure will be followed in our subsequent analyses.)

The last seven points of Deese and Kaufman's serial position curve, taken from their Figure 1 and corrected for asymptote according to Equation 2, are plotted as a function of i in Figure 3. The dashed lines in Figure 3 represent the 99% confidence limits for the probe-digit function: a standard error for each point was estimated across subjects and experimental sessions. The uncorrected data are shown in Table 1.

2. Waugh's experiments were concerned with determining the number of items freely recalled from long lists as a function of presentation time. In her first experiment, 24, 30, 40, 60, or 120 different monosyllabic English words were read to the subjects at a rate of one per second. The proportion of items recalled varied inversely with list length, so that for each length of list there is a different serial position function. The asymptotes of these functions range from approximately .08 to .20. Median serial position in recall $(m + 1)$ was calculated for each of the last six items in a list;

they invariably show a primacy effect, perhaps the result of selective attention and rehearsal.

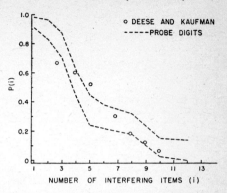

Fig. 3. Free-recall data from Deese and Kaufman (1957), corrected for asymptote and response interference.

Figure 4 shows $S(i)$ as a function of i for each of these items. The uncorrected data appear in Table 2.

In Waugh's second experiment, the subjects listened to 30 different words presented at a rate of 1, 2, 3, 4, or 6 seconds per word. In each case the presentations were either massed—that is, each word was read one, two, or three times in a row, at a rate of one word per second or of one word every two seconds—or they were distributed —each word was read once at one, two, three, four, or six different places in a list, at a rate of one word per second. The results of this experiment indicate that whether the repetitions are massed

TABLE 1

PROPORTION OF ITEMS FREELY RECALLED AS A FUNCTION
OF SERIAL POSITION AND TOTAL TIME PER LIST

Number of intervening items	List length × seconds per item						
	32 × 1	40 × 1	20 × 2	30 × 1	15 × 2	20 × 1	10 × 2
0	.72	.96	.95	.97	.97	.96	.95
1	.67	.85	.88	.89	.88	.84	.83
2	.60	.71	.75	.74	.80	.76	.71
3	.42	.51	.57	.52	.62	.62	.67
4	.32	.40	.43	.39	.58	.39	.58
5	.27	.27	.38	.33	.49	.30	.45
6	.22	.22	.38	.24	.42	.26	.45
6+[a]	.17	.12	.27	.19	.38	.15	.45

Note.—Deese and Kaufman (1957), Column 1; Murdock (1961), Columns 2–6.
[a] Entries in this row represent the asymptotic value of $R(n)$.

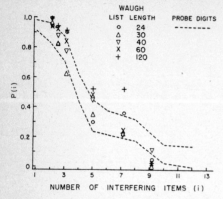

Fig. 4. Free-recall data from Waugh corrected for asymptote and response interference.

or distributed is of no importance; the probability that a word will be recalled is determined simply by the total number of seconds for which it is presented. Since this probability increases as a negatively accelerated function of presentation time, the asymptotic values of the serial position function obtained in this experiment ranged from approximately .14 (for 30 words each read once) to .45 (for 30 words each read six times). Average serial position in recall was again calculated for each of the last six items

TABLE 2

Proportion of Items Freely Recalled as a Function of Stimulus Interference and Number of Items per List

Number of intervening items	List length				
	24	30	40	60	120
0	.95	.97	1.00	.95	1.00
1	.85	.85	90	93	.95
2	.92	.69	.81	.86	.92
3	.42	.46	.51	.53	.57
4	.47	.35	.31	.32	.57
5	.21	.17	.22	.14	.14
5+[a]	.15	.17	.16	.12	.08

[a] Entries in this row represent the asymptotic value of $R(n)$.

in a list. The retention functions for massed and distributed repetitions, corrected for asymptote and response interference, are shown in Figures 5 and 6, respectively, along with the PM function obtained in our probe-digit experiment. The uncorrected data are shown in Table 2.

3. In Murdock's experiment, the subjects listened to lists of 20, 30, or 40 words read at a rate of 1 word per second and to lists of 10, 15, and 20 words read at a rate of 1 word every 2 seconds. Murdock found, as has Waugh (1963), that the probability of recalling a word that has been

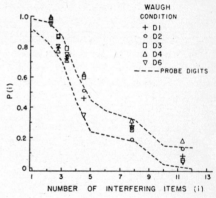

Fig. 5. Free-recall data from Waugh corrected for asymptote and response interference (1–6 distributed presentations per word).

listened to for 2 seconds is almost exactly twice the probability of recalling a word that has been listened to for 1 second. Murdock's data can therefore be grouped into three pairs of serial position curves: 10 words read at a rate of 1 every 2 seconds versus 20 words read at a rate of 1 per second; 15 words read at a rate of 1 every 2 seconds versus 30 read at a rate of 1 per second; and 20 words read at a rate of 1 every 2 seconds versus 40 read at a rate of 1 per second. Within each pair, there are two asymptotes, one of which is approximately twice the value of the other.

We have corrected Murdock's curves for asymptote—that is, for $S(i)$—and since he did not calculate serial position in recall for his words, we have plotted these corrected values of $P(i)$ against the average values of i calculated by Waugh for words recalled under similar conditions in the experiment just described (see Figures 5 and 6).[4] Murdock's uncorrected data are shown in Table 1.

It is clear that an appreciable number of the points displayed in Figures 3 through 7 fall outside the confidence limits we have set for the probe-digit function. In general, the discrepancies between theoretical and observed values of $P(i)$ appear to be unsystematic. They may have resulted from either of two possible sources which would not be reflected in the variance of the probe-digit function.

In the first place, we assume that $S(i)$ is constant for all i. While $S(i)$ does not in fact seem to vary systematically with i in the middle of a list, individual words do differ greatly in their susceptibility of storage in secondary memory: the serial position function for free recall is haphazardly jagged rather than perfectly flat. Thus, even one anomalously easy word in Location n, for instance, can greatly inflate our estimate of $R(n)$ and hence $P(n)$. The probe-digit data would presumably not be subject to this kind of variability.

A second source of errors may lie in our estimation of i, or $m + n$. We have used average position in recall—call it $\bar{m} + 1$—as our estimate of m

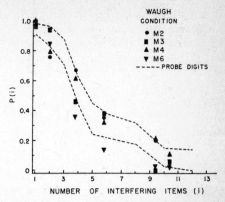

FIG. 6. Free-recall data from Waugh corrected for asymptote and response interference (2–6 massed presentations per word).

$+ 1$. Even a small error in this estimate can lead to a sizable discrepancy between a theoretical and an observed value of $P(i)$, especially around the steep early portion of the function. Errors of this sort would be reflected in Figures 4–7, where i and $P(i)$ are derived from either partially or completely independent sets of data (in Figures 4–6 and Figure 7, respectively). Furthermore, we should in any case expect some discrepancy on purely mathematical grounds between $P(i)$, where (i) is the mean of a point

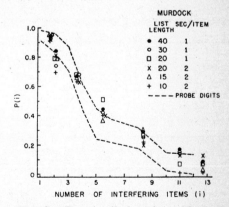

FIG. 7. Free-recall data from Murdock (1961), corrected for asymptote and response interference.

---

[4] The asymptotes for Murdock's curves were obtained by complementing his tabulated values for v (shown in his Table 2).

distribution, as in the probe-digit experiment, and $P(\bar{m} + n)$, where m can assume any of a number of values, as in the free-recall data we have analyzed. Unfortunately, we are unable to specify the magnitude of this expected discrepancy.

In view, therefore, of the likelihood of the errors we have just described, we believe that the fit between the probe-digit function and the free-recall data is fairly good and is, in fact, probably too close to attribute to chance. Actually, in one respect it is surprising that the probe-digit function should describe the free-recall data as well as it does. The probe-digit experiment tested the retention of digit pairs, whereas the free-recall experiments tested the retention of individual items. How are we justified in equating the two? One possibility is to assume that in the probe-digit experiment the subjects perceived and stored the digits as a series of overlapping pairs, rather than as single digits. In this case, the measure of interference would be given by the number of digit-pairs that follow any given pair, which is, of course, equal to the number of single digits that follow it. In the free-recall experiment, on the other hand, the subjects may have perceived the words as independent units, and the effective interference would then consist of single words, as we have in fact been assuming. The problem, then, can be restated as follows: why do pairs of digits and single words exert equal amounts of retroactive interference on like items in primary memory? There is little in the existing literature that sheds much light on this point.

Paired Associates

Our model should, of course, be able to describe ordered as well as free recall. We face serious problems, however, in attempting to apply it to serial learning: if a list is long enough to furnish a stable estimate of $S(i)$, the probability that a given item will be in PM at the time of testing is negligible, since serial items are customarily tested in the order in which they were presented. We must therefore turn to paired associates. In a recent study, Tulving and Arbuckle (1963) systematically varied the positions of the items on the recall list, and we have therefore applied our hypothesis to their data in the manner described above.

Tulving and Arbuckle presented number-word pairs to their subjects and then tested for the recall of each word by presenting only the number with which it had been paired. They were interested in measuring probability of recall after one trial as a function of an item's serial position in both the original list and the test list. We have estimated $S(i)$ by averaging the recall probabilities for $i > 13$, excluding Items 1 and 2. The value of their serial position curve is fortunately constant in this region, as it was for free recall. Note that in this task, each pair presented after a given number and before the cue for its recall actually consists of *two* interfering items: a word plus a number. We have counted all items occurring between the test item and its recall—including the test number—as interfering items. We have analyzed the proportion of items presented in Positions 1 through 6 from the end of the stimulus list and tested in Positions 1 through 6 of the response list. These proportions are shown in Tulving and Arbuckle's Tables 2 and 4; we have pooled those that correspond to a given value of i. Thus i, or $n + m$ (where $n = j$ and $m = i - j$), ranges from 1 to 11.

These data are presented in Figure 8, along with our own estimate of $P(i)$. Again, considering the variability of $S(i)$ that is not taken into account by our model, the fit between data and theory appears to be reasonably good.

In sum, then, we believe we can say that the similarity between our probe-digit function and the various other, initially disparate, serial position curves shown in Figures 3–8 is consistent with the hypothesis that there is a primary memory store that is independent of any longer term store. The capacity of the primary store appears to be invariant under a wide variety of experimental conditions which do, however, affect the properties of the longer term store.

Single-Item Retention

Much of the experimental work on memory in the past 5 years has focused on measuring the retention of a single verbal item—or of a brief list of items—over short intervals. A widely used procedure which was introduced by Peterson and Peterson (1959) is to expose an item (for example, a meaningless three-letter sequence) to a subject; have him perform some task that presumably monopolizes his attention (such as counting backwards by three's) for a specified number of seconds; and, finally, at the end of this interval, have him attempt to recall the critical item. The universal finding has been that retention decreases monotonically with the length of the retention interval. It has generally been assumed that the subject does not rehearse during the retention interval, that a number spoken by him does not interfere with a trigram previously spoken by the experimenter, and that therefore the observed decline over time in the retention of such an item reflects the pure

decay of its memory trace. This general conclusion is clearly inconsistent with our results, since we have found that the length of the retention interval as such—within the limits we tested, naturally—is of relatively little importance in determining retention loss.

In seeking for a way to account for this discrepancy, it occurred to us to question the assumption that, in an experiment of the sort described above, the numbers spoken by the subject during the retention interval do not interfere with the memory trace of the item he is supposed to retain. Some experimenters have, after all, reported that dissimilar items seem to interfere with one another just as much as do similar ones in the immediate recall of very short lists (Brown, 1958; Pillsbury & Sylvester, 1940). What would happen, therefore, if we were to define a three-digit number uttered by a subject in the course of a simple arithmetic calculation—counting backwards—as one unit of mnemonic interference? Could our model then describe the forgetting of single items over brief intervals? We have attempted to fit the data of two experimenters, Loess (in press) and Murdock (1961), by converting

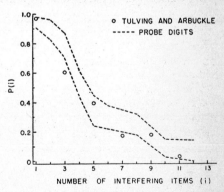

Fig. 8. Paired-associate data from Tulving and Arbuckle (1963) corrected for asymptote and response interference.

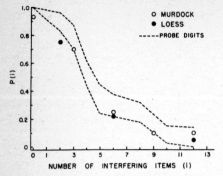

FIG. 9. The retention of three-item lists compared with the probe-digit function, (Loess' data denote the proportion of consonant trigrams recalled after various retention intervals; Murdock's data represent the average proportion of trigrams and word triads retained after a given interval.)

the retention interval into a corresponding number of interfering items. Murdock's subjects were trained to count at a steady rate of one number per second, so the number of interfering items in his experiment is equal to the retention interval in seconds. Loess' subjects counted at a rate of one number every 1.5 seconds; we have therefore multiplied the length of his retention intervals by $\frac{2}{3}$ in order to obtain the equivalent number of interfering items. We estimate $S(i)$ in both cases by the relative frequency of recall at $i = 18$.[5]

The two sets of data, corrected for asymptote, are shown in Figure 9, along with the probe-digit function. The correspondence between them is reasonably close. It is possible, of course, that this agreement between theory and fact is simply a matter of luck, depending, as it does, on the

[5] We have also tried to analyze the results of Peterson and Peterson (1959) but without success. Part of the difficulty may result from the fact that their subjects may not have adhered strictly to a prescribed rate of counting during the retention interval (L. Peterson, personal communication, 1964).

arbitrary assumption that a three-digit number generated by the subject himself is psychologically equivalent to a one-digit number presented by the experimenter during the retention interval (as in the probe-digit study). Obviously we cannot draw any firm conclusions about the effect of interference on the retention of single items until this assumption is justified empirically. We can only point out that the results of Murdock and Loess do not necessarily contradict our model.

DISCUSSION

We should at this point like to consider the general question of whether all verbal information is stored in the same system or whether, as we have assumed here, there are two independent mnemonic processes that contribute to retention even over very short intervals. The proponents of a unitary theory of memory, eloquently led by Melton (1963), have argued that recall after a few seconds is affected in very similar ways by the variables that govern recall over much longer intervals; and that therefore the distinction between a short-term memory mechanism, on the one hand, and a longer term mechanism, on the other, is purely arbitrary. The following facts have been cited in support of this argument:

1. Short-term retention improves, just as does long-term retention, when the material to be recalled is repeated before a test of retention, or when it is repeated between successive tests (Hebb, 1961; Hellyer, 1962).

2. Retention after a brief delay is subject to proactive interference, as is retention after a long delay (Keppel & Underwood, 1962; Loess, in press). Why, asks the unitary theorist, should we distinguish between short- and

long-term retention if we cannot find any quantitative and experimentally manipulatable differences between them? This question might well be disturbing if one took the position that the two processes have sharply defined non-overlapping temporal boundaries such that items recalled within some critical interval after their initial occurrence must have been retrieved from one system, whereas items recalled beyond this interval must have been retrieved from another. (Such a view would imply, interestingly enough, that an item would have to remain in a short-term storage for some specified number of seconds before passing into longer term storage, if it did so at all.)

But what if we do not require that the two systems be mutually exclusive? Then the probability that an item will be recalled will depend on both the probability that it is still in PM and the probability that it has entered into SM in the interval between its presentation and the start of the interfering sequence (or even during this sequence, if the subject is able to rehearse). All those variables that determine $S(i)$ for a given item—such as its position in a closely spaced series of tests, or the number of times it has been repeated—will then determine the observed proportion recalled after a brief interval. We believe we have shown, however, that $P(i)$ depends only on i and remains invariant with changes in $S(i)$; and we submit that most of the published data on short-term retention actually reflect the properties of both memory systems.

We would like to make one final point: the existence of some rather compelling introspective evidence in favor of two distinct mnemonic systems. PM, as we have defined it here, is best illustrated by a person's ability to recall verbatim the most recent few words in a sentence that he is hearing or speaking, even when he is barely paying attention to what is being said, or to what he is saying. Given that the flow of speech is intelligible, failures in the immediate recall of words we have just heard—errors of either omission, transposition, or substitution—are probably so rare as to be abnormal. Indeed, we believe that it would be impossible to understand or to generate a grammatical utterance if we lacked this rather remarkable mnemonic capacity. In order to recall a sentence verbatim at a later time, however, we

TABLE 3

PROPORTION OF ITEMS FREELY RECALLED AS A FUNCTION OF
STIMULUS INTERFERENCE AND PRESENTATION TIME

Number of intervening items	Seconds per item								
	Distributed					Massed			
	1	2	3	4	6	2	3	4	6
0	.96	.99	.97	1.00	.97	.98	.97	1.00	1.00
1	.82	.90	.91	.86	.89	.82	.96	.87	.91
2	.76	.81	.86	.82	.87	.75	.63	.76	.63
3	.54	.64	.73	.76	.65	.51	.58	.58	.50
4	.38	.40	.50	.57	.60	.40	.31	.51	.44
5	.21	.36	.36	.49	.48	.27	.36	.45	.44
5+[a]	.14	.26	.32	.38	.45	.25	.31	.38	.42

[a] Entries in this row represent the asymptotic value of $R(n)$.

usually have to rehearse it while it is still available in PM.

The same effect holds for meaningless arrangements of verbal items. If we present a subject with a random string of words, letters, or digits, and ask him to reproduce them in any order he chooses, he can maximize the number he recalls by "unloading" the last few items immediately. Most subjects in free-recall experiments report that these very late items tend to be lost if they are not recalled immediately, whereas items that came earlier in the list can be retrieved at leisure, if they can be recalled at all. In the colorful terminology of one such subject (Waugh, 1961), the most recent items in a verbal series reside temporarily in a kind of "echo box," from which they can be effortlessly parroted back. When an experienced subject is trying to memorize a list of serial items, moreover, he "fills up" successive echo boxes as the list is read to him and attempts to rehearse the contents of each. He will invariably lose some items if rehearsal is delayed too long or if he attempts to load his echo box with more items than it can hold. We think it very likely that the PM function describes the (variable) capacity of this mechanism. We would remind you in this connection that, within very broad limits, the rate at which someone is speaking does not affect your ability to follow his words—just as differences in the rate at which meaningless lists of digits are presented do not exert any profound effect on the PM function.

CONCLUSIONS

We have tried to demonstrate the existence of a short-term or PM system that is independent of any longer term or secondary store by showing that one function relating probability of recall to number of intervening items can describe a number of seemingly disparate sets of experimental results. In doing so, we have deliberately avoided discussing a number of problems raised in our analyses. Foremost in our list of problems is the definition of an item. Certainly the idea of a discrete verbal unit is crucial to our theory. The interference effect that we have studied seems to be invariant over a broad class of units and combinations of units—single digits, nonsense trigrams, and meaningful words. How long a string of such primitive units can we combine and still have one item? Is an item determined by our grammatical habits? Is it determined by the duration of the verbal stimulus? Is it determined by both? We do not know.

We have also avoided discussing the possible rules whereby items now in PM are displaced by later items. Are items lost independently of one another, or do they hang and fall together? It may perhaps prove difficult to answer this question experimentally, but it should not be impossible.

Finally, at what stage in the processing of incoming information does our PM reside? Is it in the peripheral sensory mechanism? Probably not. The work of Sperling (1960) indicates that "sensory memory"—to use Peterson's (1963) phrase—decays within a matter of milliseconds, whereas we have dealt in our analysis with retention intervals on the order of seconds. Does storage in PM precede the attachment of meaning to discrete verbal stimuli? Must a verbal stimulus be transformed into an auditory image in order to be stored in PM, even if it was presented visually? We refer the reader to a recent paper by Sperling (1963) for some thoughts on the latter question.

APPENDIX

A formal discussion of the interaction between PM and SM can be provided by a simple three-state Markov process. The assumptions of the model are:

1. There are three states of memory: S, P, and the null state, G.
2. The probability of recalling an item from either State S or State P is unity: items cannot be recalled from the null state, but they may be guessed with Probability g.
3. Items can only pass into State S when they are rehearsed and, for the experiments discussed in this paper, we assume that items are rehearsed only when they are presented. The probability that an item is stored in S, given that it was successfully rehearsed, is α.
4. Items in P are interfered with by later presentation of different items: the probability that an item returns to the null state on the presentation of the ith interfering item is δ_i.

The following equivalents hold between the terms defined for the Markov model and the terms defined in the body of the paper:

1. $P_i(S)$ is equivalent to $S(i)$.
2. $P_i(P)$ is equivalent to $P(i)[1 - S(i)]$.
3. δ_i is equivalent to $1 - P(i)$.

Now, define the random variable π with Value 1 if the test item is presented, and with Value 0 if some other (interfering) item is presented. (We can also let π be a probability—namely, the probability that the test item is presented. The formal statement of the model does not change with this redefinition.)

The transition probabilities for any given stimulus item (the test item) are specified by the matrix

$$
\begin{array}{c@{\quad}c@{\quad}c@{\quad}c}
 & S & P & G \\
\begin{array}{c} S \\ P \\ G \end{array} &
\left[\begin{array}{c} 1 \\ \alpha\pi \\ \alpha\pi \end{array}\right. &
\begin{array}{c} 0 \\ (1-\pi)(1-\delta_i)+\pi(1-\alpha) \\ (1-\alpha)\pi \end{array} &
\left.\begin{array}{c} 0 \\ (1-\pi)\delta_i \\ 1-\pi \end{array}\right]
\end{array}
$$

Unfortunately, it is difficult to work with transition matrices of this form (with time-varying parameters). One approximation would be to let $\delta_i = \delta$, independent of i. This approximation yields an exponential decay function of the form $P_i(P) = (1-\alpha)(1-\delta)^{i-1}$. This is clearly not correct for the results of our experiment (Figure 1); but, for some purposes, it may not be a bad approximation. A model very similar mathematically to that produced by this simple approximation for δ_i has been studied by Atkinson and Crothers (1964), who found it to be quite good for certain types of paired-associates experiments. Their model, however, is derived from quite different considerations.

For any experiments with controlled rehearsals, the probability that an item reaches State S (or SM) is completely independent of the properties of the short-term state (P or PM). This is true because, as far as State S is concerned, the general transition matrix can be reduced by combining States P and G to form the "lumped" State P'. The new matrix is

$$
\begin{array}{c@{\quad}c@{\quad}c}
 & S & P' \\
\begin{array}{c} S \\ P' \end{array} &
\left[\begin{array}{c} 1 \\ \alpha\pi \end{array}\right. &
\left.\begin{array}{c} 0 \\ 1-\alpha\pi \end{array}\right]
\end{array}.
$$

This is a simple one-element Markov model. This means that although the complete description of the verbal learning process requires a description of the short-term state, a study of only the long-term retention of items can ignore the short-term memory.

REFERENCES

ATKINSON, R. C., & CROTHERS, E. J. A comparison of paired-associate learning models having different acquisition and retention axioms. *Journal of Mathematical Psychology,* 1964, 1, 285–315.

BROADBENT, D. E. *Perception and communication.* New York: Pergamon Press, 1958.

BROWN, J. Some tests of the decay theory of immediate memory. *Quarterly Journal of Experimental Psychology*, 1958, **10**, 12–21.

BUGELSKI, B. R. Presentation time, total time, and mediation in paired-associate learning. *Journal of Experimental Psychology*, 1962, **63**, 409–412.

CLARK, L. L., LANSFORD, T. E., & DALLENBACH, K. M. Repetition and associative learning. *American Journal of Psychology*, 1960, **73**, 22–40.

CONRAD, R. Decay theory of immediate memory. *Nature*, 1957, **179**, 831–832.

DEESE, J., & KAUFMAN, R. A. Sequential effects in recall of unorganized and sequentially organized material. *Journal of Experimental Psychology*, 1957, **54**, 180–187.

HEBB, D. O. *The organization of behavior.* New York: Wiley, 1949.

HEBB, D. O. Distinctive features of learning in the higher animal. In J. F. Delafresnaye (Ed.), *Brain mechanisms and learning.* London: Oxford Univer. Press, 1961. Pp. 37–46.

HELLYER, S. Supplementary report: Frequency of stimulus presentation and short-term decrement in recall. *Journal of Experimental Psychology*, 1962, **64**, 650.

JAMES, W. *The principles of psychology.* Vol. 1. New York: Holt, 1890. Ch. 16.

KEPPEL, G., & UNDERWOOD, B. J. Proactive inhibition in short-term retention of single items. *Journal of Verbal Learning and Verbal Behavior*, 1962, **1**, 153–161.

LOESS, H. Proactive inhibition in short-term memory. *Journal of Verbal Learning and Verbal Behavior*, in press.

McGEOCH, J. A. Forgetting and the law of disuse. *Psychological Review*, 1932, **39**, 352–370.

MELTON, A. W. Implications of short-term memory for a general theory of memory. *Journal of Verbal Learning and Verbal Behavior*, 1963, **2**, 1–21.

MURDOCK, B. B., JR. The retention of individual items. *Journal of Experimental Psychology*, 1961, **62**, 618–625.

MURDOCK, B. B., JR. The serial position effect in free recall. *Journal of Experimental Psychology*, 1962, **64**, 482–488.

MURDOCK, B. B., JR. Interpolated recall in short-term memory. *Journal of Experimental Psychology*, 1963, **66**, 525–532.

PETERSON, L. R. Immediate memory: Data and theory. In C. N. Cofer, & Barbara Musgrave (Eds.), *Verbal behavior and learning: Problems and processes.* New York: McGraw-Hill, 1963. Pp. 336–353.

PETERSON, L. R., & PETERSON, M. J. Short-term retention of individual verbal items. *Journal of Experimental Psychology*, 1959, **58**, 193–198.

PILLSBURY, W. B., & SYLVESTER, A. Retroactive and proactive inhibition in immediate memory. *Journal of Experimental Psychology*, 1940, **27**, 532–545.

POSNER, M. I. Immediate memory in sequential tasks. *Psychological Bulletin*, 1963, **60**, 333–349.

POSTMAN, L. The present status of interference theory. In C. N. Cofer (Ed.), *Verbal learning and verbal behavior.* New York: McGraw-Hill, 1961. Pp. 152–179.

SPERLING, G. The information available in brief visual presentations. *Psychological Monographs*, 1960, **74** (11, Whole No. 498).

SPERLING, G. A model for visual memory tasks. *Human Factors*, 1963, **5**, 19–36.

TULVING, E., & ARBUCKLE, T. Y. Sources of intratrial interference in immediate recall of paired associates. *Journal of Verbal Learning and Verbal Behavior*, 1963, **1**, 321–334.

UNDERWOOD, B. J., & KEPPEL, G. An evaluation of two problems of method in the study of retention. *American Journal of Psychology*, 1962, **75**, 1–17.

WAUGH, N. C. Free versus serial recall. *Journal of Experimental Psychology*, 1961, **62**, 496–502.

WAUGH, N. C. The effect of intralist repetition on free recall. *Journal of Verbal Learning and Verbal Behavior*, 1962, **1**, 95–99.

WAUGH, N. C. Immediate memory as a function of repetition. *Journal of Verbal Learning and Verbal Behavior*, 1963, **2**, 107–112.

R.C. Atkinson and R.M. Shiffrin

Human memory: a proposed system and its control processes

Reprinted from K.W. Spence and J.T. Spence
(eds.) (1968) *The Psychology of Learning and
Motivation.* New York: Academic Press, **2**:92-122;
191-5

I. Structural Features of the Memory System

This section of the paper will describe the permanent, structural features of the memory system. The basic structural division is into the three components diagrammed in Fig. 1: the sensory register, the short-term store, and the long-term store.

When a stimulus is presented there is an immediate registration of that stimulus within the appropriate sensory dimensions. The form of this registration is fairly well understood in the case of the visual system (Sperling, 1960); in fact, the particular features of visual registration (including a several hundred millisecond decay of an initially accurate visual image) allow us positively to identify this system as a distinct component of memory. It is obvious that incoming information in other sense modalities also receives an initial registration, but it is not clear whether these other registrations have an appreciable decay period or any other features which would enable us to refer to them as components of memory.

The second basic component of our system is the short-term store. This store may be regarded as the subject's "working memory." Information entering the short-term store is assumed to decay and disappear completely, but the time required for the information to be lost is considerably longer than for the sensory register. The character of the information in the short-term store does not depend necessarily upon the form of the sensory input. For example, a word presented visually may be encoded from the visual sensory register into an auditory short-term store. Since the auditory short-term system will play a major role in subsequent discussions, we shall use the abbreviation a-v-l to stand for auditory-verbal-linguistic store. The triple term is used because, as we shall see, it is not easy to separate these three functions.

The exact rate of decay of information in the short-term store is difficult to estimate because it is greatly influenced by subject-controlled processes. In the a-v-l mode, for example, the subject can invoke rehearsal mechanisms that maintain the information in STS and thereby complicate the problem of measuring the structural characteristics of the decay process. However, the available evidence suggests that information represented in the a-v-l mode decays and is lost within a period of about 15–30 seconds. Storage of information in other modalities is less well understood and, for reasons to be discussed later, it is difficult to assign values to their decay rates.

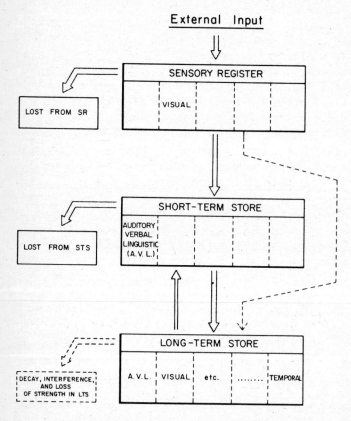

FIG. 1. Structure of the memory system.

The last major component of our system is the long-term store. This store differs from the preceding ones in that information stored here does not decay and become lost in the same manner. All information eventually is completely lost from the sensory register and the short-term store, whereas information in the long-term store is relatively permanent (although it may be modified or rendered temporarily irretrievable as the result of other incoming information). Most experiments in the literature dealing with long-term store have been concerned with storage in the a-v-l mode, but it is clear that there is long-term memory in each of the other sensory modalities, as demonstrated by an ability to recognize stimuli presented to these senses. There may even be information in the long-term store which is not classifiable into any of the sensory modalities, the prime example being temporal memory.

The flow of information among the three systems is to a large degree under the control of the subject. Note that by information flow and transfer between stores we refer to the same process: the copying of selected information from one store into the next. This copying takes place without the transferred information being removed from its original store. The information remains in the store from which it is transferred and decays according to the decay characteristics of that store. In considering information flow in the system, we start with its initial input into the sensory register. The next step is a subject-controlled scan of the information in the register; as a result of this scan and an associated search of long-term store, selected information is introduced into short-term store. We assume that transfer to the long-term store takes place throughout the period that information resides in the short-term store, although the amount and form of the transferred information is markedly influenced by control processes. The possibility that there may be direct transfer to the long-term store from the sensory register is represented by the dashed line in Fig. 1; we do not know whether such transfer occurs. Finally, there is transfer from the long-term store to the short-term store, mostly under the control of the subject; such transfer occurs, for example, in problem solving, hypothesis testing, and "thinking" in general.

This brief encapsulation of the system raises more questions than it answers. Not yet mentioned are such features as the cause of the decay in each memory store and the form of the transfer functions between the stores. In an attempt to specify these aspects of the system, we now turn to a more detailed outline, including a review of some relevant literature.

A. SENSORY REGISTER

The prime example of a sensory register is the short-term visual image investigated by Sperling (1960, 1963), Averbach and Coriell (1961), Estes and Taylor (1964, 1966), and others. As reported by Sperling (1967), if an array of letters is presented tachistoscopically and the subject is instructed to write out as many letters as possible, usually about six letters are reported. Further, a 30-second delay between presentation and report does not cause a decrement in performance. This fact (plus the facts that confusions tend to be based on auditory rather than visual similarities, and that subjects report rehearsing and subvocalizing the letters) indicates that the process being examined is in the a-v-l short-term store; i.e., subjects scan the visual image and transfer a number of letters to the a-v-l short-term store for rehearsal and output. In order to study the registered visual image itself, partial-report procedures (Averbach & Coriell, 1961; Averbach & Sperling, 1961; Sperling, 1960, 1963) and forced-choice detection procedures (Estes, 1965; Estes & Taylor, 1964, 1966; Estes & Wessel, 1966) have been employed. The partial-report method typically involves presenting a display (usually a 3 × 4 matrix of letters and numbers) tachistoscopically for a very brief period. After the presentation the subject is given a signal that tells him which row to report. If the signal is given almost immediately after stimulus offset, the requested information is reported with good precision, otherwise considerable loss occurs. Thus we infer that a highly accurate visual image lasts for a short period of time and then decays. It has also been established that succeeding visual stimulation can modify or possibly even erase prior stimulation. By using a number of different methods, the decay period of the image has been estimated to take several hundred milliseconds, or a little more, depending on experimental conditions; that is, information cannot be recovered from this store after a period of several hundred milliseconds.

Using the detection method, in which the subject must report which of two critical letters was presented in a display, Estes and Taylor (1964, 1966) and Estes and Wessel (1966) have examined some models for the scanning process. Although no completely satisfactory models have yet been proposed, it seems reasonably certain that the letters are scanned serially (which letters are scanned seems to be a momentary decision of the subject), and a figure of about 10 msec to scan one letter seems generally satisfactory.

Thus it appears fairly well established that a visual stimulus leaves a more or less photographic trace which decays during a period of several hundred milliseconds and is subject to masking and replacement by succeeding stimulation. Not known at present is the form of the decay, that is, whether letters in a display decay together or individually, probabilistically or temporally, all-or-none, or continuously. The reader may ask whether these results are specific to extremely brief visual presentations; although presentations of long duration complicate analysis (because of eye movements and physical scanning of the stimulus), there is no reason to believe that the basic fact of a highly veridical image quickly decaying after stimulus offset does not hold also for longer visual presentations. It is interesting that the stimulation seems to be transferred from the visual image to the a-v-l short-term store, rather than to a visual short-term store. The fact that a written report was requested may provide the explanation, or it may be that the visual short-term store lacks rehearsal capacity.

There is not much one can say about registers in sensory modalities other than the visual. A fair amount of work has been carried out on the auditory system without isolating a registration mechanism comparable to the visual one. On the other hand, the widely differing structures of the different sensory systems makes it questionable whether we should expect similar systems for registration.

Before leaving the sensory register, it is worth adding a few comments about the transfer to higher order systems. In the case of the transfer from the visual image to the a-v-l short-term store, it seems likely that a selective scan is made at the discretion of the subject.[1] As each element in the register is scanned, a matching program of some sort is carried out against information in long-term store and the verbal "name" of the element is recovered from long-term memory and fed into the short-term store. Other information might also be recovered in the long-term search; for example, if the scanned element was a pineapple, the word, its associates, the taste, smell, and feel of a pineapple might all be recovered and transferred to various short-term stores. This communication between the sensory register and long-term store does not, however, permit us to infer that information is transferred directly to long-term store from the register. Another interesting theoretical question is whether the search into long-term store is necessary to transfer information from the sensory register to the short-term store within a modality. We see no a priori theoretical reason to exclude nonmediated transfer. (For example, why should a scan or match be necessary to transfer a spoken word to the a-v-l short-term store?) For lack of evidence, we leave these matters unspecified.

B. SHORT-TERM STORE

The first point to be examined in this section is the validity of the division of memory into short- and long-term stores. Workers of a traditional bent have argued against dichotomizing memory (e.g., Melton, 1963; Postman, 1964). However, we feel there is much evidence indicating the parsimony and usefulness of such a division. The argument is often given that one memory is somehow "simpler" than two; but quite the opposite is usually the case. A good example may be found in a comparison of the model for free recall presented in this paper and the model proposed by Postman and Phillips (1965). Any single-process system making a fair attempt to explain the mass of data currently available must, of necessity, be sufficiently complex that the term *single process* becomes a misnomer. We do not wish, however, to engage in the controversy here. We ask the reader to accept our model provisionally until its power to deal with data becomes clear. Still, some justification

[1] Sperling (1960) has presented evidence relating the type of scan used to the subject's performance level.

of our decision would seem indicated at this point. For this reason, we turn to what is perhaps the single most convincing demonstration of a dichotomy in the memory system: the effects of hippocampal lesions reported by Milner (1959, 1966, 1968). In her words:

"Bilateral surgical lesions in the hippocampal region, on the mesial aspect of the temporal lobes, produce a remarkably severe and persistent memory disorder in human patients, the pattern of breakdown providing valuable clues to the cerebral organization of memory. Patients with these lesions show no loss of pre-operatively acquired skills, and intelligence as measured by formal tests is unimpaired, but, with the possible exception of acquiring motor skill, they seem largely incapable of adding new information to the long-term store. This is true whether acquisition is measured by free recall, recognition, or learning with savings. Nevertheless, the immediate registration of new input (as measured, for example, by digit span and dichotic listening tests) appears to take place normally and material which can be encompassed by verbal rehearsal is held for many minutes without further loss than that entailed in the initial verbalization. Interruption of rehearsal, regardless of the nature of the distracting task, produces immediate forgetting of what went before, and some quite simple material which cannot be categorized in verbal terms decays in 30 seconds or so, even without an interpolated distraction. Material already in long-term store is unaffected by the lesion, except for a certain amount of retrograde amnesia for preoperative events" (Milner, 1966).

Apparently, a short-term store remains to the patients, but the lesions have produced a breakdown either in the ability to store new information in long-term store or to retrieve new information from it. These patients appear to be incapable of retaining new material on a long-term basis.[2]

As with most clinical research, however, there are several problems that should be considered. First, the patients were in a general sense abnormal to begin with; second, once the memory defect had been discovered, the operations were discontinued, leaving only a few subjects for observation; third, the results of the lesions seem to be somewhat variable, depending for one thing upon the size of the lesion, the larger lesions giving rise to the full syndrome. Thus there are only a few patients who exhibit the deficit described above in full detail. As startling as these patients are, there might be a temptation to discount them as anomalies but for the following additional findings. Patients who had known damage to the hippocampal area in one hemisphere were tested

[2] A related defect, called Korsakoff's syndrome, has been known for many years. Patients suffering from this abnormal condition are unable to retain new events for longer than a few seconds or minutes (e.g., they cannot recall the meal they have just eaten or recognize the face of the doctor who treated them a few minutes earlier), but their memory for events and people prior to their illness remains largely unimpaired and they can perform adequately on tests of immediate memory span. Recent evidence suggests that Korsakoff's syndrome is related to damage of brain tissue, frequently as the result of chronic alcoholism, in the hippocampal region and the mammillary body (Barbizet, 1963).

for memory deficit after an intracarotid injection of sodium amytal temporarily inactivated the other hemisphere. Controls were patients without known damage, and patients who received injections inactivating their damaged side. A number of memory tests were used as a criterion for memory deficit; the easiest consisted of presenting four pictures, distracting the patient, and then presenting nine pictures containing the original four. If the patient cannot identify the critical four pictures then evidence of memory deficit is assumed. The results showed that in almost all cases memory deficit occurs only after bilateral damage; if side A is damaged and side B inactivated, memory deficit appears, but if the inactivated side is the damaged side, no deficit occurs. These results suggest that the patients described above by Milner were not anomalous cases and their memory deficits therefore give strong support to the hypothesis of distinct short- and long-term memory stores.

1. *Mechanisms Involved in Short-Term Store*

We now turn to a discussion of some of the mechanisms involved in the short-term store. The purpose of this section is not to review the extensive literature on short-term memory, but rather to describe a few experiments which have been important in providing a basis for our model. The first study in this category is that of Peterson and Peterson (1959). In their experiment subjects attempted to recall a single trigram of three consonants after intervals of 3, 6, 9, 12, 15, and 18 seconds. The trigram, presented auditorily, was followed immediately by a number, and the subject was instructed to count backward by three's from that number until he received a cue to recall the trigram. The probability of a correct answer was nearly perfect at 3 seconds, then dropped off rapidly and seemed to reach an asymptote of about .08 at 15–18 seconds. Under the assumption that the arithmetic task played the role of preventing rehearsal and had no direct interfering effect, it may be concluded that a consonant trigram decays from short-term store within a period of about 15 seconds. In terms of the model, the following events are assumed to occur in this situation: the consonant trigram enters the visual register and is at once transferred to the a-v-l short-term store where an attempt is made to code or otherwise "memorize" the item. Such attempts terminate when attention is given to the task of counting backward. In this initial period a trace of some sort is built up in long-term store and it is this long-term trace which accounts for the .08 probability correct at long intervals. Although discussion of the long-term system will come later, one point should be noted in this context; namely, that the long-term trace should be more powerful the more repetitions of the trigram before arithmetic, or the longer the time before arithmetic. These effects were found by Hellyer (1962); that is, the model predicts the probability correct curve will reach an asymptote that reflects long-term strength, and in the aforementioned experiment, the more repetitions before arithmetic, the higher the asymptote.

It should be noted that these findings tie in nicely with the results from a similar experiment that Milner (1968) carried out on her patients. Stimuli that could not be easily coded verbally were used; for example, clicks, light flashes, and nonsense figures. Five values were assigned to each stimulus; a test consisted of presenting a particular value of one stimulus, followed by a distracting task, followed by another value of the stimulus. The subject was required to state whether the two stimuli were the same or different. The patient with the most complete memory deficit was performing at a chance level after 60 seconds, whether or not a distracting task was given. In terms of the model, the reduction to chance level is due to the lack of a long-term store. That the reduction occurred even without a distracting task indicates that the patient could not readily verbalize the stimuli, and that rehearsal in modes other than the verbal one was either not possible or of no value. From this view, the better asymptotic performance demonstrated by normal subjects on the same tasks (with or without distraction) would be attributed to a long-term trace. At the moment, however, the conclusion that rehearsal is lacking in nonverbal modes can only be considered a highly tentative hypothesis.

We next ask whether or not there are short-term stores other than in the a-v-l mode, and if so, whether they have a comparable structure. A natural approach to this problem would use stimuli in different sense modalities and compare the decay curves found with or without a distracting task. If there was reason to believe that the subjects were not verbally encoding the stimuli, and if a relatively fast decay curve was found, then there would be evidence for a short-term memory in that modality. Furthermore, any difference between the control group and the group with a distracting task should indicate the existence of a rehearsal mechanism. Posner (1966) has undertaken several experiments of this sort. In one experiment the subject saw the position of a circle on a 180-mm line and later had to reproduce it; in another the subject moved a lever in a covered box a certain distance with only kinesthetic feedback and later tried to reproduce it. In both cases, testing was performed at 0, 5, 10, and 20 seconds; the interval was filled with either rest, or one of three intervening tasks of varying difficulty. These tasks, in order of increasing difficulty, consisted of reading numbers, adding numbers, and classifying numbers into categories. For the kinesthetic task there was a decline in performance over 30 seconds, but with no obvious differences among the different intervening conditions. This could be taken as evidence for a short-term kinesthetic memory without a rehearsal capability. For the visual task, on the other hand, there was a decline in performance over the 30 seconds only for the two most difficult intervening tasks; performance was essentially constant over time for the other conditions. One possibility, difficult to rule out, is that the subjects' performance was based on a verbal encoding of the visual stimulus. Posner tends to doubt this possibility for reasons that include the accuracy of the performance. Another possibility is that there is a short-term visual memory with a rehearsal component; this hypothesis seems somewhat at variance with the results from Milner's patient who performed at chance level in the experiment cited above. Inasmuch as the data reported by Posner (1966) seem to be rather variable, it would probably be best to hold off a decision on the question of rehearsal capability until further evidence is in.

2. *Characteristics of the a-v-l Short-Term Store*

We restrict ourselves in the remainder of this section to a discussion of the characteristics of the a-v-l short-term store. Work by Conrad (1964) is particularly interesting in this regard. He showed that confusions among visually presented letters in a short-term memory task are correlated with the confusions that subjects make when the same letters are read aloud in a noise background; that is, the letters most confused are those sounding alike. This might suggest an auditory short-term store, essentially the auditory portion of what has been called to this point an a-v-l store. In fact, it is very difficult to separate the verbal and linguistic aspects from the auditory ones. Hintzman (1965, 1967) has argued that the confusions are based upon similar kinesthetic feedback patterns during subvocal rehearsal. When subjects were given white noise on certain trials, several could be heard rehearsing the items aloud, suggesting subvocal rehearsal as the usual process. In addition, Hintzman found that confusions were based upon both the voicing qualities of the letters and the place of articulation. The place-of-articulation errors indicate confusion in kinesthetic feedback, rather than in hearing. Nevertheless, the errors found cannot be definitely assigned to a verbal rather than an auditory cause until the range of auditory confusions is examined more thoroughly. This discussion should make it clear that it is difficult to distinguish between the verbal, auditory, and linguistic aspects of short-term memory; for the purposes of this paper, then, we group the three together into one short-term memory, which we have called the a-v-l short-term store. This store will henceforth be labeled STS. (Restricting the term STS to the a-v-l mode does not imply that there are not other short-term memories with similar properties.)

The notation system should be made clear at this point. As just noted, STS refers to the auditory-verbal-linguistic short-term store. LTS will refer to the comparable memory in long-term store. It is important not to confuse our theoretical constructs STS and LTS (or the more general terms short-term store and long-term store) with the terms short-term memory (STM) and long-term memory (LTM) used in much of the psychological literature. These latter terms have come to take on an operational definition in the literature; STM refers to the memory examined in experiments with short durations or single trials, and LTM to the memory examined in long-duration experiments, typically list learning, or multiple-list learning experiments. According to our general theory, both STS and LTS are active in both STM and LTM experiments. It is important to keep these terms clear lest confusion results. For example, the Keppel and Underwood (1962) finding that performance in the Peterson situation is better on the first trials of a session has been appropriately interpreted as evidence for proactive interference in short-term memory (STM). The model we propose, however, attributes the effect to changes in the long-term store over the session, hence placing the cause in LTS and not STS.

At this point a finished model would set forth the structural characteristics of STS. Unfortunately, despite a large and growing body of experiments concerned with short-term memory, our knowledge about its structure is very limited. Control processes and structural features are so complexly interrelated that it is difficult to isolate those aspects of the data that are due solely to the structure of the memory system. Consequently, this paper presumes only a minimal structure for STS; we assume a trace in STS with auditory or verbal components which decays fairly rapidly in the absence of rehearsal, perhaps within 30 seconds. A few of the more promising possibilities concerning the precise nature of the trace will be considered next. Because most workers in this area make no particular distinction between traces in the two systems, the comments to follow are relevant to the memory trace in the long-term as well as the short-term store.

Bower (1967a) has made a significant exploration of the nature of the trace. In his paper, he has demonstrated the usefulness of models based on the assumption that the memory trace consists of a number of pieces of information (possibly redundant, correlated, or in error, as the case may be), and that the information ensemble may be construed as a multicomponent vector. While Bower makes a strong case for such a viewpoint, the details are too lengthy to review here. A somewhat different approach has been proposed by Wickelgren and Norman (1966) who view the trace as a unidimensional strength measure varying over time. They demonstrate that such a model fits the results of certain types of recognition-memory experiments if the appropriate decay and retrieval assumptions are made. A third approach is based upon a phenomenon reported by Murdock (1966), which has been given a theoretical analysis by Bernbach (1967). Using methods derived from the theory of signal detectability, Bernbach found that there was an all-or-none aspect to the confidence ratings that subjects gave regarding the correctness of their response. The confidence ratings indicated that an answer was either "correct" or "in error" as far as the subject could tell; if intermediate trace strengths existed, the subject was not able to distinguish between them. The locus of this all-or-none feature, however, may lie in the retrieval process rather than in the trace; that is, éven if trace strengths vary, the result of a retrieval attempt might always be one of two distinct outcomes: a success or a failure. Thus, one cannot rule out models that assume varying trace strengths. Our preference is to consider the trace as a multicomponent array of information (which we shall often represent in experimental models by a unidimensional strength measure), and reserve judgment on the locus of the all-or-none aspect revealed by an analysis of confidence ratings.

There are two experimental procedures which might be expected to shed some light on the decay characteristics of STS and both depend upon controlling rehearsal; one is similar to the Peterson paradigm in which rehearsal is controlled by an intervening activity and the other involves a very rapid presentation of items followed by an immediate test. An example of the former procedure is Posner's (1966) experiment in which the difficulty of the intervening activity was varied. He found that as the difficulty of an intervening task increased, accuracy of recall decreased.

Although this result might be regarded as evidence that decay from STS is affected by the kind of intervening activity, an alternative hypothesis would ascribe the result to a reduction in rehearsal with more difficult intervening tasks. It would be desirable to measure STS decay when rehearsal is completely eliminated, but it has proved difficult to establish how much rehearsal takes place during various intervening tasks.

Similar problems arise when attempts are made to control rehearsal by increasing presentation rates. Even at the fastest conceivable presentation rates subjects can rehearse during presentation if they attend to only a portion of the incoming items. In general, experiments manipulating presentation rate have not proved of value in determining decay characteristics for STS, primarily because of the control processes the subject brings into play. Thus Waugh and Norman (1965) found no difference between 1-second and 4-second rates in their probe digit experiment; Conrad and Hille (1958) found improvement with faster rates; and Buschke and Lim (1967) found increases in the amount of primacy in their missing-span serial position curves as input rate increased from one item per second to four items per second. Complex results of this sort make it difficult to determine the structural decay characteristics of STS. Eventually, models that include the control processes involved in these situations should help clarify the STS structure.

3. *Transfer from STS to LTS*

The amount and form of information transferred from STS to LTS is primarily a function of control processes. We will assume, however, that transfer itself is an unvarying feature of the system; throughout the period that information resides in the short-term store, transfer takes place to long-term store. Support for such an assumption is given by studies on incidental learning which indicate that learning takes place even when the subject is not trying to store material in the long-term store. Better examples may be the experiments reported by Hebb (1961) and Melton (1963). In these experiments subjects had to repeat sequences of digits. If a particular sequence was presented every several trials, it was gradually learned. It may be assumed that subjects in this situation attempt to perform solely by rehearsal of the sequence within STS; nevertheless, transfer to LTS clearly takes place. This Hebb-Melton procedure is currently being used to explore transfer characteristics in some detail. R. L. Cohen and Johansson (1967), for example, have found that an overt response to the repeated sequence was necessary for improvement in performance to occur in this situation; thus information transfer is accentuated by overt responses and appears to be quite weak if no response is demanded.

The form of the STS-LTS transfer may be probabilistic, continuous, or some combination; neither the literature nor our own data provide a firm basis for making a decision. Often the form of the information to be remembered and the type of test used may dictate a particular transfer process, as for example in Bower's (1961) research on an all-or-none paired-associate learning model, but the issue is nevertheless far from settled. In fact, the changes in the transfer process induced by the subject effectively alter the transfer function form experiment to experiment, making a search for a universal, unchanging process unproductive.

C. Long-Term Store

Because it is easiest to test for recall in the a-v-l mode, this part of long-term store has been the most extensively studied. It is clear, however, that long-term memory exists in each of the sensory modalities; this is shown by subjects' recognition capability for smells, taste, and so on. Other long-term information may be stored which is not necessarily related to any of the sensory modalities. Yntema and Trask (1963), for example, have proposed that temporal memory is stored in the form of "time-tags." Once again, however, lack of data forces us to restrict our attention primarily to the a-v-l mode, which we have designated LTS.

First a number of possible formulations of the LTS trace will be considered. The simplest hypothesis is to assume that the trace is all-or-none; if a trace is placed in memory, then a correct retrieval and response will occur. Second-guessing experiments provide evidence concerning an hypothesis of this sort.

Binford and Gettys (1965) presented the subject with a number of alternatives, one of which was the correct answer. If his first response is incorrect, he picks again from the remaining alternatives. The results indicate that second guesses are correct well above the chance level to be expected if the subject were guessing randomly from the remaining alternatives. This result rules out the simple trace model described above because an all-or-none trace would predict second guesses to be at the chance level. Actually, the above model was a model of both the form of the trace and the type of retrieval. We can expand the retrieval hypothesis and still leave open the possibility of an all-or-none trace. For example, in searching for a correct all-or-none trace in LTS, the subject might find a similar but different trace and mistakenly terminate the search and generate an answer; upon being told that the answer is wrong the subject renews the search and may find the correct trace the next time. Given this hypothesis, it would be instructive to know whether the results differ if the subject must rank the response alternatives without being given feedback after each choice. In this case all the alternatives would be ranked on the basis of the same search of LTS; if the response ranked second was still above chance, then it would become difficult to defend an all-or-none trace.

A second source of information about the nature of the trace comes from the tip-of-the-tongue phenomenon examined by Hart (1965), R. Brown and McNeill (1966), and Freedman and Landauer (1966). This phenomenon refers to a person's ability to predict accurately that he will be able to recognize a correct answer even though he cannot recall it at the moment. He feels as if the correct answer were on the "tip of the tongue." Experiments have shown that if subjects who cannot recall an answer are asked to estimate whether they will be able to choose the correct answer from a set of alternatives, they often show good accuracy in predicting their success in recognition. One explanation might be that the subject recalls some information, but not enough to generate an answer and feels that this partial information is likely to be sufficient to choose among a set of alternatives. Indeed, Brown and McNeill found that the initial sound of the word to be retrieved was often correctly recalled in cases where a correct identification was later made. On the other hand, the subject often is absolutely certain upon seeing the correct response that it is indeed correct. This might indicate that some new, relevant information has become available after recognition. In any case, a simple trace model can probably not handle these results. A class of models for the trace which can explain the tip-of-the-tongue phenomenon are the multiple-copy models suggested by Atkinson and Shiffrin (1965). In these schemes there are many traces or copies of information laid in long-term store, each of which may be either partial or complete. In a particular search of LTS perhaps only a small number or just one of these copies is retrieved, none complete enough to generate the correct answer; upon recognition, however, access is gained to the other copies, presumably through some associative process. Some of these other copies contain enough information to make the subject certain of his choice. These multiple-copy memory models are described more fully in Atkinson and Shiffrin (1965).

The decay and/or interference characteristics of LTS have been studied more intensively over the past 50 years than any other aspect of memory. Partly for this reason a considerable body of theory has been advanced known as interference theory.[3] We tend to regard this theory as descriptive rather than explanatory; this statement is not meant to detract from the value of the theory as a whole, but to indicate that a search for mechanisms at a deeper level might prove to be of value. Thus, for example, if the interfering effect of a previously learned list upon recall of a second list increases over time until the second list is retested, it is not enough to accept "proactive interference increasing over time" as an explanation of the effect; rather one should look for the underlying search, storage, and retrieval mechanisms responsible.

We are going to use a very restricted definition of interference in the rest of this paper; interference will be considered a structural feature of memory not under the control of the subject. It will refer to such possibilities as disruption and loss of information. On the other hand, there are search mechanisms which generate effects like those of structural interference, but which are control processes. Interference theory, of course, includes both types of possibilities, but we prefer to break down interference effects into those which are structurally based, and those under the control of the subject. Therefore the term *interference* is used henceforth to designate a structural feature of the long-term system.

It is important to realize that often it is possible to explain a given phenomenon with either interference or search notions. Although both factors will usually be present, the experimental situation sometimes indicates which is more important. For example, as we shall see in Section V,[4] the decrease in the percentage of words recalled in a free verbal-recall experiment with increases in list length could be due either to interference between items or to a search of decreasing effectiveness as the number of items increase. The typical free recall situation, however, forces the subject to engage in a search of memory at test and indicates to us that the search process is the major factor. Finally, note

[3] For an overview of interference see Postman (1961)
[4] Not reprinted here (Ed.)

that the interference effect itself may take many forms and arise in a number of ways. Information within a trace may be destroyed, replaced, or lessened in value by subsequent information. Alternatively, information may never be destroyed but may become irretrievable, temporarily or permanently.

In this section an attempt has been made to establish a reasonable basis for at least three systems—the sensory register, the short-term store, and the long-term store; to indicate the transfer characteristics between the various stores; and to consider possible decay and interference functions within each store.

II. Control Processes in Memory

The term *control process* refers to those processes that are not permanent features of memory, but are instead transient phenomena under the control of the subject; their appearance depends on such factors as instructional set, the experimental task, and the past history of the subject. A simple example of a control process can be demonstrated in a paired-associate learning task involving a list of stimuli each paired with either an A or B response (Bower, 1961). The subject may try to learn each stimulus-response pair as a separate, integral unit or he may adopt the more efficient strategy of answering B to any item not remembered and attempting to remember only the stimuli paired with the A response. This latter scheme will yield a radically different pattern of performance than the former; it exemplifies one rather limited control process. The various rehearsal strategies, on the other hand, are examples of control processes with almost universal applicability.

Since subject-controlled memory processes include any schemes, coding techniques, or mnemonics used by the subject in his effort to remember, their variety is virtually unlimited and classification becomes difficult. Such classification as is possible arises because these processes, while under the voluntary control of the subject, are nevertheless dependent upon the permanent memory structures described in the previous section. This section therefore will follow the format of Section I, organizing the control processes into those primarily associated with the sensory register, STS, and LTS. Apart from this, the presentation will be somewhat fragmentary, drawing upon examples from many disparate experiments in an attempt to emphasize the variety, pervasiveness, and importance of the subject-controlled processes.

A. Control Processes in the Sensory Register

Because a large amount of information enters the sensory register and then decays very quickly, the primary function of control processes at this level is the selection of particular portions of this information for transfer to the short-term store. The first decision the subject must make concerns which sensory register to attend to. Thus, in experiments with simultaneous inputs from several sensory channels, the subject can readily report information from a given sense modality if so instructed in advance, but his accuracy is greatly reduced if instructions are delayed until after presentation. A related attention process is the transfer to STS of a selected portion of a large information display within a sensory modality. An example to keep in mind here is the scanning process in the visual registration system. Letters in a tachistoscopically presented display may be scanned at a rate of about 10 msec a letter, the form of the scan being under the control of the subject. Sperling (1960) found the following result. When the signal identifying which row to report from a matrix of letters was delayed for an interval of time following stimulus offset, the subjects developed two observing strategies. One strategy consisted of obeying the experimenter's instructions to pay equal attention to all rows; this strategy resulted in evenly distributed errors and quite poor performance at long delays. The other strategy consisted of anticipating which row would be tested and attending to only that row; in this case the error variance is increased but performance is better at longer delay intervals than for the other strategy. The subjects were aware of and reported using these strategies. For example, one experienced subject reported switching from the first to the second strategy in an effort to maximize performance when the delay between presentation and report rose above .15 seconds. The graph of his probability of a correct response plotted against delay interval, while generally decreasing with delay, showed a dip at about .15 seconds, indicating that he did not switch strategies soon enough for optimal performance.

The decisions as to which sensory register to attend to, and where and what to scan within the system, are not the only choices that must be made at this level. There are a number of strategies available to the subject for matching information in the register against the long-term store and thereby identifying the input. In an experiment by Estes and Taylor (1966) for example, the subject had to decide whether an F or B was embedded in a matrix display of letters. One strategy would have the subject scan the letters in order, generating the "name" of each letter and checking to see whether it is a B or an F. If the scan ends before all letters are processed, and no B or F has been found, the subject would presumably guess according to some bias. Another strategy might have the subject do a features match on each letter against B and then F, moving on as soon as a difference is found; in this strategy it would not be necessary to scan all features of each letter (i.e., it would not be necessary to generate the name of each letter). A third strategy might have the subject compare with only one of the crucial letters, guessing the other if a match is not found by the time the scan terminates.

B. Control Processes in Short-Term Store

1. *Storage, Search, and Retrieval Strategies*

Search processes in STS, while not as elaborate as those in LTS because of the smaller amount of information in STS through which the search must take place, are nevertheless important. Since information in STS in excess of the rehearsal capability is decaying at a rapid rate, a search for a particular datum must be performed quickly and efficiently. One indirect method of examining the search process consists of comparing the results of recognition and recall experiments in which STS plays the major role. Presumably there is a search component in the recall situation that is absent in the recognition situation. It is difficult to come to strong conclusions on this basis, but recognition studies such as Wickelgren and Norman (1966) have usually given rise to less complicated models than comparable recall experiments, indicating that the search component in STS might be playing a large role.

One result indicating that the STS search occurs along ordered dimensions is based upon binaural stimulus presentation (Broadbent, 1954, 1956, 1958). A pair of items is presented, one to each ear simultaneously. Three such pairs are given, one every half second. Subjects perform best if asked to report the items first from one ear and then the other, rather than, say, in pairs. While Broadbent interprets these results in terms of a postulated time needed to switch attention from one ear to the other (a control process in itself), other interpretations are possible. In particular, part of the information stored with each item might include which ear was used for input. This information might then provide a simple dimension along which to search STS and report during recall. Another related possibility would have the subject group the items along this dimension during presentation. In any case we would expect similar results if another dimension other than "sides" (which ear) were provided. Yntema and Trask (1963) used three word-number pairs presented sequentially, one every half second; one member of a pair was presented to one ear and the other member to the other ear. There were three conditions: the first in which three words were presented consecutively on one side (and therefore the three numbers on the other), the second in which two words and one number were presented consecutively on one side, the third in which a number separated the two words on one side. Three test conditions were used: the subject was asked to report words, the numbers (types); or to report one ear followed by the other (sides); or the simultaneous pairs in order (pairs). The results are easy to describe. In terms of probability correct, presentation condition one was best, condition two next, and condition three worst. For the test conditions, "types" yielded the highest probability of correct response, followed by "sides" and then "pairs." "Sides" being better than "pairs" was one of the results found by Broadbent, but "types" being even better than "sides" suggests that the organization along available dimensions, with the concomitant increase of efficiency in the search process, is the dominant factor in the situation.

One difficulty in studying the search process in STS is the fact that the subject will perform perfectly if the number of items presented is within his rehearsal span. Sternberg (1966) has overcome this difficulty by examining the latency of responses within the rehearsal span. His typical experiment consists of presenting from one to six digits to the subject at the rate of 1.2 seconds each. Following a 2-second delay, a single digit is presented and the subjects must respond "yes" or "no" depending on whether or not the test digit was a member of the set just presented. Following this response the subject is required to recall the complete set in order. Since the subjects were 98.7% correct on the recognition test and 98.6% correct on the recall test, it may be assumed that the task was within their rehearsal span. Interesting results were found in the latencies of the recognition responses: there was a linear increase in latency as the set size increased from one to six digits. The fact that there was no difference in latencies for "yes" versus "no" responses indicates that the search process in this situation is exhaustive and does not terminate the moment a match is found. Sternberg concludes that the subject engages in an exhaustive serial comparison process which evaluates elements at the rate of 25 to 30 per second. The high processing rate makes it seem likely that the rehearsal the subjects report is not an integral part of the scanning process, but instead maintains the image in STS so that it may be scanned at the time of the test. This conclusion depends upon accepting as a reasonable rehearsal rate for digits the values reported by Landauer (1962) which were never higher than six per second.

Buschke's (1963) missing-span method provides additional insight into search and retrieval processes in STS. The missing-span procedure consists of presenting in a random order all but one of a previously specified set of digits; the subject is then asked to report the missing digit. This technique eliminates the output interference associated with the usual digit-span studies in which the entire presented set must be reported. Buschke found that subjects had superior performance on a missing-span task as compared with an identical digit-span task in which all of the presented items were to be reported in any order. A natural hypothesis would explain the difference in performance as being caused by output interference; that is, the multiple recalls in the digit-span procedure produce interference not seen in the single test procedure of the missing span. An alternative explanation would hold that different storage and search strategies were being employed in the two situations. Madsen and Drucker (1966) examined this question by comparing test instructions given just prior to or immediately following each presentation sequence; the instructions specify whether the subject is to report the set of presented digits or simply to report the missing digit. Output interference would imply that the difference between missing-span and digit-span would hold up in both cases. The results showed that the missing-span procedure with prior instructions was superior to both missing-span and digit-span with instructions following presentation; the latter two conditions produced equal results and were superior to digit-span with prior instructions. It seems clear, then, that two storage and search strategies are being used: a missing-span type, and a digit-span type. Prior instructions (specifying the form of the subject's report) lead the subject to use one or the other of these strategies, but instructions following presentation are associated with a mixture of the two strategies. It appeared in this case that the strategies differed in terms of the type of storage during presentation; the digit-span group with prior instructions tended to report their digits in their presentation order, while the digit-span group with instructions after presentation more often reported the digits in their numerical order. This indicates that the missing-span strategy involved checking off the numbers as they were presented against a fixed, numerically ordered list, while the digit-span strategy involved rehearsing the items in their presented order. It is interesting to note that if the subjects had been aware of the superiority of the missing-span strategy, they could have used it in the digit-span task also, since the two types of tests called for the same information.

It should be noted that retrieval from STS depends upon a number of factors, some under the control of the subject and some depending upon the decay characteristics of STS. If the decay is partial in some sense, so that the trace contains only part of the information necessary for direct output, then the problem arises of how the partial information should be used to generate a response. In this case, it would be expected that the subject would then engage in a search of LTS in an effort to match or recognize the partial information. On the other hand, even though traces may decay in a partial manner, the rehearsal capability can hold a select set of items in a state of immediate recall availability and thereby impart to these items what is essentially an all-or-none status. It is to this rehearsal process that we now turn.

2. *Rehearsal Processes*

Rehearsal is one of the most important factors in experiments on human memory. This is particularly true in the laboratory because the concentrated, often meaningless, memory tasks used increase the relative efficacy of rehearsal as compared with the longer term coding and associative processes. Rehearsal may be less pervasive in everyday memory, but nevertheless has many uses, as Broadbent (1958) and others have pointed out. Such examples as remembering a telephone number or table-tennis score serve to illustrate the primary purpose of rehearsal, the lengthening of the time period information stays in the short-term store. A second purpose of rehearsal is illustrated by the fact that even if one wishes to remember a telephone number permanently, one will often rehearse the number several times. This rehearsal serves the purpose of increasing the strength built up in a long-term store, both by increasing the length of stay in STS (during which time a trace is built up in LTS) and by giving coding and other storage processes time to operate. Indeed, almost any kind of operation on an array of information (such as coding) can be viewed as a form of rehearsal, but this paper reserves the term only for the duration-lengthening repetition process.

In terms of STS structure, we can imagine that each rehearsal regenerates the STS trace and thereby prolongs the decay. This does not imply that the entire information ensemble available in STS immediately after presentation is regenerated and maintained at each rehearsal. Only that information selected by the subject, often a small proportion of the initial ensemble, is maintained. If the word "cow" is presented, for example, the sound of the word cow will enter STS; in addition, associates of cow, like milk, may be retrieved from LTS and also entered in STS; furthermore, an image of a cow may be entered into a short-term visual store. In succeeding rehearsals, however, the subject may rehearse only the word "cow" and the initial associates will decay and be lost. The process may be similar to the loss of meaningfulness that occurs when a word is repeated over and over (Lambert & Jakobovitz, 1960).

An interesting question concerns the maximum number of items that can be maintained via rehearsal. This number will depend upon the rate of STS decay and the form of the trace regenerated in STS by rehearsal. With almost any reasonable assumptions about either of these processes, however, an ordered rehearsal will allow the greatest number of items to be maintained. To give a simple example, suppose that individual items take 1.1 seconds to decay and may be restarted if rehearsal begins before decay is complete. Suppose further that each rehearsal takes .25 seconds. It is then clear that five items may be maintained indefinitely if they are rehearsed in a fixed order over and over. On the other hand, a rehearsal scheme in which items are chosen for rehearsal on a random basis will quickly result in one or more items decaying and becoming lost. It would be expected, therefore, that in situations where subjects are relying primarily upon their rehearsal capability in STS, rehearsal will take place in an ordered fashion. One such situation, from which we can derive an estimate of rehearsal capability, is the digit-span task. A series of numbers is read to the subject who is then required to recall them, usually in the forward or backward order. Because the subject has a long-term store which sometimes can be used to supplement the short-term rehearsal memory, the length of a series which can be correctly recalled may exceed the rehearsal capacity. A lower limit on this capacity can be found by identifying the series length at which a subject never errs; this series length is usually in the range of five to eight numbers.[5]

The above estimates of rehearsal capability are obtained in a discrete-trial situation where the requirement is to remember every item of a small input. A very similar rehearsal strategy can be employed, however, in situations such as free recall where a much greater number of items is input than rehearsal can possibly encompass. One strategy in this case would be to replace one of the items currently being rehearsed by each new item input. In this case every item would receive at least some rehearsal. Because of input and reorganization factors, which undoubtedly consume some time, the rehearsal capacity would probably be reduced. It should be clear that under this scheme a constant number of items will be undergoing rehearsal at any one moment. As an analogy, one might think of a bin always containing exactly n items; each new item enters the bin and knocks out an item already there. This process has been called in earlier reports a "rehearsal buffer," or simply a "buffer," and we will use this terminology here (Atkinson & Shiffrin, 1965).

In our view, the maintenance and use of the buffer is a process entirely under the control of the subject. Presumably a buffer is set up and used in an attempt to maximize performance in certain situations. In setting up a maximal-sized buffer, however, the subject is devoting all his effort to rehearsal and not engaging in other processes such as coding and hypothesis testing. In situations, therefore, where coding, long-term search, hypothesis testing, and other mechanisms appreciably improve performance, it is likely that a trade-off will occur in which the buffer size will be reduced and rehearsal may even become somewhat random while coding and other strategies increase.

At this point we want to discuss various buffer operations in greater detail. Figure 2 illustrates a fixed-size buffer and its relation to the rest of the memory system. The content of the buffer is constructed from items that have entered STS, items which have been input from the sensory register or from LTS. The arrow going toward LTS indicates that some long-term trace is being built up during an item's stay in the buffer. The other arrow from the buffer indicates that the input of a new item into the buffer causes an item currently in the buffer to be bumped out; this item then decays from STS and is lost (except for any trace which has accumulated in LTS during its stay). An item dropped from

[5] Wickelgren (1965) has examined rehearsal in the digit-span task in greater detail and found that rehearsal capacity is a function of the groupings engaged in by the subject; in particular, rehearsal in distinct groups of three was superior to rehearsal in four's and five's.

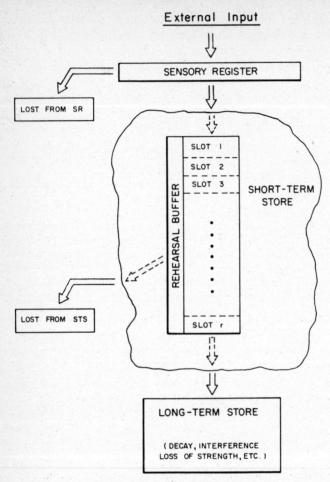

FIG. 2. The rehearsal buffer and its relation to the memory system.

the buffer is likely to decay more quickly in STS than a newly presented item which has just entered STS. There are several reasons for this. For one thing, the item is probably already in some state of partial decay when dropped; in addition, the information making up an item in the buffer is likely to be only a partial copy of the ensemble present immediately following stimulus input.

There are two additional processes not shown in Fig. 2 that the subject can use on appropriate occasions. First, the subject may decide not to enter every item into the buffer; the reasons are manifold. For example, the items may be presented at a very fast rate so that input and re-organization time encroach too far upon rehearsal time. Another possibility is that some combinations of items are particularly easy to rehearse, making the subject loath to break up the combination. In fact, the work involved in introducing a new item into the buffer and deleting an old one may alone give the subject incentive to keep the buffer unchanged. Judging from these remarks, the choice of which items to enter into the buffer is based on momentary characteristics of the current string of input items and may appear at times to be essentially random.

The second process not diagrammed in Fig. 2 is the choice of which item to eliminate from the buffer when a new item is entered. There are several possibilities. The choice could be random; it could be based upon the state of decay of the current items; it could depend upon the ease of rehearsing the various items; most important, it could be based upon the length of time the various items have resided in the buffer. It is not unreasonable that the subject knows which items he has been rehearsing the longest, as he might if rehearsal takes place in a fixed order. It is for this reason that the slots or positions of the buffer have been numbered consecutively in Fig. 2; that is, to indicate that the subject might have some notion of the relative recency of the various items in the buffer.

The experimental justification for these various buffer mechanisms will be presented in Section IV.[6] It should be emphasized that the subject will use a fixed-size buffer of the sort described here only in select situations, primarily those in which he feels that trading off rehearsal time for coding and other longer term control processes would not be fruitful. To the extent that long-term storage operations prove to be successful as compared with rehearsal, the structure of the rehearsal mechanism will tend to become impoverished. One other point concerning the buffer should be noted. While this paper consistently considers a fixed-size short-term buffer as a rehearsal strategy of the subject, it is possible to apply a fixed-size model of a similar kind to the structure of the short-term system as a whole, that is, to consider a short-term buffer as a permanent feature of memory. Waugh and Norman (1965), for example, have done this in their paper on primary memory. The data on the structure of STS is currently so nebulous that such an hypothesis can be neither firmly supported nor rejected.

3. *Coding Processes and Transfer between Short- and Long-Term Store*

It should be evident that there is a close relationship between the short- and long-term store. In general, information entering STS comes directly from LTS and only indirectly from the sensory register. For example, a visually presented word cannot be entered into STS as an auditory-verbal unit until a long-term search and match has identified the verbal representation of the visual image. For words, letters, and highly familar stimuli, this long-term search and match process may be executed very quickly, but one can imagine unfamiliar stimuli, such as, say, a nonsense scribble, where considerable search might be necessary

[6]Not reprinted here (Ed.)

before a suitable verbal representation is found to enter into STS. In such cases, the subject might enter the visual image directly into his short-term visual memory and not attempt a verbal coding operation.

Transfer from STS to LTS may be considered a permanent feature of memory; any information in STS is transferred to LTS to some degree throughout its stay in the short-term store. The important aspect of this transfer, however, is the wide variance in the amount and form of the transferred information that may be induced by control processes. When the subject is concentrating upon rehearsal, the information transferred would be in a relatively weak state and easily subject to interference. On the other hand, the subject may divert his effort from rehearsal to various coding operations which will increase the strength of the stored information. In answer to the question of what is a coding process, we can most generally state that a coding process is a select alteration and/or addition to the information in the short-term store as the result of a search of the long-term store. This change may take a number of forms, often using strong preexisting associations already in long-term store. A number of these coding possibilities will be considered later.

Experiments may be roughly classified in terms of the control operations the subject will be led to use. Concept formation problems or tasks where there is a clear solution will lead the subject to strategy selection and hypothesis-testing procedures (Restle, 1964). Experiments which do not involve problem solving, where there are a large number of easily coded items, and where there is a long period between presentation and test, will prompt the subject to expend his efforts on long-term coding operations. Finally, experiments in which memory is required, but long-term memory is not efficacious, will lead the subject to adopt rehearsal strategies that maintain the information the limited period needed for the task. Several examples of the latter experiment will be examined in this paper; they are characterized by the fact that the responses assigned to particular stimuli are continually changing, so that coding of a specific stimulus-response pair will prove harmful to succeeding pairs using the same stimulus. There are experiments, of course, for which it will not be possible to decide on a priori grounds which control processes are being used. In these cases the usual identification procedures must be used, including model fits and careful questioning of the subjects.

There are other short-term processes that do not fit easily into the above classification. They include grouping, organizing, and chunking strategies. One form that organizing may take is the selection of a subset of presented items for special attention, coding and/or rehearsal. This selection process is clearly illustrated in a series of studies on magnitude of reward by Harley (1965a, 1965b). Items in a paired-associate list were given two monetary incentives, one high and one low. In one experiment the subjects learned two paired-associate lists, one consisting of all high incentive items, the other consisting of all low incentive items; there were no differences in the learning rates for these lists. In a second experiment, subjects learned a list which included both high and low incentive items; in this case learning was faster for the high than the low incentive items. However, the overall rate of learning for the mixed list was about the same as for the two previous lists. It seems clear that when the high and low incentive items are mixed, the subject selectively attends to, codes, and rehearses those items with the higher payoffs. A second kind of organizing that occurs is the grouping of items into small sets, often with the object of memorizing the set as a whole, rather than as individual items. Typically in this case the grouped items will have some common factor. A good example may be found in the series of studies by Battig (1966) and his colleagues. He found a tendency to group items according to difficulty and according to degree of prior learning; this tendency was found even in paired-associate tasks where an extensive effort had been made to eliminate any basis for such grouping. A third type of information organization is found in the "chunking" process suggested by Miller (1956). In his view there is some optimal size that a set of information should have in order to best facilitate remembering. The incoming information is therefore organized into chunks of the desired magnitude.

C. CONTROL PROCESSES IN LONG-TERM STORE

Control processes to be considered in this section fall roughly into two categories: those concerned with transfer between short-term and long-term store and those concerned with search for and retrieval of information from LTS.

1. *Storage in Long-Term Store*

It was stated earlier that some information is transferred to LTS throughout an item's stay in STS, but that its amount and form is determined by control processes. This proposition will now be examined in greater detail. First of all, it would be helpful to consider a few simple examples where long-term storage is differentially affected by the coding strategy adopted. One example is found in a study on mediators performed by Montague, Adams, and Kiess (1966). Pairs of nonsense syllables were presented to the subject who had to write down any natural language mediator (word, phrase, or sentence associated with a pair) which occurred to him. At test 24 hours later the subject attempted to give the response member of each pair and the natural language mediator (NLM) that had been used in acquisition. Proportion correct for items on which the NLM was retained was 70%, while the proportion correct was negligible for items where the NLM was forgotten or significantly changed. Taken in conjunction with earlier studies showing that a group using NLMs was superior to a group learning by rote (Runquist & Farley, 1964), this result indicates a strong dependence of recall upon natural language mediators. A somewhat different encoding technique has been examined by Clark and Bower (personal communication). Subjects were required to learn several lists of paired-associate items, in which each item was a pair of familiar words. Two groups of subjects were given identical instructions, except for an extra section read to the experimental group explaining that the best method of learning the pairs was to form an elaborate visual image containing the objects designated by the two words. This experimental group was then given a few examples of the technique. There was a marked difference in performance between the groups on both immediate and delayed tests, the experimental group outperforming the control group by better than 40% in terms of probability correct. In fact, postexperimental questioning of the subjects revealed that the occasional high performers in the control group were often using the experimental technique even in the absence of instructions to do so. This technique of associating through the use of visual images is a very old one; it has been described in considerable detail, for example, by Cicero in *De Oratore* when he discusses memory as one of the five parts of rhetoric, and is clearly very effective.

We now consider the question of how these encoding techniques improve performance. The answer depends to a degree upon the fine structure of long-term store, and therefore cannot be stated precisely. Nevertheless, a number of possibilities should be mentioned. First, the encoding may make use of strong preexisting associations, eliminating the necessity of making new ones. Thus in mediating a word pair in a paired-associate task, word A might elicit word A' which in turn elicits the response. This merely moves the question back a level: how does the subject know which associates are the correct ones? It may be that the appropriate associations are identified by temporal position; that is, the subject may search through the associations looking for one which has been elicited recently. Alternatively, information could be stored with the appropriate association identifying it as having been used in the current paired-associates task. Second, the encoding might greatly decrease the effective area of memory which must be searched at the time of test. A response word not encoded must be in the set of all English words, or perhaps in the set of all words presented "recently," while a code may allow a smaller search through the associates of one or two items. One could use further search-limiting techniques such as restricting the mediator to the same first letter as the stimulus. A third possibility, related to the second, is that encoding might give some order to an otherwise random search. Fourth, encoding might greatly increase the amount of information stored. Finally, and perhaps most important, the encoding might protect a fledgling association from interference by succeeding items. Thus if one encodes a particular pair through an image of, say, a specific room in one's home, it is unlikely that future inputs will have any relation to that image; hence they will not interfere with it. In most cases coding probably works well for all of the above reasons.

There is another possible set of effects of the coding process which should be mentioned here. As background, we need to consider the results of several recent experiments which examine the effect of spacing between study and test in paired-associate learning (Bjork, 1966; Young, 1966). The result of primary interest to us is the decrease in probability correct as the number of other paired-associate items presented between study and test increases. This decrease seems to reach asymptote only after a fairly large number (e.g., 20) of intervening items. There are several possible explanations for this "short-term" effect. Although the effect probably occurs over too great an interval to consider direct decay from STS as an explanation, any of several rehearsal strategies could give rise to an appropriate-looking curve. Since a paired-associate task usually requires coding, a fixed-size rehearsal buffer may not be a reasonable hypothesis, unless the buffer size is fairly small; on the other hand, a variable rehearsal set with semirandomly spaced rehearsals may be both reasonable and accurate. If, on the other hand, one decides that almost no continuing rehearsal occurs in this task, what other hypotheses are available? One could appeal to retroactive interference but this does little more than name the phenomenon. Greeno (1967) has proposed a coding model which can explain the effect. In his view, the subject may select one of several possible codes at the time of study. In particular, he might select a "permanent" code, which will not be disturbed by any other items or codes in the experiment; if this occurs, the item is said to be learned. On the other hand, a "transitory" code might be selected, one which is disturbed or eliminated as succeeding items are presented. This transitory code will last for a probabilistically determined number of trials before becoming useless or lost. The important point to note here is the fact that a decreasing "short-term" effect can occur as a result of solely long-term operations. In experiments emphasizing long-term coding, therefore, the decision concerning which decay process, or combination of decay processes, is operative will not be easy to make in an a priori manner; rather the decision would have to be based upon such a posteriori grounds as good-ness-of-fit results for a particular model and introspective reports from the subject.

2. Long-Term Search Processes

One of the most fascinating features of memory is the long-term search process. We have all, at one time or another, been asked for information which we once knew, but which is momentarily unavailable, and we are aware of the ensuing period (often lasting for hours) during which memory was searched, occasionally resulting in the correct answer. Nevertheless, there has been a marked lack of experimental work dealing with this rather common phenomenon. For this reason, our discussion of search processes will be primarily theoretical, but the absence of a large experimental literature should not lead us to underestimate the importance of the search mechanism.

The primary component of the search process is locating the sought-for trace (or one of the traces) in long-term store. This process is seen in operation via several examples. The occasionally very long latencies prior to a correct response for well-known information indicates a non-perfect search. A subject reporting that he will think "of it the moment he thinks about something else" indicates a prior fixation on an unsuccessful search procedure. Similarly, the tip-of-the-tongue phenomenon mentioned earlier indicates a failure to find an otherwise very strong trace. We have also observed the following while quizzing a graduate student on the names of state capitals. The student gave up trying to remember the capital of the state of Washington after pondering for a long time. Later this student quickly identified the capital of Oregon as Salem and then said at once that the capital of Washington was Olympia. When asked how he suddenly remembered, he replied that he had learned the two capitals together. Presumably this information would have been available during the first search if the student had known where to look: namely in conjunction with the capital of Oregon. Such descriptive examples are numerous and serve to indicate that a search can sometimes fail to uncover a very strong trace. One of the decisions the subject must make is when to terminate an unsuccessful search. An important determiner of the length of search is the amount of order imposed during the search; if one is asked to name all the states and does so strictly geographically, one is likely to do better than someone who spews out names in a haphazard fashion. The person naming states in a haphazard fashion will presently encounter in his search for new names those which he has already given; if this occurs repeatedly, the search will be terminated as being unfruitful. The problem of terminating the search is especially acute in the case of recalling a set of items without a good natural ordering. Such a case is found in free-verbal-recall experiments in which a list of words is presented to the subject who must then recall as many as possible. The subject presumably searches along some sort of temporal dimension, a dimension which lets the subject know when he finds a word whether or not it was on the list presented most recently. The temporal ordering is by no means perfect, however, and the search must therefore be carried out with a degree of randomness. This procedure may lead to missing an item which has a fairly strong trace. It has been found in free-verbal-recall experiments, for example, that repeated recall tests on a given list sometimes result in the inclusion on the second test of items left out on the first test. In our own experiments we have even observed intrusions from an earlier list that had not been recalled during the test of that list.

It would be illustrative at this point to consider an experiment carried out by Norma Graham at Stanford University. Subjects were asked to name the capitals of the states. If a correct answer was not given within 5 seconds following presentation of the state name, the subjects were then given a hint and allowed 30 seconds more to search their memory. The hint consisted of either 1, 2, 4, 12, or 24 consecutive letters of the alphabet, one of which was the first letter in the name of the state capital. The probability correct dropped steadily as the hint size increased from 1 to 24 letters. The average response latencies for correct answers, however, showed a different effect; the 1-letter hint was associated with the fastest response time, the 2-letter hint was slower, the 4-letter hint was slower yet, but the 12- and 24-letter hints were faster than the 4-letter hint. One simple hypothesis that can explain why latencies were slower after the 4-letter hint than after the 12- and 24-letter hints depends upon differing search processes. Suppose the subject in the absence of a hint engages in "normal" search, or N search. When given the first letter, however, we will assume the subject switches to a first letter search, or L search, consisting of a deeper exploration of memory based upon the first letter. This L search might consist of forming possible sounds beginning with the appropriate letter, and matching them against possible city names. When the size of the hint increases, the subject must apply the L search to each of the letters in turn, obviously a time-consuming procedure. In fact, for 12- or 24-letter hints the probability is high that the subject would use up the entire 30-second search period without carrying out an L search on the correct first letter. Clearly a stage is reached, in terms of hint size, where the subject will switch from an L search to N search in order to maximize performance. In the present experiment it seems clear that the switch in strategy occurred between the 4- and 12-letter hints.

In the above experiment there were two search-stopping events, one subject-controlled and the other determined by the 30-second time limit. It is instructive to consider some of the possible subject-controlled stopping rules. One possibility is simply an internal time limit, beyond which the subject decides further search is useless. Related to this would be an event-counter stopping rule that would halt the subject when a fixed number of prespecified events had occurred. The events could be total number of distinct "searches," total number of incorrect traces found, and so on. A third possibility is dependent on a consecutive-events counter. For example, search could be stopped whenever x consecutive searches recovered traces that had been found in previous searches.

It was noted earlier that searches may vary in their apparent orderliness. Since long-term memory is extremely large, any truly random search would invariably be doomed to failure. The search must always be made along some dimension, or on the basis of some available cues. Nevertheless, searches do vary in their degree of order; a letter-by-letter search is highly structured, whereas a free associative search that proceeds from point to point in a seemingly arbitrary manner will be considerably less restrained, even to the point where the same ground may be covered many times. One other possible feature of the search process is not as desirable as the ones previously mentioned. The search itself might prove destructive to the sought-after trace. That is, just as new information transferred to the long-term store might interfere with previous material stored there, the generation of traces during the search might prove to have a similar interfering effect.

A somewhat different perspective on search procedures is obtained by considering the types of experimental tests that typically are used. Sometimes the very nature of the task presumes a specific search procedure. An example is found in the free-verbal-recall task in which the subject must identify a subset of a larger well-learned group of words. A search of smaller scope is made in a paired-associate task; when the set of possible responses is large, the search for the answer is similar to that made in free recall, with a search component and a recognition component to identify the recovered trace as the appropriate one. When the set of responses in a paired-associate task is quite small, the task becomes one of recognition alone: the subject can generate each possible response in order and perform a recognition test on each. The recognition test presumably probes the trace for information identifying it as being from the correct list and being associated with the correct stimulus.

It was said that the primary component of the search process is locating the desired memory trace in LTS. The secondary component is the recovery of the trace once found. It has been more or less assumed for simplicity in the above discussions that the trace is all-or-none. This may not be the case, and the result of a search might be the recovery of a partial trace. Retrieval would then depend either upon correctly guessing the missing information or performing a further search to match the partial trace with known responses. It is possible, therefore, to divide the recovery processes into a search component and retrieval component, both of which must be successfully concluded in order to output the correct response. The two components undoubtedly are correlated in the sense that stronger, more complete traces will both be easier to find and easier to retrieve, having been found.

One final problem of some importance should be mentioned at this time. The effects of trace interference may be quite difficult to separate from those of search failure. Trace interference here refers either to loss of information in the trace due to succeeding inputs or to confusions caused by competition among multiple traces at the moment of test. Search failure refers to an inability to find the trace at all. Thus a decrease in the probability of a correct response as the number of items intervening between study and test increases could be due to trace interference generated by those items. It could also be due to an increased likelihood of failing to find the trace because of the increasing number of items that have to be searched in memory. One way these processes might be separated experimentally would be in a comparison of recognition and recall measures, assuming that a failure to find the trace is less likely in the case of recognition than in the case of recall. At the present, research along these lines has not given us a definitive answer to this question.

REFERENCES

Atkinson, R. C., & Shiffrin, R. M. Mathematical models for memory and learning. Technical Report No. 79, Institute for Mathematical Studies in the Social Sciences, Stanford University, 1965. (To be published in D. P. Kimble (Ed.), *Proceedings of the third conference on learning, remembering and forgetting*. New York: New York Academy of Sciences.)

Averbach, E., & Coriell, A. S. Short-term memory in vision. *Bell System Technical Journal*, 1961, **40**, 309–328.

Averbach, E., & Sperling, G. Short-term storage of information in vision. In C. Cherry (Ed.), *Information theory*. London and Washington, D.C.: Butterworth, 1961. Pp. 196–211.

Barbizet, J. Defect of memorizing of hippocampal-mammillary origin: A review. *Journal of Neurology, Neurosurgery, and Psychiatry*, 1963, **26**, 127–135.

Battig, W. F. Evidence for coding processes in "rote" paired-associate learning. *Journal of Verbal Learning and Verbal Behavior*, 1966, **5**, 171–181.

Bernbach, H. A. Decision processes in memory. *Psychological Review*, 1967, **74**, 462–480.

Binford, J. R., & Gettys, C. Nonstationarity in paired-associate learning as indicated by a second guess procedure. *Journal of Mathematical Psychology*, 1965, **2**, 190–195.

Bjork, R. A. Learning and short-term retention of paired-associates in relation to specific sequences of interpresentation intervals. Technical Report No. 106, Institute for Mathematical Studies in the Social Sciences, Stanford University, 1966.

Bousfield, W. A. The occurrence of clustering in the recall of randomly arranged associates. *Journal of General Psychology*, 1953, **49**, 229–240.

Bower, G. H. Application of a model to paired-associate learning. *Psychometrika*, 1961, **26**, 255–280.

Bower, G. H. A multicomponent theory of the memory trace. In K. W. Spence and J. T. Spence (Eds.), *The psychology of learning and motivation: Advances in research and theory*, Vol. I. New York: Academic Press, 1967. Pp. 229–325. (a)

Broadbent, D. E. The role of auditory localization in attention and memory span. *Journal of Experimental Psychology*, 1954, **47**, 191–196.

Broadbent, D. E. Successive responses to simultaneous stimuli. *Quarterly Journal of Experimental Psychology*, 1956, **8**, 145–152.

Broadbent, D. E. *Perception and communication.* Oxford: Pergamon Press, 1958.

Brown, R., & McNeill, D. The "tip of the tongue" phenomenon. *Journal of Verbal Learning and Verbal Behavior*, 1966, **5**, 325–337.

Buschke, H. Retention in immediate memory estimated without retrieval. *Science*, 1963, **140**, 56–57.

Buschke, H., & Lim, H. Temporal and interactional effects in short-term storage. *Perception and Psychophysics*, 1967, **2**, 107–114.

Cohen, R. L., & Johansson, B. S. The activity trace in immediate memory; a reevaluation. *Journal of Verbal Learning and Verbal Behavior*, 1967, **6**, 139–143.

Conrad, R. Acoustic confusions in immediate memory. *British Journal of Psychology*, 1964, **55**, 1, 75–84.

Conrad, R., & Hille, B. A. The decay theory of immediate memory and paced recall. *Canadian Journal of Psychology*, 1958, **12**, 1–6.

Estes, W. K. A technique for assessing variability of perceptual span. *Proceedings of the National Academy of Sciences of the U.S.*, 1965, **4**, 403–407.

Estes, W. K. Reinforcement in human learning. In J. Tapp (Ed.), *Current problems in reinforcement.* New York: Academic Press, 1968.

Estes, W. K., & Taylor, H. A. A detection method and probabilistic models for assessing information processing from brief visual displays. *Proceedings of the National Academy of Sciences of the U.S.*, 1964, **52**, No. 2, 446–454.

Estes, W. K., & Taylor, H. A. Visual detection in relation to display size and redundancy of critical elements. *Perception and Psychophysics*, 1966, **1**, 9–16.

Estes, W. K., & Wessel, D. L. Reaction time in relation to display size and correctness of response in forced-choice visual signal detection. *Perception and Psychophysics*, 1966, **1**, 369–373.

Freedman, J. L., & Landauer, T. K. Retrieval of long-term memory: "Tip-of-the-tongue" phenomenon. *Psychonomic Science*, 1966, **4**, 309–310.

Greeno, J. G. Paired-associate learning with short-term retention: Mathematical analysis and data regarding identification of parameters. *Journal of Mathematical Psychology*, 1967, **4**, 430–472.

Harley, W. F., Jr. The effect of monetary incentive in paired-associate learning using a differential method. *Psychonomic Science*, 1965, **2**, 377–378. (a)

Harley, W. F., Jr. The effect of monetary incentive in paired-associate learning using an absolute method. *Psychonomic Science*, 1965, **3**, 141–142. (b)

Hart, J. T., Jr. Recall, recognition, and the memory-monitoring process. Unpublished doctoral dissertation, Stanford University, 1965.

Hebb, D. O. Distinctive features of learning in the higher animal. In J. F. Delafresnaye (Ed.), *Brain mechanisms and learning.* London and New York: Oxford University Press, 1961. Pp. 37–46.

Hellyer, S. Supplementary report: Frequency of stimulus presentation and short-term decrement in recall. *Journal of Experimental Psychology*, 1962, **64**, 650–651.

Hintzman, D. L. Classification and aural coding in short-term memory. *Psychonomic Science*, 1965, **3**, 161–162.

Hintzman, D. L. Articulatory coding in short-term memory. *Journal of Verbal Learning and Verbal Behavior*, 1967, **6**, 312–316.

Keppel, G., & Underwood, B. J. Proactive inhibition in short-term retention of single items. *Journal of Verbal Learning and Verbal Behavior*, 1962, **1**, 153–161.

Lambert, W. E., & Jakobovitz, L. A. Verbal satiation and changes in the intensity of meaning. *Journal of Experimental Psychology*, 1960, **60**, 376–383.

Landauer, T. K. Rate of implicit speech. *Perceptual and Motor Skills*, 1962, **15**, 646–647.

Madsen, M. E., & Drucker, J. M. Immediate memory by missing scan and modified digit span. *Psychonomic Science*, 1966, **6**, 283–284.

Melton, A. W. Implications of short-term memory for a general theory of memory. *Journal of Verbal Learning and Verbal Behavior*, 1963, **2**, 1–21.

Miller, G. A. The magical number seven, plus or minus two: Some limits on our capacity for processing information. *Psychological Review*, 1956, **63**, 81–97.

Milner, B. The memory defect in bilateral hippocampal lesions. *Psychiatric Research Reports*, 1959, **11**, 43–58.

Milner, B. Neuropsychological evidence for differing memory processes. Abstract for the symposium on short-term and long-term memory. *Proceedings of the 18th international congress of psychology, Moscow*, 1966. Amsterdam: North-Holland Publ., 1968, in press.

Montague, W. E., Adams, J. A., & Kiess, H. O. Forgetting and natural language mediation. *Journal of Experimental Psychology*, 1966, **72**, 829–833.

Murdock, B. B., Jr. The criterion problem in short-term memory. *Journal of Experimental Psychology*, 1966, **72**, 317–324.

Peterson, L. R., & Peterson, M. Short-term retention of individual verbal items. *Journal of Experimental Psychology*, 1959, **58**, 193–198.

Posner, M. I. Components of skilled performance. *Science*, 1966, **152**, 1712–1718.

Postman, L. The present status of interference theory. In C. N. Cofer (Ed.), *Verbal learning and verbal behavior*. New York: McGraw-Hill, 1961. Pp. 152–179.

Postman, L. Short-term memory and incidental learning. In A. W. Melton (Ed.), *Categories of human learning*. New York: Academic Press, 1964. Pp. 145–201.

Postman, L., & Phillips, L. W. Short-term temporal changes in free recall. *Quarterly Journal of Experimental Psychology*, 1965, **17**, 132–138.

Restle, F. Sources of difficulty in learning paired associates. In R. C. Atkinson (Ed.), *Studies in mathematical psychology*. Stanford, Calif.: Stanford University Press, 1964. Pp. 116–172.

Runquist, W. N., & Farley, F. H. The use of mediators in the learning of verbal paired associates. *Journal of Verbal Learning and Verbal Behavior*, 1964, **3**, 280–285.

Sperling, G. The information available in brief visual presentations. *Psychology Monographs*, 1960, **74** (Whole No. 498).

Sperling, G. A model for visual memory tasks. *Human Factors*, 1963, **5**, 19–31.

Sperling, G. Successive approximations to a model for short-term memory. *Acta Psychologica*, 1967, **27**, 285–292.

Sternberg, S. High speed scanning in human memory. *Science*, 1966, **153**, 652–654.

Waugh, N. C., & Norman, D. A. Primary memory. *Psychological Review*, 1965, **72**, 89–104.

Wickelgren, W. A. Size of rehearsal group and short-term memory. *Journal of Experimental Psychology*, 1965, **68**, 413–419.

Wickelgren, W. A., & Norman, D. A. Strength models and serial position in short-term recognition memory. *Journal of Mathematical Psychology*, 1966, **3**, 316–347.

Yntema, D. B., & Trask, F. P. Recall as a search process. *Journal of Verbal Learning and Verbal Behavior*, 1963, **2**, 65–74.

Young, J. L. Effects of intervals between reinforcements and test trials in paired-associate learning. Technical Report No. 101, Institute for Mathematical Studies in the Social Sciences, Stanford University, 1966.

M. Glanzer and A.R. Cunitz

Two storage mechanisms in free recall

Reprinted from the *Journal of Verbal Learning and Verbal Behavior* (1966) 5:351-60

Two experiments were carried out to test the hypothesis that the bimodal serial position curve in free recall is produced by output from two storage mechanisms—short-term and long-term. Experimental operations were applied that were predicted to have a distinct effect on each of these mechanisms, and the changes in the serial position curve were observed. In the first experiment, presentation rate and repetition of individual words were varied in order to affect long-term storage and thereby affect the beginning sections of the serial position curve. Presentation rate has the predicted effect of differentially raising the beginning section of the serial position curve. It does not affect the end section. Repetition, however, did not have any effect that could not be ascribed to presentation rate. It could not, therefore, be used to demonstrate independently the predicted differential effect. In the second experiment, delay between end of list and recall was varied in order to affect short-term storage and, thereby, the end section of the serial position curve. The predicted effect was clearly demonstrated. The results make it possible to systematize a number of findings in the literature.

In a free-recall task, S is presented with a series of words, which he then tries to recall. He is permitted to recall the words in any order that he wishes. The data obtained from this task characteristically show a pronounced serial position effect. The plot of the probability of recall as a function of the position of the word in presentation is U-shaped, with the beginning peak usually lower than the end peak.

The hypothesis proposed here is that the U-shaped serial position curve consists of two curves, each curve representing output from a separate storage mechanism. One is a long-term storage mechanism, the other is a short-term storage mechanism. It follows from the assumption of a long-term and short-term storage mechanism that the material recalled from the beginning of the list should be primarily output from long-term storage, that from the end of the list

primarily output from short-term storage. From the initial decline in the serial position curve and the preceding statement, it may be further asserted that the capacity of long-term storage is limited. The more items that are already in, the less likely that there will be place for a new item. By definition, the short-term storage mechanism is limited not with respect to capacity but with respect to the amount of time it can hold an item.

The proposal then is to view the usual serial position curve as a composite of two output curves—one, declining from beginning to end of list, represents output from long-term storage. The other, rising from beginning to end of list, represents output from short-term storage. The amount of overlap between the two curves in a given set of data cannot be specified at present. It is, in part, the aim of this study to develop information on this point.

The distinction between long-term and short-term storage has been developed in the work of Hebb (1949) and Broadbent (1958). Experimental work on short-term storage has been carried out by a number of investigators, starting from the work of Broadbent (1958), Brown (1958), Conrad (1957), and Peterson and Peterson (1959). This work, including a study using a two-factor approach (Waugh, 1960) that has points of similarity with the one used here, has been concerned almost wholly with fixed-order recall.[1] Surveys of the developments in the area and the theoretical questions involved may be found in recent papers by Melton (1963) and Postman (1964).

In order to support the view proposed above, the attempt will be made here to separate the two hypothesized curves. This will be done by means of experimental operations which have a differential effect on the beginning and end sections of the serial position curve. As will be pointed out subsequently, some of these differential effects have already been demonstrated in the literature.

There are well-established procedures that are used to produce long-term storage. These are rote-learning procedures. The variables that affect the efficiency of rote learning—presentation rate, number of presentations, meaningfulness, etc.—suggest the operations that should have their effect on the beginning section of the serial position curve. Short-term storage should, by definition, be affected primarily by the amount of time which has elapsed since presentation. This variable, amount of time elapsed, should therefore have its effect on the end section of the serial position curve.

The aim of this study is, then, to test the hypothesis that there are two distinct storage mechanisms that produce the serial position

curve in free recall. The strategy is to use variables which should have one effect on one storage mechanism and a different effect (either no effect or an opposed effect) on the other storage mechanism. These variables should give predictable changes in the shape of the serial position curve.

Experiment I

The purpose of this experiment was to change the shape of the beginning of the serial position curve by affecting, primarily, the efficiency of long-term storage. The two main variables used were interval between successive items, or presentation rate, and repetition of items in the list. Since an increase in the interval between items usually facilitates rote learning, an increase should raise the beginning but not the end section of the serial position curve. By the same reasoning, repeated presentation of an item should have the same effect.

Method

There were five main experimental treatments generated by two experimental variables—spacing, or the interval between successive words (S), and number of presentations of each word in the list (P): single spacing and presentation (1S/P)—each word presented once at a 3-sec rate; double spacing (2S)—each word presented once at a 6-sec rate; triple spacing (3S)—each word presented once at a 9-sec rate. There was a further subdivision of the 2S and 3S treatments noted below.

Parallel to the 2S and 3S conditions, were the 2P and 3P conditions: 2P—each word presented twice in succession, all at a 3-sec rate; 3P—each word presented three times in succession, all at a 3-sec rate. (A new word, however, appeared only every 6 or 9 sec.) Since the number of different words in each list was always the same, the total time taken to present a 2P and 2S list was the same. Similarly, the total time taken to present a 3P and 3S list was the same. The S conditions, depending on the location of the additional interitem intervals, were further subdivided into SA and SB conditions. If the 1S/P condition[2] is taken and an

[1] The task used by Peterson and Peterson (1959) is viewed here as a fixed-order recall task, since S was required to recall the letters of the trigram in the order that they had been presented.

[2] In the 1S/P condition, each list was preceded by a spoken ready signal 4 sec before the first word; it was followed by a bell signalling the start of the recall period, 3 sec after the last word. These intervals were increased, as indicated, in the SA and

additional 3-sec interval is inserted after each word, a 2SA (after) condition is obtained. If the additional 3-sec interval is inserted before each word, a 2SB (before) condition is obtained. Similar placements of an additional 6-sec interval produce a 3SA and 3SB condition. The effect of these placements made a difference only at the beginning and end of the lists. In 2SA and 3SA an additional interval occurred between the last word of the list and the signal for recall; in 2SB and 3SB the additional interval occurred between the ready signal and the first word.

The main reason for using the two forms of the 2S and 3S conditions was to determine the source of possible differences between the 2S versus 2P, and 3S versus 3P conditions. If only one form of the S conditions had been used, differences between the S and corresponding P conditions might be interpreted as a result of differences in the interval between the first presentation of a repeated word and its recall, or differences in the interval between the last presentation of a repeated word and its recall. (If the 2S condition is viewed as identical with the 2P condition except for the elimination of one of the two presentations of each word, then elimination of the second member of each pair gives the 2SA condition, while elimination of the first member of each pair gives the 2SB condition. Similarly, elimination of the last two presentations of each repeated word in the 3P condition gives the 3SA condition, while elimination of the first two presentations of each repeated word gives the 3SB condition.) A secondary reason for using the two forms of the S condition was to obtain further information on the effect of delays without an interpolated task on recall.

Procedure

All Ss were presented with two 5-word practice lists and eight 20-word main lists consisting of common one-syllable nouns, drawn from the Thorndike-Lorge (1944) AA lists. The lists, recorded on tapes, were composed of the same words in the same order. They varied for the groups only in the presentation rate, number of repetitions of the individual words, or location of the interitem intervals.

The lists were presented in succession to the Ss during the course of a single session. After each list the Ss had 2 min during which they wrote the words that they recalled, in booklets. Each list was preceded by a ready signal, and followed by a bell that signalled the end of the list and start of the recall period. The Ss were tested in groups of 20.

SB conditions. In the P conditions the intervals used in the 1S/P condition were used.

Subjects

The Ss were 240 Army enlisted men. There were 40 Ss in each of the following conditions: 1S/P, 2SA, 3SA, 2P and 3P. There were 20 Ss in 2SB and in 3SB.

Results

In scoring the lists, a word was considered correct if it was (a) the same as a list word, (b) a homonym, or (c) a recognizable misspelling of either. Thus, if the word "night" was given, "knight" or "nite" would both be scored correct. Repetitions of a word were not counted. The mean number correct for the eight lists at each serial position was computed for each S. These twenty means for each S form the basic data used in the analyses discussed below.

The serial position curves for the alternate forms of the spaced lists (2SA and 2SB; 3SA and 3SB) were examined to determine whether the placing of the interval at the end of the list had any effect. No marked or systematic differences were apparent in the curves. Analysis of variance of the data for the four groups found no significant effect of the placement of the interval ($F < 1$) and no significant interaction of this variable with the serial position effect, F (19,2204) $= 1.19$, $p > .10$. The interpretation of these findings will be discussed subsequently. Since, however, the variable of interval placement had neither an overall effect nor an effect on the shape of the serial position curve, the subsequent analyses of the data combine groups 2SA and 2SB into one group, and groups 3SA and 3SB into another group. The experimental conditions are therefore reduced to five: 1S/P, 2S, 3S, 2P, and 3P.

Examination of the serial position curves for these conditions (Fig. 1) shows a clear and systematic effect of spacing and a similar but less clear effect of repetition. The curve for the 1S/P condition appears in both the top and bottom half of the figure. As spacing increases, the probability of recall is raised in all but the last few positions of the curve. The end peak remains unaffected. As repetition increases, there is a similar effect

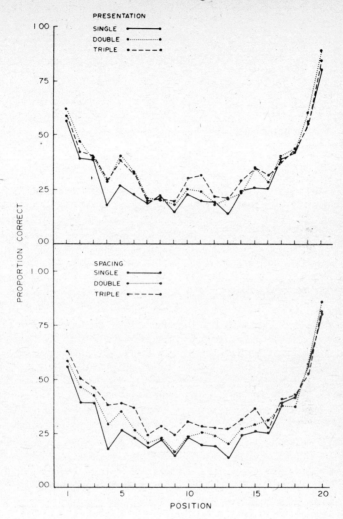

FIG. 1. Serial position curves for single (1S/P), double (2P), and triple (3P) presentation above; for single (1S/P), double (2S), and triple (3S) spacing, below. Each point represents the mean for eight lists and either 40 or 60 Ss.

in going from the 1S/P condition to the 2P condition, but no further systematic change in going from 2P to 3P. Comparison of the curves in the top half of Fig. 1 with those of the bottom half indicates that repetition has little or no effect beyond that of the spacing between new words.

The data were analyzed by analysis of variance with the five main treatments (1S/P, 2S, 2P, 3S, 3P) as a between-subjects variable and serial position as a within-subjects variable. The four degrees of freedom associated with treatments were then broken down into three components: (a) The general effect of spacing the interval between new words, whether or not repetition occurred between the new words. This was evaluated by comparing 1S/P, 2S + 2P, and 3S + 3P ($df = 2$); (b) The effect of repetitions of the words in addition to the effect of spacing *per se*. This was evaluated by comparing 2S + 3S and 2P + 3P ($df = 1$); (c) The interaction of spacing and repetition ($df = 1$).

The overall effect of treatments is significant, $F(4,235) = 2.69, p < .05$. The effect of spacing is significant, $F(2,235) = 4.61$, $p < .025$, but neither the additional effect of repetition ($F < 1$) nor the interaction of spacing with repetition, $F(1,235) = 1.34$, $p > .10$, is significant. The within-subjects effect of serial position is highly significant, $F(19,4465) = 236.66$, $p < .001$. Reduction of the degrees of freedom to 1 and 235, giving a lower-bound, conservative test for a repeated measurements design (Greenhouse and Geisser, 1959), leaves this effect significant at the .001 level. The interaction of spacing with serial position is significant at the .005 level, $F(38,4465) = 1.79$, but is no longer significant under the conservative test, with degrees of freedom reduced to 2 and 235. The remaining interactions are negligible.

The conservative test of the interaction between spacing and serial position is actually doubly conservative, since it does not focus on the specific differences expected under the hypothesis of two storage mechanisms. To focus on the predicted effects, a separate test was made of the effect of the three spacing conditions (1S/P versus 2S + 2P versus 3S + 3P) on the sum of correct responses for successive groups of five serial positions. The degrees of freedom for each of these tests are 2/235. For the first five positions $F = 23.46$, $p < .001$; for the second five, $F = 16.21$, $p < .001$; for the third five $F = 22.00$, $p < .001$. For the last five positions, however, the effect of spacing is not significant—$F = 1.71$, $p > .10$.

It might be argued that absence of significant differences in the last section of the curves is due to a ceiling effect since the

probability of recall of the last word is approximately .85. The probabilities of recall for words 15 through 19, however, run lower than the probabilities for positions 1 through 5, which do show significant differences. Comparing the sums for positions 15 through 19 gives an $F = 1.80$, $p > .10$. The ceiling effect cannot, therefore, account for the absence of differences at the end of the curve.

Discussion

The results indicate that spacing, i.e., the rate at which new words are presented, affects the shape of the serial position curve. These results agree with findings of an experiment by Murdock (1962), in which 20-word lists were given at presentation rates of a word every 1 sec and a word every 2 sec. The curves obtained for the two conditions are very similar to those on the bottom of Fig. 1, with the spacing affecting all of the positions except the last few. The presence of a regular ordering of the spacing conditions up to and including the 15th position suggests that the items are still being recruited for long-term storage well towards the end of the list.

It had been expected that adding repetition of the words in the intervals between new words would increase the differences between the serial position curves. This was clearly not so. The repetition, indeed, seems to counteract the spacing effect.

The absence of a repetition effect is surprising for two reasons. First, a preliminary check of the accuracy with which Ss could hear the words in the repeated and corresponding spaced lists indicated, as might be expected, that the Ss heard the words in the repeated lists with slightly more accuracy. The check was carried out by presenting the lists to four groups of Ss drawn from the same population as the experimental groups. Four groups, consisting of 14 to 15 Ss each, listened to the 2S, 2P, 3S, and 3P lists and recorded each new word as they heard it. The interval between the successive words gave the Ss ample time to record each new word. Comparison of the total number correctly recorded in each group indicated a tendency for more words to be recorded accurately by the groups that heard the lists with repeated words. The tendency, however, did not attain statistical significance, $F(1,55) = 3.80$, $.05 < p < .10$.

The absence of a repetition effect is also surprising because in the repeated conditions the Ss had 2 or 3 presentations to learn each word. Viewing the successive repetitions as learning trials leads to the expectation that the probability of recall of a particular word be higher in the repetition condition than in the corresponding spacing condition. It is clear both from the statistical analysis and the curves in Fig. 1 that nothing like this occurred. The curve for the 3P condition actually lies slightly lower than the curve for the 3S condition.

There are several possible reasons for the absence of this effect. One is that simple repetition without active participation by the S may not be effective for learning the words in these lists. Another possible reason is that the particular form of repetition used here—immediately successive repetition—generates effects that counter the effects of learning.

There are two aspects of the data that give information on the effects of delay when no interpolated task is imposed. One is the absence of any effect of spacing on the end peak of the serial position curve. If simple amount of time between presentation and recall were effective, then it would be expected that all points in the end peak would be lowered as spacing increased from 1S/P to 2SA to 3SA. There was no evidence for such an effect. Similarly, it would be expected that all points in the end peak, except the last one, would be lowered as spacing increased from 1S/P to 2SB to 3SB. Again, there was no evidence for such an effect. This is interpreted here as indicating that passage of time without an interpolated task has no effect on short-term storage. The finding is in line with other findings in the

literature on fixed-order recall (Brown, 1958).

Another aspect of the data that indicates that pure passage of time does not cause loss in short-term storage is the absence of differences between the 2SA and 2SB conditions, and also between the 3SA and 3SB conditions. In the 2SA and 3SA conditions, there were additional delay periods between end of list and recall. As was noted earlier, these additional delays had no effect. The relevance of these findings to the development of an effective delay procedure will be discussed further in Exp. II.

In summary, the results with the variable that was effective in the experiment—spacing or presentation rate—support the hypothesis. There is an effect on the beginning but not on the end section of the serial position. The results with a second variable, repetition, did not have any overall effect beyond that of spacing and therefore did not furnish any further information for the evaluation of the hypothesis.

EXPERIMENT II

The purpose of the second experiment was to study the separate output of the hypothesized short-term storage mechanism. The strategy again was to introduce a variable that would have a different effect on long-term and short-term storage and thus have a different effect on the beginning and end peak of the serial position curve. The variable selected was delay between the end of the list and start of recall.

Before determining the form in which this delay would be imposed, the effects of pure delay, i.e., delay without an interpolated task, were investigated further. The weight of evidence from the fixed-order recall experiments indicates that pure delay has no effect on short-term storage. The subsidiary evidence in Exp. I on the effects of pure delay also indicated that it had no effect. The effects of pure delay were, however, examined further because the interpretation of predicted differential effect of delay would be simplest if no interpolated task were used. There was reason to believe that the free recall task differed sufficiently from the fixed-order recall tasks that had been used, to make it worthwhile to investigate the effects of pure delay on the free-recall task. Moreover, even for the fixed-order recall task there is at least one instance in which pure delay results in a drop in total amount recalled (Anderson, 1960).

A pilot study was, therefore, carried out in which two groups of Ss were each given four 30-word lists, one group with no delay before recall, the other group with 30-sec delay. There was no interpolated task during the delay. A significant reduction of the end peak was found with 30-sec delay, $F(1,233) = 37.00$, $p < .001$. There was no marked effect of delay on the beginning peak, $F(1,233) = 2.67$, $p > .10$. The effect on the end peak was, however, small in magnitude, with the serial position curve showing a clear end peak after a 30-sec delay.

It was therefore decided to require the Ss to carry out a minimal task during the delay periods used in this experiment. It was expected that, under these conditions, as the amount of delay increased, the height of the end peak would decrease but the beginning peak would remain unaffected.

Method

Subjects. The Ss were 46 Army enlisted men.

Materials and Equipment. The words were shown on a screen, with an automatic slide projector. The words were 240 AA monosyllabic nouns drawn from the Thorndike-Lorge list (1944). Each word was printed in black on a light blue background.

Procedure

The S was first shown three 5-word practice lists, and then fifteen 15-word lists. Each word was shown for 1 sec with a 2-sec interval between successive words. The E read each word as it appeared. After the last word in each list, the symbol #, or a digit from 0 to 9 was shown. If the cross-hatch symbol appeared, E said "write," and the S immediately started writing all the words he could recall in his test booklet. If a number appeared, the S started counting out loud from that number until E said "write." While the S was counting, E would measure either 10 or 30 sec with a stop watch before telling him to write. Each of the delay conditions was used with each of the three practice lists and with five of the main lists. The Ss were individually tested. For each S the words were assigned at random to the lists and order of the delay conditions within the three practice lists and within the fifteen main lists was assigned at random. This meant that each S received a different set of lists and a different sequence of delay conditions.

After each list, the S was given a minimum of 1 min and a maximum of 5 min to complete his recall of each list. After the completion of each session E went over the booklet with the S to make sure that all the words were legible.

Results

The results are summarized in Fig. 2. Each curve represents 5 lists recalled by the 46 Ss. The 10-sec delay was sufficient to remove most of the end peak. With a 30-sec delay there is no trace at all of the end peak.[3]

Analysis of variance was carried with positions, and delay interval as within-subjects variables. Both variables and their interaction are significant at the .001 level or better—position $F(14,630) = 24.87$, delay interval, $F(2,90) = 19.75$, and their interaction, $F(28,1260) = 2.29$. Evaluation of the Fs with reduced degrees of freedom, here 1 and 45, leaves the effect of position and delay interval both significant at the .001 level. The interaction, however, is not significant, under this conservative test. Since, however, the effect was specifically predicted for the end peak, a separate analysis was made of the effect of the delay condition on the sum of correct responses for successive sets of five positions in the curves. The degrees of freedom for these tests are 1/45. For the first five positions, $F = 3.60$, $p > .05$; for the second five positions $F = 1.44$, $p > .10$. The effect of delay is significant only in the last five positions—$F = 22.42$, $p < .001$.

There is one characteristic of the no-delay curve that makes it differ from the usual serial position curve—the end peak is lower than the beginning peak. This may be due to the special characteristics of this experiment, in which S was exposed to delay conditions that lowered the efficiency of recall of items from the end of the list. This could have led to a strategy for handling the lists that emphasized the beginning items of the list.

[3] Since the submission of this paper, similar results have been reported by Postman, L. and Phillips, L. W., *Quart. J. exp. Psychol.* 1965, **17**, 132-138.

GLANZER AND CUNITZ

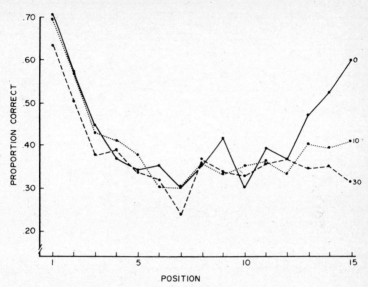

Fig. 2. Serial position curves for 0-, 10-, and 30-sec delay. Each point represents the mean for five lists and 46 Ss.

Discussion

The results of Exp. II give further support to the hypothesis of two distinct storage mechanisms. Again, it was demonstrated that an experimental operation had a predicted, differential effect on the peaks of the serial position curve.

The hypothesis furnishes a simple explanation for the serial position curve in free recall. It also furnishes a basis for further assertions about free recall which are supported by findings in the literature. Or, to say the same thing another way, the hypothesis makes it possible to systematize a number of findings in the literature:

(1) Word frequency, a variable that has an effect on rote learning, and, therefore, presumably on long-term storage, should have an effect on the beginning peak of the serial position curve. This assertion is supported by recent findings by Sumby (1963).

(2) Linguistic constraints in the words of the list, a variable that has an effect on rote learning, and therefore, presumably, on long-term storage should have an effect on the beginning peak of the curve. This assertion is supported by findings by Deese and Kaufman (1957).

(3) Requiring the S to recall the items in forward order should depress the end peak of the serial position curve. By requiring sequential recall, E imposes a delay with an interpolated task—recall of the early list items. This permits the loss of items from short-term storage. This assertion is supported by findings by Deese (1957) and Raffel (1936).

The approach used here is not presented as a complete theory for free recall. A complete theory would permit derivation of the exact form of each of the hypothesized component curves. Once such a derivation is available then it would be possible to move away from the gross distinction between short-term and long-term storage. In a complete theory, the derivation of the output curve for long-term storage would, moreover, be based on specific assumptions about the processing involved in long-term storage. This would make it possible to move away from the simple identification of long-term storage variables with those affecting rote learning. The assumptions should also permit derivation of the characteristics of recall under more complex conditions than those considered here—for example, repeated presentations of the same word list.

The attempt to build a complete theory could, of course, be based on a variety of other constructs. For example, an approach could be developed by using inhibition or interference constructs—more specifically the constructs of proactive and retroactive inhibition. Using these constructs to build towards a complete theory leads to some complexities which will be briefly pointed out here.

The application of these constructs to account for the asymmetrical, bimodal shape of the usual serial position curve would require the specification of two functions, one relating amounts of PI to each position in the list, the other relating amounts of RI to each position in the list. If RI is considered simply as a function of the number of items following a given position, and PI simply as a function of the number of items preceding a given position, then the two functions might reasonably be expected to be monotonic. Two monotonic functions of this type and a simple rule for summing the inhibitory effects will not produce the standard type of U-shaped curve such as those in Fig. 1. By using values from Fig. 1, the difficulty may be summarized as follows. The probability of recall of the first list word is approximately .60. The probability of recall of the last list word is approximately .85. It may be assumed that there has been a reduction of .40 at the first position due to RI and a reduction of .15 at the last position due to PI. The probability of recall at the middle position is approximately .25. Within an inhibitory theory, this would be viewed

as a reduction of .75 at those positions. The middle positions would be expected, if the RI and PI position functions are monotonic and if their effect is combined by addition. to have much higher probabilities of recall than those actually obtained. There are two ways of coping with this problem. One way is to move away from a simple additive system[5] allowing, for example, for interaction effects. The other way is to move away from simple functions. For example, PI for a position may be considered to be a function of both the number of items preceding the position, and the number of items following the position (time elapsing before recall).

Other complexities develop in applying inhibitory constructs to account for the systematic effects found in the experiments reported above. It is possible to use the PI construct to explain the effect of delay in Exp. II by assuming that PI is a function of both number of preceding items and the time that elapses during the delay interval. The statement of the relations involved might go as follows: Earlier items which have been extinguished recover during the delay interval and then interfere with the recall of items from the end of the list. This statement implies, however, that the effect of delay should merely alter the proportion of early and late items recalled. For every late item that is proactively blocked there should be an early item in its stead. At the very least it could be expected that there should be some increase in the probability of recall of the early items. There is no evidence at all of such an increase. The only change that occurs is that the number of items from the end of the list decreases. Again, additions or alterations can be made to handle the obtained results. Again, however, the theoretical structure grows rather complex.

---

[5] More technically, the simple additive system referred to here would be called a linear system, in which $f(RI) + f(PI) = f(RI + PI)$.

REFERENCES

ANDERSON, N. S. Poststimulus cuing in immediate memory. *J. exp. Psychol.*, 1960, **60**, 216-221.

BROADBENT, D. E. *Perception and communication.* New York: Pergamon, 1958.

BROWN, J. Some tests of the decay theory of immediate memory. *Quart. J. exp. Psychol.*, 1958, **10**, 12-21.

CONRAD, R. Decay theory of immediate memory. *Nature*, 1957, **179**, 831-832.

DEESE, J. Serial organization in the recall of disconnected items. *Psychol. Rep.*, 1957, **3**, 577-582.

DEESE, J., AND KAUFMAN, R. A. Serial effects in recall of unorganized and sequentially organized verbal material. *J. exp. Psychol.*, 1957, **54**, 180-187.

GREENHOUSE, S. W., AND GEISSER, S. On methods in the analysis of profile data. *Psychometrika*, 1959, **24**, 95-112.

HEBB, D. O. *The organization of behavior.* New York: Wiley, 1949.

MELTON, A. W. Implications of short-term memory for a general theory of memory. *J. verb. Learn. verb. Behav.*, 1963, **2**, 1-21.

MURDOCK, B. B., JR. The serial position effect of free recall. *J. exp. Psychol.*, 1962, **64**, 482-488.

PETERSON, L. R., AND PETERSON, M. J. Short term retention of individual verbal items. *J. exp. Psychol.*, 1959, **58**, 193-198.

POSTMAN, L. Short-term memory and incidental learning. In A. W. Melton (Ed.), *Categories of human learning.* New York: Academic Press, 1964. Pp. 145-201.

RAFFEL, G. Two determinants of the effect of primacy. *Amer. J. Psychol.*, 1936, **48**, 654-657.

SUMBY, W. H. Word frequency and serial position effects. *J. verb. Learn. verb. Behav.*, 1963, **1**, 443-450.

THORNDIKE, E. L., AND LORGE, I. *The teacher's word book of 30,000 words.* New York: Bureau of Publications, Teachers College, Columbia University, 1944.

WAUGH, N. C. Serial position and the memory span. *Amer. J. Psychol.*, 1960, **73**, 68-79.

F.I.M. Craik

The fate of primary memory items in free recall

Reprinted from the *Journal of Verbal Learning and Verbal Behavior* (1970) **9**:143-8

The question of whether items retrieved from primary memory (PM) are as well registered in memory as those retrieved from secondary memory (SM) was examined in a free-recall study. It was found that words in terminal serial positions were retrieved best in immediate recall but least well in a second recall session. The conclusion was drawn that PM items are less well learned than SM items, and the implications for models of memory were examined. Subsidiary findings were that auditory presentation was superior to visual presentation and written recall was superior to spoken recall in PM. Also, words retrieved late in immediate recall had the highest probability of retrieval on the second recall session.

When a subject (S) is presented with a list of unrelated words for free recall, he usually retrieves the last few words in the list right away and then augments this terminal cluster with the recall of words from the beginning and middle of the list. The better recall of terminal items (the recency effect) can be handled by one-process models of memory (Melton, 1963) by postulating that an item's strength or accessibility is very high immediately after presentation but falls off rapidly as further items are presented. In the last few years, however, several theorists have advocated two-process models of memory to describe the results of free-recall studies. For example, Waugh and Norman (1965) proposed that the last few words are retrieved from primary memory (PM) whereas earlier words are retrieved from secondary memory (SM) with greater difficulty. While generally accepting the PM/SM distinction, two-process theorists have themselves split into two camps: those postulating two stores (Atkinson & Shiffrin, 1968; Glanzer & Cunitz, 1966) and

those who argue for one memory store but two retrieval processes (Tulving, 1968).

The one-process model and the two-store model make different predictions regarding the registration in permanent memory of items presented in the middle and at the end of a list. It is known that recall of a word in free-recall learning facilitates its recall on subsequent trials (Lachman & Laughery, 1968; Tulving, 1967). Thus, since terminal items are recalled best in immediate free recall, they should receive most facilitation as a group and also be best recalled on a subsequent trial—this is presumably the prediction that one-process models must make. On the other hand, the two-store model described by Atkinson and Shiffrin (1968) predicts that terminal items should be recalled least well on a subsequent trial. This follows from the notion that the short-term store contains a rehearsal buffer which can hold 4–5 words. Once the buffer is full, further incoming items will knock out words already present—usually on the principle of "first in, first out." Words in the middle of the list will thus remain in the buffer until approximately four further words have been presented, but words at the end of the list will remain in the buffer for a shorter time on average since they are retrieved soon after presentation. The model further postulates that the strength of registration in LTM depends on the length of an item's stay in the buffer so it follows that the last words in a list, although better recalled than earlier words in immediate recall, should have the least strength in permanent memory.

The preceding argument reduces to the question of whether PM items are as well learned as SM items. Bjork (1968) explored this problem in a free-recall learning study and found better learning of words retrieved from the middle of the list than words retrieved from terminal positions. In the present experiment, Ss were given ten lists for immediate free recall and were subsequently asked to recall as many words as they could from all lists. The serial position curve of this "final recall" session was then examined to determine whether items originally in the terminal positions were recalled better or worse than items from the middle of the lists. It may be pointed out that this technique differs from that employed by Glanzer and Cunitz (1966). In their study, irrelevant material was interpolated between list presentation and free recall while the present experiment deals with words which have already been recalled once.

Other variables of interest were the modes of input and response. Previous researchers have used either auditory or visual input and either spoken or written responses with the implicit assumption that provided the words were correctly perceived, such variations should make little difference. Recent studies, however, have called this assumption into question. Murdock and Walker (1969) have shown that auditory presentation is superior to visual presentation in single-trial free recall and that this superiority is confined to the last few input positions. With regard to response mode, studies by Murray (1965) and Craik (1969) have shown a superiority of written over

spoken response in free recall. It was therefore decided to conduct the present experiment under the four combinations of auditory or visual presentation with spoken or written recall to establish either that the findings were general over input and response modes or interacted with these modes. More generally, further normative data would also be obtained on the effects of manipulating input and response modes in free recall.

METHOD

The words used in the experiment were drawn from a pool of 600 common two-syllable nouns. For each S, these 600 words were randomly sorted into forty 15-word lists. Thus each S received a unique set of lists. The S was given 10 lists in each of four sessions—each session under a different input-response combination (auditory or visual presentation; spoken or written recall). The words were presented at a 2-sec rate, and immediately following presentation S was given 1 min for free recall. For visual presentation the words were shown in a memory drum and for auditory presentation the words were read by E in time to a metronome. Responses were either written on separate sheets for each list or were spoken into a dictaphone for later transcription. After recall of the tenth list, S was given 5 min to write down as many words as he could from all 10 lists. The instructions were again for free recall.

Twenty student Ss were tested individually in each of four sessions. The sessions were at least a day apart and the order in which Ss received the four input-response combinations was counterbalanced across the group.

RESULTS AND DISCUSSION

Immediate recall scores were broken down into PM and SM components using a method described by Tulving and Colotla (1970) based on Waugh and Norman (1965). A response is regarded as a PM item if no more than a critical number of other items (either further stimulus items or responses) intervened between the item's presentation and its recall; it is regarded as an SM item if more than the critical number of stimulus items or recalled responses occurred in the item's intratrial retention interval. This method has the advantage that each word can be identified as having been retrieved from PM or SM. In the present study, the critical number of intervening items was taken as six, since that number yielded an

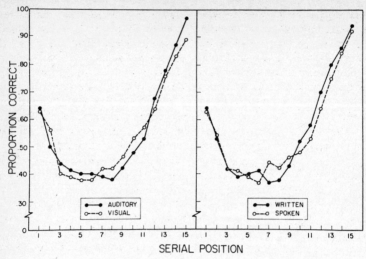

FIG. 1. Serial position curves for different input and response modes.

overall estimate of PM capacity (3.3 words) which was very close to the estimate (3.4 words) calculated by the "guessing correction" technique used by Waugh and Norman (1965).

Input and Response Modes

Figure 1 shows the serial position curves for auditory and visual presentation (combined over response mode) and for spoken and written responses (combined over input mode). The differences are slight but consistent with previous research findings: auditory presentation is superior over the last few input positions and spoken recall is poorer over these positions. An analysis of variance on the PM scores yielded a significant effect of input mode, $F(1, 19) = 6.93$, $p < .05$, and of response mode $F(1, 19) = 9.84$, $p < .01$, but no significant interaction. Thus, although PM differences were slight, they were statistically reliable. A similar analysis on SM scores yielded no significant effects.

It seems likely that the effect of input modality was small since the presentation rate was relatively slow. Murdock and Walker (1969) presented words at the rates of 2 per sec and 1 per sec and found the superiority of auditory presentation to be greater at the faster rate. Presumably input modality would have little

or no effect at presentation speeds slower than one word per 2 sec. The superiority of auditory presentation in the recency positions has been variously attributed to a larger prelinguistic store for auditorily presented material (Murdock & Walker, 1969) or to the output from a postlinguistic store augmented by retrieval of material from prelinguistic stores (Craik, 1969). The latter point of view depends on the argument that after 2–3 sec there is still usable information in the auditory prelinguistic store but none in the corresponding visual store.

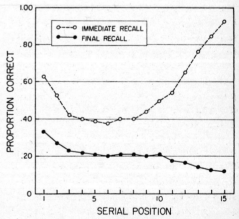

FIG. 2. Serial position curves for immediate and final recall.

The possible reasons for the superiority of written over spoken recall are even more speculative. Perhaps speaking the first few responses interferes with information remaining in PM. Another possibility is that if S is writing his responses, it is easier for him to rehearse the last few items in the list which are thus better recalled.

Immediate and Final Recall

Since the input and response manipulations had little effect on recall, scores from the different conditions were pooled to examine the serial position curves for immediate and final recall. Figure 2 shows that immediate recall yielded the classical serial position curve with a primacy effect for the first two items, a flat middle portion, and a recency effect extending over the last six or seven items. Final recall responses included some words which had not been given in immediate recall, but because of their rarity (less than 2% of the words presented) and since they were distributed over all serial positions, they were excluded from the calculation of the final recall serial position curve shown in Figure 2. Thus the final recall curve is composed entirely of words which were also recalled in immediate recall. The serial position curve in final recall consists of a primacy effect, a flat middle portion, and a slight but consistent *negative* recency effect. The reliability of this latter effect was assessed by considering the scores on the last seven serial positions since PM items typically arise from these positions (Waugh & Norman, 1965). An analysis of variance on the scores yielded a significant difference between serial positions, $F(6, 114) = 7.44$, $p < .001$, and a trend analysis of variance was also significant, $F(1, 138) = 18.82$, $p < .001$.

It thus appears that the last few words presented in a list are recalled best in immediate free recall but show the least probability of recall on a subsequent trial. This conclusion is supported by a conditional probability analysis. The probability of a word occurring in final recall given that it was also retrieved in immediate recall was $p = .37$. This value was substantially larger than the probability of final recall given that the word was not retrieved in immediate recall ($p = .04$), and this advantage to words which had already been recalled was shown by all 20 Ss. For words which were recalled in both immediate and final tests the probability of final recall given immediate recall from PM was $p = .16$ while the probability of final recall given immediate recall from SM was $p = .51$. The advantage to words recalled initially from SM was shown by all 20 Ss. Thus the retrieval of a word in the second recall session depends on whether the word was retrieved in immediate recall, and, further, whether it was retrieved initially from PM or SM.

From these results it is concluded that PM items are not as well registered as SM items in a permanent memory system. The "negative recency effect" in the final recall serial position curve is consistent with the two-store notion that terminal items are held in short-term store very briefly and thus transferred to a long-term store less effectively. Another possibility, although a less attractive one to the present writer, is that PM and SM items are equally well registered in permanent memory but that PM items are less accessible due, possibly, to the less efficient generation of semantic retrieval cues for terminal items.

From the conditional probability analysis, it may be concluded either that words which are easy to retrieve once are easy to retrieve again or that the first recall of a word has a facilitatory effect on its later retrieval. If the second explanation is true, it must be qualified by the finding that recall from PM has less of a facilitating effect than recall from SM.

Output Position in Immediate Recall

A final analysis was carried out on the relationship between *output* position in immediate recall and probability of retrieval in final recall. Words which are retrieved first in immediate recall are most likely to be PM items and so should be retrieved rather poorly in final recall. As output proceeds, so a greater proportion of the words will be retrieved from

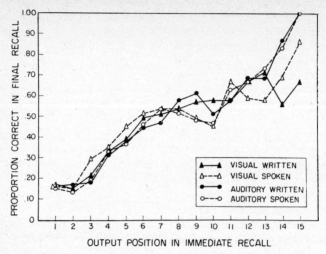

FIG. 3. Probability of retrieval in final recall as a function of output position in immediate recall.

SM, until after the sixth or seventh output position, all words are defined as being from SM. On this argument it was expected that the probability of retrieval in final recall would first rise with output position and then flatten out. However, Figure 3 shows that while there appears to be some tendency for the curves to flatten out between output positions 7–10, they rise again and even reach $p = 1.00$ in two cases. The input-response conditions are shown separately in Figure 3 to make the point that this continued increase is not an artefact of one particular condition. As might be expected, very few Ss recalled as many as 15 words in immediate recall (the total numbers of words retrieved in output positions 13, 14, and 15 were 68, 36, and 16, respectively) so the absolute values of the last few points are not to be taken too seriously. The continuing upward trend is shown in all four conditions, however, so it seems reasonable to conclude that for SM items there is an additional factor leading to the more efficient retrieval in final recall of words given late in output.

This finding goes against the notion, mentioned previously, that items which are easiest to retrieve in immediate recall are also easiest to retrieve in final recall. Presumably words in output positions 10–15 are retrieved with some difficulty, yet they have the highest probability

of retrieval in final recall. Two possible explanations for the finding may be suggested. One is that the first recall of a word acts as a second presentation and that the beneficial effects of this repetition are greatest with long lags (Melton, 1967). Alternatively, the facilitative effects of immediate recall may depend more on the process of retrieval, with difficult initial retrieval somehow being more beneficial for later retrieval.

CONCLUSIONS

The results of the present experiment and their significance may be briefly summarized. First, in a typical free-recall study, there were no large effects due to either input or response mode. Auditory presentation was superior to visual presentation and written recall was superior to spoken recall; both of these small effects were limited to PM—neither input nor response mode affected SM. It seems likely, however, that the differences would be greater at faster presentation rates.

Second, although the last words in the presentation list were retrieved best in immediate free recall, they had the lowest probability of retrieval in the final recall session. Since PM items were recalled best immediately and since it is known that recall facilitates retrieval on a subsequent trial (Lachman & Laughery, 1968;

Tulving, 1967), it seems necessary for one-process models to predict that PM items should also be recalled best in final recall. The finding that terminal items are retrieved *least* well in final recall would thus seem to pose a serious problem for one-process models. While the negative recency effect in final recall was specifically predicted from the two-store model (Atkinson & Shiffrin, 1968), the result does not constitute evidence against a theory which postulates two retrieval processes (Tulving, 1968).

Finally, it was found that the probability of retrieval in final recall was a monotonically increasing function of output position in immediate recall. At least two phenomena appear to be involved in this effect: words given early in output are more likely to be PM items, but within the set of SM items there is still a tendency for words recalled last to be retrieved best in final recall. This latter effect may be due to difficult retrieval somehow being more facilitating or it may be a special case of the repetition effect noted by Melton (1967).

REFERENCES

ATKINSON, R. C., & SHIFFRIN, R. M. Human memory: A proposed system and its control processes. In K. W. Spence and J. T. Spence (Eds.), *The psychology of learning and motivation*, Vol. 2. New York: Academic Press, 1968. Pp. 89–195.

BJORK, R. The short term and long term effects of recency in free recall. Paper presented to the Psychonomic Society, St. Louis, 1968.

CRAIK, F. I. M. Modality effects in short-term storage. *Journal of Verbal Learning and Verbal Behavior*, 1969, **8**, 658–664.

GLANZER, M., & CUNITZ, A. R. Two storage mechanisms in free recall. *Journal of Verbal Learning and Verbal Behavior*, 1966, **5**, 351–360.

LACHMAN, R., & LAUGHERY, K. R. Is a test trial a training trial in free recall learning? *Journal of Experimental Psychology*, 1968, **76**, 40–50.

MELTON, A. W. Implications of short-term memory for a general theory of memory. *Journal of Verbal Learning and Verbal Behavior*, 1963, **2**, 1–21.

MELTON, A. W. Repetition and retrieval from memory. *Science*, 1967, **158**, 532.

MURDOCK, B. B., JR., & WALKER, K. D. Modality effects in free recall. *Journal of Verbal Learning and Verbal Behavior*, 1969, **8**, 665–676.

MURRAY, D. J. Vocalization-at-presentation and immediate recall, with varying presentation rates. *Quarterly Journal of Experimental Psychology*, 1965, **17**, 47–56.

TULVING, E. The effects of presentation and recall of material in free recall learning. *Journal of Verbal Learning and Verbal Behavior*, 1967, **6**, 175–184.

TULVING, E. Theoretical issues in free recall. In T. R. Dixon and D. L. Horton (Eds.), *Verbal behavior and general behavior theory*. Englewood Cliffs, N.J.: Prentice-Hall, 1968. Pp. 2–36.

TULVING, E., & COLOTLA, V. Free recall of trilingual lists. *Cognitive Psychology*, 1970, **1**, 86–98.

WAUGH, N. C., & NORMAN, D. A. Primary memory. *Psychological Review*, 1965, **72**, 89–104.

W. Kintsch and H. Buschke

Homophones and synonyms in short-term memory

Reprinted from the *Journal of Experimental Psychology* (1969) **80**(3):403-7

Differential effects of acoustic and semantic similarity on primary and secondary memory are shown by analysis of short-term retention for sequences of 16 words containing either homophone pairs, synonym pairs, or unrelated words. After presentation of each sequence, one of the words in the sequence was given as a probe for *S* to respond with the word that followed the probe in the sequence. Recall of early words in the lists was used to estimate the secondary memory component of short-term retention. Secondary memory was strongly decreased by semantic similarity. Recall of the most recent words in the lists provided a basis for estimation of primary memory. Primary memory was unaffected by semantic similarity, but was decreased significantly by acoustic similarity.

One argument in favor of a distinction between primary and secondary memory has been that they differ in the way material is encoded. According to this view, primary memory depends upon a purely acoustic code, while such factors as meaningfulness, redundancy, and acoustic similarity are important for long-term retention. Thus, acoustic but not semantic factors should affect primary memory. Previous attempts to test this hypothesis experimentally have yielded ambiguous results. Conrad, Freeman, and Hull (1965) studied the retention of six-letter sequences that varied both in statistical predictability and acoustical confusability. They found a large effect of confusability and a very small effect of predictability (one-fifteenth of the acoustic factor). Baddeley and Dale (1966) and Baddeley (1966) reported experiments exploring the effects of semantic similarity upon short-term retention. In the first study, no effect was observed; in the second, a small effect of semantic similarity was found. However, in a short-term memory experiment by Dale and Gregory (1966), using a retroactive interference design, more intrusions were observed when the interpolated material and learning material were semantically similar.

These results may mean that semantic similarity does affect primary memory, but to a lesser degree than acoustic confusability. On the other hand, one could argue that performance in these experiments does not depend upon primary memory alone, but is jointly determined by both primary and secondary memory. This possibility is clearly implied by such theories as that of Waugh and Norman (1965). Waugh and Norman assumed that total recall can be regarded as the sum of two components, primary and secondary memory. Furthermore, they suggested a method in which the two components can be separated analytically. This method may be used to reformulate the problems discussed previously, so that the confounding between primary and secondary memory, present in any set of retention data, can be avoided. The hypothesis to be tested here is that acoustic similarity affects the primary component of retention, but semantic similarity does not. On the other hand, the secondary component of retention is surely dependent upon semantic factors, while acoustic factors may or may not play a role.

In both experiments reported here, the probe procedure of Waugh and Norman (1965) was used. A list of 16 words was presented to S, and after a warning signal, 1 word of the list was repeated. The S's task was to respond with that word in the list that immediately followed the probe. In Exp. I, the experimental lists were made from synonym pairs; in Exp. II, lists constructed from homophone pairs were used.

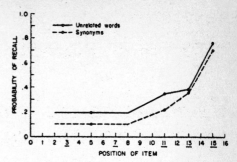

Fig. 1. Probability of recall of synonyms and unrelated words as a function of serial position.

Experiment I

Method

Subjects.—The Ss in this experiment were 30 students from the University of California at Riverside. They were paid for their participation in the experiment.

Lists.—Twenty lists of 16 unrelated words were constructed. Words were drawn from the Thorndike-Lorge (1944) count in a semirandom way, such that the sums of the Thorndike-Lorge frequencies of the words in each list differed by less than 10%. Twenty synonym lists were constructed from 160 synonym pairs obtained from a synonym dictionary. The sums of the Thorndike-Lorge frequencies of the words in the synonym lists were comparable to those of the unrelated lists. Each synonym list was made up of eight pairs arranged in random order with the restriction that the members of a pair never succeeded each other in the list.

A probe word was chosen for each list so that items in Positions 3, 7, 11, 13, and 15 were tested four times each for unrelated lists and equally often for synonym lists.

Procedure.—Lists were tape-recorded at a rate of 2 sec. per word. Before the presentation of each list, a bell signaled S to be alert. The S was instructed to fix his attention on every word as it was presented and not to rehearse old words. At the end of a list a bell sounded again, followed by the probe word. The S then attempted to respond with that word in the list that followed the probe word. The S was encouraged to guess and was given as much time as he needed to respond. Two unanalyzed practice lists preceded the 40 experimental lists. Synonym and unrelated lists were presented in random order, with 20 sec. between S's response and the start of the next list. Three 2-min. rest periods were allowed.

Results

The proportions of correct responses for each position tested are shown in Fig. 1. The data from Positions 3 and 7 have been pooled to obtain a more stable estimate of the asymptote of the retention curve. (Overall percentage correct was 15 at Position 3 and 14 at Position 7.) Connecting lines have been drawn on the assumption that the overall pattern of results would be similar to that of Waugh and Norman (1965). The total number of correct responses per S was significantly higher for unrelated words than for synonyms, $p < .01$. (Significance statements refer to the Wilcoxon matched-pairs test unless otherwise noted.)

Estimates of the secondary components of short-term retention for synonyms and for unrelated words are provided by comparison of the total number of correct responses in Serial Positions 3 and 7. As Fig. 1 shows, retention for unrelated words is almost twice that for synonyms, $p < .01$.

Although the total number of correct responses in Serial Positions 11, 13, and 15 also is greater for unrelated words than for synonyms, $p < .05$, this may be due to the difference in secondary memory rather than in primary memory since both contribute to performance in these positions. Waugh and Norman (1965) have suggested that the probability of retention of an item in Position i, $P(R_i)$, is

$$P(R_i) = P(p_i) + P(s) - P(p_i)R(s), \quad [1]$$

where $P(p_i)$ is the probability that Item i

is retained in primary memory and $P(s)$ is the probability that it is retained in secondary memory. By assumption, $P(s)$ is independent of the serial position of an item. $P(p_i)$ is highest for the last item of a list and decreases monotonically as a function of the distance from the end of the list, reaching zero with about 7–10 intervening items. If the mean probability of recall of items in Positons 3 and 7 is regarded as an estimate of $P(s)$, then Equation 1 can be used to calculate primary memory estimates for items in Positions 11, 13, and 15. These estimates are shown in Fig. 2. They do not appear to be different for unrelated words and synonyms. Evaluation of the primary memory estimates for each S (total of Positions 11, 13, and 15) confirms this impression, $p > .10$.

The performance decrement in the synonym list arises in part because Ss confuse synonyms in memory. If this were the only reason for poorer retention of synonyms, however, the difference between unrelated words and synonyms should disappear when one counts as correct the wrong member of a synonym pair given as response. When the data are reanalyzed in this way, the difference between the two conditions is no longer statistically significant, $p > .10$. However, there are only enough overt synonym confusions in the data to account for about half of the superiority of unrelated words over synonyms.

Experiment I indicates that semantic similarity interferes with the secondary component of memory, but that it has no effect on primary memory. The significance of the observation that the poorer retention of synonyms is only partly due to confusions between synonyms is discussed in connection with a similar finding in Exp. II.

EXPERIMENT II

In Exp. II, homophone pairs were used instead of synonyms. In other respects, Exp. II replicates all essential features of Exp. I.

Method

Subjects.—The Ss were 24 Stanford University undergraduates, who were paid to participate in

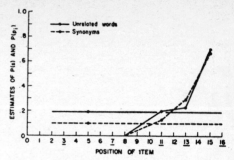

FIG. 2. Estimates of primary and secondary memory components $P(p_i)$ and $P(s)$ for the data shown in Fig. 1.

the experiment.

Lists.—Twenty lists of 16 unrelated words and 20 lists of homophone pairs were constructed. Because of the preponderance of one-syllable words among homophones, lists were constructed so that they did not contain more than two polysyllabic words. The total number of polysyllabic words was the same for unrelated lists and homophones. Rhymes, synonyms, and closely associated words were not used. The sums of the Thorndike-Lorge (1944) frequency ratings of the words in each list were constrained as in Exp. I.

The order of the words in each list was random, except that homophones were never allowed to succeed each other. In each condition, words in Positions 4 and 6 were tested once; 3, 5, and 7 were tested twice; and 11, 13, and 15 were tested four times. An additional restriction in the construction of the list required that the homophone of the test word be separated from the test word by three or four other words half of the time and by seven or eight words the other half of the time. An attempt was made to present the homophone earlier than the test word in the list as frequently as later. New randomizations and test words were prepared for every eight Ss.

Procedure.—Lists of unrelated words and homophone pairs were presented in random order on a memory drum at a 2-sec. rate. Probe words were underlined, and Ss were asked to write on their answer sheets the word in the list immediately following the underlined word. The Ss were asked to concentrate on each word as it was presented. Response times were unrestricted. Twenty seconds after a response the next list was started, except for two rest periods. Two unanalyzed practice lists were given first.

Results

Figure 3 shows the probability of recall for both homophones and unrelated words as a function of the serial position of the test word. Positions 3–7 have been pooled to

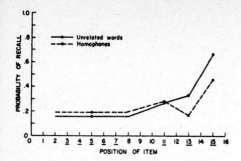

FIG. 3. Probability of recall of homophones and unrelated words as a function of serial position.

DISCUSSION

In the present experiments, words were recalled from secondary memory with a probability of slightly less than .2. Semantic similarity depressed this value to .1. The superior recall of words from the end of the list was attributed to primary memory, according to the model of Waugh and Norman (1965). The primary memory component of recall was independent of semantic factors, but was strongly depressed by acoustic similarity. It appears that only acoustic information is stored in primary memory, even if stimuli are presented visually, as in Exp. II.

Unrelated words may be recalled better than homophones because when a homophone is encoded in an auditory memory, it may be confused with the other member of the homophone pair. If this were the case, the primary memory component for homophone lists should be about half of that for unrelated words. A similar argument can be made for the recall of synonyms from secondary memory. Inspection of Fig. 2 and 4 shows that the data are not completely out of line with this hypothesis, although a strict test is not possible given the irregularity of the data in Fig. 4. There are not enough intrusions, however, to account for more than half of the deficit in the synonym and

provide a more stable estimate of the asymptote of retention. (Overall percentages correct at Positions 3–7 were 12, 19, 21, 25, and 16, respectively.) An analysis of variance showed that the position effect, the condition effect, and, most importantly, the Position × Condition interaction were highly significant statistically. The differences between the subgroups of eight Ss who received different randomizations of the lists were not statistically significant.

In order to make the analysis directly comparable to that used in Exp. I, further statistical analysis of the Condition × Position interaction was made. The secondary components of retention (Positions 3–7) were not significantly different for homophones and unrelated words, $p > .10$. On the other hand, unrelated words were much better recalled than homophones in Positions 11, 13, and 15, $p < .01$. As in Exp. I, estimates for primary and secondary memory were obtained and are shown in Fig. 4. The primary memory estimates were significantly larger for unrelated words than for homophones, $p < .01$. This difference is due only in part to confusions between homophones in memory. If a count is made of the number of times the homophone of the correct word is given as a response, approximately half of the superiority of short-term memory for unrelated words over homophones can be accounted for. This observation still holds if responses to the homophone of the probe word are counted as correct. Thus Exp. II supports the hypothesis that acoustic similarity is an important factor in primary memory.

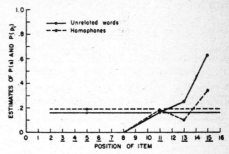

FIG. 4. Estimates of primary and secondary memory components $P(p_i)$ and $P(s)$ for the data shown in Fig. 3.

homophone conditions. Furthermore, Ss' reports do not agree with the idea that words in the homophone condition were stored in memory just as unrelated words would have been and were confused at the time of recall. Instead, Ss reported that they tried different learning strategies when they noticed that a list was made of homophone pairs. Instead of relying on primary memory as usual, they "tried to get away from the sound of the words." The Ss found this difficult and complained that the homophone lists were presented at a faster rate than the other lists and were "frustrating." Together with the intrusion data, such reports suggest that Ss did not store homophones simply in an acoustic store that they knew would be useless to them later anyway. Apparently Ss were trying to remember nonacoustic information about homophone pairs, but their capacity to do so was severely limited. The performance decrement in the homophone lists is therefore caused by two factors: First, homophones were confused when stored in primary memory; second, Ss did not rely on auditory information as much as they normally would and were unable to find an equivalent substitute. A corresponding argument can be made for the synonym lists.

On the basis of the present results, one may speculate that information may enter secondary memory without passing through primary memory. Primary memory apparently retains only acoustic information, while semantic as well as sensory and phonetic features are important for secondary memory. Therefore, information must be able to enter secondary memory directly. Primary memory appears to be a temporary acoustic store with a limited capacity. If Ss have to remember homophones, they either do not use this means of storage at all or if they do, they may confuse homophone pairs. In the case of synonyms, interference may occur because synonyms share all or most semantic and sensory features and differ only phonetically. Therefore, it is more difficult to store information in secondary memory, which suffices to discriminate among synonyms, or if insufficient information is stored, confusions may occur.

REFERENCES

BADDELEY, A. D. Short-term memory for word sequences as a function of acoustic, semantic, and formal similarity. *Quarterly Journal of Experimental Psychology,* 1966, **18,** 362–365.

BADDELEY, A. D., & DALE, H. C. A. The effects of semantic similarity on retroactive interference in long and short-term memory. *Journal of Verbal Learning and Verbal Behavior,* 1966, **5,** 417–420.

CONRAD, R., FREEMAN, P. R., & HULL, A. J. Acoustic factors versus language factors in short-term memory. *Psychonomic Science,* 1965, **3,** 57–58.

DALE, H. C. A., & GREGORY, M. Evidence of semantic coding in short-term memory. *Psychonomic Science,* 1966, **5,** 75–76.

THORNDIKE, E. L., & LORGE, I. *The teacher's word book of 30,000 words.* New York: Teachers College, Columbia University, Bureau of Publications, 1944.

WAUGH, N. C., & NORMAN, D. A. Primary memory. *Psychological Review,* 1965, **72,** 89–104.

H.G. Shulman

Encoding and retention of semantic and phonemic information in short-term memory

Reprinted from the *Journal of Verbal Learning and Verbal Behavior* (1970) **9**:499-508

A probe recognition task was used to evaluate the relative effectiveness of semantic and phonemic encoding in STM. On each trial a list of 10 words was presented at a rate of either 350, 700, or 1400 msec per word. Recognition was tested with a probe which could be a homonym, a synonym, or identical to one of the words in the list. The retention functions for all three probe types were similar in shape, supporting the hypothesis that semantic encoding is possible in STM. An interaction between type of encoding and rate occurred, indicating that encoding is a time-dependent serial process.

Because phonemic similarity is apparently a more effective variable than semantic similarity in short-term memory (STM) tasks, it is often assumed that the theoretical short-term storage (STS) system, which presumably supports STM performance, is primarily limited to the storage of phonemic information. However, Shulman (1970) argued that the differential effectiveness of the two types of similarity on STM can also be accounted for by the hypothesis that the encoding of an item takes place over time, and that features most closely related to the sensory input, e.g., phonemic features, are encoded more rapidly than semantic features. In order to maximize the time available for rehearsal and under the pressure of relatively fast presentation rates, Ss may tend to encode incoming information as quickly as possible, which implies that encoding will be based primarily on sensory attributes of the input. A subsidiary hypothesis was that semantic encoding is possible in STS when required by task de- mands or when slow presentation rates are used.

The purpose of the present experiment was to investigate the hypotheses that semantic encoding is possible in STS and that the encoding process is time dependent. A further object was to study the retention functions for semantic and phonemic information separately. Kintsch and Buschke (1969) have suggested that the effects of semantic similarity are confined to the asymptotic portion of the short-term retention function while recently presented information is encoded phonemically. Their experimental approach was to look for confusion errors based on the two types of similarity; hence, the task was not designed to require semantic encoding, just to detect it if it occurred. If it is true that the effects of semantic similarity in an STM task are mediated entirely by the contributions of long-term store (LTS) to performance, and if it is also true, as current hypotheses about the nature of this contribution have it, that

LTS contributes about equally at all except the shortest (1 or 2 sec) retention intervals, then when Ss are forced to use semantic encoding in an STM task the resulting retention function should show no recency effect and should be relatively flat over a wide range of retention intervals. Furthermore, if STS is primarily phonemic and contributes to performance as a rapidly decreasing function of retention interval, then the retention function for phonemic information should show a marked recency effect. If traces in STS contain both semantic and phonemic information, then the shape of the retention functions should be similar for both types of information.

In order to force Ss to encode items both phonemically and semantically, a probe recognition task was used in which the probe item might be either a synonym or a homonym of a presented word. In three conditions of the experiment Ss were required to make "yes" or "no" decisions of three types. These were: (a) Is the probe word *identical* to any of the presented words? (b) Is the probe word a *homonym* of any presented word? (c) Is the probe word a *synonym* of any presented word? If semantic encoding does take longer than phonemic encoding, then an interaction between presentation rate and probe type should be predicted. In particular, decreasing the presentation rate should facilitate performance in the semantic probe condition more than in the phonemic.

METHOD

The method chosen was intended to maximize the likelihood that each word presented was encoded as fully as possible. This was done by requiring judgments of similarity according to three different criteria and by informing S about which criterion to use only after presentation of the 10-word list on each trial. In addition, a system of monetary payoffs was used which heavily stressed accuracy and also placed a lesser but positive emphasis on speed.

Design

Each S had a total of 50 practice and 240 experimental trials in a single session lasting 1.5 hr. Each experimental trial consisted of the sequential visual presentation of a 1.3-sec warning signal, 10 words, a 1.3-sec instructional cue, and a recognition test word or probe. Blank periods of 100 msec separated the warning signal and the words, the words from each other, the last word from the instructional cue, and the instructional cue from the onset of the test word. The independent variables were presentation rate, serial position of the tested word, and instructional cue type, all varied factorially within Ss. On a given trial each of the 10 words was exposed for the same duration, either 250, 600, or 1300 msec, followed by the 100-msec blank interstimulus interval, resulting in presentation rates of 350, 700, and 1400 msec per word. There were 80 trials at each presentation rate. The tested word was drawn from each of the 10 serial positions with equal frequency, resulting in a total of 18 trials at each of 10 retention intervals. The remaining 60 trials were catch trials, on which a test word requiring a "no" response was presented. A third variable was the nature of the recognition test on a given trial. Thus, S was instructed that he might be asked to respond "yes" or "no" to one of the three types of questions on any trial. On any particular trial, S was informed as to which of the similarity criteria to use by the presentation of a single-letter cue for 1300 msec after the 10th word. The cues were the letters I (identical), H (homonym), or M (means the same). Each of these cues was used on 60 experimental and 20 catch trials, twice with each of the 30 combinations of serial position and presentation rate and either six or seven times on catch trials at each presentation rate. Two observations per S were made in each of the 90 combinations of cue type, presentation rate, and serial position where a "yes" response was correct.

The sequence of trials was divided into two 120-trial blocks, each containing one observation at each of the 90 combinations of cue type, rate, and serial position, and either three or four catch observations at each of the nine possible combinations of cue type and presentation rate. The order of occurrence of conditions within 60-trial subblocks was randomized with constraints imposed on runs of cue types, presentation rates, and serial positions.

Materials

The stimuli were 2580 monosyllabic or disyllabic words from three to six letters in length chosen from the list of words occurring at least once per million in the Thorndike–Lorge General Count (Thorndike & Lorge, 1944). Sixty synonym pairs were chosen from Riegel (1965), Jenkins and Palermo (1965), and by inspection of words in the Thorndike–Lorge list. Synonyms were chosen to be of maximum similarity, with preference given responses showing unimodal, peaked frequency of response distributions. Some examples are: talk-speak, leap-jump, angry-mad, nation-country, and empty-vacant. Sixty homonym pairs were chosen from Whitford (1966). Examples of these are: ball-bawl, pray-prey, board-bored, whole-hole, cereal-serial. The distributions of word lengths and Thorndike–Lorge frequencies for homonym and synonym pairs were made as nearly equal as possible. Sixty single words were chosen for the identical and catch trials which also approximated the homonyms and synonyms with respect to word frequency and length. Complete counterbalancing of the assignment of words to Rate and Serial Position conditions, within each cue condition, was achieved with 30 Ss.

Each word pair was assigned to a string of 10 words such that the nine other words used were nominally unrelated to each other and to the test pair. No more than two words per string had the same first letter, and all word lengths were represented in every string. Probe words ranged from two to eight letters in length, with 2-, 7-, and 8-letter words used rarely and equally often as correct and catch words.

Apparatus

The Ss sat in a dimly lit soundproof room containing the display and a two-key response panel. The display consisted of a linear array of 10 Burroughs Nixie tubes, measuring 31.8 cm across, placed at eye level, 137.2 cm from S. Each tube subsumed 1°20′ of visual angle; hence, a 6-letter stimulus subsumed 8° of visual angle. Preprogrammed paper tape provided a control unit with information concerning presentation rate and character set prior to each stimulus presentation. The control unit also turned on an electronic clock simultaneously with the onset of each test word. Depression of a response key stopped this clock and caused a record of S's reaction time and response to be punched on paper tape. The response panel consisted of two piano-like keys. The right key was labeled "yes," the left "no." The Ss were instructed to rest their right index finger lightly on the "yes" key and their left index finger on the "no" key.

Procedure

Prior to the 240 experimental trials, Ss were given a total of 50 practice trials. The first 20 of these involved number recognition. The next 30 trials were practice at the experimental task, using only the 350- and 700-msec rates. Strings of four words were presented and followed by either the letter I, H, or M as the cue for a particular type of test.

Each practice and experimental trial was preceded by a warning signal consisting of four asterisks which flashed at the rate appropriate for that trial. The total time taken by the presentation of this warning signal was 1300 msec in all conditions. Each test word remained visible until a response was made, and 3 sec then elapsed before the warning signal for the next trial.

Following the practice trials, the experimental sequence was administered in four segments of about 15 min each with a 2–3-min rest interval between each segment. The Ss were instructed that this would be the case, and a payoff matrix emphasizing accuracy over speed was described to them. No feedback was given S during the experiment.

Subjects

The Ss were 60 right-handed male students at the University of Michigan. They were drawn from the volunteer S pool of the Human Performance Center and were paid $1.50 per hour plus a bonus based on performance.

Instructions

Instructions emphasized the unpredictable nature of the series of trials with respect to the similarity criterion, and clear instructions were given to be prepared for any of the three types of questions (I, H, or M) on every trial, in order to maximize performance. The Ss were told that there was nothing subtle about the test, that the homonyms were words which sound identical, that the synonyms used were as close in meaning as is possible, and that when a particular instructional cue was shown, the test word would either satisfy the similarity criterion indicated by that cue or would satisfy none of the three possible criteria. Instructions were also given to refrain from speaking words out loud during their presentation.

RESULTS

Separate analyses were done for reaction times (RT) and recognition performance and for trials where "yes" and "no" were the required responses. In order to carry out an analysis of variance on the RT data, the mean RTs over groups of 10 Ss were used as the basic data. This method was chosen because at the level of individual Ss there were missing data at certain treatment combinations since the RT data were conditionalized either on correct or incorrect responses.

Figure 1 shows the proportion of correct "yes" responses as a function of probe type and serial position, averaged over presentation rates. The main effects of probe type and serial position were significant, $F(2, 116) = 50.83$, $p < .001$, and $F(9, 522) = 60.22$, $p < .001$, respectively, and a marginal interaction between probe type and serial position was

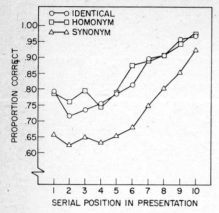

FIG. 1. Proportion correct "yes" responses as a function of serial position (10 is most recent item) with probe type the parameter.

TABLE 1

PROPORTION OF FALSE-POSITIVE RESPONSES AS A FUNCTION OF PROBE TYPE AND RATE

	Rate, msec		
Probe	350	700	1400
Identical	.074	.086	.081
Homonym	.133	.155	.183
Synonym	.271	.206	.198

present, $F(18, 1044) = 2.86$, $.05 < p < .10$. It is apparent that the effect of probe type reflects the poorer level of performance with synonym probes since homonyms and identical words did not differ from each other. Both this fact and the similarity in shape of the three functions are of interest. Since serial position and retention interval were confounded, the curves in Figure 1 and elsewhere show the retention functions in the various conditions of the experiment. In all such figures the word in serial position 10 was the most recently presented.

The poorer level of performance with synonyms might reflect either a true difference in Ss' ability to encode semantic information, a scalar difference between the similarity of synonyms to each other as compared to identical words or homonyms, or a combination of both factors. However, the fact that synonyms were correctly recognized 72.4% of the time over all serial positions and rates, and 92.8% of the time at the most recent serial position demonstrates the salience of semantic information in STM. The similarity in shape of the retention functions for the three probe types argues that all of the types of information involved are stored in functionally identical memory systems, and the strong recency effect makes plausible the identification of this system as STS.

The various conditions of the experiment resulted in variation in false-recognition rates which are shown in Table 1. These values were used to calculate estimates of P', the true probability of a correct "yes" response, as dictated by a high threshold model of recognition performance (Luce, 1963). Thus if $P(Y|Y)$ is the observed proportion of "yes" responses given that "yes" was the required response, and $P(Y|N)$ is the observed proportion of "yes" responses given that "no" was required, $P' = [P(Y|Y) - P(Y|N)]/[1 - P(Y|N)]$. This correction procedure produced no change in the pattern of results. Other correction procedures are of course dictated by other models of recognition performance, such as low threshold theory (Luce, 1963) or the theory of signal detectability (Green & Swets, 1966). There is no obvious method of estimating the parameters of either theory from the present data, and no reason to assume that either is the correct model in any case. In order to deal with the present recognition data, it is therefore necessary to assume that the available estimates of P' bear some simple monotonic relationship to true sensitivity and are therefore not misleading.

Figure 2 shows the mean RT for correct "yes" responses as a function of serial position and probe type. In order to minimize variances, RTs greater than 3.0 sec were discarded prior to this and all subsequent analyses to be reported. This procedure resulted in the loss of 355 responses (2.5% of the data) and lowered mean RTs somewhat without causing any changes in the pattern of results. The effects of probe type and serial

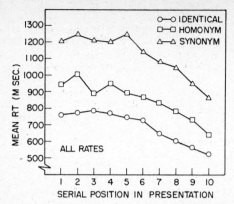

FIG. 2. Mean correct "yes" RT as a function of serial position with probe type the parameter.

position were significant, $F(2, 10) = 611.20$, $p < .001$, and $F(9, 45) = 100.08$, $p < .001$, as was the Probe × Serial Position interaction, $F(18, 90) = 1.72$, $p < .05$. This interaction was also significant when data from Serial Positions 5–10 only were analyzed, $F(10, 50) = 2.12$, $p < .05$, reflecting the fact that the serial position curve for synonyms had a greater slope than the other serial position curves.

An important feature of these data is the sizable difference in RT between identical and homonym probes, which did not differ in terms of recognition accuracy. This makes unreasonable any theory that predicts a high correlation between accuracy and latency by making them both direct measures of a single hypothetical construct such as trace strength. If the assumption is made that accuracy is some simple function of trace strength, then latency must be assumed to involve at least one other factor. The concept of memory search has been useful in explaining latency data (e.g., Sternberg, 1966) and can be used to predict latency differences where no differences in accuracy exist.

Two features of the data in Figure 2 are relevant to a search hypothesis. First, there is a large difference in the right-intercept values of the RT functions, which represent estimates of the time taken to process the probe word, and secondly the three functions are roughly the same shape. In order to precisely deter-

mine the slope and intercept values, a straight line was fitted to the mean RTs for Serial Positions 5–10. The linear correlation between serial position from the end of the list (retention interval) and mean RT was $r = .98$ for homonym probes and $r = .99$ for identical and synonym probes. The slope of the synonym function (72 msec per item) was greater than those of the homonym functions (50 and 47 msec per item) which differed only slightly. The intercept values were 472, 617, and 805 msec for identical, homonym, and synonym probes.

Smith (1968) proposed that the intercept of an RT function reflects the durations of three processes: stimulus encoding, response selection, and response execution. The slope is indicative of the time taken by the operations of searching memory and making comparisons between memory traces and the encoded test stimulus. In the data shown in Figure 2, differences in intercept must reflect differences in stimulus encoding time since the response selected and executed is the same for all of the data. Because the cue telling Ss which similarity criterion to use followed the string of words and lasted 1.3 sec, it is reasonable to assume that the encoding of the word string was completed prior to the onset of the probe word. For this reason and because of the large differences in intercept and small differences in slope between probe conditions, the differences in RT must reflect variation in the time taken to process the probe word. The data in Figure 2 also suggest that the search process for identity or homonymity proceeds at the same rate and is slightly faster than the search for semantic identity.

Table 2 shows the mean RTs for correct and incorrect responses in each of the nine combinations of probe type and rate. Correct "no" responses may be seen to vary as a function of probe type in the same manner as correct "yes" responses. Cohen (1968) has reported a similar difference in correct "no" latencies under the same three similarity criteria. This finding provides additional support for the interpretation of the intercept differences in

Figure 2 in terms of variations in the time taken to encode the probe word, since this process should be independent of S's eventual response.

TABLE 2

MEAN RT AS A FUNCTION OF RATE AND PROBE TYPE IN FOUR RESPONSE CATEGORIES [a]

Category	Rate, msec			Weighted mean
	350	700	1400	
Identical				
Correct Yes	613	699	740	683
	(520)	(610)	(664)	
Correct No	794	891	841	842
Incorrect No	899	955	1033	967
Incorrect Yes	846	1074	1090	1001
Homonym				
Correct Yes	771	860	909	846
	(661)	(732)	(793)	
Correct No	1249	1162	1261	1222
Incorrect No	1286	1368	1368	1343
Incorrect Yes	947	996	1048	1005
Synonym				
Correct Yes	1044	1105	1158	1103
	(944)	(1026)	(1081)	
Correct No	1368	1387	1513	1427
Incorrect No	1355	1420	1542	1436
Incorrect Yes	1169	1158	1436	1249

[a] Figures in parentheses are median correct "yes" RTs.

The effects of manipulating presentation rate provide further information about encoding and search processes. Figure 3 shows the effect of rate on the probability of a correct "yes" recognition response, before and after the correction for guessing. The interaction between rate and probe type is significant, $F(4, 232) = 2.86$, $p < .025$, by an analysis of variance done before the correction for guessing. The effect of Rate on mean correct "yes" RT in each probe condition is shown in Table 2. There is clearly no interaction between rate and probe type in these data, $F(4, 20) < 1$. Table 2 also shows median correct "yes" RT in each condition.

Correct "yes" RTs may be of two types, either true "yes" responses or false "yes" responses which are the result of response

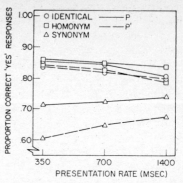

FIG. 3. Proportion correct "yes" responses as a function of rate with probe type as the parameter. Solid lines are the raw data; dashed lines are data corrected for guessing.

biases and false detections. Because there were differences between conditions in false-positive rates and RTs, as measured by incorrect "yes" responses on catch trials, the data in Table 2 may give a misleading picture of changes in the true correct "yes" RT. The median RTs in Table 2 are offered as an estimate of the variation in true correct "yes" RT as a function of probe type and rate. Medians are less sensitive than means to distortion caused by mixing false-positive RTs with true "yes" RTs and have the additional advantages of being less sensitive to varying numbers of observations and of giving a model-free estimate of the true correct "yes" RT.[1] Since the pattern of results did not change when medians were used, a reasonable conclusion is that the means in Table 2 accurately reflect changes in true "yes" RT. These data and the data in Figure 3 indicate a need to postulate mechanisms that will produce different effects of presentation rate on RT and correct recognition rates. Two processes that account for the data are time-dependent trace decay and time-dependent encoding.

[1] A correction procedure for mean RT similar to the one used for recognition rate is easily derived. However, in order to use such a procedure, it is necessary to make certain assumptions about the variances of the component RT distributions which were not met in the data.

The arguments necessary to justify these assumptions will be presented in the Discussion section of the present paper.

If slower rates have their effects on correct "yes" RT via some such decay process, then the amount of time taken per comparison in memory, that is, the search rate or slope, should become greater as items become faded in memory. Thus, the slope of the serial position function must increase as presentation rate decreases, which will be seen as an interaction of rate and serial position in the correct "yes" RT data. The predicted interaction was present and statistically reliable when all 10 serial positions were analyzed, $F(18, 90) = 2.04$, $p < .025$, and marginally when only Serial Positions 5–10 were considered, $F(10, 50) = 1.89$, $.05 < p < .10$. The data for Serial Positions 5–10 and the best-fitting straight lines are shown in Figure 4. The linear correlations between serial position from the end of the list and mean RT were .973, .998, and .993 for the 350-, 700-, and 1400-msec rates, respectively. There is a regular change in slope with rate and the intercept values of the three functions are quite close. The 350-msec intercept is slightly lower than those for 700 and 1400 msec (618 vs. 635 and 637 msec, respectively), but this seems due to the deviation of the first point on the 350-msec function from the straight line that would best fit the other five points. The increase in slope as rate decreases is roughly the same in each probe condition as evidenced by the lack of a significant Probe × Rate × Serial Position interaction, both in the data for all 10 serial positions, $F(36, 180) = 1.30$, $.10 < p < .25$, and for Serial Positions 5–10 alone, $F(20, 100) = 1.04$. These data support the hypothesis that the decay process is the same for all types of information since if the decay rate were greater in one condition than another the effect of rate on slope would be greatest in that condition.

Discussion

The present experiment constituted an effort to answer three experimental questions.

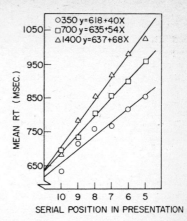

FIG. 4. Mean correct "yes" RT and best-fitting straight lines, for Serial Positions 5–10 only (10 is most recent). Presentation rate is the parameter, and the data are averaged over all probe types.

These were: (a) Can evidence for semantic encoding in STM be obtained when such encoding is a task demand? (b) Are the retention functions for semantic and phonemic information similar in shape? (c) Does the manipulation of presentation rate have a different effect on semantic encoding than on phonemic encoding? The experimental results provide affirmative answers to each of these questions.

The present data imply that the memory trace in STS is multidimensional. Because the retention functions for semantic and phonemic information resemble each other closely, and show the strong recency effect which defines STS, it is unreasonable to attribute the evidence for semantic encoding in the present experiment to the contribution of LTS to performance. This is an important result since prior demonstrations of the salience of semantic information in STM have usually used retention intervals of from 10–20 sec; hence, the possibility of LTS being responsible for the effects of semantic variables could not be ruled out.

It also seems unlikely that the recognition of synonymity in the present experiment can be attributed to the recoding of information in a phonemic STS, at the time of presentation of the probe item. Such a mechanism would increase the amount of time taken to retrieve each item in memory, hence would lead to a sizable slope difference between the synonym conditions and the others in the RT data. An estimate of the probable magnitude of this slope difference can be obtained from the intercept difference between the synonym and homonym conditions, which is attributed to a similar difference in encoding processes. Since these intercept differences average 188 msec over all rates, and since the slope differences between the synonym condition and the others in Figure 2 are about one-tenth this size, it appears unreasonable to hold the hypothesis that STS is strictly phonemic with recognition of synonyms based on recoding at the time of retrieval.

An obvious question to raise next is why evidence for semantic encoding in STM is readily found when required by the experimental procedure, but is difficult to obtain in situations that let *S* control the ways in which information is encoded into STS (cf. Kintsch & Buschke, 1969). The hypothesis offered earlier was that semantic encoding requires more time than phonemic encoding, hence is less compatible with rehearsal. Given the limited ability of *S* to engage in time-sharing between different mental tasks (Peterson, 1969) and the utility of rehearsal in an STM task, it is not surprising that phonemic encoding is generally used when semantic encoding is not required. In order to provide support for this hypothesis, evidence to the effect that semantic encoding does require more time than phonemic encoding is desirable. The data shown in Figure 3 provide this evidence. Decreasing the rate of presentation improves recognition in the Semantic Probe condition but not in the Identical or Homonym condition. This result may be attributed to an increase in the probability of encoding a word semantically as more time is provided.

Figure 3 also shows that the recognition of identical and homonym probes decreases slightly as presentation rate decreases. There is no reason to predict this finding on the basis

of a time-dependent encoding process, since the encoding of phonemic or visual information should either improve or remain constant as rate is decreased. The behavior in Figure 3, however, does not reflect the effects of encoding alone. Recognition performance also depends on how much information is retained in memory at the time of test. This suggests that the decrease in recognition of identical and homonym probes as rate decreases is due to an increasing loss of stored information. The forgetting mechanism thus seems time-dependent and may be identified either as time-dependent decay or time-dependent unlearning of critical traces and recovery from unlearning of competing traces. The unlearning hypothesis is difficult to apply in the case of recognition memory. It is not clear how to specify what associations are involved in a recognition task, hence what is unlearned. Furthermore, the concept of time-dependent decay is much simpler than unlearning and can easily be applied to the present situation.

The data in Figure 3 might be taken to suggest different decay rates for phonemic and semantic information. However, this hypothesis is strongly denied by the correct "yes" RT data in Table 2. These data reflect the effect of presentation rate on RTs for recognition of correctly encoded and successfully retained traces. Since there is a uniform decrease in performance in the three Probe conditions as rate decreases, it must be inferred that the rate of decay of information is the same for phonemic and semantic information. The interaction of Rate × Probe Type shown in Figure 3 is therefore taken to be the net result of a uniform decay process and an encoding process that interacts with presentation rate.

The correct "yes" RT serial position functions (Figures 2 and 4) show variations in slope as a function of presentation rate and, to a lesser extent, probe type. These variations indicate changes in the search rate as a function of rate and probe type. The major effect of probe type is on the intercept of the functions in Figure 2, but the synonym function also had a greater slope than the other two. This fact and the poorer recognition performance in the synonym conditions (Figure 1) are likely consequences of a difference between synonym pairs and homonym or identical pairs with respect to the degree of similarity between words in the pair. Thus, while it is virtually impossible to find two words which are truly identical in meaning, it is trivial to find phonemically or formally identical word pairs, and in fact these were used in the homonym and identical conditions. Given that meaningful identity between words is unobtainable, it follows that the decision that two words do or do not have the same meaning will take longer and be more susceptible to error than the corresponding decision with respect to phonemic identity. There also is some indication that the synonym condition results in slightly faster forgetting than the other two probe types, since correct recognition of synonyms decreases faster as a function of retention interval (serial position from the end of the list) in Figure 1. This interaction may be artifactual, since recognition at the recent serial positions in the identical and homonym conditions is constrained by the ceiling on proportion correct. An alternative explanation is that the slower search rate in the synonym condition allows more time for trace strength to decay; hence, each decision in the search and matching process takes slightly longer, producing an interaction between probe type and serial position in the recognition data. Thus, although the rate of forgetting may be greater for semantic information, there is no reason to suspect that the rate of loss of trace strength over time differs for semantic, phonemic, and possibly visual information. If complete semantic identity could be achieved, the present results give reason to believe that semantic information would be retained as well in STS as other information.

References

COHEN, G. A comparison of semantic, acoustic and visual criteria for matching of word pairs. *Perception and Psychophysics*, 1968, **4**, 203–204.

GREEN, D. M., & SWETS, J. A. *Signal detection theory and psychophysics*. New York: Wiley, 1966.

JENKINS, J. J., & PALERMO, D. S. Synonym responses to the stimulus words of the Palermo-Jenkins word association list. The Pennsylvania State University Research Bulletin No. 55, January 1965.

KINTSCH, W., & BUSCHKE, H. Homophones and synonyms in short-term memory. *Journal of Experimental Psychology*, 1969, **80**, 403–407.

LUCE, D. R. Detection and recognition. In D. R. Luce, R. R. Bush, & E. Galanter (Eds.), *Handbook of mathematical psychology*, Vol. 1. New York: Wiley, 1963.

PETERSON, L. R. Concurrent verbal activity. *Psychological Review*, 1969, **76**, 376–386.

RIEGEL, K. F. The Michigan restricted association norms. University of Michigan Research Report. National Institute of Mental Health Grant No. MH07619-OIAIO7098, April 1965.

SHULMAN, H. G. Similarity effects in short-term memory. *Psychological Bulletin*, 1970, in press.

SMITH, E. E. Choice reaction time: An analysis of the major theoretical positions. *Psychological Bulletin*, 1968, **69**, 77–110.

STERNBERG, S. High speed scanning in human memory. *Science*, 1966, **153**, 652–654.

THORNDIKE, E. L., & LORGE, I. *The teacher's word book of 30,000 words*. New York: Teachers College Press, 1944.

WHITFORD, H. C. *A dictionary of American homophones and homographs*. New York: Teachers College Press, 1966.

D. Rundus

Analysis of rehearsal processes in free recall

Reprinted from the *Journal of Experimental Psychology* (1971) **89**(1):63-77

Following the procedure previously described by Rundus and Atkinson, overt rehearsal was required during the presentation of free recall lists. This rehearsal was tape-recorded and analyzed in conjunction with written recall data. Experiment I considered rehearsal and recall of lists of unrelated nouns. The serial position effect, the order of recall of items as a function of item strength, and the organization of list items by S were examined using rehearsal and recall protocols. The introduction of distinctive items into a free recall list affects recall of the distinctive item, items adjacent to distinctive items, and the list as a whole. Experiment II examined changes in rehearsal associated with these recall effects. In Exp. III, some items of a list were repeated. Recall of repeated items increased with spacing of the repetitions; an analysis of the rehearsal protocols suggested reasons for this increase. Lists containing both categorized and unrelated items were tested in Exp. IV. Category information was used extensively by S in structuring rehearsal. Clustering in recall was related to the observed rehearsal protocols.

The interpretation of memory phenomena found in free recall studies must be based on the understanding of S rehearsal processes. The concept of rehearsal has proved to be a most intricate and enigmatic proposition, the mechanisms of which have usually been inferred from complex analyses of test results. More specifically, input variables (presentation time, item order, interitem relations) are manipulated, changes in recall are noted, and the rehearsal process is posited as a logical extension of this empirical evidence. One problem with this inferential or "black box" approach is that until sufficient data are amassed from a variety of experiments, a number of cogent descriptions of rehearsal processes can be supported. For example, it may be that items are treated more or less independently, with rehearsal serving to increase item availability (Asch & Ebenholtz, 1962), or more generally, to strengthen their memory trace (Slamecka, 1968). Several items may be considered together, with rehearsal serving to form interitem associations or strengthen preexisting ones (Bousfield, 1953). It has also been suggested that an important part of rehearsal may be the formation of mnemonics or images (Bower, 1970).

Another approach to the understanding of rehearsal has been to instruct S to use some particular rehearsal strategy. One example of this approach is to require S to repeat each item aloud several times as it is being presented. This procedure produces a reduction in overall recall and a change in the shape of the serial position curve (Fischler, Rundus, & Atkinson, 1970; Glanzer & Meinzer, 1967). In these and other similar experiments which provide strict control of S's rehearsal, it is possible to observe which rehearsal strategies are able to account for various free recall data.

It would be highly desirable, however, to determine what S is doing in rehearsal while still allowing him flexibility in his choice of strategies.

The studies reported here employed an overt rehearsal technique described by Rundus and Atkinson (1970) allowing direct observation of S's rehearsal. This procedure provides rehearsal data in a form that may be used in comparisons across Ss while imposing a minimum of restrictions on S's choice of rehearsal strategies. As a list is being presented, S is instructed to study by rehearsing aloud any item or combination of items which he has seen in the list. The resulting rehearsal protocols are tape-recorded and later analyzed in conjunction with S's free recall output.

Although, in the procedure described, the recorded rehearsal protocols for S consist only of repetitions of items, this does not imply that S is rehearsing by simple repetition. Higher order strategies used by S should be reflected in the rehearsal data. If items are being "associated," if words are being coded with mnemonics, or if images of word groups are formed, then items in these groups should appear together in the rehearsal protocols. Thus the exact coding strategy would be unknown, but any organization of the list by S should be observable.

The dual-storage model proposed by Atkinson and Shiffrin (1968) provides a framework for much of the discussion to follow. The model assumes that recall of an item is based upon the retrieval of information from both a temporary but highly available short-term store (STS) and a more permanent long-term store (LTS). Of special interest is a proposed rehearsal buffer consisting of a limited number of items in STS which S has chosen to rehearse actively. When a new item is presented for study, that item enters STS. This new item may then be chosen for inclusion in the rehearsal buffer. Due to the limited capacity of the rehearsal buffer, the entry of a new item into a full buffer necessitates the deletion of one of the items currently in the buffer. Rehearsal of an item is assumed to maintain that item in STS. This rehearsal serves a twofold purpose. First, if an item is still being rehearsed at the time of test, information about the item will be retrievable from the highly available STS. Second, the model postulates that transfer of information about an item to LTS occurs only while that item resides in STS. Since the probability of recalling an item from LTS is assumed to be a positive function of the amount of LTS information about the item, it follows that the longer an item is maintained in STS via rehearsal, the higher will be its recall probability.

The primacy and recency effects, usually observed in the U-shaped serial position curves of free recall studies, prove amenable to the dual-storage assumptions of a model such as the one described. The recency effect refers to the high recall probability of the last few items of a list. Since the time between presentation of these items and the recall test is short, information about them should still be retrievable from STS. Any activity between study and test which disrupts STS should minimize retrieval of useful information from STS and thus reduce the recency effect. Such a reduction was observed in studies by Postman and Phillips (1965) and Glanzer and Cunitz (1966). In both experiments, a mathematics task was interpolated between the study of a list and its test. The recency effect was virtually eliminated while little change was observed in the rest of the serial position curve.

The primacy effect, the high probability of recall observed for initial list items, is more difficult to explain. It is highly unlikely that S would maintain the initial list items in STS until the time of test; therefore, primacy must be a LTS phenomenon. At the beginning of list study there are few items competing for S's attention and thus these items should receive a good deal of rehearsal. In addition, the initial list items may be maintained in rehearsal as later items are being shown, thus gaining rehearsal at the expense of items from the middle of the list. Since LTS information, and consequently recall probability, is assumed to increase with rehearsal, a major component of the primacy effect may be the extensive rehearsal accorded initial items. Fischler, Rundus, and Atkinson (1970) tested this interpretation by attempting to equate rehearsal of all list items. This was accomplished by instructing S to fill his study time by overtly repeating, at a steady rate, only the item being displayed. This procedure sharply reduced the primacy effect while only slightly lowering recall for middle list items and leaving the recency effect unchanged. The observed decrement in primacy supports the interpretation that additional rehearsal accorded initial list items is a main factor in the primacy effect. Even with rehearsal thus equated, a slight primacy effect persisted. This suggests that other factors such as the distinctiveness of the initial study positions or the importance of initial items in S's organizational scheme contribute to primacy.

Structural features of rehearsal, the relationship between rehearsal and recall, output order as a function of item strength, and subjective organization in lists of unrelated words were examined in Exp. I. The next two experiments involved manipulations of items within a list of unrelated words. Experiment II considered changes in rehearsal and recall caused by introducing distinctive items into the study list. The effects of repeating items within a list and varying the spacing between the repetitions were explored in Exp. III. The final experiment examined the nature of S's rehearsal, the relationship between rehearsal and recall, and features of output for lists containing categories.

General Method and Analysis

The procedure involved in the collection and analysis of S's rehearsal protocols was common to all studies. Methodology particular to each experiment will be described in the section dealing with that experiment.

Subjects.—Female undergraduate volunteers from the introductory psychology course at Stanford University served as Ss. Class credit was given for participation. Each S served in one, 50-min. session.

Procedure.—During a session, S was shown 11 lists of nouns. The order of presentation of lists during a session and the order of words within a list were randomized for each S. Following presentation of a list, S was given a 2-min. written free recall test on that list. List items were printed on 4 × 6 in. index cards, one word per card. During study, cards bearing each list item were displayed one at a time, each card being shown for 5 sec. A timer-generated tone followed each 5-sec. interval and signaled the display of a new item. The Ss were instructed to study by repeating aloud items from the current list during the 5-sec. study intervals. There were no restrictions placed upon the choice of items to be rehearsed or the rate of rehearsal as long as S's rehearsal filled each interval. No S reported difficulty in following these instructions. A cassette tape recorder was used to record S's rehearsal on all lists.

Analysis.—The recorded rehearsal protocols were coded numerically and analyzed on a computer. The tone pulses that had served to signal the display of a new item were used to partition the rehearsal from each trial into rehearsal sets (RS). An RS was associated with each item of the list and consisted of all rehearsals recorded during the 5 sec. while that item was being presented. If an item was repeated more than once in a given RS, each occurrence was counted in determining the total number of rehearsals accorded that item. Within each experiment, the first list presented to each S was the same and was used as a practice list. The data from this list were excluded from analysis.

Experiment I

This study was designed to replicate and extend the findings of Rundus and Atkinson (1970) concerning free recall following a single presentation of a list of unrelated words.

Method.—Twenty-five Ss were each presented 11 free recall lists. Each list consisted of 20 "unrelated" nouns with Thorndike and Lorge frequencies of occurrence from 10 to 40 per million. Recorded rehearsal protocols and written free recall data were collected. The order of presentation of the lists and item order within a list were random for each S. The first list was the same for all Ss and was not included in analysis.

Results and discussion.—In Fig. 1, the recall probability of an item, $P(R)$, is shown as a function of its serial position in the study list. The U-shaped function exhibits both primacy and recency effects. Also shown in Fig. 1 is a plot of the mean number of rehearsals given an item as a function of its serial position. Number of rehearsals is seen to be quite high for the

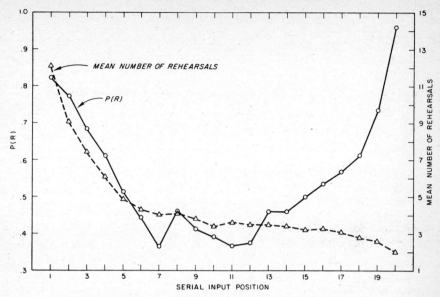

FIG. 1. The mean probability of recall, $P(R)$, and the mean number of rehearsals of an item as a function of its serial input position.

early list items and to decrease steadily as a function of serial position. Although not explicitly instructed to do so, S nearly always rehearsed an item at least once during the 5-sec. interval while it was being shown. The probability that an item was rehearsed while being presented was .996.

An item did not always appear in a continuous succession of RSs. An item might be entered into rehearsal, be absent from one or more RSs, and reappear in a later RS. Thus there are three types of items which may be included in RS: (a) the item being presented, (b) items from the immediately preceding RS, and (c) items not in the immediately preceding RS which have been returned to rehearsal after being absent from some number of intervening RSs. The mean proportions of the items in an RS from the middle of a list (Positions 4–18) which belong to these three classes were .31, .47, and .21, respectively. While it may be seen that the bulk of RS is made up of the new item and items from the immediately preceding RS, nearly one-fourth of the items in RS were returned to rehearsal following an absence. The

proportions of these returned items which had been absent from rehearsal for 1, 2, 3, 4, 5, or 6 + intervening RSs were .57, .19, .10, .05, .05, and .05, respectively.

Figure 2 presents $P(R)$ for an item as a function of the last RS in which that item appeared. This function is fairly flat for the first two-thirds of the list and then rapidly increases to a high probability for items being rehearsed at the end of the study list. Recall probability was the same (.96) for all items present in the final RS. This $P(R)$ was the same as that observed for the final list item, suggesting that it is the presence of an item in rehearsal at the end of list study which gives rise to the recency effect.

Figure 3 presents $P(R)$ for an item as a function of the mean normalized number of rehearsals accorded the item during list study for items from serial positions 1–4, 5–10, 11–16, and 17–20. The measure of normalized number of rehearsals is found by dividing the number of rehearsals of an item by the total number of rehearsals for all items in that particular S list. Thus the normalized number of rehearsals is a measure of the proportion of the total

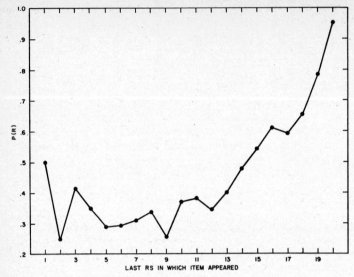

FIG. 2. The mean probability of recall, $P(R)$, of an item as a function of the last RS in which that item appeared.

rehearsals of a given S list which were accorded an item. This measure avoids a possible confounding due to different average rehearsal rates of different Ss. For all curves in Fig. 3, $P(R)$ is seen to increase with amount of rehearsal. The curves for items from the first 16 serial positions are virtually identical. For a given amount of rehearsal, items from the initial serial positions have no better recall than items from the middle of the list. It thus appears that the primacy effect derives from the additional rehearsal accorded the initial list items. The curve for items from Serial Positions 17–20 is, at all points, above the other curves. This is not unexpected since items from the last list positions should have a high probability of being present in S's rehearsal at the time of test and thus be retrievable on the basis of both STS and LTS information. Previous studies (Rundus & Atkinson, 1970; Rundus, Loftus, & Atkinson, 1970) have produced results similar to those shown in Fig. 3 and provide support for the conclusion that amount of rehearsal accorded an item is a good indicator of the memory strength of the item.

The relationship between the order in which items are recalled and their strength in memory has been the subject of some controversy. Data have been presented

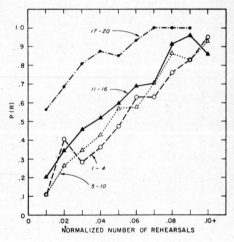

FIG. 3. The probability of recalling an item, $P(R)$, as a function of the mean normalized number of rehearsals accorded the item. (Shown for items here from Serial Positions 1–4, 5–10, 11–16, and 17–20. The circled numbers indicate the approximate mean number of rehearsals corresponding to a given mean normalized number of rehearsals.)

(Bousfield, Whitmarsh, & Esterson, 1958; Underwood & Schulz, 1960) which suggest that the strongest or best learned items are recalled first; while Battig, Allen, & Jensen (1965) present results supporting an opposite hypothesis. There is also evidence (Shuell & Keppel, 1968) that terminal list items appear early in recall. A dual-storage model might suggest that Ss first recall items from the temporary STS and then attempt to recall on the basis of LTS strength those items which are no longer in STS. In the present study, it was observed that 93% of the time the first item recalled was present in the final RS. Figure 4 shows the proportion of those items present in the final RS which appear at various output positions. It is evident that items in the final RS appear early in output. The same function for items whose final rehearsal was in an earlier RS (the 15th RS was chosen as representative) is also shown in Fig. 4. A comparison of these two functions supports the hypothesis that items in STS

at the time of test appear early in the output protocol.

The positive relationship between $P(R)$ and rehearsal (see Fig. 3) suggests that amount of rehearsal provides a good indicator of memory strength. It should be possible, therefore, to use the rehearsal data to relate the position of an item in the output protocol to its strength relative to other recalled items. In Fig. 5, the normalized number of rehearsals accorded an item is shown as a function of the Vincentized proportion of the output protocol in which the item appeared. In the Vincentizing procedure (Hilgard, 1938), the output protocol for each S list is divided into equal parts, in this case sixths. The mean normalized number of rehearsals for items in each part is then computed. The average for each sixth of output is then calculated across all S lists, yielding a single curve in which each S contributes equally to each point.

When all list items are included in the analysis, the curve is seen to rise rapidly

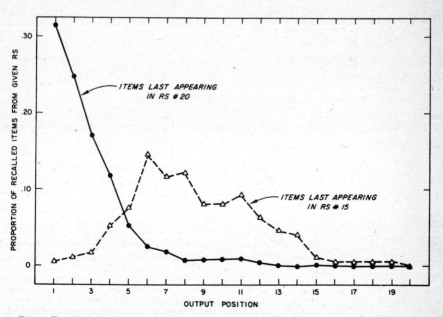

Fig. 4. For all recalled items whose last rehearsal occurred in RS #20, the proportion of those items recalled at various output positions is shown as a function of output position. (Also shown for items last rehearsed in RS #15.)

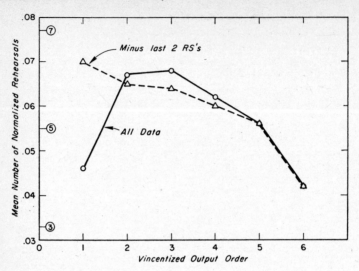

FIG. 5. The mean normalized number of rehearsals of recalled items is shown as a function of the sixth of the Vincentized output protocol in which the item was recalled. (Shown for all items and for all items not appearing in either of the final two RSs. The cricled numbers indicate the approximate number of rehearsals corresponding to a given mean normalized number of rehearsals.)

to a peak and then decline with output position. This function contains items recalled from both STS and LTS. The STS component may be minimized by deleting those items which appeared in final RSs. The function obtained when items present in the final two RSs are deleted is also shown in Fig. 5. With the STS component deleted, the order of recall is seen to be a function of item strength, with the items which received the most rehearsal appearing earliest in output.

A study of Rundus et al. (1970) provides further support for the observed relation between item strength and output order. In their study, Ss were given single free recall trials on 10 lists of words. Three weeks later, Ss returned and were given a recognition test on all of the words previously presented. The probability of recognizing an item was then plotted as a function of the position of the item in the output protocol for the list in which it appeared. The result was an inverted U-shaped curve indicating a low recognition probability for the initial items recalled (STS items), a high recognition probability for the

middle items output (the initial items recalled from LTS), and a low probability of recognizing the final items of the recall output protocol. It appears, then, that S initially recalls any items available from STS with subsequent items recalled as a negative function of their LTS strength.

There are indications, in both rehearsal and output protocols, of S's attempt to organize the list presented. Evidence for the subjective organization of lists of unrelated words was first presented by Tulving (1962), and a summary of much of the work to date is provided by Shuell (1969). Measures of subjective organization such as the one suggested by Tulving (1962) are based on the similarity in the order of words on successive recall trials and are thus only suited for multitrial, free recall procedures. In the current study, S is left free to choose which words rehearse together. The organization reflected in this choice may be compared with the order of words in recall, making it possible to observe organization in a single, free recall trial. If the organization observed during rehearsal is related to that seen in recall, then it might be expected that the probability of adjacent recall of any two items would be a positive function of the number of times these two items appeared together in rehearsal. This was indeed observed to be the case. For any pair of items appearing in a given recall protocol (excluding any items which appeared in the final RS), the mean probability that the pair would appear adjacently in recall as a function of the number of adjacent rehearsals of the pair was .07, .20, .23, and .30 for 0, 1, 2, 3+ adjacent rehearsals. There are many possible artifacts in a conditional analysis of this sort and several analyses (Rundus, 1970) were performed to examine these potential confoundings. All further analyses proved confirmatory to the hypothesis that adjacent rehearsal of two items was highly correlated with their subsequent adjacent recall.

Experiment II

Von Restorf (1933) demonstrated that when an item in a study list is distinctive, its recall probability is notably higher than that for other list items. In the present study some items of a list were printed in red, distinguishing them from the remainder of the items which were printed in black. Of particular interest were the changes in rehearsal and recall seen for (a) the emphasized items, (b) those items adjacent in list position to the emphasized items, and (c) the list as a whole.

Method.—Fifteen Ss were each shown 11 free recall lists. The lists each consisted of 20 unrelated nouns with Thorndike and Lorge frequencies of occurrence of 10 to 40 per million. Either 0, 1, 2, or 3 of the words in a list were printed in red; the remaining words were printed in black. The words selected to be printed in red were chosen randomly for each S. The list conditions (number of red words in the list) were assigned randomly across all lists for all Ss. One-third of all the experimental lists contained 1 red word, one-third contained 2 words, one-sixth contained no red words, and one-sixth contained 3 red words. The serial position of the red words was randomly chosen with the restriction that red words could appear only in Positions 5–16 with no more than 2 red words in any block of five serial positions. The Ss were told that red words might appear, and if so, to be sure that red words might appear, and if so, to be sure

TABLE 1

RECALL AND REHEARSAL FOR ALL ITEMS, RED ITEMS, AND N ITEMS

Number of red items in list	All items		Red items		N items	
	P(R)	$\bar{X}$ number of re-hearsals	P(R)	$\bar{X}$ number of re-hearsals	P(R)	$\bar{X}$ number of re-hearsals
0	.62	4.15	—	—	.62	4.15
1	.46	4.17	.72	6.52	.45	4.06
2	.47	3.85	.70	6.82	.44	3.60
3	.45	3.29	.53	4.81	.43	3.11

to remember them. Recorded rehearsal protocols and written recall were collected. The order of presentation of the lists and the order of items within a list were random for each S. The first list presented was always the same and contained 2 red words. This list was not included in analysis.

Results and discussion.—Table 1 presents the mean probability of recall and the mean number of rehearsals per item for (a) all items, (b) the red (R) items, and (c) the nonred (N) items in lists containing 0, 1, 2, or 3 R items. Both probability of recall and mean number of rehearsals were higher for R items than for N items. The additional rehearsal accorded the R items was not massed, but derived from a longer maintenance of these items in S's rehearsal. This fact is best illustrated in those lists containing a single R item, where it was observed that the mean number of RSs in which the R item appeared was 4.5, while for N items the mean was 2.3. For these same lists, it was also noted that when the R item was presented, S did not drop all other items being rehearsed and con-centrate solely on the R item. The mean number of different items in RS was 2.9 when an R item was being shown and 3.1 when an N item was displayed.

From the first two rows of Table 1, it may be seen that the introduction of a single R item sharply reduces overall probability of recall (Column 2), while rehearsal of the list remains about the same (Column 3). As more R items are included in a list, both recall and mean number of rehearsals tend to decrease for both R and N items. In general, then, the introduction of distinctive items into a

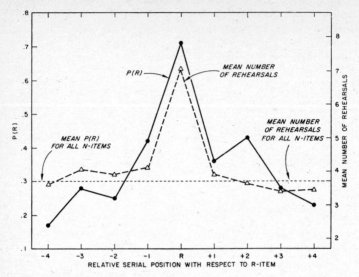

FIG. 6. The probability of recall, $P(R)$, and mean number of rehearsals for R items and N items in serial positions adjacent to the R item. (Shown for lists containing one R item.)

list impairs performance on the list. When comparing lists with zero and one R item (Rows 1 and 2 of Table 1), overall mean recall probability is seen to fall from .62 to .46; however, there is no apparent change in S's overall rehearsal. It is possible that the reduction in S's performance may be due to a disruption of S's organization of the study list as the result of the introduction of a distinctive item.

Figure 6 shows both the probability of recall and the mean number of rehearsals for the R item and the N items in serial positions adjacent to the R item in lists containing one R item. A line indicating the mean probability of recall and mean number of rehearsals for all N items in Positions 4–17 in single R-item lists is also shown for reference. Recall appears to be best for those N items immediately adjacent to the R item and declines with distance from the R item. Mean number of rehearsals declines slightly for items appearing after the R item.

The main effects of introducing a distinctive item into a free recall list thus appear to be: (a) an increase in both rehearsal and recall probability for the distinctive item, (b) a decrease in overall performance on the list, and (c) some enhancement of items presented adjacent to the distinctive item.

Experiment III

Melton (1967) found that when an item is presented twice in a free recall list, its recall probability increases as a function of the number of items intervening between the two presentations. This spacing effect has been observed in several other studies (e.g., Glanzer, 1969; Tulving, 1969), while others employing somewhat different procedures fail to find the effect (Underwood, 1969; Waugh, 1967). The present study, using lists containing repeated items, incorporated an observable rehearsal procedure with the expectation that analysis of S's rehearsal would provide evidence as to the nature of the spacing effect.

Method.—Eleven Ss were each presented 11 free recall lists. Each list consisted of 25 presentations: 20 different words, 5 of which were repeated once. The words used were unrelated nouns having Thorndike and Lorge frequencies of occurrence from 10 to 40 per million. A list contained

1 of the 5 repeated words in each of five lag conditions of zero, one, two, four, or seven intervening items between presentations. The order of lists and of items within a list were random for each *S*. The serial positions of the repeated items were balanced within each *S* using a Latin-square design. An *S* received each lag condition in every serial position once during the session. When thrree were insufficient items remaining at the end of a list to satisfy one of the lag conditions (e.g., when the item in Serial Position 22 was to be repeated at Lag 7), the second presentation of the repeated item was given at the end of the study list and data from that item was not included in analysis. The *S*s were told that some items might be repeated. Recorded rehearsal protocols and written free recall data were collected for each *S*. The first list presented to all *S*s was the same and was not included in the analysis.

Results and discussion.—In Fig. 7, the probability of recalling an item is shown as a function of the lag between presentations of the item. N items refer to those items which appeared only once in the list.

To minimize recency and primacy effects, the items included in this analysis were restricted to those receiving their first presentation in Serial Position 6 or greater, and their last presentation before Serial Position 22. Recall probability generally increased with lag providing a confirmation of the spacing effect described by Melton (1967). Also shown in Fig. 7 is the mean number of rehearsals accorded an item as a function of its lag condition. This function is seen to be highly correlated with the recall probability function.

In Table 2, the rehearsals accorded an item in each lag condition are broken down into first and second presentation components. Column 2 shows the mean number of rehearsals of an item during its initial 5-sec. presentation period. As expected, no differences in rehearsal as a function of condition appear in this interval. Column 3 displays the mean number of rehearsals accorded an item following the initial 5-sec. presentation and prior to the second presentation. The increase observed over lag is expected since the length of this inter-

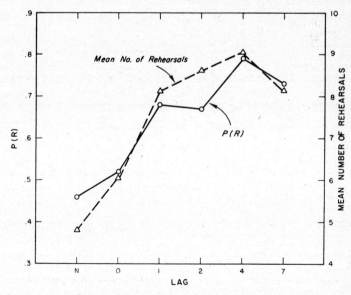

Fig. 7. The probability of recall, $P(R)$, and mean number of rehearsals of list items as a function of the lag between repetitions. (N refers to items which were not repeated.)

TABLE 2

REHEARSAL DURING AND AFTER FIRST AND
SECOND PRESENTATIONS OF AN ITEM

Lag	$\bar{X}$ number of rehearsals during initial presentation of item	$\bar{X}$ number of rehearsals following initial presentation and prior to 2nd	$\bar{X}$ number of rehearsals during 2nd presentation	$\bar{X}$ number of rehearsals following 2nd presentation
N	2.14	2.66	—	—
0	2.24	—	1.95	1.86
1	2.12	.83	1.95	3.25
2	2.16	1.35	1.73	3.40
4	2.00	1.77	1.65	3.58
7	2.14	1.62	1.98	2.44

presentation period (and hence the opportunity for rehearsal) increases with lag. Column 4 shows the mean number of rehearsals of an item during the 5-sec. interval while it was being presented for the second time. In an attempt to explain the inferior recall of Lag 0 items, as compared with items at greater lags, it may be hypothesized that S pays less attention to a Lag 0 item during its second presentation period. The results shown in Column 4 would not support this interpretation: Lag 0 items receive no fewer rehearsals during their second presentation than do items with longer lags. The final column of the table displays the mean number of rehearsals accorded an item following its second 5-sec. presentation interval. With the exception of Lag 7, rehearsals are seen to increase with lag.

For this study, then, the probability of recalling a repeated item and the amount of rehearsal of the item both increase with spacing of the repetitions. From Table 2, at least two loci of the spacing effect may be noted. First, items repeated at zero lag receive far fewer rehearsals following their second presentation than do items repeated at longer lags. Second, the increased opportunity for rehearsal between presentations (Column 3) provided by the longer lags contributes to the additional rehearsal and better recall for items repeated at these spacings.

Experiment IV

The free recall paradigm in which the lists employed contain words related either associatively or categorically has proven useful in the study of organization in memory. The related words in such lists are usually clustered in S's recall with both structural features of the study list and cues during recall having important effects on S's performance (see Shuell, 1969, for a review of both methods and results). The present study was designed to examine the effects of categorically related words on S's rehearsal. Additionally, by including both related and unrelated items in each list, comparisons can be made between S's treatment of the two types of items during study and recall.

Method.—Twenty Ss each received 11 free recall lists. Each list consisted of two, 6-item categories (C1 and C2) and 12 "unrelated" words (NC). The labels C1 and C2 were solely notational and were not related to any characteristics of the categories or their presentation order. The category words were the 6 most frequently given members of 22 noun categories from the norms of Battig and Montague (1969), and the 132 "unrelated" items were nouns with Thorndike and Lorge frequencies of occurrence "A" and "AA." Recorded rehearsal protocols and written free recall data were collected for each S. The first list was the same for each S and was not included in the analysis; the order of all other lists and the order of items within a list were randomized for each S.

Results and discussion.—Clustering of the three types of list items (C1, C2, and NC) was observed in the output protocols. A repetitions measure of clustering (Bousfield & Bousfield, 1966) was calculated for each S list. This measure computes the difference between the observed number of adjacent recalls of items in each category and an expected value based upon the total number of items recalled in each category. Any difference value greater than zero indicates some clustering. In the present study, each of the three item types was considered as a category. A difference measure was found for each S list and the mean computed. There was a mean of 5.7 more repetitions observed than expected. The observed clustering may also be expressed as the ratio of the observed difference in repetitions to the maximum possible difference given perfect clustering (Gerjouy & Spitz, 1966). A value of 1.0 for this ratio would indicate maximal

TABLE 3

Probability of Inclusion in the RS for Possibile Types of Items

Item presented	Probability that the RS will contain the item being presented	Probability that a C1 item will be included in the RS		Probability that a C2 item will be included in the RS		Probability that an NC item will be included in the RS	
		C1 items from the immediately prior RS	C1 items not in the immediately prior RS	C2 items from the immediately prior RS	C2 items not in the immediately prior RS	NC items from the immediately prior RS	NC items not in the immediately prior RS
C1	.94	.73	.59	.17	.06	.22	.07
C2	.96	.14	.06	.75	.61	.20	.06
NC	.95	.22	.10	.21	.07	.42	.15

clustering. The observed mean value of this ratio in the present study was .70.

The organization of items by category was observed in rehearsal as well as recall. For RSs in Serial Positions 5–20 the proportion of the items in RS (excluding the item being shown) which belonged to C1, C2, or NC were calculated conditional upon the type of item being presented. The observed proportions of RS items which were from C1, C2, and NC, respectively, were .64, .12, and .25 when a C1 item was shown; .11, .72, and .22 when a C2 item appeared; and .20, .19, and .61 when an NC item was presented. Thus about three-fourths of the items in a given RS were from the same class. There are at least two possible explanations for the similarity in treatment of NC and category items. First, the NC items may be treated as a third "category" defined by S as all items not belonging to C1 or C2. Alternatively, S may tend to rehearse a category item only when a member of the same category is presented and not when an NC item or an item from the other category is shown. The result of such a rehearsal strategy would be the rehearsal of NC items when an NC item is presented.

Table 3 presents a more detailed analysis of the types of items included in RS. Data included in this analysis were from RSs in Serial Positions 5–20. The rows of the table correspond to the type of item which was being shown during the 5-sec. RS, whereas the columns indicate the types of items which may be included in RS. Table 3 entries represent the probability of inclusion of the various types of items in RS. From Row 1 of Table 3 it may be

seen, in Column 3, that when a C1 word is presented, there is a high probability (.73) that any C1 items which appeared in the immediately previous RS will be maintained in S's rehearsal. In fact, their likelihood of remaining in rehearsal is about 4 times as great as that for other types of items. The entry in Column 4 indicates that when a C1 word is shown, C1 items presented earlier but dropped from rehearsal (i.e., not present in the previous RS) are nearly 10 times more likely to be reentered into rehearsal than are other items which had been dropped from rehearsal. Similar but weaker effects were again observed for the NC items.

Examination of the rehearsal protocols indicate that S is definitely using information about the category membership of an item. In fact, S appears to structure the contents of each RS to match the item being shown rather than simply including the new item in some ongoing rehearsal pattern.

Overall probability of recall was observed to be higher for category words (.67) than for noncategory words (.40). Category words also received a higher mean normalized number of rehearsals (.035) than did noncategory words (.028). This latter result, in conjunction with previous observations that the structure of S's rehearsal is highly dependent upon categorical features of the list, suggests that the higher recall probability for category words is based, at least in part, upon superior storage of information about these items. The curves shown in Fig. 8 plot the probability of recalling an item as a function of the normalized number of rehearsals accorded that item. For both category and noncategory items, recall probability is seen to increase with amount of rehearsal. For a given amount of rehearsal, however, recall is better for the category words, suggesting that categorical information may be of value in retrieval. For this study, then, the superior recall of category items appears to be due to both storage and retrieval factors.

In Exp. I, it was observed that following recall of items from STS, the order of recall for the remaining items was a function of their LTS strength: the more rehearsal accorded an item the earlier that item appeared in output. If output order is indeed correlated with item strength, then, in the present study, recall of items within a category should proceed in order from most to least rehearsed. To look at data relevant to this question, three separate output protocols, one for each type of item (C1, C2, NC), were formed from the recall data of each S list. These sub-protocols contained the output order of items within each item type relative to all recalled items of the same class (i.e., first C1 item recalled, second C1 item, etc.). To minimize the STS component, all items appearing in the last two RSs were excluded from the analysis. The subprotocols for each item type were then combined across Ss using a Vincentizing procedure. The mean normalized number of rehearsals accorded items in the first, second, third, and fourth Vincentized quarters of the output protocols were .062, .052, .037, and .029 for C1 items; .062, .047, .038, and .033 for C2 items; and .062, .049, .040, and .032 for NC items. For all item classes, output order is a negative function of amount of rehearsal. This result provides striking support to the hypothesis that recall of items from LTS proceeds from strongest to weakest.

In the present study, item strength was not the only observed determinant of output order. As was previously mentioned, Ss tended to recall category items in clusters. If recall of a cluster of items from one category was followed by recall of items from the second category, then

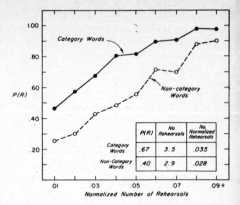

	$P(R)$	No. Rehearsals	No. Normalized Rehearsals
Category Words	.67	3.5	.035
Non-Category Words	.40	2.9	.028

FIG. 8. The probability of recall, $P(R)$, of an item as a function of the mean normalized number of rehearsals accorded the item. (Shown for category and noncategory items. The inserted table shows mean $P(R)$, mean number of rehearsals, and mean normalized number of rehearsals for category and noncategory words.

the results described above would suggest that the final item of the first cluster might have a lower strength than that of the initial item recalled from the second category. To examine this possibility, a subprotocol for each S list was formed by deleting all NC items from the recall protocol of the list. All items appearing in the last two RSs were also deleted to minimize STS effects. The resulting sub-protocol consisted of all C1 and C2 items not rehearsed in the final two RSs, in the order in which they were recalled. As an example, this subprotocol would be: $C2_1$, $C2_2$, $C2_3$, $C1_1$, $C1_2$, $C1_3$, $C1_4$, $C2_4$. The first item of the subprotocol could be from either C1 or C2. This item would then be followed by from zero to five other items of the same category prior to the appearance of the first item from the other category. This initial series of items from one of the categories was designated as the first cluster (FC) of the subprotocol. In the example given above, FC was of size three and consisted of the three C2 items which appeared prior to the first C1 item. The comparison of interest in this analysis is between the amount of rehearsal accorded the last item of FC ($C2_3$ in the example) and that given the first item of the other list category (Cl_1 in the example). The mean normalized number of rehearsals accorded both the final item of FC and the initial item recalled from the other category were calculated conditional upon the number of items in FC and were observed to be, respectively, .051 and .069 for FC of one or two items, .043 and .067 for FC of three or four items, and .031 and .061 for FC of five or six items. For all sizes of FC, the final item of FC received less rehearsal than the initial item recalled from the second category. In addition, as the size of FC increases this difference is observed to increase. Thus, while it was shown in Fig. 5 that the order of recall within a category proceeds as a function of item strength, S will recall an item of low strength within a category cluster prior to the recall of a higher strength item of a different category. This provides another indication of S's use of category information during recall.

Conclusion

At least two points should be kept in mind when considering the results of the studies just described. First, the recorded rehearsal procedure was designed to be an unobtrusive monitor allowing S freedom to rehearse any list items he chose as often as he chose. Thus at no time were the number of rehearsals of an item directly manipulated. Any relationship involving number of rehearsals is therefore correlational and should be regarded with care. Second, it was not intended that S's overt rehearsals of an item should be thought of as the sole *causes* for memory of that item. Indeed, Ss were instructed to feel free to study the lists in any manner they chose. Their instructions were that whenever they were "thinking about" one of the list items they should overtly rehearse that item. Thus the role of the overt rehearsals was to serve as *indicators* of what S was doing during list study. It was hoped that the number of overt rehearsals accorded an item might be a good measure of the number of times S "attended to" or "thought about" that item during list presentation.

A number of writers (e.g., Mandler, 1967; Tulving, 1968) have proposed that recall depends upon organization. In addition to providing a monitor of the accumulation of "strength" for individual items of a free recall list, the recorded rehearsal photocols also provided an indicator of S's attempts at list organization. In the study involving categorized lists, there was a pronounced tendency for S to rehearse together items from the same category. Presentation of a word from one of the categories not only increased the probability of other words from the category remaining in rehearsal, but perhaps more importantly, triggered the return to active rehearsal of words from that category which had been dropped from rehearsal. This latter result may help to explain the observation that in lists of "unrelated" words, items would often be dropped from rehearsal and later reappear. It is possible that these words were returned to rehearsal because S saw them as in some way related to a newly presented item and chose to include the old words with the new one in an organizational scheme.

The organization observed in rehearsal was also reflected in S's recall. In Exp. IV, S's tendency to rehearse together items of the same category was mirrored by the clustering of these items in recall. It was noted that once S had begun to recall a cluster of items from one of the categories, she would continue recalling those items even though the last item recalled in that cluster was, on the average, weaker than the first item recalled in the next cluster. Organization was also noted in lists of unrelated words in Exp. I. From the recorded rehearsal protocols, it was observed that the more often two items appeared adjacently in rehearsal, the higher was their probability of adjacent recall. Examination of S's rehearsal thus made it possible to note the emergence of organization during study and its manifestation in recall.

In conclusion, it was obvious, both qualitatively to the listening E and quantitatively in the data analysis, that S was not treating a list in a simple, mechanical fashion. To adequately understand performance in a free recall task, it is therefore imperative to gain some knowledge of S's strategies of rehearsal organization. To this end the procedure for the observation of rehearsal described here has proven, and should prove eminently useful in providing, access to S's rehearsal processes.

REFERENCES

Asch, S. E., & Ebenholtz, S. M. The principle of associative symmetry. *Proceedings of the American Philosophical Society*, 1962, **106**, 135–163.

ATKINSON, R. C., & SHIFFRIN, R. M. Human memory: A proposed system and its control processes. In K. W. Spence & J. T. Spence (Eds.), *The psychology of learning and motivation: Advances in research and theory.* Vol. II. New York: Academic Press, 1968.

BATTIG, W. F., ALLEN, M., & JENSEN, A. R. Priority of free recall of newly learned items. *Journal of Verbal Learning and Verbal Behavior*, 1965, **4**, 175–179.

BATTIG, W. F., & MONTAGUE, W. E. Category norms for verbal items in 56 categories: A replication and extension of the Connecticut category norms. *Journal of Experimental Psychology*, 1969, **80** (3, Pt. 2).

BOUSFIELD, A. K., & BOUSFILED, W. A. Measurement of clustering and of sequential constancies in repeated free recall. *Psychological Reports*, 1966, **19**, 935–942.

BOUSFIELD, W. A. The occurrence of clustering in the recall of randomly arranged associates. *Journal of General Psychology*, 1953, **49**, 229–240.

BOUSFIELD, W. A., WHITMARSH, G. A., & ESTERSON, J. Serial position effects and the Marbe effect in the free recall of meaningful words. *Journal of General Psychology*, 1958, **59**, 255–262.

BOWER, G. H. Organizational factors in memory. *Cognitive Psychology*, 1970, **1**, 18–46.

FISCHLER, I., RUNDUS, D., & ATKINSON, R. C. Effects of overt rehearsal processes on free recall. *Psychonomic Science*, 1970, **19**, 249–250.

GERJOUY, I. R., & SPITZ, H. H. Associative clustering in free recall: Intellectual and developmental variables. *American Journal of Mental Deficiency*, 1966, **70**, 918–927.

GLANZER, M. Distance between related words in free recall: Trace of the STS. *Journal of Verbal Learning and Verbal Behavior*, 1969, **8**, 105–111.

GLANZER, M., & CUNITZ, A. R. Two storage mechanisms in free recall. *Journal of Verbal Learning and Verbal Behavior*, 1966, **5**, 351–360.

GLANZER, M., & MEINZER, A. The effects of intralist activity on free recall. *Journal of Verbal Learning and Verbal Behavior*, 1967, **6**, 928–935.

HILGARD, E. R. A summary and evaluation of alternative procedures for the construction of Vincent curves. *Psychological Bulletin*, 1938, **35**, 282–297.

MANDLER, G. Organization and memory. In K. W. Spence & J. T. Spence (Eds.), *The psychology of learning and motivation.* Vol. I. New York: Academic Press, 1967.

MELTON, A. W. Repetition and retrieval from memory. *Science*, 1967, **158**, 532.

POSTMAN, L., & PHILLIPS, L. W. Short term temporal changes in free recall. *Quarterly Journal of Experimental Psychology*, 1965, **17**, 132–138.

RUNDUS, D. An analysis of rehearsal processes in free recall. (Tech. Rep. No. 159) Palo Alto, Calif.: Stanford University, Institute for Mathematical Studies in the Social Sciences, 1970.

RUNDUS, D. & ATKINSON, R. C. Rehearsal processes in free recall: A procedure for direct observation. *Journal of Verbal Learning and Verbal Behavior*, 1970, **9**, 99–105.

RUNDUS, D., LOFTUS, G. L., & ATKINSON, R. C. Immediate free recall and three-week delayed recognition. *Journal of Verbal Learning and Verbal Behavior*, 1970, **9**, 684–688.

SLAMECKA, N. An examination of trace storage in free recall. *Journal of Experimental Psychology*, 1968, **76**, 504–513.

SHUELL, T. J. Clustering and organization in free recall. *Psychological Bulletin*, 1969, **72**, 353–374.

SHUELL, T. J., & KEPPEL, G. Item priority in free recall. *Journal of Verbal Learning and Verbal Behavior*, 1968, **7**, 969–971.

TULVING, E. Subjective organization in recall of "unrelated" words. *Psychological Review*, 1962, **69**, 344–354.

TULVING, E. Theoretical issues in free recall. In T. R. Dixon & D. L. Horton (Eds.), *Verbal behavior and general behavior theory.* Englewood Cliffs, N. J.: Prentice-Hall, 1968.

TULVING, E. Distribution and repetition effects in memory for discrete events. Paper presented at the meeting of the Midwestern Psychological Association, Chicago, May 1969.

UNDERWOOD, B. J. Some correlates of item repetition in free recall learning. *Journal of Verbal Learning and Verbal Behavior*, 1969, **8**, 83–95.

UNDERWOOD, B. J., & SCHULZ, R. W. *Meaningfulness and verbal learning.* Philadelphia: J. B. Lippincott Co., 1960.

VON RESTORF, H. Uber die Wirkung von Bereichsbildungen im Spurenfeld. *Psychologische Forschung*, 1933, **18**, 299–342.

WAUGH, N. C. Presentation time and free recall. *Journal of Experimental Psychology*, 1967, **73**, 39–44.

PART 2

Dimensions of encoding

Introduction

The concept of coding is fundamental to understanding the contemporary advance in memory theory and research. As Melton (1973) points out, coding refers to what is stored in memory during learning, and the concept implies that there is not a one-to-one correspondence between the information, as presented and scored by the experimenter, and the information as processed by the subject between presentation and test. Underwood (1963) had drawn attention to this point in distinguishing between the nominal stimulus and the functional stimulus, where the nominal stimulus is that which is presented by the experimenter and the functional stimulus is that which is stored in memory by the subject.

The emphasis on coding processes is important in several ways. It serves to relate perceptual processes, memorial processes, and the general background of verbal-linguistic knowledge which the individual has permanently available. It focuses our attention on the 'interface' between particular experimental tasks and the individual's knowledge about words, relations among words, their properties and concepts, and the structure and function of language. Instead of attempting to 'decouple' memory and investigate memory processes as distinct from 'perception', 'language', or 'thinking', (Reitman, 1970), our attention is focused on how such traditionally distinct processes interact. Thus, in a general sense, the concept of coding has enriched and elaborated earlier conceptions of memory processing and considerably broadened the scope of memory research.

In a typical free recall experiment, for example, the subject's task is not to learn a set of words—the words are already highly familiar—but to store such information as will serve to discriminate the set of words presented from the large population of words permanently stored in memory (Postman, 1972; Tulving, 1968). Such information may include temporal and spatial attributes, modality of presentation, and associative-semantic features (Underwood, 1969). Evidence that 'the word' itself is not the ultimate unit stored comes from an adaptation of the Shepard-Teghtsoonian recognition paradigm, in which the subject is presented with a very long list of words and has to decide whether or not each successive word in the list has been presented previously. When a new word shares some significant features with a word previously presented (e.g. as an associate, or a synonym), subjects tend to identify the new word as having been presented before (Anisfeld and Knapp, Reading 11). Such findings imply that subjects code words in terms of such features and that, in retrieval, the features encoded serve to reconstruct the presentation event.

One major task of the coding theorist is to identify the various coding dimensions which subjects utilize, and to evaluate their relative salience in memory performance. Wickens (Reading 10) has reviewed a considerable body of evidence which has been widely interpreted as meeting those goals. The technique employed by Wickens and his associates capitalizes upon the rapid build-up of proactive inhibition (PI) which occurs in the Brown-Peterson paradigm (Keppel and Underwood, 1962) to determine the extent to which subjects can utilize a specific change in the nature of the to-be-remembered material to reduce the cumulative effects of PI. The amount of recovery in performance (or 'release from PI') which occurs on the critical trial provides an index of the relative effectiveness of encoding the particular dimension along which the to-be-remembered material is changed.

One general conclusion emerging from the release from PI studies is that changes along semantic dimensions (e.g. taxonomic category) are, on the whole, more effective than changes along a physical dimension (e.g. word length). This result has also been obtained in incidental learning studies (Hyde and Jenkins, Reading 12). Incidental learning studies acquire a new importance in the study of coding processes. Typically, the subject is required to attend only to certain specific features of the material in an initial orienting task, and since the subject does not anticipate a subsequent memory test, differences in memory performance following the orienting task can be attributed directly to the coding effectiveness of the features to which the subject attended. More recent evidence suggests that such differences cannot be attributed to the difficulty of the orienting task or to the processing times involved in carrying out the task (Gardiner, 1973; Hyde and Jenkins, 1973; Walsh and Jenkins, 1973).

The use of the coding concept to specify the nature of the trace stored in memory in turn implies that what is retrievable from the memory store is determined by the encoding process. The heuristic value of distinguishing between storage and retrieval processes gained a considerable boost from the paper by Tulving and Pearlstone (Part 3, Reading 16) in which it was shown that the provision of category labels as retrieval cues led to better recall of categorized word lists than when the category names were not provided. This result demonstrates that more information is available in the memory store than can be accessed (or retrieved) at a given test. The paper by Tulving and Osler (Reading 13) employs weak associates of the to-be-remembered words as retrieval cues, and showed that, whenever these cues were present at both the presentation and test phase, recall was enhanced, and whenever the cues were given at the test phase alone, they did not facilitate recall. On the basis of this finding, Tulving and Osler put forward a strong hypothesis concerning the relation between initial encoding and subsequent retrieval. They stated that specific retrieval cues will facilitate recall if, and only if, the information about them and their relation to the to-be-remembered word is stored at the same time as the to-be-remembered word itself. This encoding specificity hypothesis has been further examined by Tulving and Thomson (1973).

The cueing procedure described by Slamecka (Reading 14) involves the re-presentation at recall of a subset of intra-list items. Slamecka found that intra-list cueing had no beneficial effect upon recall, and he suggested that list items are stored independently and are reconstructed at recall by means of a retrieval plan based on general list structure. Intra-list items may, however, be useful cues in the case of categorized word-lists by providing access to more categories than subjects can recall unaided (Slamecka, 1972).

While the emphasis in the papers discussed above has been on coding processes with reference to verbal-linguistic information, interest in coding processes has also redirected our attention towards the relatively literal representation of the physical features of perceptual events. The readings in Part 2 begin with two articles which are concerned with such representational coding. Kroll, Parks, Parkinson, Bieber and Johnson (Reading 9) demonstrate, using a shadowing technique, that visual information may persist for as long as 25 seconds. Earlier studies may have led to an underestimate of the persistence or durability of representational information since only brief intervals were employed between presentation and test. Also, while representational information may be lost rapidly if not attended to, attention to visual (or auditory) features may lead to their preservation. Posner, Boies, Eichelman and Taylor (Reading 8) developed a matching technique which provides an index of the time taken to code the stimulus at a level of coding selected by the experimenter. For example, it takes longer to match nominal identity (Aa) than physical identity (AA). Further exploitation of the matching technique (Posner, 1969; Posner and Warren, 1972) indicates that visual and name codes are independent and may be retained in parallel.

Surface forms of coding are discussed in Chapter 2 of Herriot's *Attributes of Memory*, and the following two chapters in his text deal with deeper forms of coding and conditions of coding respectively.

References

GARDINER, J.M. (1973) Levels of processing in word recognition and subsequent free recall. *Journal of Experimental Psychology* **102**: 101-5.

HYDE, T.S. and JENKINS, J.J. (1973) Recall for words as a function of semantic, graphic, and syntactic orienting tasks. *Journal of Verbal Learning and Verbal Behavior* **12**: 471-80.

KEPPEL, G. and UNDERWOOD, B.J. (1962) Proactive inhibition in short-term retention of single items. *Journal of Verbal Learning and Verbal Behavior* **1**: 153-61.

MELTON, A.W. (1973) The concept of coding in learning-memory theory. *Memory and Cognition* **1**: 508-12.

POSNER, M.I. (1969) Abstraction and the process of recognition. In G.H. Bower and J.T. Spence (eds.) *The Psychology of Learning and Motivation* **3**. New York: Academic Press.

POSNER, M.I., and WARREN, R.E. (1972) Traces, concepts and conscious constructions. In A.W. Melton and E. Martin (eds.) *Coding Processes in Human Memory*. Washington, D.C.: Winston.

POSTMAN, L. (1972) A pragmatic view of organization theory. In E. Tulving and W.A. Donaldson (eds.) *Organization of Memory* New York: Academic Press.

REITMAN, W. (1970) What does it take to remember? In D.A. Norman (ed.) *Models of Human Memory* New York: Academic Press.

SLAMECKA, N.J. (1972) The question of associative growth in the learning of categorized material. *Journal of Verbal Learning and Verbal Behavior* **11**: 324-32.

TULVING, E., and THOMSON, D.M. (1973) Encoding specificity and retrieval processes in episodic memory. *Psychological Review* **80**: 352-73.

UNDERWOOD, B.J. (1963) Stimulus selection in verbal learning. In C.N. Cofer and B.S. Musgrave (eds.) *Verbal Behavior and Learning: Problems and Processes* New York: McGraw-Hill.

UNDERWOOD, B.J. (1969) Attributes of memory. *Psychological Review* **76**: 559-73.

WALSH, D., and JENKINS, J.J. (1973) Effects of cued orienting tasks on free recall in incidental learning: 'Difficulty', 'effort', and 'process' explanations. *Journal of Verbal Learning and Verbal Behavior* **12**: 481-8.

M.I. Posner, S.J. Boies,
W.H. Eichelman and R.L. Taylor

Retention of visual and name codes of single letters

Reprinted from the *Journal of Experimental Psychology Monograph* (1969) **79**(1) Part 2:1-16

If a stored letter can be matched more rapidly with a physically identical letter (e.g., AA) than it can with a letter having only the same name (e.g., Aa), then the stored representation must preserve something of the visual aspect of the letter. Immediately after the presentation of a letter, a physical match is about 90 msec. faster than a name match and this difference is lost after 2 sec. An interpolated information processing task abolished the difference between physical and name match RTs, but visual noise alone does not affect this difference. When the visual aspect of the letter is made a completely reliable cue, the efficiency of a physical match is maintained more adequately. If only the name of the first letter is presented, *S*s show the ability to recode the information into a form which is as efficient as a physical match and more efficient than a name match. Consideration is given to the relevance of these findings to the general questions of decay, rehearsal, and generation of visual codes.

If an *S* is required to respond whether or not two letters are the same, the rate of his response will reflect the type of information required for the match. For example, it is about 70 msec. faster to respond *same* to a pair of letters which are physically identical, e.g., AA, than it is to respond to a pair which have only the same name, e.g., Aa (Posner & Mitchell, 1967).

This technique can be used to examine the components of a letter present in the memory code which are used to make the match. If only the name of a letter is present in store, it should make no difference whether or not the new letter has the same physical form. On the other hand, if full visual information was used in the match, reaction time (RT) should be much faster when the input matches the stored code in physical form.

This basic notion was tested in an experiment which has been reported briefly (Posner & Keele, 1967). The results of that study showed that, immediately after presentation, a physical identity match was about 80 msec. faster than one which was based on the name, and that this difference was reduced to about zero after 1.5 sec.

The first section of the present paper seeks to replicate the previous findings with respect to delay between the two letters. Changes in the relative speed of physical and name matches are observed at intervals up to 2 sec. following presentation of the first visual letter. The second section considers the role of interpolated activity in the efficiency of the two types of match. A comparison is made between an interpolated visual noise field and a brief visual addition task. Differences between these two interpolated conditions could bear on the relation of visual information as inferred from this technique and the visual memory systems studied by other methods (Averbach & Coriell, 1961; Sperling, 1960). In most previous work, visual memory is studied during the time when S is in the process of acquiring the name of the letters. In the present technique it is possible to expose the first letter for sufficient time to be named by S. The relative importance of the visual and name codes can be manipulated. The third section reports the use of pure (uppercase letters only) and mixed (upper- and lowercase) lists to vary the degree to which S can rely on the visual form as a cue for making the match. If Ss are able to preserve the visual information by attending to it during the delay interval, physical matches in pure lists should maintain their efficiency better than physical matches in mixed lists. The final set of experiments compare visual and auditory presentations of the first letter. Sternberg (1967) has suggested that acoustic representations in memory might be converted into the appropriate visual form during the process of character recognition. This suggests that Ss receiving the name of a letter can generate a visual code appropriate for matching visual input. A comparison of auditory-visual and visual-visual matching as a function of delay interval seems to provide the opportunity to observe such code changes.

A background statement introduces each section of this paper. The final section considers the relevance of these techniques and results to questions of decay, rehearsal, and generation of visual information. The relationship between this work and other analyses of visual memory also is discussed.

CHANGES OVER TIME

In a previous report (Posner & Keele, 1967) a single uppercase letter was followed after intervals of 0, .5, 1, or 1.5 sec. with a letter which was either physically identical, had only the same name, or was different. The physical match was initially about 80 msec. faster than the name match. This difference was lost if a 1.5-sec. delay was introduced between the two letters. In that study

the first letter was always uppercase while the second letter could be either upper- or lowercase. Thus, the physical identity conditions were confounded with the second letter being a capital. While there was strong evidence that this did not markedly affect the decay function, it seemed important to balance this variable. Moreover, the previous study used time intervals which were run in blocks. This might have led to differential storage strategies with different delay intervals and it was thought important to eliminate this possibility. The current experiment corrects these deficiencies.

The study also was designed to compare conditions where S could anticipate the case of the second letter (pure list) with those where he could not do so (mixed list). In the pure conditions, S knows after the first letter is presented whether or not a physical match will be possible. It was thought that he might be more inclined to concentrate on the visual aspect of the first letter when he knew this would be a reliable cue (pure physical match) than when he did not know whether this could be a reliable cue (mixed physical match).

EXPERIMENT I
Method

Subjects.—The Ss were 16 students obtained through the employment service of the University of Oregon and paid $1.50 per hour. Each S was run individually for 3 consecutive days at the same hour in sessions of about 50 min.

Material.—The stimuli were the upper- and lowercase letters A, B, F, H, and K. There were three different lists of stimuli. The mixed list (M) consisted of 160 pairs of letters and was divided into two blocks of 80. Within each block, the number of "same" and "different" responses was equal. Within each response category, there were equal numbers of upper-upper-, upper-lower-, lower-upper-, and lower-lowercase combinations. For the physically identical "same" response, each letter occurred twice in each block. For the name identity, "same" (e.g., Aa), each letter occurred four times, twice in each order. The order of items within blocks was randomized with the exception that no response could occur four successive times.

The pure uppercase list consisted of 80 pairs and was a modification of the mixed list. The first letter remained mixed (either upper or lower) while the second letter was always a capital letter. In the pure lowercase list the first letter remained mixed while the second letter was always small.

Each list was recorded with elite type on the memory drum tape.

Procedure.—The lists were presented on a Stowe memory drum. When the drum rotated, a letter was exposed on the left side of the drum[1] and remained present during the trial. A Hunter interval timer timed the interstimulus intervals (ISI) of 0, .5, 1, or 2 sec., lifted the shutter exposing a letter on the right side of the tape, and started a standard timer. The S responded to each pair by pressing one of two microswitches under his index fingers which stopped the timer.

The Ss were run individually for 3 days. They were instructed to respond "same" if the two letters had the same name. The "same" key was always on the left. The first day was a practice day and each S received 40 trials of the mixed (M) list, followed by 40 trials of each pure list. On the second day, half the Ss received 80 trials of M and 80 trials of one pure list and half had M and the other pure list. On Day 3 all Ss again received 80 trials of M and the opposite pure list to the one used on Day 2. Each day, half the Ss had M first and half had the appropriate pure list. The Ss were fully informed as to the list with which they were working for each block of trials. However, they never knew which ISI was involved on a particular trial. The ISIs were assigned so that each ISI occurred an equal number of times with each response class and so that each particular pair of letters was assigned to each of the four ISIs an equal number of times.

A trial began with E saying "ready." After a short delay, E presented S with the first stimulus. After the ISI, the second stimulus was automatically exposed. The Ss were instructed to respond as soon as possible after the second stimulus appeared. A trial ended with E telling S his response latency and whether or not the response was correct. There was about 5 sec. between trials. After each block of 20 trials, S was given a brief rest while E changed the tape.

Results

Results for the mixed condition will be presented first. The patterns of results for the 2 experimental days were rather similar and will, therefore, be collapsed. Table 1 indicates the mean RTs, standard errors, and error rates for the mixed conditions. The results for "same" responses will be discussed first. The two conditions which constitute a physical match (upper-upper and lower-lower) are nearly identical. In general this also is true for the name match though the lower-upper sequence is some-

[1] The letters were separated by 10° of visual angle. The S was required to shift his eyes in order to see the second letter.

TABLE 1

MEAN RTs, STANDARD ERRORS, AND ERROR RATES FOR "SAME" AND "DIFFERENT" RESPONSES WITH MIXED LISTS AS A FUNCTION OF TIME INTERVAL: EXP. I

Match Type	Letter Case		ISI[b]			
	First	Second	0	.5	1	2
Physical	Upper	Upper	858	461	478	473
Physical	Lower	Lower	860	470	479	491
Physical		$\bar{X}$	859	466	479	482
		SE^a	17	14	14	12
	Percentage of Error		4	3	3	1
Name	Upper	Lower	950	520	497	496
Name	Lower	Upper	960	513	525	494
Name		$\bar{X}$	955	517	511	495
		SE	20	15	15	10
	Percentage of Error		13	6	2	3
Different	Upper	Upper	920	551	551	550
Different	Upper	Lower	909	535	516	528
Different	Lower	Upper	912	553	524	518
Different	Lower	Lower	936	567	537	533
Different		$\bar{X}$	919	551	532	532
		SE	21	21	22	18
	Percentage of Error		3	3	3	3

Note.—Mean RTs in milliseconds.
[a] In all cases standard errors are based on between-S variation.
[b] ISI in seconds.

what worse at 1 sec. Due to the lack of systematic differences between these subconditions, they were combined.

The delay function is shown in Fig. 1. This function is obtained by plotting the difference between physical identity and name identity "same" at each ISI. The closed circles represent the results of the present experiment while the open circles show data obtained from a previous study (Posner & Keele, 1967). An analysis of variance of the differences between physical and name "same" responses indicated a significant decline with interval, F (3, 42) = 11.6. A comparison of the mean scores for physical and name matches was made at each ISI. Sign tests show that at 0, .5, and 1 sec. the physical match is significantly better than the name match. At these intervals at least 13 of the 16 comparisons are positive, $p < .02$. At 2 sec. the difference between physical and name match is not significant, $p > .08$, and is only about 15 msec.

Data on "different" response times and error rates also are included in Table 1. In

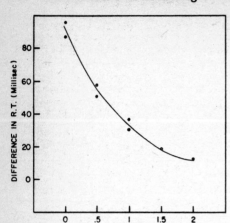

Fig. 1. Difference between physical and name identity matches as a function of interval between the two letters. (Solid and open circles represent two different experiments.)

general, the "different" responses go along with the response times for name level "same" responses as has been found in previous work (Posner & Mitchell, 1967). They tend to be somewhat longer, however, and their difference from physical "same" RTs does not approach zero in the interval studied. Since the "same" responses always were assigned to the left hand, there is some difficulty in making comparisons between the two responses. Therefore, relatively little emphasis is placed on these data in this report. Error rates tend to be rather small except for the name match with zero delay, and generally increase with the increasing RT.

TABLE 2

Mean RTs for Physical and Name "Same" Responses in Pure and Mixed Lists: Exp. I

Match	Condition	ISI[a]			
		0	.5	1	2
Physical	Pure	863	475	460	476
Physical	Mixed	859	466	479	482
Name	Pure	939	508	477	494
Name	Mixed	955	517	511	495

Note.—Mean RTs in milliseconds.
[a] Interstimulus interval in seconds.

Table 2 provides the basic data from the pure list matches. For purposes of comparison the mean RTs from the mixed condition also are included. There are no significant differences in RT between physical matches in pure and mixed lists. A comparison of name matches in the two conditions also shows relatively little difference.

Conclusions

The results obtained in the mixed list conditions replicate previous findings (Posner & Keele, 1967). In this study the cases of both first and second letters were randomly mixed so that objection to the previous findings based on confounding physical matches with upper-case letters is eliminated. Moreover, the time-delay intervals also were randomized. In the previous study the absolute RTs increased markedly between .5- and 1.5-sec. delay, while in this study they were virtually flat. Thus, the effect of temporal uncertainty on the absolute times was very different in the two experiments. Yet the difference scores plotted in Fig. 1 are similar. It would seem unlikely that changes in the difference scores could be due to an artifact of temporal uncertainty.

The pure list conditions did not result in any major differences from the mixed list. In this design Ss never knew whether the visual form would be a sufficient cue until after the first letter was presented. This might not have given sufficient time to use information concerning the case of the second letter. Experiments III and IV represent a further effort to study the effects of pure lists.

Unlike most studies of visual memory (Averbach & Coriell, 1961; Sperling, 1960). Ss in this experiment may have available both a visual code and the name of the letter. The results indicate that the matches based on the visual information become relatively less efficient over time. This could be because the visual code loses clarity over time, because it becomes less salient, or because the name information improves in efficiency. One method of manipulating stored information is to control the interval between presentation and recall. The next experiment explores this method.

Interpolated Activity

Sperling (1963) argued that the effective length of visual experience of stimuli was ended by the presentation of visual noise. Neisser (1967) disputed the contention that the icon (in his terms) was ended by the presentation of a noise field. Neisser's position was based on what seemed to him to be the excessive rate of read-in which was required if the stimulus exposure ended with the presentation of the noise field. There is evidence supporting his position available from a different source. Posner and Konick (1966) studied the ability of *S*s to retain the position of a point on a line. They argued from the accuracy of recall and from introspective data that this information was stored in a visual code. They found that reading and recording visually presented digits during the interval had little effect on the level of retention, but having to add or classify the digits had much greater effect. If their arguments are accepted, the visual information processing involved in reading the numbers was not an effective means of terminating the visual code, but the control of processing capacity through mental operations was effective.

This experiment was designed to compare the effect of visual noise and mental addition on the efficiency of physical and name matches.

EXPERIMENT II

Method

Subjects.—The *S*s were 12 students obtained and paid as in Exp. I. Each *S* participated in one practice session and four experimental sessions.

Apparatus.—The materials were presented by a Scientific Prototype three-channel tachistoscope. Exposure illumination for all fields was set at about 20 ftl.

Material.—Two random lists of 80 trials were prepared. Each trial consisted of an uppercase A, B, F, H, or K followed by one of those letters in either upper- or lowercase. The letters were transferred from Deca-Dry 18-point gothic templates and subtended a visual angle of less than .5 degrees. The 80 trials were divided into 20 pairs which were physically identical, 20 pairs which had only the same name, and 40 pairs which were different. These were randomized separately for the two lists.

Procedure.—The first letter was presented for 1 sec. This was followed by a .5-sec. interpolated interval and then by the second letter for 2 sec. The reaction time began with the presentation of the second letter and was stopped by *S* pressing one of the two microswitches under his index fin-

TABLE 3

MEAN RTs FOR PHYSICAL AND NAME MATCHES FOR EACH INTERPOLATED CONDITION: EXP. II

S	Blank		Mask		Addition	
	P[a]	N[b]	P	N	P	N
1	356	422	390	459	426	465
2	403	434	385	431	542	552
3	416	458	411	458	480	467
4	458	500	503	628	539	661
5	336	376	391	381	396	434
6	495	625	531	587	791	722
7	360	415	394	428	591	586
8	312	390	330	410	399	438
9	344	347	339	371	360	372
10	339	348	362	392	391	381
11	341	419	383	446	563	558
$\bar{X}$	378	430	402	454	498	512
SE	18	24	19	25	38	34
N − P	52		52		14	

Note.—Mean RTs in milliseconds.
[a] P = physical match.
[b] N = name match.

gers. The "same" response was always on the left. Three conditions of interpolated interval were used. Either the interval was filled by a blank field of the same intensity as the letters (blank), by a black and white random noise field (mask),[2] or by two pairs of digits grouped around the center of the field (addition). If the numbers were present, *S* had to add the upper pair. He could report the sum together with or after his response to the RT task.

On each day *S*s received 80 trials. From both random lists of 80 trials, three sublists were constructed so that each trial was assigned once to the three interpolated conditions. The interpolated conditions were randomized but occurred equally often with each letter pair. During the 4 experimental days, *S*s received four of the sublists. If the complete design of 12 *S*s had been run, each sublist would have been used eight times. Since 1 *S* did not complete the experiment, the sublists occurred either seven or eight times. Over the 4 days, each *S* had a total of 80 "same" pairs at each level (physical and name identity) which were evenly divided over the three interpolated conditions (26 or 27 pairs per condition).

All *S*s were run individually. They were instructed to respond "same" if the two letters had the same names and, otherwise, "different." After each trial, *S*s were told whether they were correct on matching and addition (if the numbers had been present) and also told their times for the RT task.

[2] The noise field consisted of random black and white ⅛-in. squares. The field covered 2 sq. in. superimposed on the letter and was displayed at an intensity setting equal to the first field.

Results

Table 3 gives the mean times for physical and name matches for each *S* and interpolated condition collapsed over the 4 days. While there are some practice effects within this period, the pattern of results for the first 2 and the last 2 days are almost identical. During the practice day, some *S*s had trouble with the addition task but they all learned to do this after a few trials.

The interpolated conditions have significant effect on the overall RTs. The mask condition increases the time for physical and name matches (each by 24 msec.). This increase occurs in 16 of 21 individual comparisons ($p < .05$). As would be expected, the addition task elevates the RTs even further. With one exception, every *S* shows an increase in RT to both physical and name matches with the interpolated addition task. However, by the last 2 days of practice, the RTs in the addition condition are, on the average, only about 100 msec. longer than the other two conditions. There were also very few errors in the addition task itself. Error rates in the RT task varied from 5% to 9%, with the larger percentage of error occurring with interpolated addition. "Different" response times are similar to the name "same" RTs and show the same effects of interpolated task.

The differences between physical (P) and name (N) RTs (N − P) for the three interpolated conditions are shown in Table 3. For the blank and mask conditions, the difference between physical and name identity is 52 msec. This compares with a difference of 51 msec. obtained with a .5-sec. delay in Exp. I. Name identity RT is greater than physical identity for every *S* in the blank condition and for 10 of 11 in the mask condition. These differences are significant by sign test, $p < .01$. There is clearly no difference between the blank and mask conditions. In the addition condition, the difference between physical and name identity is only 14 msec. which is not different statistically from zero by sign test.

Conclusions

It seems clear that visual noise alone does not affect the presence of visual information as defined by the difference between physical and name RTs. However, the mask does appear to be effective since the visual noise does act to delay the processing of the second stimulus. This is indicated by the finding that physical and name identity RTs are equally slowed when the mask is present. Delayed processing of a letter which appears following noise would be expected from considering the role of signal-to-noise ratio on RT (Sternberg, 1967).

The finding that the difference between physical and name identity is almost entirely lost with the interpolated addition task suggests that the control of central processing capacity (attention) has a greater effect on the retention of visual information from the first letter than it does on the name.

Several alternative accounts for this effect are possible. One is that the number stimuli have a greater *visual effect* than the mask field. Since the mask has *no* selective effect on the visual information, it does not seem likely that the numbers are operating mainly as a visual mask. It would be useful to determine the effectiveness of addition of numbers presented aurally. A second possibility is that the addition task delays processing the second letter so that the increased ISI causes a reduction in the relative efficiency of the visual code (see Fig. 1). This might account for effects on the first day when the addition RTs are delayed several hundred milliseconds. However, during the experimental days, the RTs for the addition conditions are only 100 msec. longer than for the other conditions. Using the function obtained in Fig. 1, this would not seem sufficient to allow such a large loss in the difference between physical and name identity. Moreover, on the last 2 days, when the absolute increases in RT due to addition are smallest, only 5 of the 11 *S*s show faster RTs to physical identity. Another explanation advanced for the addition task findings is that *S*s finish the physical match before the name match but the response cannot be emitted until the addition task is finished. This interpretation requires parallel processing of addition and the matching task. It cannot be eliminated by the present data. Perhaps if *E* had instructed *S*s to report the addition only after making the response, the likelihood of this interpretation would be lessened. However, allowing *S* to report as he desired seemed the most natural and least difficult instruction to follow.

In some ways the most striking aspect of the data is the consistency between results in this experiment with the blank field and in Exp. 1

for the .5-sec. delay. While the higher level of practice in this study produces faster absolute times, the difference between physical and name identity is almost identical to Fig. 1. This occurred despite the fact that the first letter was present for a full second in this study, while Ss could have had only a brief glimpse of it before making the eye movement in the previous study. There are also great differences in illumination and in the requirement for an eye movement in the first study. The consistency of results suggests that the technique reported here is relatively unaffected by type of apparatus, exposure duration, and illumination. Since the difference scores vary systematically with delay interval, it does not appear that the method is simply insensitive. These results challenge the view that the duration of a visual code is necessarily related to exposure duration (Neisser, 1967), luminance, or level of visual noise (Averbach & Coriell, 1961; Sperling, 1960). However, the visual code inferred from the present method may be at a different level of processing than that studied by most previous experiments.

Pure versus Mixed Lists

The first experiment indicated that the relative efficiency of a physical match declines rapidly over time. The second experiment suggests that this decline is greater when an interpolated addition task requires a portion of Ss' attention during the interval. The interpolated task has a larger effect on the physical than on the name match. It seems reasonable to ask if there are conditions under which Ss would be better able to maintain the efficiency of the physical match.

It was hypothesized that the effect of time shown in Fig. 1 was due, in part, to the conditions which tended to focus Ss' attention on the name of the letter rather than on its visual form. Within the list, half the "same" responses were based on the name. In addition, half the responses are "different." In such a mixed design, only on .25 of the trials is the physical form of the letter a sufficient basis for responding. This might well encourage S to pay attention primarily to the name. In fact, Ss run in mixed conditions report repeating the name of the letter as the main means of retaining it. The pure lists used in Exp. I provided a test of this

notion. However, in that design S never knew whether or not the visual information would be a reliable cue for making the match until the first letter was presented. These conditions are perhaps too difficult to incline Ss to use such a cue. In the experiment presented below, Ss were exposed to blocks of trials where only physical matches were used (pure lists) and blocks where there were both physical and name matches (mixed list).

Experiment III

In Exp. III, the first letter of a pair to be matched could be presented either aurally from a tape recorder (auditory condition), or visually by an in-line display (visual condition). Only the data from the visual condition is relevant to the present question and is discussed in this section.

Method

Subjects.—The Ss were 12 right-handed males obtained from the same source as in previous studies. They served for four 1-hr. sessions.

Apparatus.—Visual letters were presented from an in-line display. They were about 1 in. high and viewed from a distance of about 1 ft. subtended about 5 degrees. Audio information was presented from one channel of a Wollensak tape recorder and heard over Koss earphones. If the first letter was visual, its onset was controlled by the second channel of the audio tape so that it was present for .5 sec. and disappeared simultaneously with the offset of the audio digit. The auditory letter had a mean presentation time of about .5 sec. The offset of the first letter started a Hunter interval timer which presented the second letter after ISIs of 0, .5, and 1 sec. The second letter was always visual and was displayed by the same in-line cell. If S was in the visual condition, the sound to the earphones was interrupted so that he saw but did not hear the first letter. In the auditory conditions, the first letter was heard but was not displayed visually. In all conditions, S responded by pressing one of two keys as quickly as possible following the second letter.

Materials.—The letters consisted of A, B, F, H, and K. The first letter was either an uppercase letter presented visually (visual) or an auditory letter (auditory). The second letter was always visual and could be either upper only (pure list) or mixed upper and lower (mixed list). There were four lists of 40 pairs. For each list, there were 20 "same" pairs (4 for each letter) and 20 "different" pairs. The order of the pairs within the list was randomized.

Design.—Each S was run in all conditions on each of 4 days. The conditions were auditory

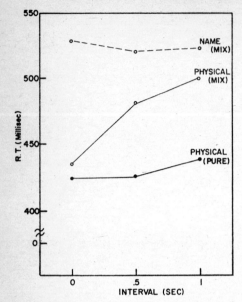

FIG. 2. Reaction time for physical matches in pure and mixed lists and for name matches in the mixed list as a function of interstimulus interval (Exp. III, all days combined).

pure, auditory mixed, visual pure, and visual mixed. One of the four lists was assigned to each condition on each day. On any given day, half the Ss had 80 auditory trials followed by 80 visual trials and half the reverse. Within an auditory or visual block, half the Ss had pure followed by mixed and half the reverse. Moreover, Ss who had auditory first on Day 1, had visual first on Day 2. Thus, the order of the four conditions was counterbalanced across Ss and within Ss. The three ISIs were randomized within the four blocks so that a given S had either six or seven "same" responses at each ISI for all four conditions every day.

Procedure.—Trials began with the presentation of the first letter for .5 sec. either aurally or visually. After an ISI of 0, .5, or 1 sec., the second letter was presented. The S responded by pressing either "same" (left hand) or "different" (right hand). The E recorded the response and RT and provided feedback. After 10 sec., the next trial was presented. The Ss were fully informed about the list with which they were working. On the first day they received a general instruction to consider an auditory letter as a capital and always to respond "same" if the two letters had the same name.

Results

The mean RTs, standard error, and error rates for "same" and "different" responses

are presented in Table 4. Only the conditions where the first letter is visual are presented in Table 4 and discussed in this section. The data are given separately for the first 2 and last 2 days of training.

Figure 2 presents the RTs for physical matches in pure and mixed lists and for name matches in the mixed list. The RTs are collapsed over the 4 days of training.

It is clear that the mixed condition results are similar to those presented in Exp. I. Immediately after presentation, physical matches are about 85 msec. faster than name matches, and this advantage is lost rapidly over the 1-sec. interval. These results are especially clear because most of the change over time is in the physical matches. On the last 2 days of the experiment there is a tendency for the "name" and "different" RTs to improve. The physical matches increase over the 1-sec. interval on all days.

The role of Ss' attention to the visual cue may be examined by comparing the difference in RT between physical matches with mixed and with pure lists over time intervals. On the first 2 days the pure physical match RTs do not increase at all, while on the last 2 days they increase at about half the rate of the mixed physical match RTs. This divergence is borne out by a significant interaction between time in store and type of list, $F (1, 11) = 14.9$, $p < .01$. The pure matches are significantly faster than the mixed physical matches at both .5 and 1 sec. by sign test, $p < .01$, but not at zero interval, $p > .05$.

Conclusions

The main change in the mixed condition is for the physical matches to get worse over the interval. This result is, of course, free of the eye movement artifact which makes it difficult to interpret the absolute times in Exp. I. It suggests that the time-delay function shown in Fig. 1 is due primarily to the visual information underlying the physical match becoming less efficient over time. There is a tendency for the name matches and different responses to improve, but this is confined to the last 2 days only.

A comparison of physical matches in pure and mixed lists shows that under proper conditions Ss can reduce the tendency for physical

TABLE 4

MEAN RTs, STANDARD ERRORS, AND ERROR RATES FOR "SAME" AND "DIFFERENT" RESPONSES: VISUAL CONDITIONS OF EXP. III

Interval	Day 1-2					Day 3-4				
	Pure List		Mixed List			Pure List		Mixed List		
	Match					Match				
	Physical Same	Different	Physical Same	Name Same	Different	Physical Same	Different	Physical Same	Name Same	Different
0										
$\bar{X}$	464	545	463	564	575	385	470	411	491	520
SE	24	23	22	30	19	23	16	17	18	19
Percentage of E	4	11	1	9	13	6	10	1	12	7
.5										
$\bar{X}$	454	525	524	555	582	396	456	434	482	504
SE	19	26	21	25	21	13	22	17	18	22
Percentage of E	3	5	1	8	5	3	4	3	10	5
1										
$\bar{X}$	466	513	524	582	575	410	451	461	463	484
SE	20	20	43	32	24	19	15	14	17	14
Percentage of E	3	3	8	12	6	3	3	3	9	8

Note.—Mean RTs in milliseconds.

matches to become less efficient over time. Since the two types of physical matches are not different at Time 0, it is difficult to account for the interaction on the basis of greater uncertainty in the mixed list. Since the retention interval shows a slight effect on the name match and a dramatic effect on physical matches, it seems unlikely that temporal uncertainty can be playing a major role here. It is, of course, possible that there is some complex combination of temporal and event uncertainty which accounts for the interaction. However, it seems more reasonable that the reliability of the visual cue in the pure lists induces Ss to attend to this feature and, thus, either to preserve its clarity or render it more available for the match.

This experiment taken together with Exp. I and II suggests that the effectiveness of visual retention in this situation is related to the attention which S gives to processing the visual aspects of the letter. If he is given relatively little incentive for maintaining the visual aspect, as distinct from the name, he shows a rapid decline in the relative efficiency of a physical match (Exp. I). If his attention is controlled during the interval, the decline is increased still further (Exp. II). If, however, the physical form is made more salient by a pure list, the efficiency of the physical match is better maintained.

AUDITORY VERSUS VISUAL PRESENTATION

Neisser (1967) suggested that Ss can scan for a target letter or letters without involving focal attention. His idea was that analyzers can be prepared which respond to various features of the letters falling within the positive set. Presumably, S can learn to set these detectors on the basis of prior experience. Sternberg (1967) studied the time required to classify a noisy digit as an instance of a positive set. His results suggested that the positive set was either stored in visual form or that it was translated from some other storage mode into visual form as part of the recognition process.

If such translations are made, it should be possible to observe their effects by the matching procedure described in the previous experiments. The results of previous studies have indicated that in some circumstances a physical identity match is based on the retention of a visual code. In order to provide evidence for this, the authors found conditions where a physical match took place more rapidly than a name match. If Ss can produce a visual code, they should be able to show RTs with the generated visual code which resemble the physical identity matches following visual stimulation. For the pure lists this means that the "same" response for the auditory condition should be as fast as the "same" response for the visual condition. With mixed lists, it suggests that "same" RTs in the auditory conditions should, under some circumstances, equal the physical identity "same" RTs and be faster than "same" RTs based on the name.

Experiment IV

Experiment IV was designed to compare auditory-visual with visual-visual stimulation. As in Exp. III, there was either auditory or visual presentation of the first letter. Moreover, the second letter could be either always uppercase (pure) or either upper- or lowercase (mixed).

The basic interest in this study was to compare the time required to match auditory-visual pairs with RT to visual-visual pairs. If Ss were able to convert the auditory stimulus into a visual code, the matches following auditory stimulation would be as efficient as physical identity matches following visual presentation. The auditory matches would be superior to name identity matches following visual stimulation. In order to be certain that the physical matches were based on a visual code, and not merely on the letter name, it was necessary to look at the relationship between physical and name matches in the visual mixed condition. It was hoped that under the conditions of this experiment, the physical identity matches in the mixed condition would be significantly faster than the name identity matches.

Method

Subjects.—The Ss were 12 right-handed males with normal uncorrected vision. They were paid volunteers from the same source as in previous studies.

Apparatus.—The apparatus was identical to that used in Exp. III. The only difference was that time intervals for both visual and auditory letters were controlled directly from the audio tape. The time, therefore, varied with the recorded duration of the auditory letter. The average duration of the first letter was 500 msec. with a standard deviation

of 96 msec. The interval between stimuli had a mean of about 750 msec. with a standard deviation of 125 msec. The second letter was shown for approximately 500 msec.

Materials.—The letter population was the same as in Exp. III and the lists were constructed in the same way as in Exp. III. Within each block of 40 trials, there were 20 "same" and 20 "different" responses. In the mixed condition the 20 "same" responses were divided into 10 where the second letter was uppercase and 10 where the second letter was lowercase.

Procedure.—Each S was run individually for 4 days. On each day Ss received 40 trials under each of the four conditions: pure-auditory, pure-visual, mixed-auditory, and mixed-visual. The two visual conditions and two auditory conditions were always adjacent so that S always received 80 trials of visual followed by 80 trials of auditory or vice versa. Within the 80 visual trials, one block of 40 was pure and the other mixed. These were counterbalanced so that a given S would receive auditory first followed by visual on one day, and on the next day visual followed by auditory. In the same manner, he received pure followed by mixed on one day and mixed followed by pure on the next. Days 1 and 2 and Days 3 and 4 were identical for each S and were counterbalanced across Ss so that all conditions appeared in each order.

The Ss were always told in which condition they were running. They were instructed on the first day to consider an auditory letter as a capital and to respond "same" if the two letters had the same name. They were told to respond as rapidly as possible, trying to keep errors to a minimum. After each response, Ss were informed whether or not they were correct and told the length of time required to make the response. As in previous experiments, the "same" response was always assigned to the left hand. The intertrial interval was approximately 10 sec.

Results

Table 5 gives the mean reaction times, standard errors, and error rates for "same" and "different" responses in each of the conditions separately for the first 2 days and last 2 days of the experiment. Since no practice day was given prior to Day 1, it was hoped that the first 2 days would represent unpracticed Ss, while Days 3 and 4 would indicate the results for relatively practiced Ss. The data from Days 1 and 2 will be considered separately from Days 3 and 4.

First, it is necessary to determine whether there is evidence for matching based on physical characteristics of the letter. The visual mixed condition provides the oppor-

TABLE 5

MEAN RTs, STANDARD ERRORS, AND ERROR RATES FOR "SAME" AND "DIFFERENT" RESPONSES: EXP. IV

Days of Training	Visual					Auditory				
	Pure List		Mixed List			Pure List		Mixed List		
	Match									
	Physical Same	Different	Physical Same	Name Same	Different	Physical[a] Same	Different	Physical[a] Same	Name[a] Same	Different
Day 1–2	369	424	438	465	466	405	433	422	428	477
SE	8	8	9	8	13	10	14	11	13	21
Day 3–4	329	392	376	402	426	342	398	376	373	418
SE	7	10	14	12	12	7	12	8	7	11
Overall Percentage of Error	7	7	6	12	7	7	7	7	10	8

Note.—Mean RTs in milliseconds.

[a] For auditory conditions "Physical Same" means the second letter is uppercase and "Name Same" indicates that the second etter is lowercase.

tunity to see the relationship of these data to those obtained in previous experiments. Physical identity matches in the mixed condition were faster than name identity matches by 27 msec. on the first 2 days and by 26 msec. on the second 2 days. These results can be compared with the data from Exp. I (Fig. 1) and Exp. III (Fig. 2). In all of these experiments, physical identity matches are about 25–40 msec. faster than name identity matches when ISI is .75 msec. The value of 25 msec., though small, is statistically significant on the first 2 days, t (11) = 2.49, $p < .05$, and nearly so on the second two, t (11) = 2.09, $.05 < p < .10$.

The data also indicate the advantage of pure over mixed lists. The difference between pure physical matches and mixed physical matches in the visual condition is 69 msec. on the first 2 days and 47 msec. on the second 2 days. These differences are shown by every S and agree with values at .75-sec. intervals interpolated from Fig. 2. In this experiment the authors do not have any evidence that the pure and mixed physical matches would be similar at zero interval, but this is the case in Fig. 2.

A comparison of the efficiency of auditory and visual conditions can be made with

"same" responses in the pure lists. During the first 2 days the visual matches in the pure condition are 36 msec. faster than the auditory matches. This difference is significant, t (11) = 6.31, $p < .01$. However, on Days 3 and 4, the visual matches are only 13 msec. faster than the auditory matches, t (11) = 1.56, which is not significant. The "different" RTs for auditory and visual conditions are about equal on all 4 days. Thus, after practice, Ss are able to make matches about as rapidly when the first stimulus was auditory as when the first stimulus was visual. Moreover, for all Ss, both auditory and visual pure list matches are significantly faster than the name identity RTs obtained from the mixed list.

Striking evidence also comes from the mixed conditions. The auditory matches are equal in RT to the visual physical identity matches. This is true on both the first 2 and last 2 days. In the auditory condition there is virtually no effect of the case of the second letter.

The instruction to consider an auditory letter as uppercase was given in order to bias Ss toward the same distinction between physical and name matches which is obtained with prior visual stimulation. It was ex-

TABLE 6

MEAN RTs, STANDARD ERRORS, AND ERROR RATES FOR "SAME" AND
"DIFFERENT" RESPONSES: AUDITORY CONDITIONS OF EXP. III

Interval	Day 1–2					Day 3–4				
	Pure List		Mixed List			Pure List		Mixed List		
	Match					Match				
	Physical[a] Same	Different	Physical[a] Same	Name[b] Same	Different	Physical[a] Same	Different	Physical[a] Same	Name[b] Same	Different
0										
$\bar{X}$	553	612	526	583	632	440	504	444	468	518
SE	59	24	20	38	27	14	19	15	44	15
Percentage of E	9	9	6	8	8	8	10	4	5	10
.5										
$\bar{X}$	500	562	535	528	583	419	497	448	449	496
SE	25	21	29	23	25	15	21	26	19	14
Percentage of E	6	12	8	6	12	5	6	8	9	6
1										
$\bar{X}$	515	553	509	520	584	415	478	428	440	498
SE	21	25	27	23	21	16	12	18	18	15
Percentage of E	8	8	6	5	8	6	8	9	5	8

[a] Physical same trials are those where the second letter is uppercase.
[b] Name same trials are those where the second letter is lowercase.

pected that the auditory mixed condition would only be as fast as the visual physical match when the second letter was uppercase. However, the data show that the case of the second letter had no effect in the auditory conditions. This could mean that Ss ignored the instruction.

To obtain a better idea of what is going on during the interval between the two letters, it is necessary to return to the data presented in Exp. III. In that experiment, the auditory-visual and visual-visual conditions were compared at 0, .5, and 1 sec. The detailed design of the experiment and apparatus was presented previously and only the results relevant to the question of generation will be considered here.

Discussion of Generation: Exp. III

Table 6 presents the RTs, standard errors, and error rates from the auditory conditions of Exp. III. Similar data from the visual conditions are presented in Table 4.

Figure 3 compares the mean difference in RT for pure list "same" responses under auditory and visual conditions. On all days the visual pure matches are faster at Time 0 and show a reduction in their relative advantage over the 1-sec. interval. On Days 3 and 4,

the difference between auditory and visual pure matches reaches nearly zero at 1 sec. An analysis of variance of the difference scores shows a significant effect of conditions, $F (1, 11) = 25.6$, $p < .01$, and a significant Condition $\times$ Interval interaction, $F (1, 11) = 7.74$, $.01 < p < .05$. These data are in close agreement with those found in Exp. IV. Both results show that with practice the advantage which visual matching has at Time 0 is quickly lost, so that with an interval of .5–1 sec. the auditory matches are equal to the visual matches. The

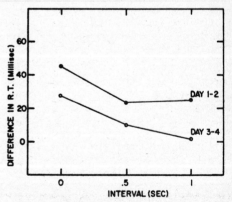

FIG. 3. Difference in RT between visual and auditory conditions with pure lists as a function of interval and days of practice (Exp. III).

individual components are shown in Fig. 4. The "same" RTs in the auditory condition show an increase in speed of about 25 msec. while the visual pure condition RTs show a decrease in speed of about the same amount. It should be noted that the "different" responses in the auditory and visual pure list conditions show a similar trend over time, but not as striking.

Since the evidence from the pure lists indicate that auditory RTs are equal to visual only after Ss have practiced (Days 3 and 4), the analysis of the auditory mixed condition is confined to the last 2 days of training. Complete data for all 4 days are provided in Tables 4 and 6. The major analysis is of the "same" responses from Days 3 and 4 which are shown in Fig. 4. Here the mean reaction times for the auditory mixed and pure conditions are compared with the times for the physical and name matches in the visual pure and mixed conditions. The bottom two curves were described previously and make up the components of the difference function which is shown in Fig. 3. The two auditory mixed conditions are marked A UPPER and A LOWER. The remaining two curves are from the visual mixed condition for physical (V UPPER) and name (V LOWER) matches.

The mixed auditory condition RTs are always somewhat worse than those from the pure auditory condition. This tendency is confirmed by statistical test, t (11) = 2.23, $p < .05$. In Exp. III the two auditory mixed condition RTs did not differ. In the current data it is clear that the instruction to consider the auditory letter as a capital is effective only at Time 0 if at all. At Time 0, there is a tendency for more efficient matching when the second letter is uppercase than when it is lowercase. This difference of 23 msec. is not significant, t (11) = 2.1, $.05 < p < .1$. No tendency in this direction is found at .5 and 1 sec. in the present experiment or at .75 sec. in Exp. III.

The trials where the second letter is uppercase will be considered first. An analysis of variance comparing auditory and visual conditions shows a significant Conditions × Time Interval interaction, F (2, 22) = 5.06, $p < .05$. At Time 0, the auditory condition lies midway between visual physical and name matches. After 1 sec., the auditory condition tends to be below the visual name match, t (11) = 2.06. This is confirmed by a nearly identical tendency for the auditory condition to be faster than the visual name match at .75 sec. in Exp. IV, t (11) = 4.0. There is a tendency for the audi-

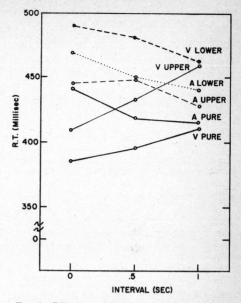

Fig. 4. RTs from visual and auditory conditions as a function of interstimulus interval (All data are from the last 2 days; Exp. III).

tory match to lie below the visual physical match, $t = 1.82$. In agreement with Exp. III the visual physical RTs cross the auditory RTs at about .75 sec.

The comparison of visual and auditory conditions also can be made where the second letter is a small letter. Here the effects are not striking. Both conditions show a slight tendency to improve over the interval. However, an analysis of variance shows no significant effects of interval, condition, or their interaction. The auditory match shows a non-significant tendency to lie below the visual name match at all time intervals. Since this same tendency is apparent in Exp. IV, it seems likely that both auditory conditions are faster, at least after 1 sec., than the visual name match.

Conclusion

The results of Exp. III and IV indicate that auditory matches can become as efficient as visual physical matches. Looking first at the pure list conditions, practiced Ss are able to match a new visual letter as rapidly when the first letter was auditory as when it was visual. This requires an ISI of approximately .75 to 1 sec. The Ss never produce auditory matching that is equivalent to visual matching at Time 0. The visual match at any delayed interval is always less efficient than it is at the zero interval. Matching following auditory information is as efficient as a physical identity match based on a visual signal of the same age, but it is not as efficient as a physical match at Time 0.

The results of the mixed list raise somewhat more complex questions. The hypothesis outlined at the start of this section suggested that if auditory information could be placed into a visual code, RTs in the auditory conditions would be as fast as those for physical identity and faster than name identity RTs following visual stimulation. The first proposition is confirmed by the data. After an interval of .75 sec., the auditory matches are as fast as the visual physical match. At this point, the visual physical match is faster than the visual name match and thus gives evidence of being based on a visual code. When, after 1 sec., the visual physical match no longer provides evidence of being based on a visual code, the auditory matches are faster.

It is clear that the auditory condition where the second letter is uppercase is faster than the visual name condition. There is more question about the other auditory condition, but on the whole it also provides faster RTs than the visual name condition. These findings appear to confirm the second proposition, but they raise two difficult problems.

The first problem for the notion of generation is that the auditory conditions seem to produce faster RTs even at the start of the interval than do the visual name "same" responses. It should be borne in mind that the first signal in Exp. III and IV lasts about 500 msec. Thus, the zero interval plotted in Fig. 2 and 4 is 500 msec. after the *initiation* of the first letter. If, as would be expected, S is doing some of the processing during the presentation of the first signal, the zero interval may already be subject to a certain amount of generation. This could explain why the auditory mixed conditions tend to lie below the name identity visual conditions, even at Time 0. Another explanation of this phenomenon might be that the visual name match requires an incompatible response. The Ss have to call "same" something that actually has a physical difference. It could be argued that the advantage the auditory conditions have over the visual name matches with longer ISIs also might rest on this type of competition. However, such an interference explanation could not handle the data presented in the previous paragraphs in which the auditory matches are as efficient as visual matches for the pure lists.

Moreover, the similarity of physical and name match RTs 1 sec. after visual stimulation argues that the case of the prior stimulus has no effect either facilitating or interfering after that interval.

Another problem is the lack of difference between auditory matches as a function of the case of the second letter. The E's instruction suggested that Ss think of the auditory letter as uppercase. Nonetheless, after a delay of .75–1 sec., the two auditory conditions were almost equal. One possibility is that Ss generate both the upper- and lowercase forms of the letter. If this were so, the difference which was obtained between the two conditions at Time 0 would tend to indicate that the uppercase was generated first. Moreover, the advantage of pure list auditory matches over mixed list matches might suggest that generating two letters was more difficult than generating a single letter. Perhaps the similarity of the upper- and lowercase forms of the letters F, H, and K also helps to explain why Ss are efficient in matching both cases of the same letter.

General Conclusions

Decay

Immediately after the exposure of a visual letter, Ss have a relatively complete visual description of that experience. This conclusion seems to be warranted from the fast matching at the physical identity level. As time passes, the relative advantage of the physical match is lost (see Fig. 1). The term "decay" might be used to describe the reduced efficiency of the physical match. It is difficult, however, to say whether this loss in the relative advantage of a physical match corresponds closely with loss in the ability to state whether the letter was upper- or lowercase. It is possible that Ss who show no faster reaction time for physical than for name identity would be able to recall better than chance the case of the letter. Indeed the information required from the visual representation for a fast RT might be greater than would be required in order to tell whether the letter is uppercase or lowercase. It is conceivable that a very seriously decayed visual representation would still be sufficient, given unlimited time, for Ss to retrieve information concerning the case of the letter.

Both Sperling (1960) and Averbach and Coriell (1961) found rates of decay from visual store which were generally faster than those shown in Fig. 1. However, our studies show that the rate of decay depends on the degree to which S's attention is focused on the visual experience. Since the Averbach and Sperling experiments used large arrays of visual information, it would be expected that relatively little attention could be given to the process of preserving an individual visual letter. It seems, therefore, that the decay functions in the present RT experiments are not out of line with those obtained from studying error rates.

The technique presented in this paper may be more closely related to that used by Sokolov (1963) to explore what he calls a "neural model." This, he suggests, serves as a description of the current stimulus situation. The neural model represents the material that is most salient at a given moment, but information not currently in the neural model may still be present in memory in some other way. It is possible that the decay function shown in Fig. 1 represents primarily the salience of the visual information or its representation in some particularly accessible store and does not represent a loss of availability or clarity of that visual information. More research will be necessary in order to delineate the relationship between the loss of accessibility of visual information for the matching task and the loss of the ability to recollect the visual nature of the prior stimulus. Nevertheless, the term "decay" may be used to describe the loss in efficiency of the visual match whatever proves to be the exact mechanism.

Rehearsal

It seems abundantly clear that Ss maintain visual information with varying degrees of efficiency depending on the conditions of the experiment. The degree of efficiency can be said to depend on rehearsal because it is related to the processing capacity which S allocates to the preservation of the visual information. Rehearsal may be serving to maintain the availability of the visual information or only its accessibility. In these studies the information is visual, but the same definition of rehearsal has been used previously to apply to verbal (Posner & Rossman, 1965) and kinesthetic (Posner, 1967) information. Under the conditions of Exp. I, Ss have both visual and name matches within the same list. They report an active attempt to retain the names of the letters, but there are relatively few verbal reports of efforts to retain the visual form of the letter. Under these conditions, decay is very rapid. Even under these conditions, however, some attention may be given to the visual information, since the decay process can be increased

still more if S's attention is distracted to another task. Thus, the conditions of Exp. II, in which the efficiency of a physical match is lost within $\frac{1}{2}$ sec., represent perhaps a low point on the rehearsal continuum. When Ss have pure lists, much more attention can be focused on the visual representation of the letter and indeed subjective reports of visual representation are more frequent. In these cases, Ss are more efficient in the retention of visual information over a 1-sec. interval. This is shown in Fig. 2 where there is a significant divergence between physical identity matches made under mixed list conditions and under pure list conditions. Attention to the visual aspect of the figure can be manipulated by the experimental situation, and it in turn varies the efficiency with which the visual match can be made.

There are two consequences which are usually thought to flow from the rehearsal of information in other situations. These are the ability to retain information for longer periods of time than would occur without rehearsal and the consolidation of information into a memory system which no longer depends on rehearsal. The authors have not shown either of these consequences in the present experiments. Indeed, the rapid loss of the visual information when attention is taken away, as in Exp. II, and the relative insensitivity of the visual match to the exposure duration of the first stimulus both seem to argue that the visual information is not consolidated, at least within the system that underlies visual matching. It is, however, possible that longer exposure to the visual information increases the probability that visual information is available in some other memory system. Moreover, the authors have not established conditions where it is possible to tell whether rehearsal can extend beyond 1–2 sec.

Generation

Experiments III and IV indicate that Ss are able to operate on auditory information to produce highly efficient matches. We have labeled this process the generation of visual information. Perhaps this production of visual information is related to the operations of lower-level visual analyzers, such as proposed in the pattern recognizer "pandemonium" (Selfridge & Neisser, 1960). Generation in this sense can be seen as the activation of such pattern analyzers. It is not possible for us to tell the detail of the visual analyzers available as a result of generation. For example, it would be possible for S to generate only certain features which would allow him to distinguish between different letters of the alphabet. It also is possible that the generated information preserves very specific details of the stored letter.

The results of Exp. III and IV may indicate that Ss are able to produce information which underlies the detection of two cases of the same letter. This finding seems intuitively to conflict with the idea that the generated material is in the form of an image. In any case, the authors cannot be sure of the relation of generated visual information in the sense of these studies to the subjective experience called imagery. It is probably better to view the visual information as a program for analyzing visual features. The efficiency of the generated code depends on the time S has prior to the occurrence of the second letter.

It should be possible to develop a perceptual analysis of generated visual information in very much the same way that other experiments have attempted to work on the perception of external visual information. One should be able to tell, e.g., whether generated visual information preserves such features of letters as size, orientation, color, etc. Such experiments would do much to relate the generation of visual codes to their perception.

Compulsory and Optional Processes

Atkinson and Shiffrin (1967) have distinguished between properties of memory systems which are obligatory and control processes which may be varied with the particular task requirements. These distinctions have applicability to the present experiments. The present data suggest that the registration of visual information and its decay under conditions of relatively low attention are compulsory features of the visual matching situation. Almost every S, for whom there is sufficient data, shows faster physical identity than name identity matches, and shows loss of this difference over time. The striking consistency of these results across Ss and conditions seems to argue for them as basic features of human information processing.

On the other hand, rehearsal and generation seem to be better described as control processes. It is possible for Ss either to attend or not to attend to the visual features of individual letters. Attention to the visual features leads to their preservation, and lack of attention leads to their loss. Whether or not, under a particular condition, Ss choose to attend to the

visual features seems to be something that E can manipulate by incentive or by varying the task conditions.

If Ss consistently and easily generated visual information, they might very well override the decay processes found in Exp. I. Why, for example, if Ss are able to generate, don't they generate a visual code for the name matches under the conditions of Exp. I? The data seem to suggest that the process of generation is sufficiently difficult that the proper conditions must be set up by E before Ss will show such generation. Much more needs to be done in order to explore the conditions under which Ss may choose to generate visual information from one or more letters.

REFERENCES

ATKINSON, R. C., & SHIFFRIN, R. M. Human memory: A proposed system and its control processes. Technical Report 110, 1967, Institute for Mathematical Studies in Social Sciences.

AVERBACH, E. The span of apprehension as a function of exposure duration. *Journal of Verbal Learning and Verbal Behavior*, 1963, 2, 60–64.

AVERBACH, E., & CORIELL, A. S. Short term memory in vision. *Bell Systems Technical Journal*, 1961, 60, 309–328.

NEISSER, U. *Cognitive psychology*. New York: Appleton-Century-Crofts, 1967.

POSNER, M. I. Characteristics of visual and kinesthetic memory codes. *Journal of Experimental Psychology*, 1967, 75, 103–107.

POSNER, M. I., & KEELE, S. W. Decay of visual information from a single letter. *Science*, 1967, 158, 137–139.

POSNER, M. I., & KONICK, A. F. Short-term retention of visual and kinesthetic information. *Organizational Behavior and Human Performance*, 1966, 1, 71–88.

POSNER, M. I., & MITCHELL, R. F. Chronometric analysis of classification. *Psychological Review*, 1967, 74, 392–409.

POSNER, M. I., & ROSSMAN, E. Effect of size and location of informational transforms upon short-term retention. *Journal of Experimental Psychology*, 1965, 70, 496–505.

SELFRIDGE, O. G., & NEISSER, U. Pattern recognition by machine. *Scientific American*, 1960, 203, 60–68.

SOKOLOV, YE. N. *Perception and the conditioned reflex*. London: Pergamon Press, 1963.

SPERLING, G. The information available in brief visual presentation. *Psychological Monographs*, 1960, 74(11, Whole No. 498).

SPERLING, G. A model of visual memory. *Human Factors*, 1963, 5, 19–31.

STERNBERG, S. Two operations in character recognition: Some evidence from reaction time experiments. *Perception and Psychophysics*, 1967, 2, 45–53.

N.E.A. Kroll, T. Parks, S.R. Parkinson, S.L. Bieber and A.L. Johnson

Short-term memory while shadowing: recall of visually and of aurally presented letters

Reprinted from the *Journal of Experimental Psychology* (1970) 85(2):220-4

Ten male Ss were given a single letter of the alphabet to remember while shadowing (repeating aloud) female-voiced letters of the alphabet. The memory letter was either presented visually for .4 sec., or aurally by substituting a letter read in a male voice for one of the shadow letters. After a retention interval of 1 sec., visual memory letters (VMLs) and the aural memory letters (AMLs) were recalled equally well, suggesting that they had been perceived equally well. However, after a retention interval of 25 sec., all Ss recalled more VMLs than AMLs. The VMLs may have been less subject to retroactive interference from the auditory shadowing task because they were stored differently than were the AMLs.

Conrad (1964) established the importance of auditory memory in short-term memory (STM) through his finding of a high correlation between the memory errors of visually presented letters and the perceptual errors of aurally presented letters. Many current theorists make auditory memory the cornerstone of their STM models (e.g., Atkinson & Shiffrin, 1968; Laughery & Fell, 1969; Norman, 1969; Sperling, 1967), implying that most, if not all, STM is accomplished via subvocal auditory rehearsal, while restricting visual STM to a rapid-decaying trace.

While there is a great deal of evidence to support the position that humans are capable of auditorily encoding material that is presented visually, introspection suggests that it may also be possible to store such material in visual form for more than the fraction of a second found by Sperling (1960). Indeed, some authors have argued that visual

materials are stored at least differently from auditory materials for somewhat longer periods (e.g., Dornbush, 1968; Margrain, 1967; Murdock & Walker, 1969; Posner & Keele, 1967). Unfortunately, their results have extended the time course of such storage only a few seconds at most. Those studies which have shown even longer duration memory for visual stimuli relatively uncontaminated by auditory memory (e.g., Bahrick & Boucher, 1968) involve only a *recognition* measure of retention.

The present experiment attempted to demonstrate the existence of highly persistent visual storage. The Ss were required to shadow (repeat aloud) letters they heard while trying to remember a particular letter (the "memory letter") that had been presented either visually or aurally. If a visually presented memory letter were encoded and remembered auditorily, it would be subject to approximately as much retroactive interference (RI) from the shadow task as would be an aurally presented memory letter. Thus, both would show approximately the same forgetting curve. If, however, less forgetting were to be found for visual memory letters, there would be reason to believe that the visually presented memory letters were less subject to RI from the shadow task, as would be the case if they were being stored in visual form.

METHOD

Subjects.—Ten male students, enrolled in introductory psychology courses at the University of California at Davis, served as Ss in the experiment and were paid for their participation.

Apparatus.—The Ss wore stereo headphones (Sharpe, Model HA-10A) and sat at a table facing a rear-projection read-out unit (Industrial Electronics Engineers, Series 80,000), which was modified to allow rapid changing of the film plate. The shadow material and the aural memory letter (AML) were presented binaurally via one track of stereo tape recorder, while signals on the other track of the tape activated a timer (Hunter, Model 111-B) which controlled the onset and offset of the visual memory letter (VML) on the read-out unit. The particular letter shown was controlled by E according to a predetermined schedule.

Materials.—The material to be shadowed consisted of lists of letters of the alphabet (excluding the three-syllable "W") recorded by a female reader. All lists were presented at a rate of 120 letters/min, with the exception of the first three shadow practice lists, which were presented at a rate of 108 letters/min.

The item to be remembered was a single letter of the alphabet. This memory letter was presented aurally during half of the memory tests by a male voice saying one of the letters of the shadow list. The instructions required Ss to shadow *all* letters in the list and to remember the male-voiced letter. Notice that contrary to earlier studies (e.g., Mowbray, 1964; Norman, 1969), the AML was *not* presented simultaneously with the shadow letters on a separate channel. In the present study, the AML was made part of the shadow task, and both the AML and the shadow letters were presented binaurally. It was thought that this method of presentation would improve the perception of the AML by preventing interference from the opposite channel. The letter used as the memory letter of a list was not repeated in that list.

The memory letter was presented visually during the other half of the memory tests. The same shadow lists were paired with the same memory letters in the visual memory tests as in the auditory memory tests. The VML was presented in the same temporal position of the lists as the AML had been and remained on the screen for .4

sec. The male-voiced letter, which was shadowed in the auditory memory task, was replaced with a female-voiced letter drawn from the same population as the other shadow letters of the list.

Lists within a session were separated by 5 sec. After the last shadow letter of a memory list, S recorded what he remembered as the memory letter of the list just ending. The instructions asked that S guess if he could not remember the memory letter.

Lists, except for the practice lists, were classified as either "low similarity" or "high similarity." A low-similarity list was one where the shadow letters were chosen from those letters not easily confused acoustically with the memory letter. A high-similarity list was one where at least every third letter was one easily confused acoustically with the memory letter. The degree of confusion was determined from Conrad's (1964) "Listening-Errors" matrix, with allowances for the American pronunciation of "Z" ("zee" rather than "zed").

Procedure.—Each S had one training session, followed by two experimental sessions. The sessions were separated by at least 4 hr., but not more than 48 hr.

The first session was a training session. The S first received tape-recorded instructions for shadowing, which included the suggestion to allow a lag of two letters between hearing a letter and saying that letter. Next, S practiced shadowing on lists which were 52 letters long. There were 17–38 shadow practice lists, depending on how much difficulty S experienced in learning to shadow. After the shadow practice, instructions for the aural memory task were given. The instructions emphasized that S should not allow shadowing performance to deteriorate while hearing or remembering the male-voiced letter. The 16 practice aural memory lists were followed by the instructions for the visual memory task (which again emphasized the importance of maintaining good shadow performance) and 16 practice visual memory lists. The memory letters were drawn from the population: H, I, J, K, L, R, U, Y, and Z. The shadow letters were drawn randomly from the alphabet (excluding "W" and the memory letter of that particular list). The number of shadow letters preceding the memory letter varied from 8 to 16 letters among lists. There were four lists at each of the following retention intervals: 1, 5, 10, and 20 sec. (i.e., 2, 10, 20, or 40 shadow letters following the memory letter).

Two sets of 30 lists were used for the two experimental sessions. The memory letters for these lists were drawn from the population: A, B, C, D, E, F, G, M, N, O, P, Q, S, T, V, and X. The number of lead-in items varied from 8 to 14 letters. Each set of lists had 10 lists with each of three retention intervals: 1, 10, and 25 sec. (i.e., 2, 20, and 50 shadow letters following the memory letter). In addition, half of the lists at each interval were low-similarity lists and half were high-similarity lists. Over the two sets, each

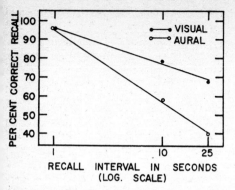

FIG. 1. Percentage of correct recall of visually and aurally presented memory letters as a function of recall interval.

memory letter was given with at least two different retention intervals, and each memory letter except "O" was given with both low- and high-similarity lists.

On Experimental Tape 1, the first set of 30 lists was given as an aural memory task and the second set was a visual memory task. On Experimental Tape 2, the first set was given as a visual memory task and the second set as an aural memory task. For half of the Ss, Tape 1 was used during their first experimental session and Tape 2 during their second experimental session, while for the other half of the Ss the order of the tapes was reversed. A short rest was given between sets within each session.

Shadowing performance was recorded on a second tape recorder.

RESULTS AND DISCUSSION

Visual versus auditory memory letters.
The finding of major interest was of a very definite superiority of recall performance for visual, as compared to auditory, memory letters (see Fig. 1). With 10- and 25-sec. retention intervals, the superiority of memory following visual presentation was so uniform across Ss that sign tests were used to demonstrate the reliability of the effect. At the 25-sec. interval, all 10 Ss recalled more VMLs than AMLs ($p < .001$). At the 10-sec. interval, 8 Ss recalled more VMLs, while 2 recalled more AMLs ($p < .055$). Mowbray (1964) found similar differences, but attributed the better recall of visual material to its being better perceived than the auditory material. Equal perception of the two modalities seems to have occurred in the present experiment, as evidenced by the

nearly equal percentage of correct recall after a 1-sec. retention interval (96.5% for visual, 96.0% for aural; 4 Ss recalled more visual material, 3 recalled more aural material, and 3 recalled an equal amount of visual and aural).

In Mowbray's (1964) experiment, the perception of the AML might have been relatively poor since the AML was presented simultaneously with a shadow letter to the other ear. The present experiment avoided this problem by making the AML one of the letters to be shadowed, thus insuring initial perception of the AML. However, this technique produced a difference in procedure between AML and VML trials in that the VML was not verbalized. Rather, Ss were aurally presented with another letter to shadow during the presentation of the VML. While it was thought that this procedural difference favored the memory of the AML over the memory of the VML, it is also possible, though unlikely, that the verbalization of the memory letter actually detracted from the memory of that letter (e.g., by making the letter more subject to interferences from the shadow task). To check for this possibility, a subsequent group of five male Ss were run who verbalized the VML as well as the shadow list. These Ss performed no worse than the group which did not verbalize the VML. The mean performance levels of the VML verbalization group were 100% correct responses at 1 sec., 92% at 10 sec., and 88% at 25 sec. The performances of the two visual conditions did not differ reliably even at the 25-sec. retention interval, t (13) = 1.92, $p > .05$.

Neither can the superiority of visual recall be attributed to Ss tending to ignore the shadow task in the visual condition. During the 10-sec. retention interval, the mean percentage of shadow errors (intrusions, inversions, omissions, and mispronunciations) was 15.6 with a VML and 19.0 with an AML. During the 25-sec. retention interval, the mean percentage of errors was 8.8 with the VML and 10.6 with the AML. The tendency for Ss to make more shadow errors with the AML would be expected if the AML is rehearsed auditorily while the

VML is stored in some other way.

However, Ss do shadow the AML better than they shadow the letter presented simultaneously with the VML. Averaged over 10- and 25-sec. retention conditions, there was a mean error percentage of 8.6 of the AML, and of 19.7 of the shadow letter presented with the VML. This should not be surprising since, in the aural memory condition, S is shadowing the letter he is trying to store in memory and his attention is not diverted elsewhere. In the visual memory condition, S must divide his attention between the storing of the VML and the shadowing of a different letter. On the other hand, even if these occasional errors in shadowing represent deliberate, half-second abandonment of the shadowing task (in favor of subvocal encoding of a VML), they could not account for the observed superiority of visual recall performance. That is, subsequent recall performance would not be expected to be superior to that for the AMLs which had been repeated aloud (Peterson & Peterson, 1959).

Thus, the simplest explanation of the observed difference in recall performance would appear to be that the shadow material provided more RI for the AML than for the VML because the AML was encoded and rehearsed auditorily, while the VML was encoded and rehearsed visually. This explanation is substantiated by the comments made by Ss after their participation. Eight Ss were asked how they remembered the memory letter. Five of these Ss reported that they remembered the AML by saying it covertly, but that they remembered the VML by keeping an "after-image." They also reported that the shadow task made auditory rehearsal difficult, but that they could usually hold the "after-image" unless visually distracted. Two Ss reported trying to associate the memory letter. One of these said he found this very difficult while trying to shadow and often used the same technique as the above-mentioned five. The second made very few memory errors of either type, but did make a great many shadow errors. Only one S reported having great difficulty in holding a visual memory and resorting to auditory encoding of the

VML. This S had one of the poorer visual recall scores.

Acoustic similarity. Wickelgren (1966) found the acoustic similarity of the shadow material to the memory material affected the the memory of aurally presented material. It was hypothesized that the present procedure would also find acoustic similarity to affect RI with AMLs, but not with VMLs. This would have been further evidence that the VMLs were not being remembered via auditory encoding. As would be expected under this hypothesis, there seemed to be little, if any, effect of similarity on performance following visual presentations. Correct recalls occurred on 73.5% and 74.5% of all trials with high- and low-similarity lists, respectively (10- and 25-sec. intervals combined). A very small tendency was found for the level of similarity to effect the recall of auditory items (49.5 as compared to 54.0), but that tendency appeared in the performance of only 6 of the 10 Ss and was, therefore, clearly unreliable. However, the failure to find a strong similarity effect with the AML does not seriously detract from the overall conclusions that visually and auditorily presented stimuli may be stored differently.

In conclusion, it must be noted that these results should not be taken as evidence against the position that humans can, and often do, auditorily encode a visual stimulus. Indeed, auditory encoding and rehearsal might be the best strategy in a great many situations, particularly if the stimulus is easily labeled and pictorially complex (e.g., several letters or numbers rather than a single letter). However, the present results do seem to suggest that humans also have some ability to hold a visual image for at least 25 sec.

REFERENCES

ATKINSON, R. C., & SHIFFRIN, R. M. Human memory: A proposed system and its control processes. In K. W. Spence & J. T. Spence (Eds.), *The psychology of learning and motivation: Advances in research and theory.* Vol. 2. New York: Academic Press, 1968.

BAHRICK, H. P., & BOUCHER, B. Retention of visual and verbal codes of the same stimuli. *Journal of Experimental Psychology,* 1968, **78**, 417–422.

CONRAD, R.   Acoustic confusions in immediate memory. *British Journal of Psychology*, 1964, **55**, 75–83.

DORNBUSH, R. L.   Shadowing in bisensory memory. *Quarterly Journal of Experimental Psychology*, 1968, **20**, 225–231.

LAUGHERY, K. R., & FELL, J. C.   Subject preferences and the nature of information stored in short-term memory. *Journal of Experimental Psychology*, 1969, **82**, 193–197.

MARGRAIN, S. A.   Short-term memory as a function of input modality. *Quarterly Journal of Experimental Psychology*, 1967, **19**, 109–114.

MOWBRAY, G. H.   Perception and retention of verbal information presented during auditory shadowing. *Journal of the Acoustical Society of America*, 1964, **36**, 1459–1469.

MURDOCK, B. B., JR., & WALKER, K. D.   Modality effects in free recall. *Journal of Verbal Learning and Verbal Behavior*, 1969, **8**, 665–676.

NORMAN, D. A.   *Memory and attention.*   New York: Wiley, 1969.

PETERSON, L. R., & PETERSON, M. J.   Short-term retention of individual verbal items. *Journal of Experimental Psychology*, 1959, **58**, 193–198.

POSNER, M. I., & KEELE, S. W.   Decay of visual information from a single letter. *Science*, 1967, **158**, 137–139.

SPERLING, G.   The information available in brief visual presentations. *Psychological Monographs*, 1960, **74**(11, Whole No. 498).

SPERLING, G.   Successive approximations to a model for short-term memory. In A. F. Sanders (Ed.), *Attention and performance.* Amsterdam: North-Holland Publishing Company, 1967. (A special edition of *Acta Psychologica*, 1967, **27**, 285–292.)

WICKELGREN, W. A.   Short-term recognition memory for single letters and phonemic similarity of retroactive interference. *Quarterly Journal of Experimental Psychology*, 1966, **18**, 55–62.

D.D. Wickens

Encoding categories of words: an empirical approach to meaning

Reprinted from the *Psychological Review* (1970)
77(1):1-15

This article reports a series of studies investigating the dimension along which words are encoded, using the "release from proactive inhibition" in short-term memory technique.   The results of the experiments indicate that different dimensions vary in their effectiveness for proactive inhibition release. In general, semantic dimensions (taxonomic categories or semantic differential) are highly effective, whereas physical characteristics such as word length or figure-ground colors of the slide presentation are relatively ineffective in releasing proactive inhibition.   The results of this technique of measuring encoding are related to other types of experiments on verbal material as well as to the topic of subception and imageless thought.

The basic purpose of the research presented here has been to discover something about how an individual encodes a single word which he hears or sees.   I shall begin with the statement of a point of view about encoding that I have developed as a consequence of several of my researches.   Essentially the point of view—which is basically the same as one espoused by Bower (1967) —is that when a person hears or sees a word, the process of perceiving this word consists of encoding it within a number of different aspects, attributes, or conceptual psychological dimensions.   I assume that when a person hears the word "horse," it is encoded into the broader categories of beasts of burden, four-legged creatures, mammals, warm-blooded animals, and finally of animals in general.   In short, I suspect that the encoding process functions in the manner of a good player of Twenty Questions, but in more or less the reverse direction.

I do not think we have, at present, any notion of the richness of the encoded material, but I suspect it is far richer than most of us imagine.   Further, I do not think that the identity of the many encoding attributes or dimensions enter very much into the individual's consciousness.   Consequently, we are unaware intellectually of the richness of the encoding of a single word.   If we were to consciously recognize this richness, then so much time would be required for the perceptual ingestion of a single word that we would find it next to impossible to listen to a series of words and remember any but the first and last of them.   We handle the intellectual and conceptual meaningful reactions to common words with the same kind of automatic skill as the veteran big league outfielder who turns his back to a hard-hit fly ball, runs at top speed, and then without stopping and almost without looking, raises his gloved hand at exactly the right instant and in exactly the right location to grasp the ball.

The ball player's marvelous competence

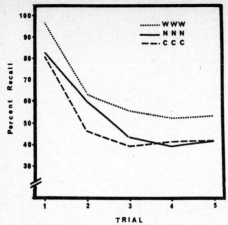

FIG. 1. Proactive inhibition effects for three classes of material.

is the product of his years of experience in the bush leagues, in the training camp, and in the big league ball parks themselves. So, too, our automatic ability to transform the sounds or the sight of a word into many attributes is the product of the many, many experiences we have with words in this highly verbal world of ours. We are more complex and facile in our reactions than we witness ourselves as being, and in our dealing with words, much of an intellectual nature goes on about which we are cognitively blind, deaf, and therefore mute.

Most, but not all, of my basic research methodology is to be found in the now popular field of short-term memory (STM), and in particular in a slight modification of the type of design which was introduced by Peterson and Peterson (1959); but for the purposes of this paper, the most relevant STM experiment is one performed by Keppel and Underwood (1962) in which they showed that proactive inhibition is involved in the Peterson and Peterson type of task. This is indicated by the fact that with retention interval held constant, performance declines from the first to the third or fourth trial. Figure 1 illustrates this decline in performance for three types of materials: CCCs (a trigram of three consonants), NNNs (three numbers), and three common unrelated words. The curves are taken from control groups run in several different

experiments in my laboratory, and the retention interval is not the same for all the groups; it is 20 seconds for the words and only 10 seconds for the CCCs and NNNs. This fact is unimportant for the present purpose, which is simply to demonstrate that all the materials show a decline in performance during the first few trials. Quite obviously, dealing with the early materials interferes with the retention performance of the subsequent target items, a maximum of interference being reached after three or four items.

The next relevant experiment is one by Wickens, Born, and Allen (1963), which suggests that this inhibitory effect may be specific to the class of materials employed in the target presentation. In that experiment, groups of subjects were given CCCs for three trials and then shifted to NNNs on the fourth trial. Obviously another group began with NNNs and shifted to CCCs, and the control groups remained on the same class of material throughout the four trials. Figure 2 shows the results of such an experiment. They are not the results of the Wickens et al. study, but are from a comparable study done by Wittlinger (1967). This discussion includes only two of his curves, the one labeled "class" and the one labeled "control." The procedure for the control group was very simple; half re-

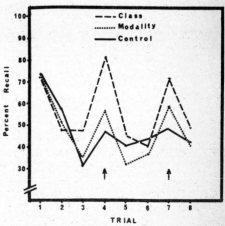

FIG. 2. The effect of shift in class of material and modality of presentation on STM performance.

ceived NNNs throughout the eight plotted trials, and half received CCCs. The results of both groups are combined in the presentation. The retention interval was 20 seconds, during which time the subjects were making difficult discriminations of four auditory stimuli. The curve is less smooth than one would like, but it is obvious that proactive inhibition developed quite rapidly and remained more or less constant. The experimental groups started out on one class of material—NNNs for half and CCCs for the other half—and remained on this class for the first three trials. Then on Trial 4 they were shifted to the other class of material on which they stayed until Trial 7 when each half was shifted back to the original class of material. The Trial 8 material was the same as the Trial 7 material. Needless to say, the necessary counterbalancing of particular NNNs or CCCs across trials was employed for all groups, and the N per major group was 80. Quite clearly there was a marked improvement in performance as a consequence of both the first and second class shift, and the experimental groups were significantly superior ($p < .05$) to the control group on each shift trial. Wittlinger's study very clearly confirmed what Wickens et al. (1963) had found.

As a consequence of the results obtained in the Wickens et al. experiment, the authors tentatively concluded—overgeneralizing somewhat—that in the STM situation, triads or trigrams, all elements of which are homogeneous with respect to a psychological class, seem to be encoded not only as unique items but also as members of the same psychological class. If the next item is drawn from a different class, then interference no longer exists—or is minimized—and performance is raised. Further reasoning and speculating suggested the possibility that the shift procedure could be used as something of a projective technique of cognitive organization; a way of asking the subject what classes are being employed without requiring him to identify and label them—or even, as we shall see later, of being aware of them.

For the sake of clarity, these assumptions can stand repetition. The process of perceiving a word involves encoding that word

into positions within many categories; if a series of items comes from the same set of categories, they will interfere with each other and depress retention performance. They do so, however, only for items which are similarly encoded, and if a new set of items is encoded into a different category, or categories, interference is reduced and retention performance will increase.

The strategy of the research is simple. One chooses two classes of words, the classes being based on linguistic rules, a logical assumption, or some more sophisticated means of identifying psychological categories. Triads of items are then chosen from one class and these are presented to a group of subjects for three or four trials and then the group is shifted to a triad drawn from the other class. If there is first a decline in performance across early trials and then a significant improvement on the shift trial, one can assume that there is a common way of encoding within a class (accounting for the decline) which differs between the two classes (accounting for the gain on the shift trial). The strategy of the research is based on the assumption that the more psychologically similar the classes are, the more they will interfere with each other. There is a fair amount of evidence from the field of long-term memory as well to support this assumption (Friedman & Reynolds, 1967; McGeoch & McDonald, 1931; Postman, Keppel, & Stark, 1965).

Encoding by Grammatical Class

Since our early days in school, we all have been made aware of the various grammatical classes of words of the English language. Most college students given a deck of cards with various words on them could sort them into correct grammatical piles of pronouns, verbs, adjectives, and so on (Cofer & Bruce, 1965). It seems plausible to assume that an individual might encode or tag single words according to their grammatic class along, of course, with the semantic aspects of the word. Indeed there is even evidence from classical introspective work that the "state of mind" aroused by various grammatical classes differs (Rowland, 1907). What would be more logical than to expect that one would obtain an upward shift in performance when one moved from the presentation of triads of one grammatical class to triads of another?

We began such an experiment with the intent of contrasting the class nouns with the class verbs, but soon discovered, in the search for good triads, that so many verbs are also nouns and nouns are also verbs that we felt forced to shift to verbs and adjectives where there is little ambiguity of dichotomous classification. After several false starts in which we seemed to find weak evidence in support of grammatical encoding, we finally did the experiment in a proper fashion. A set of 60 verbs and 60 adjectives were chosen in which half of each were Thorndike-Lorge (1944) high-frequency words and half low-frequency words, and half in each subset were one-syllable words and half were disyallabic. Four triads of words, homogeneous with respect to grammatical class, frequency, and syllable length, were given. Then the subjects were switched to a triad of the other grammatical class which matched the original triads in frequency and syllabic characteristics. Switching was done from verbs to adjectives and adjectives to verbs and control groups were run for which the same grammatical class was maintained throughout the five trials. The triads were counterbalanced so that each triad appeared equally often in each position. A total of 400 subjects were run, 200 in the control and another 200 in the experimental group. Half of the controls were run on adjectives and half on verbs, while half of the experimentals shifted to verbs and half shifted to adjectives (Wickens, Clark, Hill, & Wittlinger, 1968).

The overall results of this study are shown in Figure 3, and if ever a pair of groups appear to behave alike, these do. An examination of the various subgroups showed all of them to be consistent with the major trend. In a subsequent informal experiment conducted by Ronald Huff, he first ask his subjects to sort a miscellaneous set of words according to grammatical class in an effort to give the subject a set to respond to words grammatically and then ran them in a verb-adjective shift experiment. Once again the

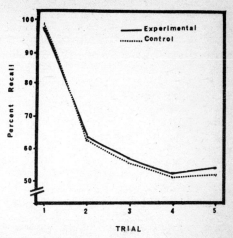

Fig. 3.   The effect of shifting grammatical class.

subjects gave no evidence of using grammatical form as an encoding tag.

It is quite obvious that at the present time I cannot make the statement that single words are not encoded by grammatical class, since we have tested only two categories. I have also been told that the linguist would be more inclined to predict differential encoding for nouns and verbs than for the two classes we used. I rather imagine that pronouns, prepositions, and conjunctions may be encoded grammatically, but I would hesitate to use them in an experiment because they are so limited in number and because they would also differ so much in frequency of usage. As I shall point out later, word frequency serves also as an encoding category. In summary, I suspect that grammatical class is not a dominant attribute for the encoding of a single word. Perhaps the story would be a different one if the word were to appear in a grammatical context, that is in a sentence or phrase, a circumstance which would necessarily impart a grammatical flavor to each word.

Connotation and encoding. According to Osgood, Suci, and Tannenbaum (1957), connotative meaning may be described by the word's location in a sphere which has three orthogonal axes. The three axes are identified as Evaluation, Potency, and Activity. All axes, of course, have a positive and a negative pole. Heise (1965) has published a monograph in which 1,000 common English words are rated on each of the three dimensions. By a careful selection of the words, it is possible to find groups of words which are rated high or low on a particular dimension and are close to neutral on the other two dimensions. Thus, one can create triads of words all of which are relatively homogeneous with respect to their connotative meaning as defined by their location on the axis of each one of the three dimensions.

In an experiment conducted by Wickens and Clark (1968), triads of words were formed from each end of each Osgood dimension in such a way as to avoid the use of synonyms or antonyms and obvious acoustic similarities across all triads. The technique was, of course, to present the subject with homogeneous word triads for four trials and on the fifth to shift to a triad drawn from the other end of the dimension. Separate groups were run for each dimension with half of them shifting from the high end to the low end and half in the reverse directions. Obviously six control groups who remained at the same end of the dimension were required. The nonrehearsal activity was subtraction by 3s and the retention interval was 20 seconds. A sample of the words representative of the various dimensions are:

> *Evaluative positive*—religious, success, nice, knowledge, true, enjoy
> *Evaluative negative*—kill, danger, worry, lose, disease, debt
> *Potency positive*—steel, mountain, science, college, officer
> *Potency negative*—kiss, voice, beautiful, flower, baby, dream
> *Activity positive*—sailor, party, pull, tough, inventor, quick
> *Activity negative*—dead, soft, moon, later, egg, silence

The results are shown in the next three figures where the various subgroups have been combined. That is, the positive and negative controls were averaged together as also were the experimentals who shifted in opposite directions, giving a total of 100 Ss in each group. Figure 4 presents the results for the Evaluative scale. It is clear that proactive inhibition built up across the first

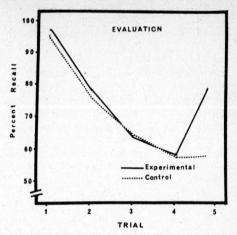

FIG. 4. The effect of shifting from one end to the other end of the Evaluative dimension.

four trials and in the same way for both groups. The experimental group gained markedly on the shift trial and was superior to the control group at the $p < .01$ level. The same story is told for the Potency dimension as well as for the Activity dimension.

It may be worth noting that although there was indeed a performance gain concurrent with the shift trial, the level of performance on that trial was not as high as it was on the first trial, indicating that the effect of this type of response class shift is

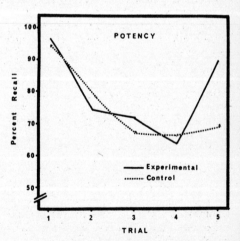

FIG. 5. The effect of shifting from one end to the other end of the Potency dimension.

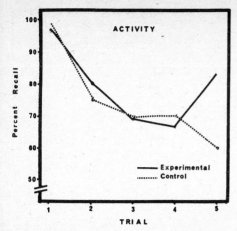

FIG. 6.   The effect of shifting from one end to the other end of the Activity dimension.

not as great as one finds in going from CCCs to NNNs.   It seems quite reasonable to believe that there is a greater difference between the categories of consonants and numbers than between classes of meaningful words.

Some tentative work has been done by Simpson (1967), who shifted groups from one dimension to another.   Not surprisingly a similar performance increase on the shift trial was found, but a complete experiment comparing an intradimensional shift with an extradimensional is yet to be done.   It is feasible, but a tiresome number of subgroups is required for a perfect design.

What I have to say by way of interpreting these results is fairly obvious.   It is simply that subjects do encode materials by some meaning characteristic which is associated with the extremes of each of the Osgood dimensions.   They seem to do it, as data to be presented later will imply, quite automatically and without being fully aware of the intelligent richness and complexity of their own discriminative reactions.

Encoding by Other Characteristics

Other studies on the effect of shifts have been conducted at the Ohio State University laboratories and at other universities.   The researches have been on semantic shifts, on shifts in the physical characteristics of words, and on shifts in the manner of pre-

sentation of the material.   Since, in general, the procedures for these studies have been similar, and since the experiments have been, or probably will be, published elsewhere, they will not be described in detail.   However, a few statements concerning the methods which were consistently used in our studies are in order.

Counterbalancing was always employed to insure that each trigram or triad of words appeared equally often in each trial position.   Shifts were made in both directions, as in the above-mentioned semantic differential study, and since in all cases the shift effects seemed to operate in the same manner in either direction, they have been combined in the graphic presentation to follow.   An attempt was made to equate the words with respect to other variables which might themselves lead to a release from proactive inhibition.   For example, save in a study on frequency shift itself, Thorndike-Lorge word frequency was matched in the two classes of materials.   Semantic matching was also employed in some circumstances; in a study of the effect of syllabic length, words such as STEEL-*iron* and LAKE-*river* were paired against each other in the two lists.   A fairly large sample of words characterizing any class was chosen in an effort to secure class representativeness.   Finally, the N in each group, although varying from experiment to experiment, did not run less than 48 for any experimental or for any control group.   With one exception, the retention interval was 20 seconds, and the intertrial interval was always 30 seconds.

The data of the experiments are summarized in the form of a bar graph in Figure 7.   The values for the graph were determined in the following fashion.   The amount of decline from Trial 1 to the shift trial was obtained for the control group.   This figure was then divided into the value of the difference between the control and experimental groups on the critical shift trial to give a percentage gain resulting from the shift.   This procedure corrects for the fact that the groups in the different experiments varied somewhat in the level of performance on the shift trial.   The minimal value required for significance at the .05 level on a

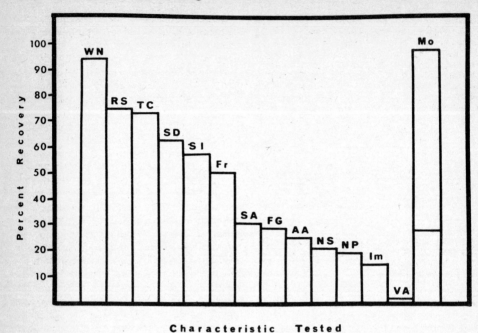

Fɪɢ. 7. A summary of the shift effectiveness of various aspects of the triad.

two-tailed test is about 25%. It should be emphasized that the control and experimental groups always had exactly the same materials on the shift trials and differed only in their histories up to that trial. The different types of data presented in the bar graph are enumerated below according to the order of magnitude of gain in the shift trial.

1. *Class shift* (W-N). Reutener (1969) studied the effect of shifting between triads of miscellaneous nouns and triads of spelled-out numbers.

2. *Representing symbol* (RS). These data also come from research by Reutener (1969). The change was between arabic numerals and spelled-out numbers.

3. *Taxonomic class* (TC). This value on the bar graph was estimated from the first shift trial in the Loess (1967) study. Specifically, Loess presented triads of words drawn from one Bousefield, Cohen, and Whitmarsh (1958) taxonomic class names of birds, or trees, or occupations—and after three trials of the one class, shifted to another.

4. *Semantic differential* (SD). The data for all three dimensions of the semantic differential experiment, mentioned above, were combined to produce a single value.

5. *Sense impression* (SI). Underwood and Richardson (1956) have presented data on the sense impression evoked by various nouns. Reutener[1] investigated shifts made between one pair of these sense impressions, "round" (barrel, knob, doughnut), and another, "white" (chalk, lint, salt).

6. *Frequency shift* (Fr). In a study by Swanson,[2] shifts were made between Thorndike-Lorge high-frequency verbs and nouns (AA) to verbs and nouns of low frequency (below 15 per million). The words were chosen to be heterogeneous in meaning to avoid confounding a semantic shift with the frequency shift. The retention interval was 15 seconds.

7. *Slide background area* (SA). The graph value is taken from the work of Turvey and Egan (1969). This study shifted the white background areas of the projected slide, the areas being approximately 85 or 24 square inches on a screen 3.5 feet from the subject. The materials were CCCs, and they maintained the same size regardless of background area. The scoring system used by these authors is slightly different from that employed in the Ohio State studies, but this probably does not produce a great disparity between values computed by the two methods.

8. *Figure ground* (FG). Word trigrams or CCCs were shifted between a black-on-white display and a white-on-black display (Reutener, 1969).

[1] D. Reutener. Sense impression as an encoding category in STM. Unpublished study, 1968.

[2] J. Swanson. Preprocessing on the basis of

frequency of occurrence. Unpublished study, 1969.

9. *Acoustic-articulatory* (AA). Baldwin (1969) shifted between groups of words whose pronunciation would be described as "open," "back" (harsh, north), and words described as "closed," "front" (fierce, east). Since the words were spoken aloud by the subject when they were presented on the screen, the shift classification must be considered as both auditory and articulatory.

10. *Number of syllables* (NS). Baldwin (1969) also shifted between one- and two-syllable words, as NURSE-*doctor*, GOLD-*silver*. Since the words were presented visually, physical length is somewhat confounded with syllabic length.

11. *Number of phonemes* (NP). Triads of one-syllable words of two to three phonemes and triads of one-syllable words of four and five phonemes were used for a shift dimension by Baldwin (1969). The words were presented orally by tape recorder in order to avoid confounding with visual extent.

12. *Imagery* (Im). Words of high imagery-concreteness and low imagery-abstractness were selected from the monograph by Paivio, Yuille, and Madigan (1968). The two sets of words were matched in *m* value, number of syllables, and Thorndike-Lorge value. Although the retention of the high-imagery items was superior to the low-imagery items, the shift effect with a total *N* of 256 was not significant (Engle, 1969).

13. *Verbs-adjectives* (VA). This study (Wickens & Clark, 1968) has been described in an earlier portion of this paper.

14. *Presentation modality* (Mo). This aspect has been presented last and out of order of magnitude because of the somewhat conflicting results obtained in two experiments. Wittlinger (1967), in the study mentioned above, shifted between auditory and visual presentation of NNNs and CCCs, and obtained a release from PI of about 28%. Rubin (in press) found increments of close to 100% as he shifted between these modalities. There are a number of differences between the two experiments, but it is not clear why the results of the two should be so disparate.

Summary of the STM Research

One generalization which seems clear in the data of Figure 7 is that changes in semantic content produce a considerable amount of release from proactive inhibition, whereas the physical characteristics of words —their lengths and sounds—produce only a slight effect. Changing certain characteristics of the presentation—background area or figure ground—is relatively ineffective, but changing the language of the symbol itself— arabic numerals to spelled-out numbers— is highly effective. Insofar as modality changes are concerned, their power seems to be dependent on subtle differences in the experimental procedures, but modality shifts are clearly effective.

Although an interpretation of the increases in performance as a result of these changes is not critical to the use of this STM technique for identifying the encoding attributes of words, it is of interest to speculate on the matter.

One explanation which has been advanced is that the subject is perceptually alerted by the shift item, and either learns it better or makes a greater (and more successful) effort to retain this item than the previous one. There are several arguments against this position. One is that the interpretation would seem to account for the decline in performance on the second, third, and fourth trial by a decreasing effort on the subject's part. Examined carefully, this position becomes difficult to accept in view of the fact that the subject will have been in the situation for only about 2 minutes at the time the shift occurs. It seems doubtful that college students would have become so bored and indifferent to the situation in so short a period of time and after such a small number of trials. In general, experimenters report that subjects are well motivated and challenged by the task. Finally, as will be pointed out later, subjects are very frequently unaware of the differences between different types of materials. One would almost certainly expect that a perceptual alerting would enter into consciousness.

A very plausible interpretation of the phenomenon is that the altered materials, differing as they do from the preceding materials, supply a new, and for one trial, a unique retrieval cue. Therefore, interference between the last item and the preceding items at the time of retrieval is reduced. That at least a certain amount of the recall difficulty is a retrieval problem during the short "paced" recall interval is indicated by the fact that at the completion of the experiment, subjects can, when asked to do so by the experimenter, recall many of the words or even triads which they had not given on the trial recall. Whether the retrieval cue interpretation alone will be sufficient to account for all the data is a matter for further research to answer.

Other Evidence for Encoding

I should like, very briefly and with no pretenses of having covered the field in a thorough fashion, to present other data suggestive of encoding of the sort of which I have been speaking.

1. Free recall. There is an interesting parallel between the results obtained in the shift experiments and those in free recall. Wickens and Clark obtained no effect of the shift with grammatical classes and Cofer and Bruce (1965) obtained no clustering by grammatical classes in free recall. There is a great deal of evidence of clustering by taxonomic category (Bousfield et al., 1958). Loess (1967) obtained clear shift effects as his subjects were moved from one to another category in the STM situation. Hudson (1968) has demonstrated that subjects will cluster according to sense impression, and the study of Reutener (see Footnote 3) found that a shift from one to another dimension produced a release from proactive inhibition.

2. Recognition memory. Two studies in recognition memory support the notion of the higher level encoding of single words. The method used in the two studies, one by Underwood (1965) and the other by Kimble (1968), was essentially the same. The subjects were read a large group of words and were asked to judge whether or not they had heard the word previously in an earlier portion of the list. Imbedded in the later portions of the list were words which bore certain relations to some of the earlier words. The relationships were antonyms of previous words, high associates of previous words, the categorical names of previous specific examples, or, finally, they were words which named a sense impression that might have been produced by the earlier words (barrel, doughnut, globe, and spool could create the sense impression of "roundness"). The question these experimenters asked was whether false positive recognitions would be given to the new words which had been foreshadowed in one way or another by earlier related words. The two experi-

ments do not completely overlap in the relationships employed and I shall not linger over all the results, but the Underwood experiment found evidence for false recognition of category names and associates and the Kimble study noted, in addition, significant recognition errors based on sense impression—though, I should add, Underwood's subjects did not produce errors attributable to this aspect of the stimulus.

3. Transfer of training. It is possible that, in the STM situation, the presentation of several triads of words which are homogeneous with respect to some class have an accumulative effect and prime the subject to encode in a particular way, and this form of encoding would not occur for a single word. The hypothesis that single words are categorically encoded was investigated by Ory (1968) in an experiment using typical transfer-of-training designs.

For those who are not familiar with the alphabet soup of the verbal learner, a brief description of the basic paradigms employed may be in order. Two paired-associate lists may have nearly any kind of relationship to each other. They may have completely different stimuli and responses, the same stimuli and different responses, the obverse of this arrangement, or similar stimuli and the same or similar response and so on almost ad infinitum. Certain conventional abbreviations have been developed to describe these relationships. The first list which is learned is usually referred to as the A-B list, A representing the stimulus, and B the response term. If the second list is called A-C, then it means the second list has the same stimuli but different responses—C rather than B; whereas a D-C list would have both different stimuli and different responses. If the responses of the second list are referred to as B', this means that the responses of the two lists are similar in some manner; or if the second list stimuli are referred to as A', it means they are similar to the first-list stimuli. One further paradigm must be described, and it is the A-B$_r$ design. This symbol means that the same stimuli and responses are present in both lists but that the pairing of them

TABLE 1

Sample of Words and S-R Arrangements Used for the Measurement of Transfer by Taxonomic Category

List 1	List 2
A-B'	A-B
21 England	21 France
13 Head	13 Arm
88 Train	88 Bus
16 Lake	16 River
A-B$_r$'	A-B
21 Head	21 France
13 Train	13 Arm
88 Lake	88 Bus
16 England	16 River
A-C	A-B
21 Diamond	21 France
13 Maple	13 Arm
88 Priest	88 Bus
16 Window	16 River
D-C	A-B
18 Diamond	21 France
12 Maple	13 Arm
45 Priest	88 Bus
22 Window	16 River

differs in the two lists. The "r" stands for re-paired.

In the usual transfer of training design, the D-C group is the control group, the A-B' paradigm produces positive transfer effects, the A-C group negative transfer effects, and the A-B$_r$ group is ordinarily even more negative. The Ory experiment employed these paradigms using items from taxonomic categories—that is, word classes —as response terms, the stimulus term being a two-digit number.

A sample pair used by each of the four groups in the experiment is presented in Table 1, together with the paradigm designation of the various groups. The responses of the first group are different in the two lists, and in that sense it is an A-C list. But it will be noted that the responses paired with the same numbers are related to each other by membership in the same taxonomic category. In this sense the relationship between the two lists is an A-B' one, and if the subject engages in category encoding, positive transfer should occur for this group. Group 2 uses the same stimuli and the same responses in the two lists but they are re-paired, so category encoding should lead to

negative transfer effects. Finally for Group 4 the two lists are neutral with respect to both stimuli and responses and this group serves as the base line with which to compare the other groups. Note, incidentally, that since one was interested primarily in the performance on List 2—the transfer test—this list is the same for all groups, and it is the first list that differs among groups. Twenty subjects were run in each group and after they reached a criterion of two perfect trials on List 1, they were given the second list to learn to the same criterion. The results in terms of the number of correct responses during each of the first five trials are presented in Figure 8.

A statistical analysis of the total number of correct responses during these trials showed the A-B$_r$' group to be inferior to all the other groups, with the A-B' group superior to the A-C. In summary, there appears to be evidence of categorical encoding which is somewhat helpful to the A-B' group and which is clearly detrimental to the A-B$_r$' group.

After the experiment was completed, we asked the subjects how they went about learning the second list. Most of the subjects in Group A-B' recognized the relationship between the responses of the two lists and many reported that they intentionally used the first-list responses as mediators.

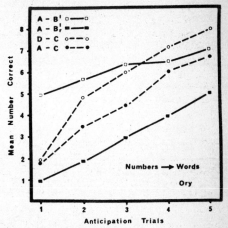

Fig. 8. Transfer in various paradigms as a function of word class of the response in paired-associate learning.

TABLE 2

SAMPLE OF WORDS AND S-R ARRANGEMENTS USED
FOR THE MEASUREMENT OF TRANSFER BY
ACOUSTIC SIMILARITY

List 1	List 2
A-B′	A-B
10 SNEEZE	10 TEASE
25 CRYSTAL	25 PISTOL
60 VOTE	60 BOAT
36 WRITE	36 BRIGHT
A-B$_r$′	A-B
10 WRITE	10 TEASE
25 SNEEZE	25 PISTOL
60 CRYSTAL	60 BOAT
36 VOTE	36 BRIGHT
A-C	A-B
10 JAM	10 TEASE
25 LEMON	25 PISTOL
60 PUBLIC	60 BOAT
36 MINUTE	36 BRIGHT
D-C	A-B
33 JAM	10 TEASE
16 LEMON	25 PISTOL
50 PUBLIC	60 BOAT
95 MINUTE	36 BRIGHT

This behavior facilitated performance in the early trials, but did not do so toward the end of the learning, and actually the A-B′ group averaged a few more trials to reach complete mastery than did the control or D-C group. In the same subsequent query, the A-B$_r$′ group, on the other hand, seemed to be innocent of any knowledge about the relationship of the responses of the two lists. It is obvious, however, that they were affected by this relationship, for otherwise they would have behaved in the manner of the A-C group. It would appear that the responses of List 1 had been encoded in a categorical fashion and this interfered with List 2 learning where once again categorical encoding occurred, but now different numbers were the stimuli for the older categories.

I believe that the performance of the A-B$_r$′ group is especially critical to the supposition that responses are richly encoded, and much of the encoding is achieved quite automatically and can serve us for ill without our necessarily being aware of what is occurring. Finally and most significantly, the experiment suggests that the categorical encoding occurs for single words and does not require a priming from other words of the same word class for its effect to occur.

One final experiment in the same vein is in order, this one conducted by Graf (1968). The basic design was the same as was the transfer experiment described above, except in this case we were working with acoustic similarity. The groups and lists employed are shown in Table 2. Once again we used the A-B′ design—where dimension of similarity was phonetic rather than semantic—the A-B$_r$′ paradigm, the A-C, and the D-C. The lists and results are shown in Table 2 and in Figure 9.

There is a tendency for all experimental conditions to lead to negative transfer effects, although it is significant only for the A-B$_r$′ group. The A-B′ group did report an awareness of the rhyming of the responses of the two lists, and they also said that it seemed to hinder them, as indeed the data faintly suggest. The performance of the A-B$_r$′ group quite clearly points toward acoustic encoding in long-term memory, but it seems to produce less separation among the groups than does the semantic encoding, measured in the parallel experiment by Ory. More research is needed before a precise specification of the effect of acoustic as opposed to semantic encoding can be stated.

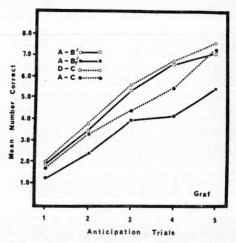

FIG. 9. Transfer in various paradigms as a function of acoustic similarity of the response in paired-associate learning.

Encoding and Word Perception

The research which I have reported makes a commentary on two psychological processes—the process of word perception and the process of memory; but at this time I wish to emphasize only the perceptual aspect of the research, and to speculate about the mechanisms of word perception.

In reacting to the symbol which we call a word, the perceiver has available to him a vast amount of experience with and knowledge about the object, event, or action which the symbol represents. This knowledge is most variegated and it comes from both direct and vicarious experience with the symbol's referent. It is used to code the sensory impress of the referent, frequency of its occurrence, its relationship to other referents, its coordinate or subordinate symbols, its affective connotations, as well, undoubtedly, as other dimensions or attributes of experience. In addition to these more abstract dimensions of encoding, the symbol itself is encoded according to its particular physical characteristics—its phonetics, perhaps its length, and even how it is now physically represented. In the split second while the symbol is processed by the individual, it is granted a locus on many of these dimensions or aspects—encoded, in short, in a multiplicity of ways. Given all of these multiple aspects along which a word can be encoded, only a few locations on each dimension would suffice to produce a large number of unique symbolic experiences— this is the word's meaning. Because other symbols may have the same locus in several dimensions, confusions occur, but because there are so many attributes for identification, recognition errors do not abound, as the above-mentioned studies by Underwood and by Kimble show.

One may assume that some of these dimensions are more salient than others and that the speed of encoding as well as the rate of forgetting of the symbol's location on the dimensions is not the same over all dimensions. I would expect that with ingenuity one could discover experimental means of demonstrating these suppositions.

The process of encoding symbols into these multiple dimensions is done—I be-lieve—with tremendous alacrity and proficiency, the entries into the many different attributes being achieved almost simultaneously, and with the deftness and automaticity associated only with a highly practiced skill. Thus it is, and only thus, that we are able to understand the rapid and variegated flow of conversation.

Encoding and Consciousness

My interpretation of the encoding process under the circumstances of our experiments has been one which assumes that the categorizations are achieved with very little conscious awareness on the part of the subject of what he is doing. This conclusion has grown from two sources, one empirical and the other historical.

At the empirical level are the data which we have acquired from questioning subjects at the close of many of our experiments. In the instance of the semantic differential research, and especially in the study of sense impression, we asked the subjects if they could identify any differences in the kind of words which were presented to them, or if the words of some triads were related to each other in any particular way. The overwhelming majority of these subjects were completely unable to verbalize the differences in the kinds of materials they had experienced, yet obviously they behaved differently toward the different classes of words. In the instance of the sense impression words, they readily recognized, when told by the experimenter, that some sets of words referred to round objects and some to white objects, but they reported that they were unaware of this fact during the experiment proper. Thus these empirical data strongly support the view that the subjects were encoding appropriately without being conscious of the fact that they were doing so.

At the historical level, I turn for support to the reports of a group of psychologists who undoubtedly knew more about the contents of consciousness than did any group before or since, namely those who employed the Method of Introspection as their tool for the investigation of psychological events. It must be obvious to you as it is to me that the concept of word encoding is very closely related to the older term of meaning, a topic which occupied the attention of the introspective psychologists quite intensively, so it is appropriate to turn to some of their comments on this topic.

Of meaning, Titchener (1909) made the following statement in one of his lectures on the experimental psychology of the thought processes:

But I go farther. I doubt if meaning need necessarily be conscious at all—if it may not be "carried" in purely physiological terms. In rapid reading, the skimming of pages in quick succession; in the rendering of a musical composition . . . in these and similar cases I doubt if meaning necessarily has any kind of conscious representation. It very well may; but I doubt if it necessarily does. There must be an *Aufgabe,* truly, but then the *Aufgabe,* as we have seen, need not either come to consciousness [p. 178].

Later, Moore (1915) was to do an experiment in which his subjects indicated when they first obtained the meaning of a word shown to them, and also when the first image evoked by the word entered into consciousness. According to my calculations of the data he presents, meaning takes an average of a half second to develop, and the image about a second and a half. A few of the introspective reports are as follows:

To the word "steamship," Kulpe reported that

Immediately on the exposition of the word, auditory-kinesthetic image thereof, and a realization of the meaning in the sense of "a means of transport by water." This time there was no trace of any image.

The word "scissors" brought out the following introspection from Moore:

At first, a feeling of familiarity was present and then a feeling of certainty that I know what the word signifies without having analyzed its meaning any further. First, during the reaction itself there came the further thought "something with which one cuts."

It is interesting to note that both observers encoded categorically. To Kulpe a steamship was "a means of transport by water," and the scissors were "something with which one cuts" to Moore.

The introspective reports are also of interest in the light of my view that much of the richness of the encoding does not enter into consciousness, and remains, to be technical, a part of the imageless thought that was so much a matter of concern and controversy in the early years of this century. Kulpe's encoding statement would include such diverse items as canoes, rowboats, and Yankee clippers, while Moore's description would encompass a meat cleaver, a cutlass, and a carving knife. Although there is nothing in their introspective protocols which would exclude these items, it seems most improbable that Kulpe or Moore would confuse the word they had seen with these other words on a multiple-choice recognition test given to them at the completion of their observations. It would appear that consciousness has time or need only to recognize the broad category into which the symbol falls and not the other attributes which make that symbol unique, even though the total psychological reaction certainly does include an encoding of these other characteristics.

Therefore, to one who is even mildly versed in the history of psychology, it should not come as a surprise to learn that our subjects were usually unable to verbalize the encoding categories which they used. These particular results were foreshadowed many times in the introspective protocols in the early days of experimental psychology; they were anticipated not only in the paucity of conscious content in the studies of meaning, but in the word association research as well; and these findings led to the introduction of such words as *Bewusstseinslagen,* determining tendencies, and *Aufgabe.* It would appear that where the Method of Introspection failed, information about the richness of the word-perceiving process can be indirectly evaluated through the study of man's failing memory, using what might be called the Method of Unwitting Self-Incrimination.

Multidimensional Encoding and Subception

Some 10 to 20 years ago there was a considerable flurry of research on the topic of subception (Lazarus & McCleary, 1951). Quite simply, the concept of subception dealt with the finding that when words were presented for brief tachistoscopic exposures, subjects might classify correctly the word as referring to a pleasant or unpleasant state of affairs, even though they could not identify the word itself (Eriksen, Azuma, & Hicks, 1959) ; or again they might report that they saw the word "sacred" when the actual word in the tachistoscope was "Easter" (Postman, Bruner, & McGinnis, 1948).

This general class of findings, and its interpretation, was somewhat hotly debated and vigorously researched. It implied that one could perceive without awareness, and one interpretation held that the empirical results demonstrated a capacity for the unconscious to defend the ego (equated with the conscious state) from recognizing materials to which it was inimicable.

The view that words are encoded on a multiple number of dimensions—and it is only after the entries are made in all the pertinent dimensions that the complete and unique word meaning is achieved—can account for these results quite readily. Each encoding process, I assume, takes some small but finite amount of time, and it is not done simultaneously for all aspects of the word. If the word is withdrawn before it is completely encoded, or leaves traces which can then be encoded, the perception is incomplete, and the meaning which accrues for the symbol is but a fragment of the world's total meaning. Given the requirement to define the word, the subject responds with a word which is consonant with the encoded fragment. Thus, if only the religious aspect of the word "Easter" has been encoded, the subject could readily respond with the word "sacred." I do not as of now have direct evidence of successive multiple encoding, but certainly such a process would predict not only the subception data, but also the occurrence of intrusion errors in other situations, errors which match the misperceived word on some semantic, sensory, or structural attribute.

In concluding, there is one other feature of this research that I should like to mention, namely, that it has an immediate practical value to it. This is so unusual of my research that I cannot avoid dwelling on it for a brief moment. Its utility comes from the fact that it can be used to evaluate a joke. The joke is an old one, and I first heard it from my advisor, J. F. Dashiell, in my graduate school days, but apparently it has the quality of agelessness about it, for it appears in the recent Hilgard and Atkinson (1967) introductory text in their chapter entitled "Remembering and Forgetting." I shall quote from their book:

A story told about Stanford University's first president illustrates this theory of interference. David Starr Jordan was an authority on fish. As the president of a new university, he began to call the students by name, but every time he learned the name of a student he forgot the name of a fish. Hence, it is said, he gave up learning the names of students.

My research permits me to conclude that either the story is apocryphal, or that the Stanford students in David Starr Jordan's time looked a good deal less human than they do today.

REFERENCES

BALDWIN, R. Release from PI and the physical aspects of words. Unpublished master's thesis, Ohio State University, 1969.

BOUSFIELD, W. A., COHEN, B. H., & WHITMARSH, G. A. Associative clustering in the recall of words of different taxonomic frequencies of occurrence. *Psychological Reports*, 1958, **4**, 38–44.

BOWER, G. A multicomponent theory of the memory trace. In K. W. Spence & J. T. Spence (Eds.), *The psychology of learning and motivation*. New York: Academic Press, 1967.

COFER, C. N., & BRUCE, D. R. Form-class as the basis for clustering in the recall of nonassociated words. *Journal of Verbal Learning and Verbal Behavior*, 1965, **4**, 386–389.

ENGLE, R. High and low imagery words in short-term memory. Unpublished master's thesis, Ohio State University, 1969.

ERIKSEN, C. W., AZUMA, H., & HICKS, R. B. Verbal discrimination of pleasant and unpleasant stimulus prior to specific identification. *Journal of Abnormal and Social Psychology*, 1959, **59**, 114–119.

FRIEDMAN, M. J., & REYNOLDS, J. H. Retroactive inhibition as a function of response-class similarity. *Journal of Experimental Psychology*, 1967, **74**, 351–355.

GRAF, S. Acoustic similarity in long-term memory. Unpublished master's thesis, Ohio State University, 1968.

HEISE, D. R. Semantic differential profiles for 1000 most frequent English words. *Psychological Monographs*, 1965, **79**(8, Whole No. 601).

HILGARD, E. R., & ATKINSON, R. C. *Introduction to psychology*. New York: Harcourt, Brace & World, 1967.

HUDSON, R. L. Category clustering as a function of level of information and number of stimulus presentations. *Journal of Verbal Learning and Verbal Behavior,* 1968, **7**, 1106–1108.

KEPPEL, G., & UNDERWOOD, B. J. Proactive inhibition in short-term retention of single items. *Journal of Verbal Learning and Verbal Behavior,* 1962, **1**, 153–161.

KIMBLE, G. A. Mediating associations. *Journal of Experimental Psychology,* 1968, **76**, 263–266.

LAZARUS, R. S., & McCLEARY, R. A. Autonomic discrimination without awareness: A study of subception. *Psychological Review,* 1951, **58**, 113–122.

LOESS, H. Short-term memory, word class and sequence of items. *Journal of Experimental Psychology,* 1967, **74**, 556–561.

McGEOCH, J. A., & McDONALD, W. T. Meaningful relation and retroactive inhibition. *American Journal of Psychology,* 1931, **43**, 579–588.

MOORE, T. V. The temporal relations of meaning and imagery. *Psychological Review,* 1915, **22**, 177–224.

ORY, N. Transfer as a function of response and stimulus encoding in the learning of paired associates. Unpublished master's thesis, Ohio State University, 1968.

OSGOOD, C. E., SUCI, G. J., & TANNENBAUM, P. H. *The measurement of meaning.* Urbana: University of Illinois Press, 1957.

PAIVIO, A., YUILLE, J. C., & MADIGAN, S. Concreteness, imagery, and meaningfulness values for 925 nouns. *Journal of Experimental Psychology,* 1968, 76(1, Pt. 2).

PETERSON, L. R., & PETERSON, M. J. Short-term retention of individual verbal items. *Journal of Experimental Psychology,* 1959, **54**, 157–173.

POSTMAN, L., BRUNER, J. S., & McGINNIS, E. Personal values as selective factors in perception. *Journal of Abnormal and Social Psychology,* 1948, **43**, 142–154.

POSTMAN, L., KEPPEL, G., & STARK, K. Unlearning as a function of the relationship between successive response classes. *Journal of Experimental Psychology,* 1965, **69**, 111–118.

REUTENER, D. Background, symbolic and class shift in short-term memory. Unpublished doctoral dissertation, Ohio State University, 1969.

ROWLAND, E. H. The psychological experiences connected with the different parts of speech. *Psychological Review,* 1907, **14**(Monogr. Suppl. 32).

RUBIN, S. M. *Proactive and retroactive inhibition in short-term memory as a function of sensory modality.* (Technical Report) Human Performance Center: University of Michigan, in press.

SIMPSON, H. F. The semantic differential and the release of proactive inhibition in short-term memory. Unpublished master's thesis, Ohio State University, 1967.

THORNDIKE, E. L., & LORGE, I. *The teacher's word book of 30,000 words.* New York: Teacher's College, Columbia University, Bureau of Publications, 1944.

TITCHENER, E. B. *Lectures on the experimental psychology of the thought-process.* New York: Macmillan, 1909.

TURVEY, M. T., & EGAN, J. Contextual change and release from proactive interference in short-term verbal memory. *Journal of Experimental Psychology,* 1969, **81**, 396–397.

UNDERWOOD, B. J. False recognition produced by implicit verbal responses. *Journal of Experimental Psychology,* 1965, **70**, 122–129.

UNDERWOOD, B. J., & RICHARDSON, J. Some verbal materials for the study of concept formation. *Psychological Bulletin,* 1956, **53**, 84–95.

WICKENS, D. D., BORN, D. G., & ALLEN, C. K. Proactive inhibition and item similarity in short-term memory. *Journal of Verbal Learning and Verbal Behavior,* 1963, **2**, 440–445.

WICKENS, D. D., & CLARK, S. E. Osgood dimensions as an encoding class in short-term memory. *Journal of Experimental Psychology,* 1968, **78**, 580–584.

WICKENS, D. D., CLARK, S. E., HILL, F. A., & WITTLINGER, R. P. Grammatical class as an encoding category in short-term memory. *Journal of Experimental Psychology,* 1968, **78**, 599–604.

WITTLINGER, R. P. Phasic arousal in short-term memory. Unpublished doctoral dissertation, Ohio State University, 1967.

M. Anisfeld and M. Knapp

Association, synonymity and directionality in false recognition

Reprinted from the *Journal of Experimental Psychology* (1968) **77**(2):171-9

When asked to indicate whether each of 200 orally presented words had appeared before (+) or not (−), students gave more plusses to common associates and synonyms of preceding words than to control words. In a 2nd experiment, false recognition errors were obtained when the preceding words associatively elicited the test words and when the associative relation was bidirectional but not when only the test words elicited the preceding words. The results of the 2nd experiment were taken as an indication that initial coding of words contributes to false recognition and that the phenomenon is not merely an artifact of testing for it. The occurrence of false recognition errors was taken as support for a characterization of words as complexes of attributes or features.

Even the bulkiest dictionaries present vocabulary as a list of unrelated items. Linguists, however, have made it clear that although the lexical component of language manifests less systematicity than syntax or phonology, it nevertheless has much more structure than is suggested by the arrangement of words in dictionaries (e.g., Chomsky, 1965, especially Ch. 4.; de Saussure, 1959; Katz & Fodor, 1963; Weinreich, 1964). Within the generative approach to language (Chomsky, 1965) a theory of semantics has recently been developing which has as its central notion the cross classification of words into syntactically relevant categories, such as animate-inanimate, and human-nonhuman.

Psychologists too have recognized that words are organized and they have concerned themselves with the analysis of the psychological processes underlying this organization and with its consequences in verbal behavior. Experiments on semantic generalization (Feather, 1965), clustering in free recall (e.g., Cofer, 1965), not to mention work on free and controlled associations (e.g., Deese, 1965), can all be viewed as reflecting this concern. In these areas of psychological investigation, there is a general tendency, with some notable exceptions (e.g., Deese, 1965), to explain findings by reference to associative bonds between words. The present study was designed to challenge this approach.

In particular, our interest was aroused by a study of Underwood

(1965) in which he used a method of continuous recognition originally introduced by Shepard and Teghtsoonian (1961). Underwood had *S*s indicate for each of 200 words, presented by a tape recorder, whether it had occurred earlier in the list or not. He found that common associates of words which appeared earlier in the list were falsely recognized more often than control words.

The purpose of the first experiment to be reported below was to investigate whether relations of synonymity have similar effects to those of association. The constant use of paraphrasing in everyday life communication suggests that in coding for memory under normal conditions speakers retain primarily the semantic content of a message. Since synonyms have a large area of meaning in common, they would seem natural candidates for confusion in the kind of task used by Underwood. Of course, this experimental situation, unlike everyday life, puts a premium on verbatim coding, but it was reasoned that since associates proved to intrude in this situation synonyms certainly should.

The second experiment was suggested by Razran's study (1949) on semantic generalizations of conditioned responses. He found greater generalization when the test word strongly evoked, in a free association task, the conditioned word than when the conditioned word strongly evoked the test word. For instance, when a salivary response was conditioned to the word *dog* there was less generalization to the superordinate *animal* than to the subordinate *terrier*. In a free association task, subordinates tend to evoke superordinates more strongly than superordinates evoke subordinates. His finding led Razran to the conclusion that semantic generalization was

not an automatic process taking place during original conditioning but rather was an artifact of subsequent testing. Using unidirectional and bidirectional associates the present authors attempted to see whether false recognition was due to processes involved in initial coding of the stimulus or to confusion resulting from the presentation of its associate.

Method

Subjects

There were 28 male university students in the first experiment and 34 female students in the second.

Materials and procedure

Each of the two experiments contained 200 words which were recorded on magnetic tape at 10-sec. intervals. Each word was recorded twice in immediate succession to make sure that it would be heard. The tape was played to groups of five or six *S*s. For each word, *S* had to indicate by a + or − whether it was "old" or "new." The *S*s were instructed to guess when in doubt. The lists were constructed to contain three major categories of words: Preceding (P) words, Experimental (E) words, and Control (C) words. For each P word the list contained one or two E words, and for each E word one C word.

Experiment I.—The E words in the first experiment related to the P words in two ways: 24 as common associative responses (As) and 25 as synonyms (Ss). Table 1 presents the list of words used in this experiment. The words included as As were given as responses to their respective stimuli in a free association test by 27–70% of the 500 male college students Palermo and Jenkins (1964) used for their association norms. The words used as Ss were given as snynonyms by 30–86% of the 50 students Jenkins and Palermo (1965) used for their synonym norms. As can be seen in Table 1, the E words were of four kinds: 15 As and 15 Ss had common P words (e.g., P: chair, A: table, S: seat), 4 As were related to Ps which had no obvious synonym (e.g., P: bed, A: sleep), 5 Ss were related to Ps which had no common associates (e.g., P: baby, S: infant), and in five cases the same E word was both

TABLE 1

Words Used in Exp. I, Their Ordinal Positions and Number
of False Recognition Errors

	P		A			CA		S			CS	
Word	Position[a]		Word	Position[b]	Error	Word	Error	Word	Position[b]	Error	Word	Error
always	40		never	74	1	beside	1	forever	64	1	carefully	0
black	142		white	185	4	soft	3	dark	169	4	cold	1
girl	119		boy	167	6	air	5	female	157	1	marble	1
chair	60		table	88	7	valley	2	seat	78	0	job	2
high	132		low	173	1	ill	1	tall	163	2	safe	1
king	141		queen	181	4	dance	0	ruler	191	0	statue	0
live	32		die	52	1	see	3	exist	68	2	inform	0
needle	129		thread	153	2	nest	3	pin	175	1	jar	1
scissors	89		cut	110	0	look	0	shears	128	1	brine	0
thirsty	44		water	86	3	paper	0	dry	67	0	nice	0
whiskey	95		drink	135	7	spend	2	alcohol	115	1	corridor	0
bath	158		clean	186	5	small	3	shower	198	3	humor	1
now	145		then	176	2	near	9	immediately	192	2	certainly	4
over	36		under	61	1	within	0	above	83	4	early	2
tell	79		me	107	0	it	0	relate	123	2	deceive	0
Error Subtotals					44		32			24		13
anger	166		mad	199	1	rough	3	mad	199	1	rough	3
carpet	159		rug	179	2	shed	2	rug	179	2	shed	2
eagle	111		bird	151	5	guard	3	bird	151	5	guard	3
kitten	54		cat	100	2	wool	0	cat	100	2	wool	0
swift	39		fast	58	0	third	0	fast	58	0	third	0
Error Subtotals					10		8			10		8
bed	114		sleep	149	2	guess	0					
green	47		grass	91	2	heart	0					
his	97		hers	136	2	grim	1					
stem	35		flower	55	0	journal	0					
Error Subtotals					6		1					
baby	134							infant	160	3	drama	1
citizen	37							member	57	2	winter	1
have	144							own	193	4	go	0
jump	49							hop	75	0	fetch	0
make	162							create	182	3	reduce	2
Error Subtotals										12		4
Grand Totals					60		41			46		25

[a] The positions indicated are for the third token of each P word.
[b] The positions indicated are for the first order.

an A and an S (e.g., P: carpet, A, S: rug).

Our procedure for selecting control words differed from that employed by Underwood. Underwood's control words were common associates whose stimuli did not appear in the list. For instance, he used *down* as a control word because it is commonly given as a response to *up*, but *up* was not included in the list. This method does not provide a specific control word for each experimental word. Also, it implies that the only variable conceivably relevant to false recognition is associative connection—a stronger hypothesis than Underwood's experiment was designed to test. The large number of errors to the control words in Underwood's study suggests that factors other than associative relation influence false recognition. Because of these considerations, our C words were

selected so that each one of them would be similar to its experimental counterpart with respect to part of speech, frequency of usage as reflected in the Thorndike and Lorge (1944) G count, and number of syllables. In addition, the C words had to have no obvious relation to other words in the list.

The list thus contained 29 P words, 44 E words, and 44 C words. Each P word appeared three times in different positions before its E counterpart was heard. The three tokens of each P word were within 10–20 positions of each other, and the E word appeared within 18–50 positions after the last token of its corresponding P word. In the 15 cases where a single P word had two E counterparts, one A and one S, the two E words were located within 10–22 positions of each other. Each C word was

TABLE 2
WORDS USED IN EXP. 2, THEIR ORDINAL POSITIONS AND NUMBER OF FALSE RECOGNITION ERRORS

P	Position[a]	E	Position	Errors	C	Position	Errors
P◄————————►E							
List 1							
black	120	white	169	1	fine	168	2
boy	70	girl	99	1	bird	101	0
chair	177	table	199	5	duty	198	3
king	82	queen	116	0	field	118	2
health	127	sickness	147	0	aspect	148	1
butter	79	bread	114	3	fault	115	2
high	131	low	164	5	all	162	4
square	102	round	142	4	young	144	3
green	104	grass	124	6	town	122	0
cold	159	hot	188	2	full	190	2
List 2							
white	120	black	169	1	fresh	168	1
girl	70	boy	99	0	car	101	0
table	177	chair	199	6	page	198	1
queen	82	king	116	3	star	118	1
sickness	127	health	147	0	church	148	1
bread	79	butter	114	3	evening	115	1
low	131	high	164	4	each	162	1
round	102	square	142	0	real	144	1
grass	104	green	124	1	large	122	1
hot	159	cold	188	2	just	190	1
Error Subtotals				47			28
P————————►E							
List 1							
bitter	125	sweet	155	2	best	153	0
fingers	78	hand	108	1	fact	107	1
how	156	now	180	5	why	179	2
long	130	short	161	1	rich	160	2
swift	149	fast	178	5	kind	176	6
bloom	154	flower	187	7	answer	189	4
sky	133	blue	166	1	free	167	0
whiskey	87	drink	121	1	break	119	1
tell	62	me	90	0	it	91	0
door	96	window	135	0	building	136	5
List 2							
appear	98	see	138	1	add	139	1
cottage	163	house	185	8	time	183	1
dream	75	sleep	111	4	price	113	0
heavy	69	light	93	2	stone	92	0
lift	72	carry	97	0	follow	95	0
loud	128	soft	157	4	glad	158	1
therefore	152	because	181	2	either	182	1
stomach	151	food	184	2	law	186	1
infant	143	baby	174	3	army	173	1
scissors	105	cut	146	1	ask	145	3
Error Subtotals				50			30
P◄————————E							
List 1							
see	98	appear	138	1	begin	139	0
house	163	cottage	185	0	feather	183	3
sleep	75	dream	111	4	grant	113	0
light	69	heavy	93	2	double	92	1
carry	72	lift	97	0	drop	95	0
soft	128	loud	157	2	fair	158	2
because	152	therefore	181	0	without	182	0
food	151	stomach	184	0	lecture	186	0
baby	143	infant	174	1	jacket	173	0
cut	105	scissors	146	0	parchment	145	0
List 2							
sweet	125	bitter	155	1	active	153	1
hand	78	fingers	108	0	corners	107	0
now	156	how	180	3	yet	179	2
short	130	long	161	6	late	160	3
fast	149	swift	178	0	cruel	176	1
flower	154	bloom	187	0	crash	189	0
blue	133	sky	166	3	art	167	1
drink	87	whiskey	121	0	antique	119	0
me	62	tell	90	0	play	91	3
window	96	door	135	0	book	136	0
Error Subtotals				23			17
Error Grand Totals				120			75

[a] The positions indicated are for the second token of each P word.

within two positions of its E word, with half the Cs preceding and half following the E words. The Cs for As will be referred to as CAs and those for Ss as CSs. The positions of P, E, and C words are indicated in Table 1.

In addition to words in these three categories, the list also contained 22 filler words. Of these, 20 appeared once each, one—twice, and one—three times. The fillers had no apparent relation to any of the other words in the list. They occupied positions 1–10 and other positions mostly in the first quarter of the list. The list was recorded in two orders. For the first order, the words were randomly arranged, within the constraints outlined above. The second order was identical to the first, except that the positions occupied by Ss and CSs were replaced by their respective As and CAs, and vice versa. This interchange was, of course, possible only for the words which had common Ps.

Experiment II.—In the second experiment there were 30 E words and all of them had an associative relation to the P words. The words used in this experiment and their positions can be seen in Table 2. The As were drawn from two sources. Some were given as responses to their respective stimuli by 22–73% of the 500 female college students in the Palermo and Jenkins (1964) norms and others by 26–74% of the 1,349 airmen in the Bilodeau and Howell (1965) norms. The 30 E words fell into three categories in terms of their relation to P words. In 10 P-E pairs, the E words were common responses to the P words as stimuli but they did not commonly elicit the P words as responses (e.g., bitter $\rightarrow$ sweet, P $\rightarrow$ E). In 10 other cases, the E words commonly elicited the P words as responses but this relation was not reciprocated by the P words (light $\leftarrow$ heavy, P $\leftarrow$ E). Finally, in 10 cases, the associative link went in both directions (king $\leftrightarrow$ queen, P $\leftrightarrow$ E). Most of the words considered as nonassociates were given by less than 10% of the respondents in the norms used and only one word reached 22% response commonality. For instance, while *sweet* was given by 53% of the Palermo-Jenkins Ss in response to *bitter*, only 2% gave *bitter* as a response to *sweet.* The words (List 1) that served as Ps for about half (16) of the Ss served as Es for the rest of the Ss (18, List 2), and vice versa. The mean association values for the directions indi-

cated are: P $\leftrightarrow$ E $= 53\%$, P $\rightarrow$ E $=$ P $\leftarrow$ E $= 42\%$. In Exp. II, as in Exp. I, the characteristic that distinguished a P word from an E word was its ordinal position in the list: the P word came before its corresponding E word. Because each E word had a specific C word, the Cs for the two lists had to be different. In Exp. II, each P word appeared only twice. Thus, the distribution of words in the list was as follows: 60 positions were occupied by the Ps, 30 by the Es, and 30 by the Cs. The rest, 80 positions, were held by filler words. Thirty-five fillers appeared once each, 19—twice each, one—three times, and one—four times. The first 49 positions were taken by fillers, the rest of the fillers were scattered throughout. The second token of each P word was within 10–20 positions of the first token, and each E word was placed 20–50 positions following the second token of its P counterpart. In other respects the design of the second experiment was similar to that of the first.

RESULTS

Two types of errors were possible in these experiments: (*a*) identification of a new item as an old one (positive errors, or false recognition errors), and (*b*) identification of an old item as a new one (negative errors). Negative errors could have been made to the repetitions of the P words and filler words. False recognition errors could have been made to all other words. The number of errors of any kind was minimal. In Exp. II, it amounted to 6% out of the possible number of errors, and in Exp. I the number of errors reached only 5%.

Our interest in this paper is focused on the comparison of the number of errors made to the E words vs. the number made to the C words. The errors made in these two categories of words can be seen in Tables 1 and 2 for Exp. I and II, respectively. Inspection of the distribution of errors in Exp. I showed an atypically large number of errors to the P word "bath" (12 errors, while the next highest figure for a P word was 6) and to the CA word "near" (9, next highest in this category being 5). For Exp. I, therefore, the comparisons between E and C words excluded the two rows (10 words) in which these two words appeared. After this exclusion, both the association and synonymity variables produced significant results, for the S-CS difference, t (27) = 2.94, $p <$ .01, and for the A-CA difference, t (27) = 2.52, $p < .02$. Comparisons for the complete data without exclusions yielded significant results for S-CS, t (27) = 2.42, $p < .05$, but not for A-CA, t (27) = 1.85, $p < .10$.

The exclusions thus do not alter the status of synonymity as a relevant variable, they affect seriously only the association variable. Since the main object of this study was to weaken the omnipotence of associative relations in verbal behavior, the exclusion procedure seems theoretically conservative. As will be seen below, another type of experimental error, "misperception," militated in the present study against the association variable.

The means for the 23 entries involved in the S-CS comparison are: S = 1.46, CS = .71, and the means for the 22 A-CA entries are: A = 1.89, CA = 1.03. The five E words which were related to the P words as both associates and synonyms, and their corresponding C words, were included in both the A-CA and the S-CS comparisons, but as can be seen in Table 1 these words contributed very little to the differences obtained.

The higher error rate for the A and CA categories as compared to the S and CS categories may be due to the higher frequency of these words. While only 5 A and 5 CA words had Thorndike-Lorge frequencies under AA, 16 S words and 15 CS words fell below this level. The more frequent the words,

the greater the likelihood that they will have interrelationships amongst themselves. Such relationships, beyond those under experimental control, will tend to contribute to false recognition. Generally, it is practically impossible to construct a list of 200 words which will not contain relations other than those built-in experimentally. The best one can achieve is the elimination of any glaring nonexperimental relations and then depend on chance to distribute the remaining relations equally among all conditions.

In Exp. II, the statistical analysis for the pooled data of Lists 1 and 2 reveals that significantly more false recognition errors were made to the E words than to the C words when the E words were bidirectionally associated with P words, $P \leftrightarrow E$; means: E = 1.38, C = .82, t (33) = 2.81, $p < .01$, and when the associative link was in the forward direction, $P \rightarrow E$; E = 1.47, C = .88, t (33) = 2.23, $p < .05$, but not when the association was backward, $P \leftarrow E$; E = .68, C = .50, t (33) = .65, ns. In separate analyses for List 1 and List 2, the pattern of results for List 2 was identical to the pattern for the pooled data but none of the E-C comparisons for List 1 reached significance.

Why was the pattern of results in List 2 not duplicated in List 1? It may be seen by inspecting Table 2 that the number of errors to the E words in List 1 was roughly the same as in List 2. The difference between the two lists is that the number of errors to the C words in List 1 was more than double that in List 2 for the $P \leftrightarrow E$ and $P \rightarrow E$ categories. It is possible to blame the higher error score of the C words in List 1 on gratuitous relations between some of these words and other words in the list. For instance, *kind* which was used as a control for the adjective *fast* contributed a very high number of errors (6). This control could have been perceived by Ss as a synonym of the noun *type* which appeared earlier in the list as a filler. Although such ad hoc explanations are of little value, because one can probably find some nonexperimental relation for most of the words in the list, the point stands that uncontrolled (and uncontrollable) relations, whatever they are, played a role in this experiment, and could account for the disproportionate number of errors in the C category of List 1.

After completion of the experiments the suspicion arose that some words may not have been heard as the words they had been intended to be. To check on this possibility, different Ss were asked to listen to the tapes and to write down what they heard. Eight Ss did this for the tape used in Exp. I and four for the tape used in Exp. II. This test revealed some misperception, mostly due to homophones. The misperceptions of one or more Ss were distributed among the word categories as follows: Exp. I, two P words, four A words, six CA words, one S word, and one CS word; Exp. II, seven P and E words, and four C words.

It is apparent that in Exp. I there was a greater concentration of misperceptions in the A category words than in the other categories. Because of this it is likely that the t value for the difference between A and C words underestimates the true contribution of associative relations to false recognition. However, this problem is not too serious for the present study because its purpose was not to ascertain the exact weight of associations in determining false recognition but rather to introduce synonymity as an additional variable.

DISCUSSION

In interpreting the results of the second experiment it must be kept in mind that the forward $(P \rightarrow E)$ and backward $(P \leftarrow E)$ conditions differed not only in temporal order of the free association stimuli and responses relative to each other but also in the number of times the associative stimuli appeared. In the forward condition where the associative stimuli served as P items, they appeared twice, but in the backward condition, where they served as E items, they appeared only once. For this reason it is not possible to conclude that backward associative relations cannot produce false recognition. But one can conclude that forward relations do result in such an effect, thus establishing that initial coding plays a role in false recogniton, and that it is not merely an artifact of testing for it. The discrepancy between this conclusion and Razran's is not too disturbing, because of the basic methodological flaws in his experiment recently summarized by Feather (1965). In fact, despite the gadgetry involved in semantic generalization experiments—perhaps, because of it —it seems that the judgmental procedure employed in the present experiments taps the underlying semantic processes more directly than the semantic generalization procedure. In semantic generalization, the CR transfers, according to this view, to words judged, mistakenly in the case of the test words, by Ss (not necessarily in full awareness) as having been previously conditioned. The generalization gradient, whenever it obtains, may reflect the degree of confidence associated with such judgments. Such mistaken judgments reflect underlying processes of word coding.

What are these processes? A model is needed that would account both for Ss' pronounced ability to recognize correctly new and old words and for the systematic false recognition errors found. It is clear that S must somehow mark off the words on the list from the tens of thousands of words in his vocabulary. This marking off may be achieved in the following way. Assume that, when activated, the neural processes giving a word its identity leave a trace which is "dark" and "heavy" at first and with the passage of time wears out and becomes fainter and fainter. A mechanism of this sort would keep the time of words and enable S to judge each word as to whether it was heard in the experimental session or prior to it. On the basis of this information S could classify a word as new or old.

This timing notion can thus account for Ss' correct identification of words. But it cannot explain why Ss made the systematic false recognition errors described. In order to account for these errors it must be assumed that the word is not the ultimate unit of coding. If it were, associates and synonyms should not produce more errors than control words. Rather, our finding, along with the common phenomenon of paraphrasing and related observations (e.g., Broadbent, 1964; Brown & McNeill, 1966; Yavuz & Bousfield, 1959), supports the conception of words as complexes of features. According to this view, each word consists of a set of features or attributes which uniquely characterize it and distinguish it from all other words in the vocabulary system. The features are of many different kinds and involve semantic, syntactic, phonological, and for literates, orthographic aspects. For instance, the feature characterization of *table* would describe it as "a piece of furniture," "a noun," "having a [t] sound in initial position," "an ⟨e⟩ letter in final position," etc. On this conception, the encoding of a word would correspond to a *simultaneous* activation of a set of features. Many of the semantic features and all of the features in the other three categories would be common to large segments of S's lexicon, but some semantic features would be specific to a single item or to a small group of items (see Katz & Fodor, 1963). The general features serve to relate various lexical items to each other. For instance, many English words begin with a ⟨t⟩, and all these words constitute, in some sense, a category whose members share this feature. But the fact that a *table* stands at a certain height, broadly defined, in relation to its other dimensions could be thought of as an idiosyncratic feature.

Within the framework of the feature analysis, different responses to the same word share to a great extent the same processes. When an S is asked in a free-association test to give the first word that comes to his mind, he focuses on some of the features of the word, perhaps the ones which appear to him most salient at the time. When he is asked to give a synonym, he focuses again on a subset of the feature complex. In this case the features relevant for the determination of the response are semantic. When he is asked to produce rhymes, he focuses on phonological features, and when asked to respond with words of the same letter length as the stimuli, he focuses on orthographic features. According to this view, associative responses and so-called categorical responses do not entail totally different processes, they result mainly from different selections of features.

The idea of feature coding can account for the false recognition errors resulting from associative and synonymy relations. When a new word is heard which shares some significant features with an old word, S may be led mistakenly to "disregard" the distinguishing features and consider the two as identical. The assumption implied here is that not all features carry equal weight. When a word is heard, some of the features potentially associated with it may not get activated and even if activated not all features leave noticeable traces.

In conclusion, we would like to restate the hypothesis that words are not stored as words but as complexes of features. When words are used they are not reproduced from memory but rather reconstructed from their component features.

REFERENCES

Bilodeau, E. A., & Howell, D. C. Free association norms by discrete and continued methods. Technical Report No. 1, 1965, Tulane University, Contract Nonr. 475 (10), Office of Naval Research, New Orleans.

Broadbent, D. E. Perceptual and response

factors in the organization of speech. In A. V. S. de Reuck & Maeve O'Connor (Eds.), *Disorders of language; Ciba Foundation Symposium.* Boston: Little, Brown, 1964.

BROWN, R., & McNEILL, D. The "tip of the tongue" phenomenon. *J. verbal Learn. verbal Behav.,* 1966, **5,** 325–337.

CHOMSKY, N. *Aspects of the theory of syntax.* Cambridge: M.I.T. Press, 1965.

COFER, C. N. On some factors in the organizational characteristics of free recall. *Amer. Psychologist,* 1965, **20,** 261–272.

DEESE, J. *The structure of associations in language and thought.* Baltimore: Johns Hopkins Press, 1965.

DE SAUSSURE, F. *Course in general linguistics.* (Trans. by W. Baskin) New York: Philosophical Library, 1959.

FEATHER, B. W. Semantic generalization of classically conditioned responses: A review. *Psychol. Bull.,* 1965, **63,** 425–441.

JENKINS, J. J., & PALERMO, D. S. *Synonym responses to the stimulus words of the Palermo-Jenkins word association list.* (Res. Bull. No. 55). University Park: Department of Psychology, Pennsylvania State University, 1965.

KATZ, J. J., & FODOR, J. A. The structure of a semantic theory. *Language,* 1963, **39,** 170–210.

PALERMO, D. S., & JENKINS, J. J. *Word association norms; grade school through college.* Minneapolis: University of Minnesota Press, 1964.

RAZRAN, G. Semantic and phonetographic generalizations of salivary conditioning to verbal stimuli. *J. exp. Psychol.,* 1949, **39,** 642–652.

SHEPARD, R. N., & TEGHTSOONIAN, M. Retention of information under conditions approaching a steady state. *J. exp. Psychol.,* 1961, **62,** 302–309.

THORNDIKE, E. L., & LORGE, I. *The teacher's word book of 30,000 words.* New York: Teachers College, Columbia University, 1944.

UNDERWOOD, B. J. False recognition by implicit verbal responses. *J. exp. Psychol.,* 1965, **70,** 122–129.

WEINREICH, U. Webster's third: A critique of its semantics. *Int. J. Amer. Ling.,* 1964, **30,** 405–409.

YAVUZ, H. S., & BOUSFIELD, W. A. Recall of connotative meaning. *Psychol. Rep.,* 1959, **5,** 319–320.

T.S. Hyde and J.J. Jenkins

Differential effects of incidental tasks on the organization of recall of a list of highly associated words

Reprinted from the *Journal of Experimental Psychology* (1969) 82(3):472-81

In three experiments involving 17 groups, the amount and organization of recall of word lists varied with the type of incidental task performed by Ss during presentation of the list. All Ss heard a randomized list of high-strength primary word associates. When the incidental task required using the word as a semantic unit (rating the word as to its pleasantness), recall and organization were equivalent to those of a control group with no incidental task. When the incidental task involved the word as an object (checking for certain letters or estimating the number of letters in the word), recall and organization were greatly reduced. The effects were unaltered by incidental-plus-recall instructions, doubling presentation time, and presenting the list twice.

The value of the free recall situation for studying the organization of verbal materials in memory is well known. Substantial differences in amount of recall can be produced by varying stimulus materials and, ordinarily, these differences can be attributed to differences in the organization imposed by Ss on the material recalled. Such recall-facilitating organization is variously referred to as secondary organization, subjective organization, clustering, etc. Reviews of this literature may be found in Cofer (1965), Mandler (1967), and Tulving (1968).

In general, it appears that meaningful relations (taxonomic classes, logical classes, and prior associative relations) lead readily to well-organized recall. Repetition of the materials in new random orders and successive recall attempts also lead to increasing degrees of organization even in seemingly unrelated materials.

A problem of particular interest now is the elucidation of the mechanisms which bring this organization about. If, along with Melton (1963), we conceptualize the memory sequence as trace formation, trace storage, and trace retrieval, a first step in choosing among mechanisms might be: Where in this input, storage, and output model shall we suppose the organization occurs?

Some studies have assumed that the organization takes place via mediation during the activity of recall itself. This view, which was explicitly advanced by Jenkins and Russell (1952), is compatible with Deese's (1959) work and is echoed in Cofer's (1965) review. It holds that once a word is recalled, it acts as an auxiliary stimulus to help elicit another word that was on the list.

Tulving (1962, 1964, 1966), on the other hand, views such organization as a storage phenomenon, with the list of items being stored under higher order units corresponding to the relations existing in the stimulus lists. Organization in free recall reflects the organization within the memory storage itself.

Cohen (1966) and Slamecka (1968) suggested mechanisms of still a different sort. Slamecka, e.g., postulated that traces of individual items are stored independently, but that S also encodes some general representation of the list structure as a retrieval plan or strategy which guides the recall of the items. Highly organized stimulus lists produce greater recall and more organization because they are more amenable to some highly organized and efficient retrieval plan or strategy.

Both Cofer (1965) and Tulving (1968) suggested that it might be profitable to vary the intraexperimental situation and look for differences in organization of recall while holding the stimulus materials constant. If large and consistent differences in organization can be produced with intraexperimental manipulations, it may be possible to separate the roles played by encoding, storage, and retrieval in the production of organization. The present study is an effort in that direction.

The experiments reported here were modeled on a study by Postman, Adams, and Bohm (1956) which compared the recall of high-strength primary associates in groups that performed incidental tasks during presentation of the words. The Ss whose task was to rate the words as to frequency of usage in English showed lower recall than Ss given standard recall instructions. Reduced recall was not, however, accompanied by any reduction in the relative amount of secondary organization (clustering of pairs).

Pilot work for the present study was similar in design to the Postman et al. (1956) experiment, but the results were quite different. Several types of incidental tasks were found to effect a marked reduction in both the organization and amount of recall. Other tasks had little or no effect on either dependent variable as compared to a control group which performed no incidental task.

The guiding hypothesis, arising from these pilot studies, was that clustering in recall depends on the use to which Ss put the words during the incidental tasks. Tasks that involved meaningful interpretation of the stimulus materials (words as semantic units) were expected to have little or no effect on clustering, while tasks which required nonmeaningful treatment of the stimuli (words as objects) were expected to effect a reduction in organization (clustering) and a corresponding decrement in recall.

METHOD

In all experiments there were three basic groups: The recall only group simply heard the words, with the instructions that they were to recall the words later. The incidental group was given some task to perform on the stimulus materials during their presentation. The incidental + recall group performed the same task as that performed by the appropriate incidental group, but Ss were also told that they would have to recall the words later. The major variable of interest within each experiment was a comparison of the amount and organization of the recall of the word list by the groups of Ss who performed different types of incidental tasks during presentation of the words.

All Ss were students in sections of a course in introductory laboratory psychology at the University of Minnesota. All experiments were conducted in the classroom. Each separate section made up one group. Assignment of students to sections was not systematic with respect to academic ability, college, major department, interest, aptitude, sex, or any other variable known to be relevant to the learning of verbal material.[1] Experimental conditions were randomly assigned to the sections, with the restriction that all seven incidental groups were run first, in order to keep the true nature of the experiment from becoming known to these Ss.

Stimulus materials consisted of the 12 pairs of primary associates used by Jenkins, Mink, and Russell (1958) in their high-strength recall list. These were the Kent-Rosanoff pairs with the highest associative strength in the early Minnesota norms (Russell & Jenkins, 1954). The mean frequency of response for these pairs was 70.9%, with a range from 60.5% to 83.3%. The words were presented to Ss in a random order, with the restriction that primary associates could not occur together in the list. All groups in the first two experiments were presented with a list of the same word order. In the third experiment, where the words were presented twice, the second reading

[1] Group assignment does not appear to have resulted in distorted findings. Pilot data on 350 Ss who were randomly assigned to groups from the general S pool of introductory psychology students is in complete accord with the data presented here.

of the list was a different randomization. All word lists contained four "filler" words, two at the beginning and two at the end. Fillers were selected from the Minnesota norms so that they showed no appreciable associative strength with any of the 24 stimulus words. Filler words were not counted in any data analyses.

All stimulus materials were recorded and presented to Ss via tape recorder during the experiment. Within each experiment the same tape was used for all groups.

Although all experiments were conducted simultaneously and any condition may be compared to any other, for the sake of the reader, the findings are presented as three experiments, grouped on presentation conditions.

EXPERIMENT I

Seven groups of Ss in the first experiment were presented with one reading of the stimulus words at a rate of one word every 2 sec. The Ss in the recall-only group were read the list of words with the instruction that they would have to recall them as soon as E finished his presentation. The remaining six groups differed from each other in two respects. Three of them were incidental groups and three were incidental + recall groups. The former groups were not prewarned about the recall task, while the latter groups were. Within each of these conditions there were three different incidental tasks. It was hypothesized that one task (pleasant–unpleasant) would facilitate recall and clustering, while the other two tasks would adversely affect recall and clustering. The three tasks performed by Ss were as follows:

1. The pleasant–unpleasant task. Two groups of Ss rated the words as to their pleasantness or unpleasantness on a simple check list with one line for each stimulus word.

2. The "E" task. Two more groups were given the task of detecting Es in the words that were read to them. The Ss had a check list with spaces for each stimulus word. They were directed to check if the word contained an E, otherwise to leave the space blank. Eight of the 24 stimulus words contained at least one E.

3. The number-of-letters task. Two other groups of Ss estimated the number of letters in each word. They were told not to count letters, but to estimate the number and write it in the space provided for each word. The instructions for these same tasks to the subgroups in the incidental + recall condition were modified to indicate that S would have to recall the words when the task was finished. He was encouraged to do his best on both of the tasks and told that if he did not do his best on the first task, his results on the second (recall of the words) would be of little value. When the presentation of the list was finished, a set of standard recall instructions was read to all groups. The Ss were then allowed 5 min. to recall as many words as they could. Very few Ss recalled any words during the fourth and fifth minutes of the recall period.

Results and Discussion

Four different variables were analyzed:

1. Mean recall. This was the mean for each group of the total number of words recalled by each S, excluding the four filler words.

2. Percentage of clustering per opportunity. A cluster consisted of the recall of an associated pair together in either a forward or a backward order. Recall of one member of the pair constituted an "opportunity" for clustering to occur. If the other member of the pair immediately followed, the pair was scored as a cluster for that opportunity. If one member of the pair occurred alone, it was scored as an "opportunity," but not as a cluster. If the other member of the pair occurred later in recall, it was not scored as an opportunity for clustering. The score reported for each group was then the mean percentage of clustering per opportunity.

3. Mean categories. This and the following measure are the same as those used by Cohen (1966). A category was simply an opportunity for clustering. When a member of a pair occurred in recall, it was scored as one category, whether or not it was followed by its associate. If one member of a pair occurred alone in recall and was scored as a category, the later recall of the other member of the pair was not scored as a category. The value reported for each group was the mean of the number of such categories recalled by each S in the group.

TABLE 1

MEANS AND STANDARD DEVIATIONS FOR ALL VARIABLES FOR EXP. I

Variable	Group						
	Incidental			Incidental + Recall			Recall
	Pleasant–Unpleasant (1)	E (2)	Number of letters (3)	Pleasant–Unpleasant (4)	E (5)	Number of letters (6)	Control (7)
Mean recall	16.3	9.4	9.9	16.6	10.4	12.4	16.1
SD	3.1	3.5	3.5	3.1	4.0	3.9	3.9
Percentage of clustering	67.5	26.3	30.9	71.5	41.7	40.3	63.7
SD	23.7	23.8	22.8	21.8	27.1	27.8	28.4
Mean categories	8.9	6.3	6.5	9.0	6.2	7.6	9.1
SD	1.5	1.6	1.6	1.5	1.9	1.9	1.9
Mean IPC	1.8	1.5	1.5	1.9	1.6	1.6	1.8
SD	.2	.3	.3	.1	.4	.2	.2
N	43	32	39	29	38	39	37

4. Mean items per category (IPC). This was simply the mean items per category for Ss in each group. This measure was the total recall for each S divided by the number of categories that he recalled. This measure differed from the clustering measure in that words did not have to occur together, i.e., clustered, to be counted as members of the same category.

Results for the first experiment are reported in Table 1. The means and standard deviations for each of the four variables are given for each group, as well as the number of Ss. In the table the groups are numbered from one to seven to facilitate the statistical analysis.

One-way analysis of variance indicated statistical significance for each of the four variables across the seven groups. All F values far exceed the .001 level of significance.

Mean recall.—Contrasts on individual cell means yielded consistent results across the four variables. Consider first the mean recall variable within the incidental condition. Group 1 (pleasant–unpleasant task) was significantly different from Groups 2 (Es) and 3 (number of letters), $F (1, 250) = 67.778$, $p < .01$; $F (1, 250) = 65.069$, $p < .01$. Groups 2 and 3 did not differ significantly from each other. Group 1 did not differ significantly from the recall-only group (Group 7). Both Groups 2 and 3 were significantly different from Group 7, $F (1, 250) = 59.718$, $p < .01$; $F (1, 250) = 56.151$, $p < .01$.

Results were almost identical for the mean recall within the incidental + recall condition. Group 4 (pleasant–unpleasant) differed significantly from Groups 5 (Es) and 6 (number of letters), $F (1, 250) = 50.241$, $p < .01$; $F (1, 250) = 23.064$, $p < .01$. Within this condition, Group 5 recalled fewer words than did Group 6, $F (1, 250) = 5.223$, $p < .05$. Group 4 did not differ from the recall-only group (Group 7). Groups 5 and 6 were both significantly different from Group 7, $F (1, 250) = 44.253$, $p < .01$; $F (1, 250) = 20 196$, $p < .01$.

Analyzing differences within tasks across the intentionality conditions, only the number-of-letters task showed a significant difference, $F (1, 250) = 9.176$, $p < .05$, indicating that recall prewarning had a positive effect. Differences between Groups 1 and 4 and between 2 and 5 were not significant.

Clustering.—Results for the second variable, percentage of clustering, were almost identical to those reported for the first variable, mean recall. Within the incidental subdivision the results were exactly the same as for the first variable. All significant F values far exceeded the .01 level of significance. Within the incidental + recall subdivision there was a return to the general regularity; Groups 5 and 6 were not significantly different as they had been with mean recall. In analyzing differences within tasks across the intentionality condition, results were also slightly different from the first variable. Groups 3 and 6 (number of letters) were not significantly different as they had been with mean recall. Instead, Groups 2 and 5 (Es) were significantly different, F (1, 250) = 6.472, p < .05. In all other respects the results were the same as for mean recall. All significant F values far exceeded the .01 level of significance.

Categories.—The results for the third variable, mean categories, followed the same pattern as the results from the first two variables. Within the incidental condition the results were identical to those found with the first two variables. The pleasant–unpleasant task yielded as many categories as the recall-only group, while the other two tasks resulted in fewer categories recalled. Within the incidental + recall condition Groups 5 and 6 were significantly different (as they had been on mean recall), F (1, 250) = 14.006, p < .01. No differences were found within tasks across the intentionality condition, i.e., Group 1 vs. 4 (pleasantness), 2 vs. 5 (Es), and 3 vs. 6 (number of letters) were not significantly different. In all other respects the results were the same as with the first two variables. All F values far exceeded the .01 level of significance.

Items per category.—The results for mean IPC followed the general pattern. Within the incidental condition, results were identical with those for the other three variables. The Ss in the pleasant–unpleasant group recalled more items per category than did Ss performing the other two tasks. Within the incidental + recall condition, results mirrored those found for the second variable (clustering), i.e., Groups 5 and 6 were not significantly different. As with the third variable, there were no differences within tasks across the intentionality conditions. In all other respects the results were exactly the same as for the other three variables. All F values far exceeded the .01 level of significance, except a comparison between Groups 4 and 5 which yielded an F (1, 250) = 6.750, p < .05.

Interpretation.—The results for the four variables showed a consistent pattern for the experiment. For all of the variables considered, the pleasant–unpleasant task was not appreciably different from the recall-only

group, within either the incidental or the incidental + recall condition. The E task and the number-of-letters task were never different from each other in the incidental condition, but were different from each other within the incidental + recall condition for mean recall and mean categories. In all cases the E task and the number-of-letters task differed from both the recall-only group and the pleasant–unpleasant group. In most comparisons the tasks themselves did not have different effects on the groups in the incidental and the incidental + recall conditions. For mean recall, the number-of-letters task showed a small but significant difference, and for the percentage-of-clustering variable the E task showed a small but significant difference. For the last two variables, mean categories and mean IPC, none of the tasks showed a difference across these conditions.

Alternative analysis.—One possible explanation for the differences in organization and recall produced by the different tasks that immediately presented itself was that the two tasks, E and number of letters, that lowered organization were leading Ss into some type of counterorganization during recall. To evaluate this hypothesis, the E condition was taken as a test. The recall characteristics of words containing the letter E were analyzed for the first experiment (see Table 2). Three measures were employed for this analysis: (*a*) recall of words containing an E; (*b*) mean recall of words containing an E as a percentage of total recall; and (*c*) percentage of clustering of words containing an E.

Results of these three variables are presented in Table 2. One-way analysis of variance on the first variable, recall of Es, yielded an F (6, 250) = 13.148, p < .01. Results indicated that the recall of Es mirrored exactly the mean total recall for each group. In all cases where the mean recall was significantly different between groups, so was the mean recall of words with an E. All differences exceeded the .01 level of significance.

When the recall of words containing an E was corrected for total recall, a much different pattern emerged. Groups 2 and 5 that

TABLE 2

MEANS AND STANDARD DEVIATIONS OF THE ANALYSIS OF THE WORDS
CONTAINING THE LETTER E FOR EXP. I

Variable	Group						
	Incidental			Incidental + Recall			Recall
	Pleasant–Unpleasant (1)	E (2)	Number of letters (3)	Pleasant–Unpleasant (4)	E (5)	Number of letters (6)	Control (7)
Mean recall	5.4	3.8	3.4	6.1	3.8	4.2	5.4
SD	1.7	1.4	1.8	1.4	1.7	1.8	1.9
Percentage of mean recall/total recall	32.7	42.2	33.5	36.1	39.1	33.5	32.9
SD	7.9	18.0	11.0	7.3	15.3	8.0	9.7
Percentage of clustering	50.9	40.4	41.3	53.6	45.5	42.8	44.8
SD	28.9	34.0	38.6	18.8	31.4	32.2	23.2
N	43	32	39	29	38	38	37

performed the task of looking for Es now showed much higher recall of the words with E. One-way analysis of variance on the second variable, mean recall of words with E expressed as a percentage of total recall, yielded an F (6, 250) = 3.596, $p < .01$. Within the incidental condition, Group 2 (Es) was significantly greater than Groups 1, 3, and 7, F (1, 250) = 11.231, $p < .01$; F (1, 250) = 10.138, $p < .01$; F (1, 250) = 12.454, $p < .01$. Within the incidental + recall condition, Group 5 (Es) was significantly greater than Groups 6 and 7, F (1, 250) = 4.623, $p < .05$; F (1, 250) = 5.025, $p < .05$. Group 5 did not, however, differ significantly from Group 4.

Analysis of the third variable, percentage of clustering of words containing an E, yielded statistically unreliable results. The rather high percentage of clustering found in all groups (see Table 2) can be explained as being due to the fact that half of the words containing an E occurred in words that were primary associates.

Groups that looked for Es showed higher proportional recall of words with an E. In the organizational measure, however, there were no differences. The Ss who performed the task of looking for Es did not show a significantly greater tendency to organize their recall around this dimension.

EXPERIMENT II

In the second experiment, Ss were given a much longer time interval per word during stimulus input. The words were read at a rate of one word per 4 sec. rather than at one per 2 sec. as in the first experiment. This was the rate of presentation used by Postman et al. (1956) and was the major difference, other than the type of task, between our pilot work and Postman's experiment. This condition was run as both a systematic replication of the first experiment, and, also, as an attempt to clear up differences in results found between the pilot work and Postman's experiment.

The number-of-letters task was dropped from the study at this point. This made a total of five groups in all. The control group was similar in all respects to the control group in the first experiment, except that the words were read at a slower rate. The four remaining groups were made up of the two remaining incidental tasks, the pleasant–unpleasant task, and the task in which Ss looked for letters. These were again subdivided into two subgroups across the intentionality condition. The task in which Ss looked for letters was changed slightly to fill up the longer time interval; instead of checking the response sheet for the presence of the letter E, Ss now looked for either Es or Gs and made a check if either or both of these letters were present in the word.

Instructions for all groups were changed slightly to accommodate the new conditions,

TABLE 3

MEANS AND STANDARD DEVIATIONS FOT ALL VARIABLES FOR EXP. II

Variable	Group				
	Incidental		Incidental + Recall		Recall
	Pleasant–Unpleasant (8)	E-G (9)	Pleasant-Unpleasant (10)	E-G (11)	Control (12)
Mean recall	17.0	8.9	18.2	11.5	16.6
SD	3.7	2.8	2.4	3.7	3.5
Percentage of clustering	78.8	17.3	68.7	38.0	67.4
SD	22.4	18.1	20.8	28.8	28.0
Mean categories	9.1	6.4	9.7	6.9	9.8
SD	1.2	1.8	1.1	1.7	1.9
Mean IPC	1.7	1.4	1.9	1.6	1.8
SD	.3	.3	.1	.3	.2
N	34	33	29	32	33

and Ss were told that they would have plenty of time for the task.

Results and Discussion

Results for the second experiment are reported in Table 3. The results are almost identical to those in the first experiment. One-way analysis of variance showed highly significant results with all four of the variables. All F values far exceeded the .001 level of significance.

Comparisons of individual means yielded results that were consistent across the four variables and also consistent with the results for Exp. I.

Mean recall.—Within the incidental condition, Group 9 (E-G) was significantly different from both Groups 8 (pleasant–unpleasant) and 12 (recall only). Group 8 did not differ significantly from Group 12. Within the incidental + recall condition, the same pattern of differences emerged: Group 11 (E-G) was significantly different from Groups 10 (pleasant–unpleasant) and 12 (recall only), while Group 10 did not differ from Group 12. Within tasks across the intentionality conditions, the E-G task showed a significant difference, but Groups 8 and 10 (pleasant–unpleasant) were not significantly different. All significant F values were beyond the .01 level of significance.

Percentage of clustering.—Exactly the same pattern of results obtained for the second variable, percentage of clustering. All significant F values far exceeded the .01 level of significance.

Mean categories.—Results for the third variable, mean categories, were identical with the earlier findings except that the E-G task showed no difference across the intentionality conditions; i.e., the Group 9 vs. 11 comparison was not statistically significant. All significant F values far exceeded the .01 level of significance.

Mean IPC.—Results for the last variable, mean IPC, were the same in all respects as those for the first two variables. All significant F values far exceeded the .01 level of significance. It is again clear that the pattern is consistent for all four variables and the overall pattern is the same as for the first experiment.

EXPERIMENT III

In the third experiment, the conditions were the same as in the first experiment except that the word list was read twice to Ss at a rate of one word per 2 sec. The first randomization of the list was the same as in the first two experiments; the second time through the list a second randomization was used. Treatments were arranged as in the second experiment. Instructions were the same as those in the first experiment except that Ss were told that many of the words would be read more than once. Response sheets included spaces to respond to 52

TABLE 4

MEANS AND STANDARD DEVIATIONS FOR ALL VARIABLES FOR EXP. III

Variable	Group				
	Incidental		Incidental + Recall		Recall
	Pleasant–Unpleasant (13)	E (14)	Pleasant–Unpleasant (15)	E (16)	Control (17)
Mean recall	18.7	13.1	18.5	13.3	17.9
SD	2.2	2.7	3.0	4.8	2.5
Percentage of clustering	74.4	35.3	74.1	39.4	72.9
SD	17.9	23.1	19.0	25.3	24.9
Mean categories	10.0	7.9	10.0	8.0	9.6
SD	1.0	1.2	1.3	2.2	1.3
Mean IPC	1.9	1.7	1.9	1.6	1.9
SD	.1	.3	.2	.2	.2
N	30	33	34	27	40

words, rather than 28 as in the first two experiments.

The third experiment was primarily a systematic replication of the first two experiments, across a different intraexperimental variable (repetition) known to have an effect on clustering in recall.

Results and Discussion

Results for the third experiment, reported in Table 4, mirror those of the first two experiments. All consistent findings of the earlier experiments were significant far beyond the .001 level.

Mean recall.—Results for the mean recall variable confirmed the earlier major findings. Group 14 (E) was significantly different from Groups 13 (pleasant–unpleasant) and 17 (recall only). Groups 13 and 17 did not differ significantly. Within the incidental + recall condition, the same pattern of results occurred; Group 16 (E) was significantly different from Groups 15 (pleasant–unpleasant) and 17 (recall only), while Group 15 did not differ significantly from Group 17. Differences within the tasks across the intentionality variable were not statistically significant.

Other variables.—The results for the other three variables were identical in all respects to those for mean recall. All significant F values far exceeded the .01 level of significance.

GENERAL DISCUSSION

The major finding from these three experiments is that the tasks performed by Ss while they listen to verbal stimuli greatly effect both amount of free recall and the apparent organization of the material recalled. Two of the tasks studied here, having Ss look for the letter E in the words and having Ss estimate the number of letters in the words, greatly reduced mean recall and the organization in recall as measured by percentage of clustering. The other task, rating words as pleasant or unpleasant, reduced neither recall nor organization in recall as compared to the recall-only group. Rather surprisingly, this result was obtained for both the incidental and the incidental + recall conditions. Furthermore, the effects attributable to the nature of the task were very large and reliable. For example, the differences in percentage of clustering between the pleasant–unpleasant and the E group within the incidental condition were 40% or greater.

The E and the number-of-letters task sometimes showed higher recall and higher percentage of clustering in the incidental + recall condition than they did in the incidental condition. These differences were small, however, and often failed to reach statistical significance.

One possible explanation for the differences in organization and recall produced by the different tasks is that the two tasks, E and number of letters, somehow led to some type of "counterorganization," which was inefficient. To check this hypothesis, the occurrences in recall of words containing the letter E were analyzed. It was found that Ss showed no tendency to organize their recall around those words containing an E, so it appears that we must look elsewhere for an explanation of these differences.

What can be said about the differences in the tasks which produced such widely different results in organization in recall? Before a definitive division can be made between tasks that produce decrements in recall organization and tasks that do not, more research on many different types of tasks is needed. Current findings suggest to us that when S is performing some task where he is using the word as a semantic unit, organization in recall and, consequently, recall itself are not adversely affected. In the present experiments the pleasant–unpleasant task is of this type. The task used in the Postman et al. (1956) experiment where Ss rated the words as to their frequency of usage in the English language appears also to be of this type.

What about the other "type" of task? In the other two tasks, the present Ss appear to use words as objects or collections of letters rather than as units of meaning. This type of task seemed to lower the organization in recall consistently to a very great degree.

What do these results have to say with regard to the several mechanisms suggested to account for organization in recall? It seems that no matter how we characterize the differences between the tasks (the way S uses the word, amount of attention required of S, etc.) that produce differences in organization in recall, we are led to the same locus of the effect— the nature of the stored trace.

The first mechanism discussed was the notion that the organization in free recall is a primarily mediational phenomenon taking place during recall itself. The results of the present experiments do not lend support to such a postulation. During recall all the groups in the study were under essentially the same conditions. It is hard to explain, therefore, why all the groups did not show the same degree of organization in recall. This suggests, rather, that the groups were somehow unequal with respect to organization before the recall process began.

Cohen (1966) and Slamecka (1968) emphasize the input stage, suggesting that S is acquiring both the individual words and also some representation of the general structure of the list (Slamecka) or codes corresponding to the categories (Cohen). This seems more plausible since it deals with the locus of the present experimental manipulations, but still fails to be very persuasive as an explanatory device. The most damaging part of the present results to such an interpretation is the lack of any consistent difference in organization within the

same tasks across the intentionality variable. The differences within the tasks across the incidental and incidental + recall conditions were small and more often than not failed to show statistical significance. The incidental + recall condition produced decrements in organization nearly equal to the incidental condition for the two tasks that interfered with organization. If the organization in recall is due to some encoding of a general representation of the list structure, the group that knew they were going to have to recall the words ought to have superior organization in recall. Even if such a process is covert and more or less automatic, any instructions that the words are to be recalled should produce a set in Ss conducive to the operation of such a mechanism. (Incidentally, questioning of the 244 Ss in the seven incidental groups after the experiment showed only 10 Ss suspected that they might be required to recall the words.) The failure to find a difference associated with intention does not encourage us to believe we have a simple input variable.

The final suggestion as to a mechanism is that of Tulving (1962, 1966), who suggested that it is the traces of the words themselves that are stored together in some fashion that serves to facilitate organization in recall. The present work, like Tulving's, seems to fit with some type of storage suggestion more easily than with any other type of suggestion. The large differences between tasks, as well as the lack of differences along the intentionality condition, seems to suggest that differences in organization found in recall reflect differences in the way traces of individual items are arranged in storage. It is tentatively suggested that when words are used as units of meaning (the pleasant–unpleasant task, and the Postman et al., 1956, frequency estimation task), the semantic components of the words are activated. If the associates are strongly related semantically (and we know they are), this assures that common structures are activated in the task. Thus on the search for recall, the items to be recalled are found together. On the other hand, when words are used by Ss as a collection of symbols devoid of meaning (at least as far as the task is concerned), the common structures are not activated and the recall is unorganized. The effect may be further augmented by some general superiority of semantic activity in processing materials for later recall.

REFERENCES

COFER, C. N.   Some factors in the organizational characteristics of free recall.   *American Psychologist*, 1965, **20**, 261-272.

COHEN, B. H.   Some-or-none characteristics of coding behavior.   *Journal of Verbal Learning and Verbal Behavior*, 1966, **5**, 182-187.

DEESE, J.   Influence of inter-item associative strength upon immediate free recall.   *Psychological Reports*, 1959, **5**, 305-312.

JENKINS, J. J., MINK, W. D., & RUSSELL, W. A.   Associative clustering as a function of verbal association strength.   *Psychological Reports*, 1958, **4**, 127-136.

JENKINS, J. J., & RUSSELL, W. A.   Associative clustering during recall.   *Journal of Abnormal and Social Psychology*, 1952, **47**, 818-821.

MANDLER, G.   Organization and memory.   In K. W. Spence & J. T. Spence (Eds.), *The psychology of learning and motivation.* Vol. 1.   New York: Academic Press, 1967.

MELTON, A. W.   Implications of short-term memory for a general theory of memory.   *Journal of Verbal Learning and Verbal Behavior*, 1963, **2**, 1-21.

POSTMAN, L., ADAMS, P. A., & BOHM, A. M.   Studies in incidental learning: V.   Recall for order and associative clustering.   *Journal of Experimental Psychology*, 1956, **51**, 334-342.

RUSSELL, W. A., & JENKINS, J. J.   *The complete Minnesota norms for responses to 100 words from the Kent-Rosanoff Word Association Test.*   (Tech. Rep. No. 11, Contract N8-ONR-66216) Washington, D. C.: United States Government Printing Office, 1954.

SLAMECKA, N. J.   An examination of trace storage in free recall.   *Journal of Experimental Psychology*, 1968, **76**, 504-513.

TULVING, E.   Subjective organization in free recall of "unrelated" words.   *Psychological Review*, 1962, **69**, 344-354.

TULVING, E.   Intratrial and intertrial retention: Notes towards a theory of free recall in verbal learning.   *Psychological Review*, 1964, **71**, 219-237.

TULVING, E.   Subjective organization and effects of repetition in multitrial free recall learning.   *Journal of Verbal Learning and Verbal Behavior*, 1966, **5**, 193-197.

TULVING, E.   Free recall.   In T. R. Dixon & D. L. Horton (Eds.), *Verbal behavior and general behavior theory.*   New Jersey: Prentice-Hall, 1968.

E. Tulving and S. Osler

Effectiveness of retrieval cues in memory for words

Reprinted from the *Journal of Experimental Psychology* (1968) **77**(4):593-601

*S*s had to memorize lists of 24 to-be-remembered (TBR) words. The TBR words were exposed for study on a single input trial, in presence or absence of cue words—weak associates of the TBR words. Recall of TBR words was tested in presence or absence of these cue words. The findings showed that (*a*) cue words (retrieval cues) facilitated recall of TBR words when they were present both at input and output, (*b*) retrieval cues did not enhance recall of TBR words when they were present only at output, and (*c*) 2 retrieval cues presented simultaneously with each TBR word were no more effective in facilitating recall than single cues. The main conclusion was that specific retrieval cues facilitate recall if and only if the information about them and about their relation to the TBR words is stored at the same time as the information about the membership of the TBR words in a given list.

When a person studies a list of to-be-remembered (TBR) words with the intention of recalling them at a later time, appropriate mnemonic information is stored in his memory. This stored information is used at the time of attempted recall to reproduce the original input. The success of recall, broadly speaking, depends on two factors: the amount and organization of the relevant information about the TBR words in the store at the time of attempted recall (availability of information), and the nature and number of retrieval cues which provide access to the stored information (accessibility of information; Mandler, 1967; Tulving & Pearlstone, 1966). The distinction between these two factors can be demonstrated under conditions

where different groups of *S*s are treated identically (given identical instructions, presented with identical material, asked to engage in identical activity interpolated between input and output, etc.) up to the beginning of the recall period, and then provided with different kinds of retrieval cues. The availability of relevant information is equal for different groups under these conditions and consequently any variation in recall must be attributed to differences in accessibility of this information.

An earlier experiment in the present series (Tulving & Pearlstone, 1966) provided an experimental demonstration of the distinction between availability and accessibility. The *S*s were presented with lists of TBR words which they had to memorize. At input the TBR words were accompanied by the names of conceptual categories of which the words were members. When these category names were given to Ss at output as retrieval cues, Ss recalled more words than when no experimentally manipulated retrieval cues were present at output. This finding demonstrates that retrieval depends upon the completeness of reinstatement, at the time of output, of the stimulating conditions present at the time of input (Melton, 1963), but it does not provide much insight into the underlying mechanisms.

The experiment reported in this paper was designed to provide some empirical evidence relevant to speculations about the nature of these mechanisms. This evidence takes the form of answers to four specific questions. First, is it possible for cue words that are only weakly associated with the TBR words to facilitate recall of TBR words? In the Tulving and Pearlstone (1966) experiment, the average frequency of occurrence of TBR words, as responses, to category names as stimuli, according to the Connecticut Restricted Word Association norms (Cohen, Bousfield, & Whitmarsh, 1957) was 6.5%, and in every case the connection between the category name and the TBR word was quite obvious. What would happen if the strength of the associative connection is weaker and less obvious?

Second, given that a retrieval cue is effective if it is present both at input and at output, is it equally effective if it is provided to S only at the time of attempted recall of the TBR word? It is conceivable that a preexperimental associative bond between the cue and the TBR word is sufficient to make the retrieval cue effective. On the other

hand, it may be necessary that information about the relation of the retrieval cue to the TBR word be specifically stored at the time of the input of the TBR word.

The third question is related to the second: If a TBR word is paired with a certain cue at input and its recall then tested in presence of a different but preexperimentally equivalent cue, would such a changed cue also be as effective as the original cue? To the extent that the effectiveness of a retrieval cue depends on the existence of a preexperimental associative bond between the cue and the TBR word, the changed cue would still be expected to facilitate recall. If, on the other hand, information about the relation of the cue to the TBR word has to be stored at the same time as information about the TBR word, the changed cue would not be expected to be effective.

The fourth and final question has to do with the effectiveness of double cues. Given A and B as two different but associatively equivalent cues for a given TBR word, would the presentation of both A and B at input as well as at output produce greater facilitation of retrieval of the TBR word than each of them separately? Some data from an experiment on tachistoscopic identification of words—selection of words from the long-term store—would lead one to expect that double cues are more effective than single cues (Tulving, Mandler, & Baumal, 1964). It is also conceivable, however, that even though E presents two words as both input cues and retrieval cues for a given TBR word, S may treat the two words as a single unit, comparable to a single-word cue, and no greater facilitation of recall would occur.

METHOD

Design.—Lists of 24 TBR words were presented to *S*s for study and subsequent recall on a single trial. Four input conditions were combined factorially with five output conditions, except that one input condition was associated with only four output conditions. The input conditions were: (*a*) the TBR words were presented alone (Input Cond. 0), (*b*) each TBR word was accompanied by Cue A (Input Cond. A), (*c*) each TBR word was accompanied by Cue B (Input Cond. B), and (*d*) each TBR word was accompanied by both Cues A and B (Input Cond. AB). The output conditions were: (*a*) noncued recall of TBR words (Output Cond. 0), (*b*) recall of TBR words in presence of Cues A (Output Cond. A), (*c*) recall of TBR words in presence of Cues B (Output Cond. B), (*d*) recall of TBR words in presence of both Cues A and B (Output Cond. AB), and (*e*) free recall of TBR words *and* of all cues shown at the time of input (Output Cond. WC). The Output Cond. WC was not used in conjunction with Input Cond. 0, since in the latter condition no cues had been presented. Thus there was a total of 19 experimental treatment combinations. Each combination can be designated in terms of its input and output conditions. Thus, for instance, Cond. 0—0 was a standard free recall condition—TBR words shown alone and tested in absence of any cues; in Cond. B-AB each TBR word was presented in presence of Cue B and tested for recall in presence of both Cues A and B; in Cond. AB-WC each TBR word was presented in presence of both Cues A and B and *S* had to recall TBR words and both Cues A and B in absence of any experimentally provided aids to retrieval, etc.

Independent groups of *S*s were used in each of the 19 treatment combinations. The design is reflected in the organization of the data in Table 1.

Materials.—Two equivalent lists of TBR words (I and II) were used to provide for sampling of materials. Each list consisted of 24 words selected from among the stimulus words in the Minnesota Free Association Norms (Russell & Jenkins, 1954). For each TBR word two other words were selected to serve as cues. These were low-frequency responses from the associative hierarchy of each TBR word. Each cue

had been given as a response to the stimulus words in the Minnesota norms by fewer than 1% of *S*s. Of the two cues thus selected for each TBR word, one was arbitrarily labelled as Cue A and the other as Cue B. The two sets of cues, A and B, for each list were thus approximately equally related to the TBR words. Some examples of A and B cues and TBR words are: fat, LEG—MUTTON; village, DIRTY—CITY; dark, GIRL—SHORT; body, VIGOR—HEALTH; empty, HURT—STOMACH; emblem, SOAR—EAGLE.

Independently of the present experiment, free association data were collected for cue words of this experiment as stimuli. The *S*s were 278 high school students in the same school system in Metropolitan Toronto where the present experiment was carried out. One-third of these *S*s were presented with 48 A cues, another third with 48 B cues, and the remaining one-third with each pair of corresponding A and B cues presented simultaneously (double cues). The *S*s were instructed to write down for each single or double stimulus word some other word that the stimulus word or words made them think of. The observed proportions of responses corresponding to the TBR words used in this experiment (the total number of TBR words given to their respective cues, divided by the product of number of words and number of *S*s) were as follows: A cues—.011, B cues —.015, and double cues—.025.

The Ss' assignment to experimental conditions.—The Ss were 674 boys and girls from 23 eighth grade classes in 10 different elementary schools in the Metropolitan Toronto area. (Original design called for testing of *S*s in 24 classes, but *S*s were lost in 1 class because of apparatus failure) They were tested in intact groups in their own classrooms, classes varying in size from 22 to 36. Each of the four input conditions was administered to 6 classes, each in a different school. Three classes in each input condition were tested with List I, and 3 with List II. (Because of the apparatus failure, Input Cond. 0 was given to only 2 classes with List I). In each class, *S*s were assigned to the five output conditions (four in the case of Input Cond. 0) on the basis of a random distribution of five (four) kinds of recall booklets to the seats in the classroom. Thus, each of the 19 experimental groups, corresponding to the 19 treatment combinations, consisted of *S*s from 6 different classes, each in a different school. The sizes of the 19 experimental groups varied 32–39, with a median size of 36.

Procedure.—Upon entering each classroom recall booklets were first distributed. These booklets contained pages for *S*s' recording of their recall, different sections of booklets being of different colors and separated by blank pages. The *E* then gave some general information to *S*s about the study of memory conducted by the psychology department of the University of Toronto and about the nature of the task, explaining how the material to be "learned" was to be presented, how *S*s were to write their recall at the proper time in their recall booklets, and how they were to work independently. A practice list, consisting of 24 adjectives as used by Tulving and Pearlstone (1966) was then administered. Words were projected on the screen by means of a film-strip projector, at the rate of 2 sec/word, and *S*s were allowed 3 min. to record their recall in the booklets. The *S*s were then asked to turn to the next (blank) page in the recall booklet and were given *study instructions* with respect to the "second part of the experiment," memorization of the experimental list proper.

Study instructions varied according to input conditions. The *S*s were told that they had to study and try to remember words projected in capital letters on the screen. In Input Cond. A, B, and AB, they were told that each of the capitalized words was to be accompanied by another word which was "somehow related to the capitalized word. . . ." (two other words in Cond. AB) typed in smaller case letters above the capitalized word. They were told that although their memory was going to be tested only for words typed in capital letters (TBR words) they should also pay attention to the words typed in lower case letters (cue words), because these "may help you to remember the capitalized words later on." They were also told to try "to see how each word and its accompanying cue (cues) are related."

The list was projected on the screen in front of the classroom, at the rate of 5 sec/frame in all input conditions. Each frame contained one TBR word in capital letters, and, in Input Cond. A, B, and AB, one or two cue words in lower case letters above the TBR word. After all 24 frames had been shown, *S*s were asked to turn to the next page in their recall booklet, read the

recall instructions on the top of the page, and then to record their recall. Recall instructions in the booklets varied according to the output condition to which *S* had been assigned. The first sentence in all instructions was, "Now write down all the capitalized WORDS you remember," and the final sentence was, "The important thing is to get as many WORDS correct as possible." Some examples of the rest of the instructions follow:

Condition 0—0: "write them down in any order you like. . . ."

Conditions 0—A and 0—B: "the words you see written on this and on the following sheet may help you to remember the WORDS since each of them is related to one of the capitalized WORDS. If you can, put each of the WORDS you remember opposite the word to which it is related. If you find this too difficult, however, put down the WORDS you remember anyhow, anywhere on this sheet or on the following sheet. . . ."

Conditions A-A and B-B: "the cue words you saw are given on this sheet and on the following sheet. If you can, write down each WORD on the line opposite the cue word. If you remember a WORD but you do not remember which cue word it went with, put it down anyhow, anywhere on this sheet or the following sheet. . . ."

Conditions A-B and B-A: "each of the words you see on this sheet and on the following sheet is related to one of the capitalized WORDS in more or less the same way as the cue words which appeared on the slides together with the WORDS you had to remember. If you can, put each of the WORDS you remember opposite the word to which it is related. If you find this too difficult, however, put down the WORDS you remember anyhow, anywhere on this sheet or the following sheet. . . ."

Conditions A-WC and B-WC: "write them down in any order you like in the blank spaces on the right hand side of this sheet and the following sheet. If you can, you should also write down as many of the cue words as you remember. Write the cue words in the blank spaces on the left side of this sheet and the following sheet. If you can, write each capitalized WORD on the line opposite the cue word that went with it. But if you do not remember the connection between a WORD and its cue word, write both of them anyhow, anywhere on this sheet or on the following sheet. . . ."

The 24 words in each of two lists were shown in the same constant order to all Ss. In Output Cond. 0, the recall sheets in the booklet consisted of 24 consecutively numbered lines on two successive pages. In Output Cond. WC, there were two columns of 24 numbered lines, the left one for cue (cues) and the right one for TBR words. In Output Cond. A, B, and AB, the cues were shown in the same order in which their corresponding words had appeared in the input list.

In each group, 6 min. were allowed for recall. Recall booklets were then collected and Ss permitted to ask questions they had about the experiment, problems of memory, or psychology. Finally, Ss were asked not to discuss the experiment with other students at the school until the next day and reasons for this request were given.

RESULTS

The mean number of words correctly recalled from the practice list of 24 adjectives was 6.19 for all 674 Ss. The same list administered under comparable conditions to 948 high school Ss in the Tulving and Pearlstone (1966) study had yielded a mean recall score of 9.48. This difference indicates that the authors are here dealing with a different population of Ss and that therefore no direct comparisons of the main data between the two experiments would be very useful. The mean scores on the practice list for different experimental groups varied from 5.74 to 6.69.

The primary data are provided by the mean number of TBR words correctly recalled. "Lenient" scoring was used throughout. The S was given credit for recall of a TBR word regardless of whether or not the word was paired with its appropriate cue.

The data on correct recall of TBR words were pooled over Lists I and II and are summarized in Table 1. Table 1 shows the number of Ss in each experimental group (n), the mean number of TBR words recalled (M), and the standard deviation of the distribution of the correct recall scores (SD). The last column in Table 1, Output Cond. WC, also shows the mean number of cue words correctly recalled. Thus, for instance, the entry 8.45 + 5.88 in the cell corresponding to Cond. A-WC means that the mean number of TBR words recalled was 8.45 and the mean number of cues recalled was 5.88. The figure for the standard deviation, however, applies only to the distribution of TBR word scores.

Table 1 contains all the data needed to answer the four questions posed in the introduction. First, is it possible for cue words that are only weakly associated with the TBR words to facilitate recall of TBR words? The answer to the question is affirmative. When single cues were present at

TABLE 1

NUMBER OF Ss-(n), MEAN NUMBER OF WORDS RECALLED-(M), AND STANDARD DEVIATION-(SD) FOR EACH EXPERIMENTAL CONDITION

Input Condition	Output Condition				
	0	A	B	AB	WC
0					
n	37	38	39	37	
M	10.62	8.39	8.64	8.43	
SD	(2.79)	(2.97)	(2.43)	(2.68)	
A					
n	37	36	36	36	33
M	9.00	14.94	6.94	14.81	8.45 +5.88
SD	(2.96)	(3.50)	(2.68)	(3.72)	(2.87)
B					
n	36	37	35	37	35
M	8.44	7.95	14.91	14.84	8.86 +6.63
SD	(2.94)	(3.23)	(4.14)	(4.76)	(2.72)
AB					
n	32	34	34	33	32
M	9.06	11.24	11.79	14.33	8.31 +5.91
SD	(4.08)	(3.69)	(3.86)	(4.05)	(3.15)

Note.—For explanation of entries in column WC, see the text.

input, cued recall (Cond. A-A and B-B) was approximately 70% higher than noncued recall (Cond. A-0 and B-0). With the data pooled over Input Cond. A and B, the two means are 14.93 and 8.73, respectively.

Second, does an otherwise effective retrieval cue still facilitate recall if it is provided to S only at the time of output? This question receives a negative answer. When single or double cues were present at output, but not at input (Cond. 0-A, 0-B, and 0-AB), recall was lower than in the absence of cues at both input and output (Cond. 0–0). With the data pooled over relevant conditions, the two means are 8.49 and 10.62, respectively.

Third, would a changed cue, pre-experimentally equivalent to the cue paired with the TBR word at input, be as effective as the original cue? This question is also answered negatively. Recall of TBR words in Cond. A-B and B-A was not only considerably lower than in Cond. A-A and B-B (means of 7.45 and 14.93, respectively), but also lower than in Cond. A-0, A-WC, B-0, and B-WC (pooled mean of 8.70) in which the cue present at input was simply omitted at output.

Fourth, does the presentation of two cues at input as well as at output facilitate recall of TBR words to a greater extent than do the single cues? Again the answer is negative. The mean number of TBR words recalled in Cond. AB-AB was 14.33, while in Cond. AB-0 and AB-WC it was 8.68. Thus, with input conditions held constant, recall in presence of two retrieval cues per TBR word was approximately 65% higher than in absence of these cues. The facilitation of recall by double cues thus is of the same order

of magnitude as that observed in the case of single-cue input conditions (70%).

Statistical analyses, in the form of one-way analyses of variance within each input condition and subsequent contrasts of individual means using Scheffé's method, were found to support all of the above statements at least at the .05 level of significance and will not be reported in detail. Some additional observations, however, may be of interest and will be mentioned briefly.

In Cond. A-A and B-B, e.g., over 96% of all TBR words correctly recalled were paired with their cues on recall sheets, while in Cond. 0-A and 0-B only 39% of recalled words, and in Cond. A-B and B-A 34% were so paired. The two latter figures are probably inflated because of the correspondence between input positions of words and the ordering of cues on the recall sheets. These data again demonstrate that otherwise potent retrieval cues are quite ineffective in facilitating recall if they are not presented together with tne TBR words at input.

When two cues were presented with each TBR word at input, but recall was tested in presence of only one of those cues (Cond. AB-A and AB-B), recall was lower than in presence of both cues (Cond. AB-AB). This finding is reminiscent of stimulus selection in paired associate learning (Underwood, 1963), although alternative interpretations are possible.

When TBR words were accompanied by cues at input but had to be recalled in absence of any cues, recall was approximately equal in Output Cond. 0 and WC. The mean recall of TBR words in Cond. A-0, B-0, and AB-0 was 8.83, and in Cond. A-WC, B-WC, and AB-WC it was 8.55.

Thus, the requirement that S retrieve cue words in addition to TBR words produced the same level of recall as the requirement that S select for recall only the TBR words from the total input. The lower recall of cues than of TBR words in Output Cond. WC, however, does suggest that Ss paid less attention to cues than to TBR words at input, i.e., that they believed E's instructions. Of all the cues recalled, 93% were paired with their corresponding TBR words.

Finally, the number of repetitions of TBR words was negligible (674 Ss gave a grand total of 106 repetitions), but the frequency of extralist intrusions was relatively high. In the seven noncued recall conditions the mean number of extralist intrusions per S was .58, while in the 12 cued recall conditions this average was 1.77.

Discussion

An earlier experiment in the present series (Tulving & Pearlstone, 1966) demonstrated that category names of TBR words can serve as effective retrieval cues. In that experiment category names accompanied the TBR words at input, and recall of TBR words was tested either in presence of category names (cued recall) or in absence of these cues (noncued recall). Cued recall was higher—in some cases considerably higher—than noncued recall. A part of the design of the present experiment replicated the paradigm used by Tulving and Pearlstone, namely Cond. A-A and B-B (cued recall) and A-0 and B-0 (noncued recall). The data from this part of the experiment fully corroborated the earlier findings.

Some other evidence available in the literature (Earhard, 1967a, 1967b; Tulving, 1962) indicates that initial letters of TBR words can also function as potent retrieval cues. In these experiments, the multitrial free-recall paradigm was

used, and Ss were instructed to think about the intial letters of TBR words at input and to generate the letters of the alphabet as retrieval cues on their own at output. Such "alphabetic recall" was found to be higher than free recall. In addition, several smaller experiments the authors have done at Toronto have shown that synonymic cues of TBR words (BENT—*twisted*, BRIDGE—*bond*, SOFT—*pliable*, etc.), as well as descriptions of graphemic features of TBR words (a long word—*understanding*, a word ending in *ly*—*intimately*, a word with a double consonant in the middle—*summer*, etc.), also facilitate recall if the cues are present both at input and at output. It thus appears that a wide variety of experimentally manipulable specific retrieval cues that are meaningfully related to the TBR words can provide access to stored information about the TBR words that is available but not accessible under the noncued recall conditions.

While the meaningfulness of the connection between the cue and the TBR word—the meaningfulness obviously being determined by Ss' preexperimental knowledge of the language—may be a necessary condition for the effectiveness of retrieval cues, it does not seem to be a sufficient condition. It may be necessary in that a random pairing of cues and TBR words will probably not enhance cued recall when compared with noncued recall, and it is not sufficient in that the presence of cues only at output (Cond. 0-A, 0-B, and 0-AB of the present experiment) does not facilitate recall of TBR words. The overall pattern of the data reported in this paper was completely consistent in showing that whenever the cues accompanied the TBR words at input, their presence at output facilitated recall, and whenever they were absent at input, their presence at output did not serve any useful purpose. In fact, the presence of cues only at output, or changing of cues from input to output, appeared to interfere with recall of the TBR words. This phenomenon may merit further study, but for the present purposes the important finding is the lack of recall facilitation by cues presented to Ss for the first time at the time of recall. This finding, in conjunction with the finding that the same cues were quite effective when presented at both input and output, suggests that specific retrieval cues facilitate recall if and only if the information about them and about their relation to the TBR words is stored at the same time as the information about the membership of the TBR words in a given list. The authors would like to offer this suggestion as the main conclusion of the present experiment.

At first blush, this conclusion may appear to be inconsistent with the results of experiments (e.g., Bilodeau & Blick, 1965; Fox, Blick, & Bilodeau, 1964; Lloyd, 1964) in which retrieval cues have been provided to Ss only at the time of recall and which have showed such retrieval cues to facilitate recall. The inconsistency disappears, however, if it is remembered that appropriate coding of input words may take place even if E does not explicitly suggest to S how he is to code the TBR items, that is, what additional information he has to store with the TBR item at the time of input. If the TBR word is *bulb*—to use an example given by Bilodeau and Blick (1965)—at least some Ss are quite likely to think of it as something to do with light. If "light" is then presented by E as a retrieval cue, it is effective for those Ss in the same way as it would have been if it had been presented together with *bulb* at input.

Thus, if E leaves S free to code the input subjectively, or lets S make his own differential responses to stimuli (Postman, Adams, & Phillips, 1955), the effectiveness of specific retrieval cues provided by E at output presumably depends on the extent of the overlap between the cues and such subjective coding responses that have occurred at input. Experimental manipulation of cues at the time of the presentation of TBR items simply restricts the ways in which various Ss code the input and thus provides E with greater control over what is stored, but the underlying mechanisms are probably the same in both cases. Regardless of whether S codes the TBR items subjectively or follows the suggestions for coding given by E in the form of input cues, a retrieval cue is effective only if the information about it and its relation to the TBR item is stored at the same time with the TBR items. This conclusion is quite consistent with the principle that retrieval depends upon the completeness of reinstatement of original stimuli at the time of recall (Melton, 1963).

Finally, a few words about the effectiveness of double cues. To the extent that specific retrieval cues provide access to the information about TBR items not accessible in absence of such cues, one might expect that the use of multiple retrieval cues would lead to more effective recall performance than the use of single cues. The attempt to demonstrate this relation in the present experiment, however, ended in failure. Double-word cues were found to be no more effective than single-word cues, even though each member of the double-word cue was shown to be quite effective in other parts of the experiment, and even though the double-word cue produced a somewhat higher frequency of "correct guesses" in the free-association task. It looks as if Ss in the present experiment treated the double-word cue as a single unit of information which was as potent in effecting retrieval of the TBR word as was a single-word unit. It is still conceivable, however, that double cues are more effective than single cues if the two members of the double cue are presented separately, rather than simultaneously, at input. Bevan, Dukes, and Avant (1966) have shown, in the terminology of the present paper, that non-cued recall of TBR words repeated within a list is higher for words accompanied by multiple cues than for words accompanied by single cues. The same phenomenon may well hold for cued recall as well.

REFERENCES

BEVAN, W., DUKES, W. F., & AVANT, L. L. The effect of variation in specific stimuli on memory for their superordinates. *American Journal of Psychology*, 1966, **79**, 250–257.

BILODEAU, E. A., & BLICK, K. A. Courses of misrecall over long-term retention intervals as related to strength of preexperimental habits of word association. *Psychological Reports*, 1965, **16** (Monogr. Suppl. 6).

COHEN, B. H., BOUSFIELD, W. A., & WHITMARSH, G. A. Cultural norms for verbal items in 43 categories. Technical Report No. 22, 1957, University of Connecticut, Contract Nonr-631 (00), Office of Naval Research.

EARHARD, M. Cued recall and free recall as a function of the number of items per cue. *Journal of Verbal Learning and Verbal Behavior*, 1967, **6**, 257–263. (a)

EARHARD, M. The facilitation of memorization by alphabetic instructions. *Canadian Journal of Psychology*, 1967, **21**, 15–24. (b)

FOX, P. W., BLICK, K. A., & BILODEAU, E. A. Stimulation and prediction of verbal recall and misrecall. *Journal of Experimental Psychology*, 1964, **68**, 321–322.

LLOYD, K. E. Short term retention as a function of recall point coding. *Psychological Reports*, 1964, **14**, 752–754.

MANDLER, G. Organization and memory. In K. W. Spence & J. T. Spence (Eds.), *The psychology of learning and motivation.* New York: Academic Press, 1967

MELTON, A. W. Implications of short-term memory for a general theory of memory. *Journal of Verbal Learning and Verbal Behavior*, 1963, **2**, 1–21.

POSTMAN, L., ADAMS, P. A., & PHILLIPS, W. Studies in incidental learning: II. The effects of association value and of the method of testing. *Journal of Experimental Psychology*, 1955, **49**, 1–10.

RUSSELL, W. A., & JENKINS, J. J. The complete Minnesota norms for responses to 100 words from the Kent-Rosanoff Word Association Test. Technical Report No. 11, 1954, University of Minnesota, Contract No. Nonr-66216, Office of Naval Research.

TULVING, E. The effect of alphabetical subjective organization on memorizing unrelated words. *Canadian Journal of Psychology*, 1962, **16**, 185–191.

TULVING, E., MANDLER, G., & BAUMAL, R. Interaction of two sources of information in tachistoscopic word recognition. *Canadian Journal of Psychology*, 1964, **18**, 62–71.

TULVING, E., & PEARLSTONE, Z. Availability versus accessibility of information in memory for words. *Journal of Verbal Learning and Verbal Behavior*, 1966, **5**, 381–391.

UNDERWOOD, B. J. Stimulus selection in verbal learning. In C. N. Cofer & B. S. Musgrave (Eds.), *Verbal behavior and learning: Problems and processes.* New York: McGraw-Hill, 1963.

N.J. Slamecka

An examination of trace storage in free recall

Reprinted from the *Journal of Experimental Psychology* (1968) **76**(4):504-13

A series of 6 free recall experiments was carried out to determine if traces of stored items are organized in relation to each other, or whether they are stored independently. The procedure involved providing one group with some of the list items at recall, and comparing its recall of the remainder with that of a group which had no items provided. Results strongly indicated that trace storage in these tasks was independent. A dual-component memory hypothesis was discussed in which perception of the general list structure forms the basis for a retrieval plan which then operates upon the independently stored traces.

Conceptualization of the memory sequence postulates three consecutive phases. At the theoretical level these have been designated in terms of *traces* as, trace formation, trace storage, and trace utilization or retrieval, in that order (Melton, 1963).

If the construct of trace storage is to afford maximum theoretical usefulness, then suitable analytical procedures must be developed for distinguishing between the characteristics of stored traces and the characteristics of retrieval processes. The only way to gain such information appears to be through the overt products of the retrieval phase. However, uncritical reliance upon features of recall performance as prima facie indicators of the nature of storage, risks the confounding of characteristics of storage with characteristics of retrieval. Some findings from free recall experiments illustrate this point.

It is known that free recall is not characterized by random retrieval, but rather that items are recalled in sequences showing associative clustering (Jenkins, Mink, & Russell, 1958; Jenkins & Russell, 1952), category clustering (Bousfield, 1953; Cohen, 1966), or subjective organization (Tulving, 1962b). Behind such phenomena lies the question of whether item traces are originally arranged into such cohesive groups during storage, as is sometimes suggested,[1] or whether this organization comes into being only at recall. It is conceivable, and consistent with such findings, that traces are stored independently of each other and that a systematic *retrieval* strategy is adopted

---

[1] "It is as if the list items . . . are rearranged in the storage in the course of trial-by-trial practice [Tulving, 1964, p. 234]." "This organization apparently determined the arrangement of words in the storage . . . [Tulving and Pearlstone, 1966, p. 390]."

by *S* to promote maximum recall. This alone would produce nonrandom output sequences. The view that recall is a matter of data retrieval and that certain search plans may be more effective than others has been discussed, for example, by Yntema and Trask (1963). From this viewpoint the positive correlations obtained in multitrial tasks, between amount recalled and degree of organization (Tulving, 1962b, 1964), may indicate only that systematic retrieval plans constitute relatively efficient search devices. Indeed, when *S*s are suddenly asked to order their output according to an alphabetical schema, recall rises dramatically (Tulving, 1962a). The fact that output organization increases across trials within a list, as well as between successive lists (Mayhew, 1967; Tulving, McNulty, & Ozier, 1965), may be interpreted as evidence for learning how to organize items in storage, but such facts are also consistent with an interpretation that *S* is learning to develop more efficient strategies for retrieval.

Other studies have permitted *S* to sort items into as many categories as he pleased before a recall test was given (Mandler, 1967; Mandler & Pearlstone, 1966), with the result that recall was positively correlated with the number of classificatory categories used. Yoked *S*s, constrained to a prescribed number of categories, also displayed the recall-category number correlation. Did the categorization task serve to arrange traces into similar subdivisions in storage, or did it serve to suggest a plan for subsequent retrieval? The correlation may indicate that increasing fineness of classification, up to a point, provides a better basis for effective retrieval.

Another experiment found improved performance when category names were provided as cues at recall (Tulving & Pearlstone, 1966). Were the cues effective because they mirrored the organization among traces, or because they facilitated the execution of plans for retrieval? Yet another study showed that adding to the length of an already learned list retarded the learning of the expanded list, as compared to a control group (Tulving, 1966). Was the retardation due to a necessity for reorganizing stored items when the list was expanded, or to the necessity for devising a new retrieval plan for the enlarged list? One cannot know, and it seems that neither analyses of output organization nor the other methods described are likely to provide answers to questions about storage.

How may the nature of items in storage be characterized theoretically? Several possibilities exist. Traces might be stored in total independence of each other, as discrete noninteracting units. Or they could be in touch with each other, either through associative bonds, or clustered into categorical groups, or tagged with markers that relate them to each other, or by other mnemonic devices. These possibilities are not exhaustive, but they do suggest a major line of division.

The present study analyzed trace storage in free recall tasks employing one recall trial along the lines of a dichotomy called independence vs. dependence. Storage *independence* means that traces are functionally isolated, so that the fate of one does not influence the fate of any other. Thus, if some items are made directly accessible at recall this should not change the probability of retrieving the rest. This type of assumption is found in some mathematical models of free recall (Miller & McGill, 1952; Waugh & Smith, 1962). Storage *dependence* means that traces are associated with or in contact with each other, so that the fate of one affects the status of another. In such cases, assuring the accessibility of some items at recall should increase the probability of retrieving the rest. Tulving and Pearlstone (1966, p. 390) advocate this position.

The following experiments all used the same general approach, as follows. After auditory presentation of a list the Context group opens a sheet on which is displayed a random half of the items, and is asked for a written recall of the rest in any order (items displayed on the sheet are the "context," and those which are to be recalled are the "critical" items). The Control group is given no context and is asked to recall the entire list. A comparison of Context and Control performances on the critical items provides the basis for conclusions about storage. Any recall differences must be due to the context, and not to item variations, since both groups hear the identical sequences of words and are scored on the identical critical items. It should be noted that context, as used here, refers only to display of list items, and not to any general environmental or extralist retrieval cues (Weingartner, 1964).

If dependent-trace storage is the rule, then the Context group should have superior recall. This follows from the reasonable assumption that *some* of the context words would not have ordinarily been recalled, and the ready accessibility of these should stimulate retrieval of those critical item traces with which they were in contact in storage. If independent storage is the rule, then there should be no difference in recall between the groups. This is because functionally isolated traces would be totally immune to any changes in other traces.

EXPERIMENT I

Method.—The Ss were 46 psychology students at the University of Vermont, meeting course requirements. They were tested in six groups of about eight each, assigned randomly. The materials were three lists of 30 words. The Rare list had two-syllable nouns with a Thorndike and Lorge (1944) G count of six or less. The Common list had two-syllable nouns from the T-L 1,000 most common. The Butterfly list had "butterfly" and its 29 most popular free-associates, drawn from the Russell and Jenkins (1954) norms. It can be assumed to have a high interitem associative index (Deese, 1959), in that the items would mutually arouse each other as free-associates. Each S served only in the Context or in the Control condition, and was tested once on all three lists. Counterbalancing for list sequence required three groups for each condition, a total of six.

The procedure was as follows. The Ss were told that 30 words would be read aloud twice, in a different random order each time, and that they should attempt to remember all of them. The list was read at a 2-sec. rate with an 8-sec. intertrial interval. Then, Context Ss opened a recall sheet with a random half of the words on it and were asked to write the remaining 15 in any order. Control Ss had a blank recall sheet and were asked to write all 30 words in any order. Four minutes were allowed for recall, which was ample time, since all Ss had stopped writing by then and none wished for more time.

TABLE 1

MEAN CRITICAL RECALLS AND TOTAL CONTROL RECALL FOR EACH LIST IN EXP. I

Cond.	List					
	Rare		Common		Butterfly	
	M	SD	M	SD	M	SD
Context	4.91	2.22	6.56	2.78	8.61	2.84
Control	6.39	3.00	7.78	3.31	10.00	3.50
Total Control	12.96	4.87	15.74	5.78	20.17	6.07

Note.—*N* = 23 each cell.

Results.—Table 1 shows mean critical recall and mean total Control recall. Since each total Control recall was almost exactly twice as high as its critical recall, the Context was indeed a random half of the list (this proportionality was also the case in the rest of the experiments, and will not be noted again).

Analysis of variance of conditions showed the Context group significantly *inferior* to the Control group on critical recall, F (1, 44) = 5.75, $p < .025$, and the direction of this difference was the same on every list. The effect of Lists was also significant, F (2, 88) = 41.28, $p < .001$, with recall being poorest for the Rare, better for the Common, and best for the Butterfly list. The Conditions × Lists interaction was nonsignificant, F (2, 88) < 1, showing that the effect of Conditions was not dependent upon list type. The data were then rearranged according to stage of practice and analysis indicated no influence of that variable, F (2, 88) = 1.64, $p > .10$. Virtual absence of practice gains in single-trial free recall has been reported by others (Dallett, 1963; Murdock, 1960). The Conditions × Practice interaction was nonsignificant, F (2, 88) < 1, implying that the effect of conditions was not dependent on practice level.

Since the fact that the putative "help" given the Context group was completely ineffective seemed somewhat counterintuitive, a replication across a wider range of context items was judged desirable.

EXPERIMENT II

Method.—Fifty-seven more psychology students served as Ss in six groups of about 10 each. The materials were three Rare lists, 30 words long. Rare lists were used in order to minimize possible ceiling effects. Each S was either in the Context or the

TABLE 2

MEAN PROPORTION CRITICAL RECALLS AT EACH PROPORTION OF CONTEXT IN EXP. II

Cond.	Context Proportion					
	.17		.50		.83	
	M	SD	M	SD	M	SD
Context	.38	.18	.38	.20	.36	.25
Control	.47	.18	.50	.18	.56	.30

Note.—N = 26 each Context Cell and 31 each Control Cell.

Control condition, and was tested on each list. The other variable was the number of random context words given, namely 5, 15, or 25 (or in proportions, .17, .50, and .83). Counterbalancing list sequence and context proportion took three groups for the Context conditions, and counterbalancing list sequence took three for the Control. The general procedure was the same as in Exp. I.

Results.—Table 2 shows critical recall in terms of proportions in order to provide a common framework of comparison. Analysis of variance showed the Context group again significantly inferior to the Control, F (1, 55) = 15.80, $p < .001$, consistently at every level of context. The effect of Proportions was not significant, F (2, 110) < 1 (when calculated with absolute scores it was highly significant of course, but that is uninteresting), nor the Conditions × Proportions interaction, F (2, 110) = 1.33, $p > .05$. These results support and extend the generality of the previous findings, that over a wide range of context proportion the provision of such cues does not assist recall. Since it is barely conceivable that the context presented did not, by chance, include the effective "key" items, it was decided to push the test of the amount-of-context variable to its limits by providing the maximum amount possible.

EXPERIMENT III

Method.—Forty psychology students served as Ss in four groups of 10 each. Two 30-word lists were used, one Rare and one Common. Each S was either in the Context or the Control condition, and was tested once on each list. The Context group was provided at recall with 29 of the 30 items and had only to recall the remaining one. The Controls were to recall the entire list, as usual. For each list two different critical items were chosen, one being used for half the Context Ss in a group, the other for the other half. These words were representative in the sense that their individual probability of recall in Exp. I approximated the probability of recall of the list as a whole. Counterbalancing for list sequence required a total of four groups for the experiment. This time the lists were given four consecutive readings, in a different random order each time. The rest of the procedure was the same as before.

Results.—With the Rare list, 4 Context Ss and 11 Control Ss recalled the critical item. Contingency analysis showed x^2 (1) $= 5.23$, $p < .05$. With the Common list 10 Context Ss and 16 Control Ss recalled the critical item. Analysis showed x^2 (1) $= 4.00$, $p < .05$. The results are in accord with the previous data, and taken all together, show that provision of from 5 to 29 words of context has absolutely no facilitating effect upon recall. In fact the Context condition was again significantly inferior in recall, but this aspect of the data will be examined in more detail later.

Organization in free performance has most readily and obviously been seen in the case of lists deliberately constructed with groups of words clearly belonging to separate conceptual categories (Cofer, 1965). It is possible that such E-categorized lists might respond positively to the provision of context, on the grounds that their intrinsic rational structure is easily apparent to S, and thus would foster de-pendent storage. Instead of randomly constituted lists, therefore, the next experiment used categorized lists.

EXPERIMENT IV

Method.—Fifty psychology students served as Ss in six groups of about eight each. Each S was either in the Context or the Control condition, and was tested on all three of the lists to be described. The materials were three categorized lists, 30 words in length. Each list had six words belonging to each of five supraordinate categories. Among the 18 categories represented in the lists were trees, fish, musical instruments, occupations, countries, and the like. The words were all fairly common, and were arranged randomly for both presentation trials. The other variable was the number of context words given, namely, 5, 15, or 25 (or in proportions, .17, .50, and .83), as in Exp. II, but this time the context was not drawn randomly. Rather, an equal number of words from each category was always displayed, ranging from 1 per category at the 5 context level to 5 per category at the 25 context level. These words were arranged in haphazard sequence on the recall sheet. Counterbalancing list sequence and proportion of context took three groups for the Context condition, and counterbalancing list sequences took another three for the Control. The general procedure was the same as in the other experiments.

Results.—Table 3 has critical recall expressed in terms of proportions. Analysis of conditions showed the Context group again significantly inferior

TABLE 3

MEAN PROPORTION CRITICAL RECALLS AT
EACH PROPORTION OF CONTEXT
IN EXP. IV

Cond.	Context Proportion					
	.17		.50		.83	
	M	SD	M	SD	M	SD
Context	.51	.23	.47	.14	.40	.26
Control	.66	.14	.67	.20	.62	.23

Note.—$N = 23$ each Context Cell and 27 each Control Cell.

to the Control, F (1, 48) = 67.50, p < .001, and consistent in direction at every level of context. Neither the effects of Proportions, F (2, 96) = 2.67, p > .05, nor the Conditions × Proportions interaction, F (2, 96) < 1, were significant.

The presence of output organization, as expected, was very obvious. Under all conditions where it was possible (therefore excluding the 25 context level), the clustering of items according to category membership was clearly discernible. From the total Control recall a count was made of the number of categories represented, as indicated by the presence of at least one item from a category (Cohen, 1966). Mean category recall was 4.88, indicating that practically every S recalled a correct instance of each of the 5 categories involved. A comparison with the category recall of Context Ss would be unenlightening because the latter condition perforce reduced the number of alternatives available.

These data are also consistent with those of the other experiments, and show that even with categorized lists, over a wide range of proportions, memory is not assisted by context cues. In fact the Context condition produced a small but significant interference effect at recall in all cases. This unexpected phenomenon posed a problem in and of itself; for its solution the next two experiments were designed. It was hypothesized that the source of the interference lay in the fact that Context Ss first had to scan the context list before commencing their recall, whereas Control Ss could begin recalling immediately. During the brief interval occupied by this initial scanning, a few items might have been irretrievably lost from short-term memory, or from the "echo box" (Waugh & Nor-

man, 1965). If that was the case, they would most likely have been the last items presented during original learning. Inspection of individual protocols did indeed reveal a tendency on the part of Context Ss to recall considerably fewer terminal items than did Control Ss.

An experimental test of this hypothesis could take either of two directions, both designed to equalize the groups with respect to the echo box factor. One method would be to allow both groups to engage in unhindered immediate free recall, and then to provide context to one of them afterward. Another would be to delay the start of recall on the part of the Control group by an amount of time equivalent to that spent by the Context group in their initial scanning. With either method the previously obtained recall differences should then disappear. The next experiment used the former technique.

EXPERIMENT V

Method.—Twenty-four student Ss were tested individually. The materials were two Rare lists, 30 words long. Each S had both lists and both conditions. List sequence and conditions were counterbalanced across Ss. After the two randomly ordered presentations of a list, S was given 4 min. for free recall. Then his paper was taken and all correct items were quickly checked. In the Context condition a random half of the yet unrecalled items was added to the paper, and the paper was returned with instructions to attempt recall of the remainder. In the Control condition the paper was also checked but no context was added, and the paper was similarly returned for further recall. This procedure took about 1 min., and the second recall period was 4 min.

Results.—Mean recall at the end of the first period was 13.33 items for the Context condition and 13.38 for the Control (SDs of 4.67 and 4.47, respectively) with obviously no significant difference between them. During the second period a total of 6 additional words was recalled by four Context Ss, and 11 additional by eight Control Ss. Since the Context group had only half the number of items left to recall during the second period than did the Control, the obtained 2:1 recall ratio signifies that the relative performances did not differ.

Although this outcome is in accord with the hypothesis, it is not sufficiently convincing. A full 5 min. elapsed between original learning and presentation of context, and such a relatively lengthy interval might have resulted in the dissolution of whatever connections existed among the traces. Therefore, the second of the two techniques described above was used in the last experiment.

Experiment VI

Method.—A total of 59 students served as Ss, tested in six groups, with 33 in the Context condition and 26 in the Control. The materials and all aspects of the procedure were exactly the same as in Exp. I, with just one difference. At recall the control group was delayed for a brief time by a task which was intended solely to prevent list rehearsal. As soon as the last list item was read, E gave a three-digit no. and Ss were told to write down the numbers gotten by counting backwards from it by threes, as rapidly as possible. After 15 sec. they were told to begin free recall of the list of words. The 15-sec. period represented E's best estimate of the time spent by Context Ss in initial scanning.

Results.—Table 4 shows the mean critical recalls. Analysis of conditions produced a nonsignificant F (1, 57) < 1. Lists was a significant variable as before, F (2, 114) = 51.43, p < .001, and the Conditions × Lists interaction was nonsignificant, F (2, 114) < 1.

In Exp. I the mean recall difference obtained between conditions across all levels was 1.36 items in favor of the

TABLE 4

MEAN CRITICAL RECALLS FOR EACH LIST IN EXP. VI

Cond.	List					
	Rare		Common		Butterfly	
	M	SD	M	SD	M	SD
Context	4.70	2.34	6.79	2.82	8.97	3.57
Control	5.58	2.93	7.04	2.87	8.50	2.75

Note.—N = 33 each Context Cell and 26 each Control Cell.

Control group, in Exp. II it was 1.70, and in Exp. IV it was 2.61. By imposing a short delay task on the Control group in the present experiment the magnitude of that difference was reduced to an insignificant .22 items. The results of these last two experiments are consistent with the hypothesis that the Context groups' lesser recall was caused by short-term memory loss suffered during initial scanning of the context list. The series of experiments seems to have arrived at a convenient point of termination.

Discussion

With regard to the original question of whether trace storage in these tasks is dependent or independent, the most reasonable conclusion which can be drawn from the overall findings is that the traces are stored independently of each other. The provision of context, even to the maximum degree possible, simply did not facilitate recall performance. Further, this conclusion is applicable across a number of different types of lists, and in the presence of a substantial degree of recall achieved. Across the various lists average recall ranged from about 13 to 20, or from 43% to 67% of the total possible. Thus a good proportion of the words of these supraspan lists was remembered in the absence of any demonstrable organization at the level of storage.

The fact that in the first four experiments the context situation exerted a slight interfering effect upon recall can be ascribed to a tangential procedural artifact which apparently influenced short-term memory differentially between the groups. When this extraneous factor was controlled so as to place both groups on an equal footing, there were still no beneficial effects of context to be discerned.

Since the experimental series was confined to the single-trial situation where S had only one opportunity to recall a given list, it is clear that the conclusion about independent storage is necessarily limited to that case. It might be argued that although trace storage is indeed independent in single-trial tasks, multitrial learning does produce a state of organization in the traces. This is strictly an empirical question, to be settled by empirical means, so that judgment must be reserved at this time. Nevertheless, it would be rather unlikely that such an implied discontinuity in the emergence of organization is really the case, particularly if organization is the key to successful recall performance, as Mandler (1967) repeatedly asserts. Rather, it is more reasonable to expect that organization is present to an effective degree even on the first recall trial, at least whenever a substantial proportion of the list is able to be remembered, as in the preceding experiments. And, in fact, evidence of output organization was quite obvious in the protocols of Exp. IV, in the form of considerable category clustering. If this single trial organization cannot be traced to the storage phase, then how else could it have come about? The answer might be found in the retrieval phase.

Consider the following theoretical account which is intended to illustrate how independently stored traces might nevertheless combine with other factors to eventuate in an organized output.

We assume a reasonably alert and attentive S who comes into the situation armed with an extraexperimental background of verbal and conceptual experience. During the presentation of a typical categorized list S perceives or detects (Cohen, 1966), to some degree of veridicality, its systematic structural framework. He encodes and stores this *general* representation of the list structure, while at the same time the specific item traces are being stored independently. Later, if free recall is requested, he uses this general representation of the list to form a retrieval plan which then guides his search, more or less successfully, for the independent item traces. Such a procedure should produce two related behavioral consequences. First, the use of a *plan* immediately implies that (if it is at all workable) its products will not be random, but that they will display the organization characteristically found in free-recall protocols. The pattern of output organization would reflect the nature of the retrieval scheme. Secondly, a systematic plan should result in a more thoroughgoing job of retrieval than would just a haphazard search, thereby giving rise to the often reported positive correlations between degree of organization and amount recalled. That the plan is truly one of retrieval and not merely a guide to shrewd reconstruction of the material is suggested by the fact that extraneous intrusion errors are notoriously very rare occurrences in recall performance (Underwood, 1964). One tends to find only what is there.

Anything which would enhance or inhibit the development or use of an efficient retrieval plan should be reflected in the subsequent recall performance. Thus, the difference between an incidental and an intentional learning situation could be the difference between a relatively complete vs. a relatively fragmentary general representation of the list structure, even though the specific item traces have been equally well stored in both cases. As Miller, Galanter, and Pribram (1960) expressed it: "An intention to learn means that the subject executes a Plan to form a Plan to guide recall [p. 129]." Not only should incidental recall be inferior to that obtained with intentional learning instructions, but its organization should also be lower. Further, if at time of recall the incidental learner was given a retrieval plan equivalent to that being used by the intentional learner, their recalls should be the same, indicating that item storage was not the locus of the difference.

Still other variables can be postulated as influencing the detection of general list structure, and thereby the efficiency of the subsequent retrieval plan. Block presentation of categorized lists produces better recall and more clustering than does random presentation (Puff, 1966). Degree of constraint in the choice of list items may be another factor, illustrated by the differential recall associated with the Rare and the Butterfly lists above. Formal variables such as rate of presentation, distribution of practice, and number of trials may also provide differential opportunities for detecting general list structure.

Finally, it is to be expected that parts of retrieval plans can also be forgotten, so that any means which would help to augment them at time of recall would be beneficial to performance. The Tulving and Pearlstone (1966) study can be interpreted in this light. Block presentation of categorized lists was used, and at time of recall one group was provided with the category names, and the other was not. The cued condition resulted in superior recall, and when the noncued group was later also provided with the category names, their recall increased significantly. Further, the superiority of the cued condition was most marked when the number of categories involved was maximal, at each length of list used. It is as though the retrieval plan was based upon category names, and when a large number of categories was involved, the cognitive strain was excessive and parts of the plan simply could not be remembered, unaided. Providing these names at time of recall helped to reinstate the plan, with a consequent increase in successful retrieval. When one knows what he is looking for he is more likely to find it.

The preceding dual-component analysis is admittedly no more than an exercise in post hoc theoretical interpretation, but at least it seems to do no violence to the facts in the literature, and at most it may lend further plausibility to the conclusion about independently stored item traces, and call increased attention to the potential importance of the concept of retrieval plans.

REFERENCES

Bousfield, W. A.   The occurrence of clustering in the recall of randomly arranged associates.   *J. gen. Psychol.,* 1953, **49,** 229–240.

Cofer, C. N.   On some factors in the organizational characteristics of free recall. *Amer. Psychologist,* 1965, **20,** 261–272.

Cohen, B. H.   Some-or-none characteristics of coding.   *J. verbal Learn. verbal Behav.,* 1966, **5,** 182–187.

Dallett, K. M.   Practice effects in free and ordered recall.   *J. exp. Psychol.,* 1963, **66,** 65–71.

Deese, J.   Influence of inter-item associative strength upon immediate free recall. *Psychol. Rep.,* 1959, **5,** 305–312.

Jenkins, J. J., Mink, W. D., & Russell, W. A.   Associative clustering as a function of verbal association strength.   *Psychol. Rep.,* 1958, **4,** 127–136.

Jenkins, J. J., & Russell, W. A.   Associative clustering during recall.   *J. abnorm. soc. Psychol.,* 1952, **47,** 818–821.

Mandler, G.   Organization and memory. In K. W. Spence and J. T. Spence (Eds.), *The psychology of learning and motivation.*   New York: Academic Press, 1967.

Mandler, G., & Pearlstone, Z.   Free and constrained concept learning and subsequent recall.   *J. verbal Learn. verbal Behav.,* 1966, **5,** 126–131.

Mayhew, A. J.   Interlist changes in subjective organization during free-recall learning.   *J. exp. Psychol.,* 1967, **74,** 425–430.

Melton, A. W.   Implications of short-term memory for a general theory of memory. *J. verbal Learn. verbal Behav.,* 1963, 2, 1–21.

Miller, G. A., Galanter, E., & Pribram, K. H.   *Plans and the structure of behavior.*   New York: Holt, 1960.

MILLER, G. A., & McGILL, W. J. A statistical description of verbal learning. *Psychometrica*, 1952, **17**, 369–396.

MURDOCK, B. B., JR. The immediate retention of unrelated words. *J. exp. Psychol.*, 1960, **60**, 222–234.

PUFF, C. R. Clustering as a function of the sequential organization of stimulus word lists. *J. verbal Learn. verbal Behav.*, 1966, **5**, 503–506.

RUSSELL, W. A., & JENKINS, J. J. The complete Minnesota norms for responses to 100 words from the Kent-Rosanoff word association test. Technical Report No. 11, 1954, University of Minnesota, Contract No. N8-ONR-66216, Office of Naval Research.

THORNDIKE, E. L., & LORGE, I. *The teacher's work book of 30,000 words.* New York: Teachers College, Columbia University, 1944.

TULVING, E. The effect of alphabetical subjective organization on memorizing unrelated words. *Canad. J. Psychol.*, 1962, **16**, 185–191. (a)

TULVING, E. Subjective organization in free recall of "unrelated" words. *Psychol. Rev.*, 1962, **69**, 344–354. (b)

TULVING, E. Intratrial and Intertrial Retention: Notes towards a theory of free recall verbal learning. *Psychol. Rev.*, 1964, **71**, 219–237.

TULVING, E. Subjective organization and effects of repetition in multitrial free recall learning. *J. verbal Learn. verbal Behav.*, 1966, **5**, 193–197.

TULVING, E., McNULTY, J. A., & OZIER, M. Vividness of words and learning to learn in free recall learning. *Canad. J. Psychol.*, 1965, **19**, 242–252.

TULVING, E., & PEARLSTONE, Z. Availability versus accessibility of information in memory for words. *J. verbal Learn. verbal Behav.*, 1966, **5**, 381–391.

UNDERWOOD, B. J. The representativeness of rote verbal learning. In A. W. Melton (Ed.), *Categories of human learning.* New York: Academic Press, 1964. Pp. 47–78.

WAUGH, N. C., & NORMAN, D. A. Primary memory. *Psychol. Rev.*, 1965, **72**, 89–104.

WAUGH, N. C., & SMITH, J. E. K. A stochastic model for free recall. *Psychometrika*, 1962, **27**, 141–154.

WEINGARTNER, H. The free recall of sets of associatively related words. *J. verbal Learn. verbal Behav.*, 1964, 3, 6–10.

YNTEMA, D. B., & TRASK, F. P. Recall as a search process. *J. verbal Learn. verbal Behav.*, 1963, **2**, 65–74.

PART 3

Organization and semantic memory

Introduction

Organization may be viewed as a form of higher-order coding process in that it involves relations among several to-be-remembered items rather than the transformation of single items independent of each other. This view implies that those features or attributes of single items encoded by the subject form the basis for organizational coding. It has been common to distinguish between subjective organization and 'experimenter-determined' organization. This distinction reflects the amount of latitude accorded to the subject in choosing his own organizational codings rather than adopting those either suggested by, or explicitly designated by, the experimenter. Where subjects are presented with clearly structured categorized word lists (e.g. Bower, Clark, Lesgold and Winzenz, 1969), they may organize their recall through adopting the given structure. That is, the use of organizational coding may be inferred from the correspondence between the material as presented and the material as recalled. Where, however, subjects are presented with nominally unrelated word lists to learn, organizational coding may be inferred from the finding of consistent discrepancies between the material as presented and the material as recalled (e.g. Tulving, 1962).

The papers by Tulving (Reading 15) and Tulving and Pearlstone (Reading 16) exemplify these two broad approaches to the study of organizational coding. In the Tulving paper, a transfer paradigm is employed in which the subject learns part of a list of unrelated words and subsequently is given the whole list to learn. Surprisingly, this procedure produces a negative transfer effect. That is, those subjects who have prior experience of learning part of the list before whole-list learning find the whole-list more difficult to learn than do subjects who have no prior experience of the list. Tulving argues that this negative transfer phenomenon may be attributed to the inapplicability of the organizational codings used in part-list learning for the whole-list situation. List discrimination hypotheses have also been invoked to account for the phenomenon, however, and it is apparent that whether or not negative or positive transfer effects are found depends also on how transfer is defined and measured (Slamecka, Moore and Carey, 1972; Sternberg and Bower, 1974).

In the Tulving and Pearlstone study (Reading 16) the subjects were presented with lists of words belonging to explicitly designated conceptual categories. Recall of the word lists was either in the presence or in the absence of the category names. In addition to the finding that cued recall was higher than non-cued recall, Tulving and Pearlstone also found that the number of words recalled within each category was unaffected by the cueing manipulation. This latter result indicates that category recall and words within category recall are independent processes. Tulving and Pearlstone argue that, regardless of whether the basis for organization is subjective or determined by the experimenter, the functional significance of higher-order units is that they enhance the accessibility of information in a limited retrieval system. The general conclusion that organizational coding reduces the information load in the memory system is in line with much other research on organizational processes (cf. Mandler, 1967). Further evidence that the limitation in capacity occurs at retrieval is provided by the demonstration that retroactive inhibition in free recall of categorized lists represents a state in which higher-order units of information are available in the memory store, but are not accessible (Tulving and Psotka, 1971).

In *Attributes of Memory*, Herriot argues that coding processes in general are best understood with reference to the communicative function of language. Forms of coding have the specific function of the understanding and speaking of language. In Howe's study of the recall of meaningful prose (Reading 17), subjects recalled thirty words 'correct' and fifty words 'incorrect' from a 160 word passage. That is, judged by the criterion of verbatim recall, subjects recalled far more words that were not in the original passage than they did words which were in the original. Scored in terms of meaningful units, or 'idea' units, subjects recalled far more from the passage than is revealed by the traditional measure of 'words correct'. Such results considerably reinforce Herriot's point, and are, of course, also reminiscent of earlier accounts of the reconstructive and interpretive nature of recall (Bartlett, 1932). Clearly, the processing of meaningful material is directed at comprehension, not at future verbatim recall. Comprehension is likely to involve inference. The act of comprehension involves more than the simple recovery of information present at input. It involves elaboration and the addition of extra information. The role of inference in memory for sentences is demonstrated clearly by Bransford, Barclay and Franks (Reading 18).

Tulving (1972) contrasts the memory necessary for the use of language, semantic memory, with episodic memory, which he describes as a more or less faithful record of a person's experiences. Tulving argues that traditional memory research has concentrated almost exclusively on episodic memory performance, that is, on the individuals memory for particular events occurring in an 'autobiographical' context. Recently, however, there has been a spate of models whose general aim is to specify the nature and structure of semantic memory. Among such models is that put forward by Collins and Quillian (Reading 19). Collins and Quillian propose an heirarchical structure in semantic memory. The model assumes that the meaning of a word is given by its location in an associative network which includes class-inclusion and part-whole relations. The model also assumes that words are located in the network according to the principle of cognitive economy. Thus, those properties of a word which do not define the word uniquely, but are also properties of the word's superordinate are stored at the superordinate level. For example, 'breathing', as a property of animals, is stored at the animal node rather than separately with all the words which are instances of the class of animals. The model predicts that, in judging the veracity of statements such as 'A canary can sing', and 'A canary can fly', reaction time will increase as a function of the 'distance' between the subject of the sentence and the property, (or superordinate), in the heirarchical network. The results for true sentences support the model.

Schaeffer and Wallace (Reading 20), however, using a two-word meaning comparison paradigm, find that semantic similarity, while facilitating 'same' judgements, impedes 'different' judgements. For example, the subjects took longer to judge 'hemlock' and 'daisy' as different than to judge 'hemlock' and 'parrot' as different. This result is difficult to explain in terms of the Collins and Quillian model, since 'hemlock' and 'daisy' are closer than 'hemlock' and 'parrot' in the heirarchical network. Schaeffer and Wallace propose an alternative model in which reaction times for such judgements reflect only a 'comparison process' involving the sets of attributes, or conceptual elements, of the two words presented. Reaction time is thus a function of the number of conceptual elements which the two words have in common, or attribute 'overlap'. Greater attribute overlap will facilitate 'same' judgements but impede 'different' judgements.

While reaction time has been widely used in studies of semantic memory (see also Conrad, 1972; Rubenstein, Garfield and Millikan, 1970), few studies have directly investigated the recall of information from semantic memory. Brown and McNeill (Reading 21) did so by presenting subjects with dictionary definitions of rare words and asking them to retrieve each word so defined. Brown and McNeill were particularly interested in those instances when the subjects could not retrieve the target word, but felt that they were 'close' to retrieving the word and that the word was on the 'tip-of-the-tongue'. They found that under these conditions, the subjects were able to report accurately on various characteristics of the target word, such as the number of syllables and the initial letter. The subjects were also able to produce other words similar to the target word in sound and in meaning. Yarmey (1973) has shown recently that imagery processes may also be involved in tip-of-the-tongue states. Hart (1967) described a phenomenon similar to the tip-of-the-tongue experience which he called 'feeling-of-knowing'. Hart argued that when an initial retrieval attempt fails, the subject attempts to assess whether or not the required information is, in fact, available in the memory store. The capacity of the memory system to assess its own storage states is an intriguing phenomenon. It seems likely that feeling-of-knowing and tip-of-the tongue states are mediated by knowledge of specific attributes of the inaccessible target memory (Blake, 1973; Gardiner, Craik and Bleasdale, 1973), and such effects accord well with any account of memory which regards attributes as the basic focal elements of memorial processes (e.g. Underwood, 1969).

In Herriot's *Attributes of Memory*, chapters 5 and 6 are concerned with organization and semantic memory respectively. Language and memory are discussed in his chapters 3 and 7.

References

BARTLETT, F.C. (1932) *Remembering*. London: Cambridge University Press.

BLAKE, M. (1973) Prediction of recognition when recall fails: Exploring the feeling-of-knowing phenomenon. *Journal of Verbal Learning and Verbal Behavior* **12**: 311-19.

BOWER, G.H., CLARK, M.C., LESGOLD, A.M., and WINZENZ, D. (1969) Hierarchical retrieval schemes in recall of categorized word lists. *Journal of Verbal Learning and Verbal Behavior* **8**: 323-43.

CONRAD, C. (1972) Cognitive economy in semantic memory. *Journal of Experimental Psychology* **92**: 149-54.

GARDINER, J.M., CRAIK, F.I.M., and BLEASDALE, F.A. (1973) Retrieval difficulty and subsequent recall. *Memory and Cognition* **1**: 213-16.

HART, T.J. (1967) Memory and the memory-monitoring process. *Journal of Verbal Learning and Verbal Behavior* **6**: 685-91.

MANDLER, G. (1967) Organization and memory. In K.W. Spence and J.T. Spence (eds.) *The Psychology of Learning and Motivation*. **1** New York: Academic Press.

RUBENSTEIN, H., GARFIELD, L., and MILLIKAN, J.A. (1970) Homographic entries in the internal lexicon. *Journal of Verbal Learning and Verbal Behavior* **9**: 487-94.

SLAMECKA, N.J., MOORE, T., and CAREY, S. (1972) Part-to-whole transfer and its relation to organization theory. *Journal of Verbal Learning and Verbal Behavior* **11**: 73-82.

STERNBERG, R.J., and BOWER, G.H. (1974) Transfer in part-whole and whole-part free recall: A comparative evaluation of theories. *Journal of Verbal Learning and Verbal Behavior* **13**: 1-26.

TULVING, E. (1962) Subjective organization in free recall of 'unrelated' words. *Psychological Review* **69**: 344-54.

TULVING, E. (1972) Episodic and semantic memory. In E. Tulving and W. Donaldson (eds.) *Organization of memory*. New York: Academic Press.

TULVING, E. and PSOTKA, J. (1971) Retroactive inhibition in free recall: inaccessibility of information available in the memory store. *Journal of Experimental Psychology* **87**: 1-8.

UNDERWOOD, B.J. (1969) Attributes of memory. *Psychological Review* **76**: 559-73.

YARMEY, A.D. (1973) I recognize your face but I can't remember your name: Further evidence on the tip-of-the-tongue phenomenon. *Memory and Cognition* **1**: 287-90.

E. Tulving

Subjective organization and effects of repetition in multi-trial free-recall learning

Reprinted from the *Journal of Verbal Learning and Verbal Behavior* (1966) 5(2):193-7

Some experimental evidence is presented in support of the argument that increasing recall over successive practice trials in free-recall learning (FRL) is a consequence of subjective organization and of the development of higher-order memory units (S units). Two experiments showed that mere repetition of list-items on six continuous "reading" trials has no effect on immediately following learning of these items under the standard FRL procedure. Two other experiments demonstrated that learning half of the items from a list immediately prior to the learning of the whole list under the standard FRL procedure retards the learning of the whole list.

Over the past six or seven years we have conducted a large number of free-recall learning (FRL) experiments at Toronto. One of the major problems in this research has been the elucidation of the processes involved in the learning of a list of items over successive trials. Given the fact that human memory is capable of handling only a limited number of list-items on the first trial, why is rehearsal effective in producing higher recall on subsequent trials?

A concept that has figured prominently in our attempts to answer this question is subjective organization, suggested by Miller's (1956a, 1956b) concepts of recoding and unitization. In FRL it has been commonly observed that Ss tend to group certain list-items on successive trials. Such grouping of items in recall can be regarded as suggestive evidence for the development of higher-order memory units, each consisting of two or more related items. Since the instructions given to the S in a typical FRL experiment do not prescribe any organization of output, and since it is the S's previous experience with the materials used in the experiment that seems to determine the nature and composition of higher-order memory units, we refer to the organization found in the S's output as subjective organization and to the higher-order units as subjective units (S units).

As a first approximation, we assume that the effect of rehearsal in FRL is a consequence of the development of S units. The S may not be capable of retrieving more than a limited number of S units on any given trial, but his total recall score goes up because the size of the S units increases over trials.

Some evidence in agreement with this view has come from observed correlations between subjective organization and number of recalled items, and from the findings that increases in recall over trials are closely paralleled by increases in subjective organization (Tulving, 1962, 1964). This evidence points to the primary role of organization in determining trial-by-trial increments in recall, but some critics have quite correctly argued that the evidence is only indirect and that organization need be nothing more than a side-effect of trial-by-trial practice. Carterette and Coleman (1963), for instance, have contended that increases in subjective organization *follow* performance increments and therefore cannot determine these increments. And Asch and Ebenholtz (1962) have claimed that FRL occurs in absence of specific inter-item associations. Since associative mechanisms are probably involved in at least some types of S units, Asch and Ebenholtz's claim constitutes a denial of the primary role of organizational processes in determining trial-by-trial increments in recall.

In the present paper, four experiments will be presented that are relevant to the problem of the nature of the relation between subjective organization and the effects of rehearsal. The first two demonstrate that mere repetition of material has no effect on producing higher recall and that something else is needed. The other two experiments illustrate how the learning of a part of a list prior to learning of the whole list retards the mastery of the whole list, thus suggesting that recall performance is dependent upon the existence and the nature of S units.

Mere Repetition Is Ineffective

The first experiment was designed to assess the effects of repetition under conditions where subjective organization and hence the development of S units was minimized, but where otherwise the conditions of practice were met.

In this experiment, two groups of eight Ss learned a common list of 22 randomly selected English nouns of Thorndike-Lorge (1944) frequency of more than 100 per million. Typical FRL conditions were used (viz. Tulving, 1962). Words were presented at the rate of 1-sec per word. At the end of each trial S had 60 sec for oral recall. Twelve learning trials were given.

The groups differed with respect to the treatment they received immediately prior to the learning of

the experimental list. Both groups were given a task of reading 22 pairs of items on six continuous trials, but each group read different kinds of pairs. For the Prior Acquaintance (PA) Group, the pairs consisted of the 22 nouns from the experimental list as left-hand members and single letters, randomly selected without replacement, as right-hand members. For the No Prior Acquaintaince (NPA) Group, the pairs consisted of male names and randomly selected two-digit numbers. The pairs of items were presented by means of a memory drum at the rate of 1 sec per pair. The Ss in both groups were instructed to simply read and pronounce aloud both members of each pair as they occurred. The order of pairs was systematically changed to maximize inter-pair distances over the six trials.

Thus, at the end of this prior practice, Ss in the PA Group had seen and responded to each of the 22 nouns in the experimental list six times, while the Ss in the NPA Group had seen and responded to the same number of irrelevant items. If it were just the matter of repeating the list-items in presence of a given set of environmental stimuli and in the context of other items that is responsible for the practice effect, one would expect the PA Group to do considerably better in learning the experimental list than the NPA Group. If, on the other hand, grouping of items in terms of their relatedness is the critical factor, and if, as we assumed to be the case under these conditions, such subjective organization of items by the PA Group were minimal, there would be no reason to expect differences between the groups in

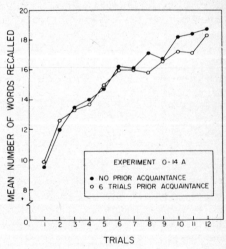

Fig. 1. Learning curves for two groups of Ss. One group (open circles) had had prior intra-experimental exposure to list-words, the other group (filled circles) had had no such prior exposure.

memorizing the experimental list.

The learning curves of the two groups for the experimental list are shown in Fig. 1. They are, for all practical purposes, indistinguishable. The mean number of words over all 12 trials was 15.14 for the PA group, and 15.44 for the NPA Group.

It could be argued that Ss in the PA Group may have incidentally learned associations between nouns and letters in the prior reading task and that these associations may have interfered with the learning of the nouns in the FRL task. To examine this possibility, a second experiment was conducted. All the conditions of this experiment were identical to those of the first one, except that groups of 12 Ss were used and that the prior reading task involved only single items. For the PA Group, the items were the same as those in the final experimental list, namely 22 high-frequency nouns. For the NPA Group, the items in the reading task were male names. Again, Ss in both groups were given six continuous trials in the prior task of reading and calling out the items presented by the memory drum.

The two learning curves were again very similar. On the first trial, the PA Group had a nonsignificant advantage over the NPA Group in the mean number of words recalled (10.42 vs. 9.25), but beginning with the second trial there were no consistent or obvious differences. Over all 12 trials, the mean recall for the PA Group was 15.71 and for the NPA Group 15.91.

The findings of these two experiments suggest that mechanical repetition by itself has no effect on recall. If the items are well integrated as independent units prior to the experiment, merely repeating them over and over does not facilitate their memorization. We conclude that only repetition that leads to the formation of higher-order S units, as it occurs under the instructions to memorize the material in a typical FRL task, is effective in permitting the S to retrieve more items on later trials than on the first one. It looks as if items in excess of the immediate memory span can be retrieved from the memory storage only through other items as cues for retrieval. However, other items can function as retrieval cues only to the extent to which the material has been organized into higher-order S units.

While alternative interpretations of the findings from the two experiments are undoubtedly possible, it seems that the obtained data cannot be readily accommodated by theories such as the one proposed by Asch and Ebenholtz (1962), according to which free recall depends on "availability" of items, where availability is mainly a function of frequency and recency. The Ss in the PA Groups in the two experiments just reported had the benefit of both frequency and recency of repetition of the relevant list items, but this did not apparently help them to recall the items.

PRIOR PART-LIST LEARNING RETARDS
SUBSEQUENT WHOLE-LIST LEARNING

If subjective organization and formation of higher-order S units is necessary for the S to be able to recall more items in an FRL task than can be handled by immediate memory, and if the number of S units that can be retrieved on any given trial is limited, then it follows that the existence of inappropriate S units may hinder rather than facilitate memorization of a set of items. It is difficult to have Ss form completely inappropriate S units under the conditions of a typical FRL task, but it is possible to induce them to form S units that are only partly appropriate for a particular task. For instance, if Ss learn only a part of a list first and then attempt to learn the complete list, the S units that have been formed during part-learning need not be most appropriate for handling the material in the whole-learning. If the number of S units that can be retrieved on any given trial is limited, formation of new S units in addition to those developed during part-learning would be ineffective for increasing recall. The S could memorize the whole list either by adding "new" words, those that did not occur in the part-list, to the existing S units, or by reorganizing and modifying the existing S units. The first expedient, adding new words, may be applicable only on a limited scale if the items in the list have been selected randomly. The second alternative, reorganizing and modifying, would probably require extra effort and time, offsetting any potential advantage of prior learning. Therefore, under the conditions of FRL, prior learning of a part of the list may have very little facilitating effect on

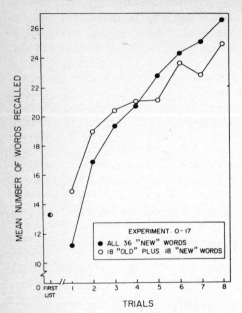

FIG. 2. Learning curves for two groups of Ss on a whole list of 36 words. One group (open circles) had learned half of the whole list before learning the whole list, the other group (filled circles) had learned an irrelevant list.

the learning of the whole list or perhaps even an inhibiting effect.

The third experiment was designed to examine the effect of part-learning on the whole-learning. Two groups of 24 Ss learned identical final lists (whole lists) of 36 familiar words on eight trials under the standard FRL procedure. Words were presented at the rate of 1 sec per word on a memory drum. After each trial Ss had 72 sec to recall the words orally.

Prior to the learning of the whole list, the Part Learning (PL) Group was given eight trials of standard FRL practice with an 18-word list. All the words in this list were taken from the whole list which the Ss were to learn later, although they were not told about this fact. Words were presented at the rate of 1 sec per word and 36 sec was given for oral recall at the end of each trial. The No Learning (NL) Group was given an irrelevant list of 18 words under the same conditions. Thus, at the end of the learning of the first, 18-word list, the Ss in Group PL had had eight trials of FRL practice with one-half of the words from the final whole list, while Ss in Group NL had had no exposure to the words in the final whole list.

The two learning curves on the whole list of 36 words are shown in Fig. 2. The point on the far left

in Fig. 2 shows the mean number of words recalled from the 18-word prior list on the eighth trial. It happened to be identical for both groups. On the whole list of 36 words Group PL had a higher recall score on the early trials than Group NL, but as Fig. 2 shows the curves cross after the fourth trial, with recall scores for the NL being higher than those of the PL Group over the last four trials. The difference in the slopes of the two curves is highly significant statictically, $F(1, 46) = 22.50$, $p < .01$. Prior part-learning aids the recall of items from the whole list on early trials only, while on later trials part-learning seems to retard memorization of the whole list.

It can be argued that the finding of the experiment just described is true only under limited conditions, such as relatively long lists and relatively small amounts of prior learning. Another experiment was therefore designed as a replication of the experiment just reported. In this experiment shorter lists were used and greater amounts of prior part-list practice given to Ss. The common final lists consisted of 18 words and prior lists of 9 words. Twelve trials were given on both the prior and final lists. Two new groups of 24 Ss were used. Words were presented at the rate of 1 sec per word. The amount of time given for recall after each trial was 18 sec for the prior list and 36 sec for the final list.

The two learning curves, shown in Fig. 3, bear a marked similarity to those from the previous experiment. The groups reached approximately the same level of performance on the 12th trial of the prior list. On the final list the PL Group started higher, but the NL Group surpassed it after the seventh trial. Judging by the slopes of the two curves it also looks as if the Ss in the PL Group might have had some real trouble ever reaching perfect performance, since they made little progress from Trial 7 to Trial 12.

The finding that learning a part of the list prior to the learning of the whole list retards the acquisition of the whole list may sound paradoxical in the light of what is commonly known and assumed about the effects of practice. But it does make sense if we assume the primary role of subjective organization and of S units in determining the amount of material that can be retrieved. The organization that develops in the course of part-learning is not always appropriate for handling the whole list. To learn the whole list, the S must reorganize some of the existing units to accommodate the new material or integrate at least some of the existing S units into larger units. To the

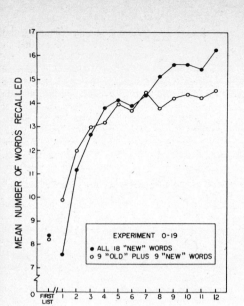

FIG. 3. Learning curves for two groups of *S*s on a whole list of 18 words. One group (open circles) had learned half of the whole list before learning the whole list, the other group (filled circles) had learned an irrelevant list.

not result in the development of higher-order S units, or where it results in the development of inappropriate S units, it fails to facilitate or may even retard the mastery of the material. At the very least it seems that the findings from these experiments are difficult to reconcile with theories that ascribe the effects of rehearsal in FRL to frequency and recency of responses corresponding to individual items, or theories that regard organizational processes in FRL as by-products of more basic phenomena. The key to the understanding of the effects of rehearsal in FRL lies in the understanding of the subjective organization and of the nature and development of S units.

extent that *S*s are incapable or unwilling to abandon or modify the S units formed during part-learning, and to the extent to which retrieval of material on any given trial is limited to a fixed number of S units, the existence of inappropriate S units precludes the successful accomplishment of the task.

CONCLUSION

We believe that the evidence presented here is consistent with the hypothesis that rehearsal is effective in producing increments in recall only if it permits the *S* to organize the material into appropriate S units. Under conditions where repetition of the material does

REFERENCES

Asch, S. E., and Ebenholtz, S. M. The process of free recall: Evidence for non-associative factors in acquisition and retention. *J. Psychol.*, 1962, **54**, 3-31.

Carterette, E. C., and Coleman, E. A. Organization in free recall. Paper presented at the Fourth Annual Scientific Meeting of the Psychonomic Society, Bryn Mawr College, August 29-31, 1963.

Miller, G. A. Human memory and the storage of information. *IRE Trans. Inform. Theory*, 1956, **2**, 129-137. (a)

Miller, G. A. The magical number seven, plus or minus two: Some limits on our capacity for processing information. *Psychol. Rev.*, 1956, **63**, 81-96. (b)

Thorndike, E. L., and Lorge, I. *The teacher's word book of 30,000 words.* New York: Teachers College, Columbia Univer., 1944.

Tulving, E. Subjective organization in free recall of "unrelated" words. *Psychol. Rev.*, 1962, **69**, 344-354.

Tulving, E. Intratrial and intertrial retention: Notes towards a theory of free recall verbal learning. *Psychol. Rev.*, 1964, **71**, 219-237.

E. Tulving and Z. Pearlstone

Availability versus accessibility of information in memory for words

Reprinted from the *Journal of Verbal Learning and Verbal Behavior* (1966) 5(4):381-91

The Ss learned, on a single trial, lists of words belonging to explicitly designated conceptual categories. Lists varied in terms of length (12, 24, and 48 words) and number of words per category (1, 2, and 4). Immediate recall was tested either in presence or absence of category names as retrieval cues. Cued recall was higher than noncued recall, the difference varying directly with list length and inversely with number of items per category. This finding was interpreted as indicating that sufficiently intact memory traces of many words not recalled under the noncued recall conditions were available in the memory storage, but not accessible for retrieval. Further analysis of the data in terms of recall of categories and recall of words within recalled categories suggested two independent retrieval processes, one concerned with the accessibility of higher-order memory units, the other with accessibility of items within higher-order units.

If a person is shown a long list of familiar words and is then asked to recall the list, he can recall some words, but not all of them. It can be assumed that the person learns each single word at the time of its presentation, in the sense that the probability of recall of the word rises from a value near zero immediately before the presentation to a value near unity immediately after the presentation. The failure to recall some of the words, therefore, reflects intratrial forgetting (Tulving, 1964).

Intratrial forgetting is a descriptive label that carries no implications as to the fate of the memory traces associated with nonrecalled words. It may be attributable to the decay of traces as a consequence of passage of time between the presentation and attempted recall of an item (Brown, 1958), or to the displacement of some of the items stored earlier by subsequently presented items (Waugh and Norman, 1965). In either case, failure to recall a certain item would be interpreted to mean that the trace of the item is no longer available in the memory storage at the time of recall. It is also possible, however, that intratrial forgetting represents a failure to "find" otherwise intact traces in the storage. According to an information processing model of memory described by Feigenbaum (1961), for instance, forgetting occurs not because information in storage is destroyed, but because learned material becomes "inaccessible in a large and growing association network." Thus, to interpret intratrial forgetting, it is useful to draw a distinction between what information or what traces are *available* in the memory storage and what are *accessible*. This distinction parallels the distinction between retention and recall, or the distinction between trace storage and trace utilization (Melton, 1963).

The present paper is concerned with a conceptual and experimental analysis of non-recall of learned items in terms of such a distinction between availability and accessibility. It describes an experiment whose primary purpose was to explore the hypothesis that a substantial part of nonrecall of familiar words under typical experimental conditions is attributable to inaccessibility of otherwise intact memory traces.

Experimental demonstrations of the distinction between availability and accessibility of information require that critical experimental treatments be administered at the time of the recall test, rather than at some earlier stage in the sequence of events involved in any memory task. Only if conditions of the experiment are held constant until the beginning of the recall period can differences in observed recall scores be attributed to differences in accessibility. While scattered examples exist in the literature of expermients satisfying these requirements (e.g., Fox, Blick, and Bilodeau, 1964; Peterson and Peterson, 1962, Exp. IV), there have been no systematic attempts to distinguish between availability and accessibility of mnemonic information. Experiments in which various "measures of retention," such as unaided recall and recognition, have been compared (e.g., Luh, 1922; Postman and Rau, 1957) lend support to the proposition that unaided recall does not tap all of the information that is available about previously learned material, but the interpretation of data in these experiments with respect to the distinction between availability and accessibility is complicated. Unaided recall requires the S to reproduce the whole item, while in recognition the correct item is given to the S and his task is to decide whether or not it occurred in the list. To distinguish between availability and accessibility of information that is sufficient for *reproduction* of a given item, comparisons between recognition and recall are only partly relevant and other methods must be used.

The experiment described in this paper uses one such other method. Categorized word lists were presented to Ss for learning, and recall of words was tested in the presence or absence of category names as retrieval cues. It was expected that a large proportion of words not accessible for recall under the unaided conditions would become accessible as a consequence of experimental presentation of such retrieval cues, thus indicating that sufficient information was available in the storage for the reproduction of these words, but that this information was not accessible. The results of the experiment thus were expected to clarify the nature of intra-trial forgetting as defined earlier. As the results turned out, they also illuminated the retrieval processes involved in a memory task such as the one used in the experiment, and had several interesting implications for other types of experiment.

Method

Design

Categorized word lists, consisting of (a) *category names,* and (b) *words* representing instances of categories, were presented to Ss once. Immediately after the presentation, two recall tests were given in succession. The Ss were instructed to try to remember as many *words* as possible.

Three independent variables were manipulated: (a) list length—L (12, 24, and 48 words), (b) number of words or items per category—IPC (1, 2, and 4 words), and (c) conditions of recall in the first recall test—cued recall (CR) and noncued recall (NCR). The second recall test was always given under the conditions of CR.

All possible combinations of L and IPC were used to yield nine lists. Lists are designated in terms of the values of these two variables. For instance, List 24-2 refers to a 24-word list in which there are two items per each of 12 categories.

All combinations of nine lists and two conditions of recall in the first recall test were used to yield 18 experimental conditions. Experimental conditions are designated in terms of the list and recall condition. For instance, condition 12-4 CR refers to List 12-4 recalled under the conditions of cued recall. Thus, the design of the experiment was 3 × 3 × 2 factorial. With respect to the first recall test the independent variables were L, IPC, and recall condition; with respect to the second recall test they were L, IPC, and recall condition of the first test. Since the second recall test was always given under identical conditions (CR), experimental groups can be uniquely defined in terms of list characteristics and recall condition of the first test. For instance, Group 48-1 NCR designates the sample of Ss who learned List 48-1 and who were first tested under the conditions of noncued recall.

Subjects and Experimental Groups

The Ss were high-school students of both sexes from Grades 10 to 12 from a number of different schools in two school systems in the Metropolitan Toronto area.

A total of 948 Ss were tested in the experiment. Data from 19 Ss had to be discarded because of incompleteness of recall protocols. The data discussed in this report are thus based on the records from 929 Ss. The age of Ss ranged from 14 to 21 years, with a great majority (94%) of Ss being between 15 and 18 years of age.

The Ss were tested in groups during a regular class period. Each of nine lists was learned by Ss in four classes. Within each class, all Ss were presented with identical material under identical conditions, but half the Ss were tested first under the conditions of CR while the other half was tested first under the conditions of NCR. The second recall test of the material, as mentioned earlier, occurred under the conditions of CR for all Ss.

The sizes of the 18 experimental groups, each composed of Ss from four different school classes, ranged from 48 to 56.

Lists

A practice list, consisting of 24 common adjectives, was administered under the typical single-trial free-recall conditions to all Ss prior to the presentation of the experimental list.

Two different sets of nine experimental lists were constructed with the aid of the Connecticut word associations norms (Cohen, Bousfield, and Whitmarsh, 1957) and with the aid of norms from a small pilot study patterned after the procedure used by Cohen et al. (1957). Two groups of Ss under each of the 18 experimental conditions learned a list from the first set, while the other two groups learned a corresponding list from the second set.

Corresponding lists in the two sets contained identical categories but different words. The words in List 48-1 represented 48 different categories, 40 taken from the Connecticut norms and eight from the pilot study. Twenty-four categories were selected randomly for Lists 24-1 and 48-2. The 12 categories represented in Lists 12-1 and 48-4 in turn were selected randomly from those occurring in Lists 24-1 and 48-2, respectively. The same general procedure was followed in the selection of categories for other lists.

Words in a given category of a list in which IPC = 4 were, in the first set, usually the second, fourth, sixth, and eighth ranking words in the norms, and in the second set, the third, fifth, seventh, and ninth ranking words in the norms, but some deviations from this general rule occurred. Words for categories containing two items or one item were selected randomly from such sets of four words.

The order of categories in a list and the order of words within categories were determined randomly. All the words within a category occurred in immediately adjacent positions. The lists presented to Ss thus consisted of a number of category names, each category name being followed by one, two, or four items appropriate to the category. For instance, List 12-2 in the first set was as follows: four-footed animals—*cow, rat;* weapons—*bomb, cannon;* crimes—*treason, theft;* forms of entertainment—*radio, music;* substances for flavoring food—*cinnamon, pepper;* professions—*engineer, lawyer.*

Procedure

The Ss recorded their recall in specially prepared recall booklets that were distributed at the beginning of the experimental session. Instructions about Ss' task, and about the use of recall booklets, as well as all lists were presented to Ss by means of a high-fidelity tape-recorder. The Ss were first informed that they were going to take "a test to find out how people remember words," and that although E was not interested in how well each of them did individually, they should do their best in the test. The standard free-recall instructions were then given for the practice list, followed by the presentation of the practice list, at the rate of 2 sec per word. Two min were given for recall.

The instructions for the second part of the test, the experimental list, informed Ss that they would next hear and try to memorize a list of nouns, or "names of various things," pairs of nouns (in case of IPC = 2), or groups of four nouns (in case of IPC = 4), and that each word (or pair of words or group of four) would be "preceded by another word or phrase that describes the word (words) to be remembered, but which in itself does not have to be remembered." Next, an illustrative list of the kind that Ss in a particular group had to learn was given as part of the instructions. This short list contained five categories (country in Europe, boy's name, city in U.S., name of a river, and statesman of our day), each category being accompanied by one, two, or four names, depending on the IPC of the experimental list. The illustrative list was read and the Ss reminded that "we want you to remember only the word (words) that followed each descriptive phrase, or category." These words that Ss had just heard, but not the category names, were then read again and referred to as the part of the list Ss would have to remember. The Ss were then told the number of words, number of categories, and number of words per category in the list they were going to learn.

Apart from the general instructions to recall as many words as possible, no information was given to Ss exactly what the conditions of the recall test were going to be nor were they told that there would be different recall conditions for different Ss in the same group.

The duration of presentation of the list varied for different lists according to the formula: $T = 3 \, NoC + L$, where T is the total duration of presentation in seconds, NoC is the number of categories (L/IPC), and L is list length. The amount of time given for recall also varied for different lists, depending on L. The Ss had 1, 2, or 4 min to recall lists of 12, 24, or 48 words, respectively.

For the condition of NCR, the recall booklets contained L consecutively numbered lines. For the condition of CR, the recall booklet listed all category names that had occurred in the list, in the same order as in the input list, and each category name was followed by one, two, or four lines, depending on IPC.

At the end of the first recall test of the experimental list, all Ss recalled all the words they could remember a second time under the conditions of CR.

RESULTS

The mean number of correctly recalled words on the practice list for the total sample of 929 Ss was 9.48 ($SD = 2.27$). The breakdown of these recall scores in terms of the 18 experimental groups showed the means to range from 8.81 to 10.06. A one-way analysis of variance of these data yielded an $F(17, 911)$ of 2.53 which is unexplainably significant at the .01 level. Since the median correlation coefficient between practice and experimental list recall was only $+ .228$ for the nine CR groups and $+ .284$ for the nine NCR groups, possible differences in ability among the groups suggested by differences in practice-list scores probably had only a minor effect on the evaluation of the effects of experimental treatments.

Recall of Words

The first analysis of the data was concerned with the number of words recalled under various experimental conditions. The stability of these data was tested in the following manner. In each of the 18 experimental groups, the Ss were randomly divided into two subgroups, the mean recall score on the first recall test computed for each subgroup, and an intraclass correlation coefficient (McNemar, 1962) between the 18 resulting pairs of means calculated. This coefficient turned out to be .997, indicating a high degree of stability of the mean recall scores for various experimental groups.

First Recall Test. Mean number of words recalled on the first recall test of the experimental lists is shown by filled (CR) and unfilled (NCR) circles in Fig. 1 as a function of L and IPC. An overall analysis of variance of the number of words recalled in the first recall test showed all three main effects and all three double interactions to be significant at better than the .001 level. The triple interaction among R, L, and IPC was not significant.

Recall of words was higher under the condition of cued recall than under the conditions of noncued recall for all nine lists. The smallest numerical difference between CR and NCR was found for List 12-4. This was not significant by t-test ($t = 1.88$), but all other differences were significant at better than the .01 level. As can be seen from Fig. 1, the superiority of CR over NCR was an increasing function of list length and a decreasing function of IPC. The largest difference (19.8 items, or 126%) was found for List 48-1.

When we consider CR and NCR separately, we find in Fig. 1 that NCR increases with IPC at all three levels of list length, but under the conditions of CR the effect of IPC depends on L. The inverse relation between CR and IPC is quite clear for the 24-word list and is also obvious when we compare recall for IPC = 1 with that for IPC

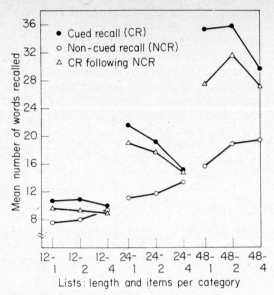

FIG. 1. Mean number of words recalled in the first recall test (circles) and the second recall test (triangles) as a function of list length and number of items per category.

= 4 for the other two lists, but there was no decrease in cued recall from IPC = 1 to IPC = 2 for the 12-word and 48-word lists. All six possible comparisons of mean recall scores between IPC = 1 and IPC = 4 yielded significant differences when tested by means of *t*-tests, five being significant at the .001 level and one (CR for the 12-word list) at the .05 level.

Second Recall Test. The second recall test was administered to all *S*s under the conditions of cued recall, where category names were available on recall sheets. For *S*s in all nine CR groups the mean number of words recalled on the second test was practically identical with the mean number of words recalled on the first test. The overall mean word-recall in all nine groups on the first test was 21.17, and on the second test 21.20. Thus there was neither any forgetting nor "reminiscence" from the first to the second test.

The mean recall scores on the second test for the NCR groups are shown by triangles in Fig. 1. These means were significantly higher than the means on the first test for all lists except List 12-4. But for none of the nine lists did the mean second test recall score in the NCR groups equal that of the CR groups, as can be seen in Fig. 1.

The second recall test was included in the design, and the data from the second test are included in this report, primarily in order to illustrate that subsequent presentation of category names as retrieval cues in the NCR groups would result in an increase in the number of retrieved words. More detailed analyses of these data, however, are not warranted, since no safe assumptions can be made about availability of information in the memory storage after different treatments in the first recall test. For this reason, data from the second recall test will be ignored in the rest of this paper.

Error Data and Guessing Bias. Errors of recall were classified into three categories: repetitions of list words, noncategorical intrusions, and categorical intrusions. Errors falling into the first two classes were few in number. On the first recall test, for instance, a total of 24 repetitions and a total of 73 noncategorical intrusions were found in all

929 recall protocols.

Categorical intrusions are extralist intrusions that are members of one of the categories used in a given list. Mean numbers of such intrusions are shown in Table 1. Three observations are of interest. First, the frequency of categorical intrusions tended to increase with IPC at all levels of L. Second, the frequency of intrusions increased with L at all levels of IPC. Third, the number of intrusions for a given list was always greater for CR than NCR, with the exception of List 12-4.

Since the frequency of categorical intrusions seems to be related to the treatment variables, "correct" recall scores may be somewhat inflated. The Ss may have received credit for recall even when they arrived at the correct word through a free association to the category name, remembered under the NCR conditions and explicitly given on recall sheets under the CR conditions. One might argue, therefore, that the differences in recall between the CR and NCR conditions might in fact be smaller than the data depicted in Fig. 1 indicate.

The extent of such possible bias can be roughly estimated by considering the probability of occurrence of our list-words as free associations in the norms of Cohen et al. For the nine lists, such mean probability varied over the range of .052 to .078, with an overall average of .065. To illustrate the small extent of the bias in recall scores attributable to guessing of words from given categories under the CR conditions, consider List 24-4 for which the difference between CR and NCR was the smallest of all lists. (We will ignore List 12-4 for which the difference was not significant.) The mean number of words recorded by Ss in Group 24-4 CR was 17.7, of which 15.1 were correct and 2.6 were categorical intrusions. The same mean for Group 24-4 NCR was 14.6, of which 13.4 were correct and

1.2 were intrusions. Thus, Ss in Group 24-4 CR put down, on the average, 3.1 more responses than Ss in Group 24-4 NCR. Since the average word in List 24-4 had occurred in the norms with the probability of .052, only .16 words of the 3.1 "extra" words given by Group 24-4 CR would be expected to match the list words and credited to correct recall. The actual difference in mean correct recall between Groups 24-4 CR and 24-4 NCR, however, was over ten times as large. It is clear, therefore, that even for the list showing the smallest difference between CR and NCR the difference could not be accounted for in terms of free associations to category names, and hence must be attributed to the facilitative effect of category names as retrieval cues.

Category and Words-Within-Category Recall

The analysis of word-recall data in an experiment such as the present one can be regarded as a first-level analysis only. It indicates the gross effects of the variables manipulated, but it does not provide much insight into the underlying relations. Some such insight, however, can be obtained from an analysis of the data in terms of two further response measures.

The first of these is referred to as category recall. This is defined in terms of the number of categories from which *at least one word* is recalled. The measure has been used earlier by Cohen (1963). We designate this measure as R_C. In lists where IPC $= 1$, R_C is identical with the number of words recalled (R_W), but in lists where IPC > 1, the two measures do not necessarily covary and usually yield different values.

The second measure is words-within-category recall, or words recalled per category recalled. It is defined in terms of the ratio of the number of words recalled to the number of categories recalled. This measure has been referred to as "mean word recall per category" by Cohen (1966). We designate this measure as $R_{W/C}$. In lists where IPC $= 1$, $R_{W/C}$ is always 1.00 by definition, given that S recalls at least one word from the list, but for higher levels of IPC, $R_{W/C}$ can assume all values between 1.00 and IPC.

The word-recall score (R_W) is a simple multiplicative function of category recall

TABLE 1

MEAN NUMBER OF CATEGORICAL INTRUSIONS IN THE FIRST RECALL TEST OF EXPERIMENTAL LISTS

List length (L)	First recall	Items per category (IPC)		
		1	2	4
12	CR	.66	.59	.77
	NCR	.21	.31	1.23
24	CR	.91	2.12	2.58
	NCR	.22	.92	1.23
48	CR	4.22	3.87	5.52
	NCR	1.59	1.29	2.92

<table>
<tr><td colspan="5" align="center">TABLE 2
MEAN NUMBER OF CATEGORIES RECALLED (R_C) IN
THE FIRST RECALL TEST OF EXPERIMENTAL LISTS</td></tr>
</table>

List length (L)	Recall condition	Items per category (IPC)		
		1	2	4
12	CR	(10.70)	5.88	2.98
	NCR	(7.70)	4.42	2.92
24	CR	(21.70)	11.16	5.79
	NCR	(11.18)	6.84	4.87
48	CR	(35.35)	20.49	11.36
	NCR	(15.57)	10.52	7.29

TABLE 3
MEAN NUMBER OF WORDS RECALLED PER CATEGORY
RECALLED ($R_{W/C}$) IN THE FIRST RECALL TEST
OF EXPERIMENTAL LISTS

List length (L)	Recall condition	Items per category (IPC)		
		1	2	4
12	CR	(1.00)	1.86	3.35
	NCR	(1.00)	1.84	3.19
24	CR	(1.00)	1.73	2.61
	NCR	(1.00)	1.73	2.75
48	CR	(1.00)	1.75	2.61
	NCR	(1.00)	1.79	2.65

score (R_C) and words-within-category recall score ($R_{W/C}$), i.e., $R_W = R_C \cdot R_{W/C}$. The word-recall data that we considered in the two preceding sections thus reflected the effects of the independent variables on both of the two components of R_W. We will now examine the data from the first recall test with respect to the two components of R_W. Table 2 shows mean R_C scores for all experimental conditions. It can be seen that R_C varies systematically with all three independent variables. It is less under the NCR conditions than under the CR conditions for all lists, but the magnitude of this difference depends on both L and IPC. At a given level of IPC the difference is an increasing function of L, and at a given level of L it is a decreasing function of IPC. In Table 2, the values of R_C for lists in which IPC $= 1$ are in parentheses to remind the reader that they are identical with the corresponding R_W values.

The mean recall scores of words recalled per category recalled ($R_{W/C}$) are shown in Table 3. Again the scores for lists where IPC $= 1$ are included for the sake of completeness, although they are always unity by the definition of the $R_{W/C}$ measure.

Table 3 shows that while $R_{W/C}$ is systematically related to IPC, it seems to be independent of recall conditions and also independent of list length for lists of 24 and 48 words. When $R_{W/C}$ scores are averaged over all six lists for which IPC > 1, the overall

means are identical at 2.32 for both CR and NCR. None of the differences in $R_{W/C}$ between CR and NCR for the six lists approaches significance by t-tests. And when the data are averaged over both recall conditions and IPC levels of 2 and 4, the mean $R_{W/C}$ for 24-word lists is 2.21 and the mean for the 48-word lists is 2.18.

Interpretation of Findings on Word-Recall.
To aid in the interpretation of some of the findings pertaining to word-recall (R_W), the data on R_W, R_C and $R_{W/C}$ are summarized in Table 4 as mean proportions of these measures relative to maximum possible scores. These proportional measures are designated as $P(R_W)$, $P(R_C)$, and $P(R_{W/C})$.

Values of $P(R_W)$ in the right-hand panel of Table 4 were obtained by dividing each of the mean R_W scores by its respective L, but these scores can also be arrived at by multiplying the corresponding $P(R_C)$ and $P(R_{W/C})$ scores given in the two left-hand panels in Table 4.

An important fact reflected in the data in Table 4 is that the relations between $P(R_C)$, and $P(R_{W/C})$ on the one hand, and IPC, on the other hand, are all monotonic, for all levels of L and for both conditions of recall, while the relation between $P(R_W)$ and IPC is not. $P(R_C)$ is always an increasing function of IPC, and $P(R_{W/C})$ is always a decreasing function of IPC, but the relation between $P(R_W)$ and IPC cannot be

TABLE 4

RECALL OF CATEGORIES (R_C), OF WORDS PER CATEGORY RECALLED ($R_{W/C}$), AND OF WORDS (R_W)[a]

Recall condi-tion	List length	R_C			$R_{W/C}$			R_W		
		1	2	4	1	2	4	1	2	4
CR	12	.892	.980	.993	(1.00)	.930	.837	.892	.912	.832
	24	.904	.930	.965	(1.00)	.865	.652	.904	.804	.630
	48	.736	.854	.947	(1.00)	.873	.652	.736	.745	.617
NCR	12	.642	.737	.973	(1.00)	.920	.797	.642	.678	.776
	24	.466	.570	.812	(1.00)	.864	.687	.466	.492	.558
	48	.324	.438	.608	(1.00)	.893	.663	.324	.391	.403

[a] Table entries are proportions based on group means relative to maximum scores possible.

stated as simply. $P(R_W)$ is an increasing function of IPC under the conditions of NCR. while under the conditions of CR it is a decreasing function of IPC for the 24-word list and, taking the sample means in Table 4 literally, it increases from IPC = 1 to IPC = 2 and decreases from IPC = 2 to IPC = 4 for both the 12-word and 48-word lists.

The relations between $P(R_W)$ and IPC become somewhat more meaningful if we remember that any change in $P(R_W)$ depends on changes in both $P(R_C)$ and $P(R_{W/C})$. An increase in $P(R_W)$ as a function of IPC means that under certain conditions $P(R_C)$ increases at a faster rate as a function of IPC than $P(R_{W/C})$ decreases. Conversely, a decrease in $P(R_W)$ as a function of IPC means that under certain conditions $P(R_{W/C})$ decreases at a faster rate as a function of IPC than $P(R_C)$ increases.

These considerations suggest that the decrease of R_W as a function of IPC under the conditions of CR, shown in Fig. 1, is probably an artifact related to lists of limited length and to limited number of categories. The $P(R_C)$ score is already so high for lists in which IPC = 1 that there can be relatively little further improvement in this measure with higher levels of IPC. Even for List 48-1, $P(R_C)$ is so high (.736, as shown in Table 4) that the maximum possible increase of .264 in this measure which would bring it to unity would not be sufficient to outweigh the decrease in $P(R_{W/C})$ from

1.00 to .652 over the range of IPC values used in this experiment.

This "ceiling effect" on $P(R_C)$ and the role it plays in determining the relations between R_W and IPC at levels of L used in this experiment is made explicit as a result of the breakdown of the word-recall measure into its two components. Inspection of the R_W curves plotted against IPC would not readily lead to the conclusion that we are dealing with an artifactual limit imposed on the Ss' recall performance, since the R_W curves have a negative slope.

The reversals in the R_W curves plotted as a function of IPC, for 12-word and 48-word lists under the cued recall conditions, can also be understood in terms of the two components of R_W, in an analogous fashion, and will not be elaborated further.

Order of Recall. Two further findings, having to do with order of recall under the conditions of NCR, where the order of recall was free to vary, will be briefly mentioned.

The first was the tendency for the words from a given category to be recalled together despite the absence of the experimentally presented category name. A measure reflecting this trend is provided by the proportion of times that a word from a given category was followed in recall by another word from the same category. This proportion varied between .92 and .95 in the three lists of IPC = 2, and between .89 and .97 in the three lists of IPC = 4.

The second finding concerned the order in which words were recalled within a given category. The general tendency was for the words to be recalled in the same order in which they appeared in the input list. As an illustration we only mention some data from List 48-2. In those cases where the Ss recalled *both* words from a category the order of recall was the same as in the input list 78% of the time (311/397) and reverse to that in the input list 22% of the time (86/397). These data show that even in the case of the longest list used in this study the Ss apparently retain a fair amount of information about the order in which two words from the same category occurred in the input list.

DISCUSSION

The most important finding of this experiment was higher recall under the conditions of cued recall than under the conditions of noncued recall. Since the experimental treatment administered to the Ss in the two recall conditions was the same, both the amount of information and the organization of this information in the memory storage at the beginning of the recall test must have been identical for the CR and NCR groups. The superiority of cued recall over noncued recall thus suggests that specific information about many words must be available in the storage, in a form sufficient for the reproduction of words, even when this information is not accessible under a given set of recall conditions.

Intratrial forgetting, defined in terms of nonrecall of words learned in the input phase of a trial, thus does not necessarily reflect the loss of relevant information from the storage, but only its inaccessibility. Accessibility of the information clearly depends on its availability, but it also depends on retrieval cues. While the present findings do not rule out the possibility that some information stored in memory in the course of presentation of a list decays over intratrial retention intervals or is erased by other incoming information, they do make clear that inferences about what is available in memory cannot be made on the basis of what is accessible.

Retrieval cues obviously constitute an extremely important factor in determining the level of recall. The presence of a single experimentally manipulated retrieval cue, the category name, resulted in large increments in the number of recalled words, particularly for longer lists. It is entirely within the realm of possibility that additional and more powerful retrieval cues would produce an even greater facilitation of recall. Experimental work on memory has largely ignored recall conditions as an important source of variance in recall. Melton (1963) has discussed three broad theoretical problems concerned with retrieval and utilization of traces, but only one of these—dependence of the retrieval on the completeness of reinstatement at the time of recall of the stimulating situation present at the time of input —involves the analytical separation of conditions affecting storage and those related to retrieval, and very little experimental work has been done on this problem.

The analysis of recall data in the present experiment in terms of the logically definable components of word recall, namely category recall and words-within-category recall, showed that category recall was greater under the conditions of CR than NCR and that it increased directly with the length of the list, while words-within-category recall was independent of recall conditions and remained invariant when list length increased from 24 to 48. The latter finding confirms the data reported by Cohen (1966) who found that mean word recall per category was constant for lists of 35, 53, and 70 words.

The fact that variations in recall conditions and list length have an effect on only one component of the word recall measure, but not on the other, suggests that the two components represent two independent processes of recall. One of these has to do with the accessibility of higher-order memory units into which material has been organized, while the other is concerned with the accessibility of individual items comprising the higher-order units. Accessibility of higher-order units depends on appropriate retrieval cues and on the total number of stored higher-order units (or list length), while accessibility of items within higher-order units is largely independent of these variables.

In the present experiment, and in other experiments with categorized word lists, the words to be memorized were organized into higher-order units by the E. This organization apparently determined the arrangement of words in the storage and their retrieval not only for Ss working under the CR conditions, but also for those working under the NCR conditions. When two or more words from a given category were recalled by the NCR subjects, almost invariably these words occurred in immediate succession.

Even when the E does not impose any particular organization on the material the S has to memorize, by selecting words for inclusion in lists randomly and by presenting them without any additional descriptive labels, Ss can and do organize the words into larger units (Tulving, 1962, 1964). Some of these subjective units (S-units) consist of words from meaningful conceptual categories, but others seem to be based on other principles—associative groupings, structural characteristics, and similarity of sound patterns—and still others appear to be determined idiosyncratically. It has been suggested previously (Tulving, 1964) that the functional significance of S-units, whatever their nature, lies in the increased accessibility of individual items constituting a unit. We do not yet know much about the mechanism underlying the retrieval of a single unit of information, be it an individual word or a larger S-unit, but it appears that if an individual list-item has been stored as a part of a larger unit it does become more accessible for retrieval when

other items in the same unit are accessible. Thus organization of material, whether suggested by the E or imposed by the S, seems to affect recall performance primarily by making the desired information more accessible in an otherwise limited biological retrieval system. It need not have any effect on the availability of the information in the storage.

REFERENCES

BROWN, J. Some tests of the decay theory of immediate memory. *Quart. J. exp. Psychol.*, 1958, **10**, 12-21.

COHEN, B. H. Recall of categorized word lists. *J. exp. Psychol.*, 1963, **66**, 227-234.

COHEN, B. H. Some-or-none characteristics of coding behavior. *J. verb. Learn. verb. Behav.*, 1966, **5**, 182-187.

COHEN, B. H., BOUSFIELD, W. A., AND WHITMARSH, G. A. Cultural norms for verbal items in 43 categories. Tech. Rep. No. 22, Nonr-631(00), 1957, University of Connecticut.

FEIGENBAUM, E. A. The simulation of verbal learning behavior. *Proc. West. Joint Computer Conf.*, 1961, **19**, 121-132.

FOX, P. W., BLICK, K. A., AND BILODEAU, E. A. Stimulation and prediction of verbal recall and misrecall. *J. exp. Psychol.*, 1964, **68**, 321-322.

LUH, C. W. The conditions of retention. *Psychol. Monogr.*, 1922, **31**, No. 142.

MCNEMAR, Q. *Psychological Statistics* (3rd Ed.). New York: Wiley, 1962.

MELTON, A. W. Implications of short-term memory for a general theory of memory. *J. verb. Learn. verb. Behav.*, 1963, **2**, 1-21.

PETERSON, L. R., AND PETERSON, M. J. Minimal paired-associate learning. *J. exp. Psychol.*, 1962, **63**, 521-527.

POSTMAN, L., AND RAU, L. Retention as a function of the method of measurement. *Univ. Calif. Publ. Psychol.*, 1957, **8**, 271-396.

TULVING, E. Subjective organization in free recall of "unrelated" words. *Psychol. Rev.*, 1962, **69**, 344-354.

TULVING, E. Intratrial and intertrial retention: Notes towards a theory of free recall verbal learning. *Psychol. Rev.*, 1964, **71**, 219-237.

WAUGH, N. C., AND NORMAN, D. A. Primary memory. *Psychol. Rev.*, 1965, **72**, 89-104.

M.J.A. Howe

Repeated presentation and recall of meaningful prose

Reprinted from the *Journal of Educational Psychology* (1970) **61(3):214-19**

In a study designed to measure the effects of repeated presentation and recall trials upon learning a 160-word prose passage, it was found that the contents of weekly attempts at written reproduction were very closely related to previous recall attempts. The contents of a given recall attempt, even when incorrect, were more likely to recur in succeeding recall trials than were nonrecalled items, despite the opportunities for self-correction provided by repeated presentations of the correct material, which produced relatively small improvements in recall accuracy. The high stability of initial meaningful retention indicates that some emphasis upon avoidance of early errors is justified.

In recent research on learning of meaningful verbal materials there has been relatively little emphasis upon the role of the individual learner in influencing the course of the acquisition process. Yet observations by Bartlett (1932), Allport and Postman (1947), and Ausubel (1968) indicate that what the learner himself brings to the learning situation is an important factor in determining the outcome. It would seem that the learner's personal cognitive structure or "frame of reference" powerfully affects the encoding of the material, and hence partially determines what is later reproduced.

The results of an experiment by Kay (1955) suggest some specifically educational implications of such interactions between the learner and meaningful verbal materials. Kay read aloud meaningful prose passages, totaling 300 words, to a group of adult subjects. Then he asked the subjects to attempt written recall of the material. Afterwards he once more read aloud the original passage. A week later he requested the subjects to make a second recall attempt, and then he read to them the correct version. Kay repeated this procedure in five subsequent sessions. Thus, on each occasion the subjects attempted recall and then listened to the correct version. As Kay points out, although such a procedure may be somewhat unusual in experimental research, it is not unrelated to the educational practice of "giving instruction in a subject, then making some examination of what has been learned, correcting it, followed by further testing at some subsequent date [p. 82]."

The availability of early feedback in Kay's experiment would appear to offer excellent opportunities for self-correction and hence lead to considerable improvements in recall performance. However, this did not occur. What happened was that from week to week a typical subject reproduced very accurately what he had recalled before, correct or incorrect, and was unable to profit much from the opportunities for correction and improvement apparently provided by the repeated presentation of the correct passage. For instance, an incorrect word that had appeared on all of a subject's recall attempts in the first 3 weeks had an 80% mean probability of occurring again in the reproduction made on Week 4. Conversely, a word omitted on one attempt was very unlikely to be recalled on the next session. Of the 97 words omitted, on the average, on Week 5, 85 were again omitted on Week 6. There was no significant overall improvement in recall between the first and seventh weekly sessions.

It can be objected that perseverance of particular words and phrases in verbatim performance need have little importance for the broader issues of meaningful learning and may relate only to linguistic coding. As Miller (1956) has noted, the process of translating information into a verbal code is "tremendously useful for repackaging material into a few chunks," and the activity of rephrasing material into "our own words" seems to be important in learning. However, deeper aspects of meaning and comprehension may be relatively untouched by such linguistic transformations, and hence it is not inevitable that the meaningful contents of recall attempts recur from week to week to any great extent. Tulving (1962) has observed that subjects impose "subjective organization" upon unstructured word lists that are presented in different orders on successive learning trials. The extent of such organization, as displayed by the tendency for items to be recalled in the same sequence on succeeding trials, has a close and probably causal relationship (Tulving, 1966) to learning performance. But there is no clear evidence that structuring of materials by individual subjects plays an equally prominent role in the learning of verbal materials that are initially organized and meaningful. However, Kay (1955) also carried out a content analysis of his data, and his findings show that for meaningful, as well as for verbatim recall, each version "bore a much greater semblance to its immediate predecessor than either was bearing to the original." It would appear that recall by Kay's subjects was based on versions of the original as interpreted and coded by each individual subject, and that the encoded versions were extremely difficult to alter or correct.

Kay's results may have broad implications for meaningful verbal learning. In general it seems that the active processes required in one's having to reproduce written material result in a stable version that is resistant to forgetting. A possible implication concerns the role of retroactive and proactive interference effects in meaningful verbal learning. Ausubel and his associates (Ausubel & Blake, 1958; Ausubel, Robbins, & Blake, 1957; Ausubel, Stager, & Gaite, 1968, 1969) have found that whereas similar materials may interfere with learning of relatively meaningless verbal passages or with verbatim learning of meaningful passages, similar adjacent materials that require subjects' attention do not interfere with meaningful learning of prose passages. However, in none of the studies were the subjects required to actually reproduce the similar materials, and Kay's findings suggest the possibility of interfering effects if reproduction of proactively or retroactively interpolated materials were required.

Before the implications for meaningful learning of Kay's (1955) findings can be explored in any detail, a replication would be desirable with some modifications in the experimental design and analysis. Kay's content analysis for meaningful learning is somewhat imprecise, and no data are provided concerning the reliability of measurement. Accordingly, the present experiment follows the broad outline of that carried out by Kay, but differs considerably in points of detail.

METHOD

Subjects

The subjects were 22 adult graduate students (Mean age 30.0 years, $SD = 11.03$ years) enrolled in a course in Educational Psychology as a requirement for the Master of Education program at Tufts University. The subjects participated as a group on each of four weekly sessions. The results of 10 additional potential subjects who attended the first session but were unable to attend all the other sessions were discarded.

Materials

The passage to which the subjects listened and

were subsequently required to recall was a 160-word prose extract from Saul Bellow's novel "Henderson The Rain King." The extract describes events that occur to the American central figure in a remote African tribal village. The particular passage was chosen because while it is entirely meaningful and presented no difficulty in comprehension, its content is sufficiently unfamiliar to all subjects to prevent capitalization on particular subject-matter knowledge. The passage contains a relatively large number of separate events and is one in which the content of later parts, if forgotten, cannot for recall purposes be easily predicted or guessed on the basis of memory for the beginning of the extract. One consideration underlying the choice of a short but relatively "difficult" passage was that recall failures were more likely to reflect simple forgetting and not other factors such as boredom and fatigue that might be the case with a longer passage with a lower concentration of substantive content. The fact that subjects had to make four separate recall attempts made this consideration especially important.

Procedure

There were four sessions, at weekly intervals. On Session 1, subjects were told to listen to the 160-word passage, which was read at a rate of 120 words per minute, and they were informed that they would subsequently be asked to recall it. Approximately 2 minutes after the passage had ceased, subjects were asked to attempt written recall of it. In the recall instructions subjects were told to concentrate on reproducing the meaningful contents of the materials. Reproduction of the precise form was to be as accurate as possible, but the primary goal was to recall the substantive content. After a 5-minute recall period (Trial 1) the subjects once more listened to the prose passage, presented at the same rate. This ended the session.

Session 2, 1 week later, began with the request that the subjects attempt written reproduction of the prose passage. After the 5-minute recall period (Trial 2), the subjects once more listened to the original passage. Exactly the same procedure was followed on Sessions 3 and 4, which took place at weekly intervals. Thus by the end of Session 4, each subject had listened to the passage on a total of five occasions (two on Session 1, plus one on each of the other sessions), and had made four attempts at written recall.

Scoring Meaningful Recall

The procedure draws upon the work of Cofer (1941). For scoring accuracy of reproduction of meaningful components of the material, the 160-word passage was divided into 20 segments, each of which was judged to have content that contributed meaningfully to the passage. The important content of each segment was reduced to a phrase of around two or three words, and segments were scored correct if the meaningful content was judged to have been reproduced. Synonyms and

alterations in phrasing were considered acceptable if they did not substantially alter the meaning of a segment. To facilitate reliable scoring, written guidelines were provided giving examples of acceptable versions. For instance, one segment of the original passage read, "In came a man from the back of the house," and the scoring instructions specified that to be scored correct a reproduction had to provide at least the equivalent of "A man came in." A measure of reliability was provided by correlating the meaningful recall scores as measured by two judges, using each subject's reproductions for one trial. The product-moment correlation of +.89 indicates that the meaningful recall measure is adequately reliable for the purposes of the present study.

RESULTS

Meaningful Recall

The mean numbers of meaningful units correctly recalled (out of 20) were 8.13, 8.50, 10.00, and 11.75 for Sessions 1, 2, 3, and 4, respectively. The week-to-week improvement is statistically significant, $F = 28.44$, $df = 3/63$, $p < .01$. Table 1 shows that items recalled on one session were likely to be recalled on the succeeding session and that items that were not recalled on a given session were much less likely to be correctly reproduced on the succeeding trial. Note that items recalled on none of the first three sessions were recalled on only .19 of occasions on Trial 4, although in such instances the subjects had heard the items in four separate presentations. This probability was very much lower than that for items presented only once but subsequently recalled correctly on Trial 1 (.71), and considerably lower even than the probability that an item presented on one occasion only (in Session 1) and not yet requested for recall, would be correctly recalled on Trial 1 (.43, since mean recall on Trial 1 was 8.13 meaningful items out of 20). Rank correlations between age and meaningful recall were −.08 for Trial 1, −.27 for Trial 4, and −.09 for the improvement (difference in recall scores) between Trials 1 and 4. None of these correlations is significant.

Verbatim Recall

The mean numbers of words correctly recalled (out of 160) were 29.77 on Trial

1, 24.95 on Trial 2, 37.32 on Trial 3, and 43.36 on Trial 4. The mean numbers of "additions" (i.e., words that appeared in a subject's recall attempts but not in the correct version) were 51.73, 55.95, 58.32, and 57.36, for Trials 1–4. Thus the mean total number of words that appeared in the subjects' reproductions (correct words plus additions) increased from 81.50 on Trial 1 to 102.72 on Trial 4.

As in the case of meaningful recall scores, words reproduced correctly on any given trial had a high probability of being recalled on the succeeding trial, although the precise numerical values are generally lower for verbatim than for meaningful repetitions (Table 1). Words that were not correctly reproduced on any given trial generally had an even lower probability of being recalled on the succeeding trial than in the case of meaningful items.

These results clearly show that with verbatim as with meaningful recall, items that had appeared on previous attempts at reproduction were much more likely to appear on subsequent recall attempts than items that had been presented in the original passage but which had not appeared in previous recall attempts. For instance, a word that had been presented once and recalled once was about four times as likely (.48 versus .11) to appear on the next recall trial than an item that had been presented on four occasions but not previously recalled.

Verbatim scores allow a further useful analysis that is not easily possible with measures of meaningful retention, since it is possible to count the number of additions and observe how often they are repeated. Additions appearing on Trials 1, 2, and 3 had mean probabilities of .21, .29, and .37 of appearing again on the respective succeeding trial. An addition occurring on both Trials 1 and 2 had a .56 probability of recurring on Trial 3. If the same addition was made on all of the first three trials, the mean probability of it occurring again on Trial 4 was .61. It is clear that the probabilities of additions that were made on one trial recurring on the next were generally much higher than the probabilities for word recall of items

TABLE 1

THE PROBABILITY THAT AN ITEM RECALLED OR NOT RECALLED ON GIVEN TRIAL(S) WILL BE RECALLED ON THE IMMEDIATELY SUCCEEDING TRIAL, FOR MEANINGFUL AND VERBATIM RECALL

Trial	Probability that the item will be recalled on the immediately succeeding trial	
	Meaningful recall	Verbatim recall
Item recalled on the trial(s) shown		
1	.71	.48
2	.64	.73
3	.89	.74
1 & 2	—	.86
1, 2, & 3	.98	.93
Item not recalled on the trial(s) shown		
1	.22	.08
2	.25	.14
3	.32	.13
1 & 2	.20	.10
1, 2, & 3	.19	.11

in the correct version that were not reproduced on preceding trials. For instance, a word presented on four separate occasions as part of the correct prose passage had only a .11 mean probability of being reproduced on Trial 4 if it had not been recalled earlier, whereas an incorrect addition that had not (by definition) occurred at all in the presentation sequence, but which had been produced by a subject on just one occasion, in Trial 1, had a mean probability of .21 being reproduced in the succeeding recall attempt.

Rank correlations were calculated to discover whether there was a significant relationship between the subjects' age and accuracy of verbatim recall. For Trial 1, $r = -.21$ (ns) and for Trial 4 $r = -.46$ $(p < .01)$. There is also a significant negative correlation between age and magnitude of improvement in recall between Trial 1 and Trial 4 (Trial 4–Trial 1), $r = -.40, p < .05$.

Relationship between Meaningful and Verbatim Recall

Product-moment correlations were calculated between meaningful and verbatim recall scores for each trial. The correlations were: Trial 1, $r = +.89$; Trial 2, $r = +.79$; Trial 3, $r = +.76$; Trial 4, $r = +.75$. In all cases $p < .01$.

DISCUSSION

The results leave no doubt that, for both meaningful and verbatim recall, items that subjects produced on a given recall trial are much more likely to be reproduced on the succeeding trial than items not previously recalled. The magnitude of the difference is shown by the fact that probabilities for reproduction of previously recalled and nonrecalled items generally differ by a factor of around three for meaningful recall and around five for verbatim recall, when appropriate comparisons are made across equivalent trials. In the case of verbatim recall scores, even incorrect additions are, on average, two or three times more likely to recur on the succeeding trial than are previously nonrecalled items to be reproduced correctly. The demonstration that memory for meaningful units as well as verbatim retention is closely related to past recall performance suggests that subjects submit the materials to relatively durable interpreting and encoding processes, and that such encoding goes well beyond the function of putting the material into one's own words, to which Miller (1956) draws attention. Indeed, subjects seems to make considerable changes in the substantive content of the material to which they listen, and such changes apparently persist in the face of the opportunities which repeated presentation provides for amending and correcting one's faulty version of the original prose passage. Thus the present results not only support and add precision to the findings of Bartlett (1932) and Allport and Postman (1947), but indicate that transformations made by subjects may be remarkably stable, even when incorrect. The fact that correlations between verbatim and meaningful scores decrease slightly from week to week suggests that subjects may become progressively less influenced by the verbatim form of the original passage. Additional, albeit anecdotal evidence concerning the persistence of the subject's versions was provided by a number of subjects who spontaneously reported to the experimenter their awareness that they were tending to reproduce very much the same material from week to week and that they found it much more difficult than they would have expected to make use of the repeated presentations of the original passage in order to correct their own retained versions. Several subjects found this very frustrating.

The high incidence of repetitions of incorrect additions in verbatim recall, which contrast with the much lower occurrence of recall of correct words not reproduced on previous recall trials, might not in itself be regarded as particularly important, since the main purpose of the experiment, stressed in the instructions to the subjects, was to examine meaningful rather than verbatim recall. However, it is clear from the high correlations between meaningful and verbatim recall scores, that especially in the first two trials the verbatim measures closely reflected what was happening at the meaningful level.

In conclusion, the present results generally agree with those obtained by Kay (1955) in finding that subjects who are required to attend to, and later recall, meaningful prose material appear to encode the materials in ways that have stability and permanence to an extent which may interfere with subsequent efforts to increase the accuracy of learning. Skinner's (1958) claim that students are liable to repeat their own errors, which he uses as an argument for the use of systems that minimize the incidence of errors, appears to have validity, although further evidence would be necessary to establish whether the tendency for meaningful reproductions to persist extends to the typically short student responses required in the sort of frames that Skinner advocates in programmed learning. The possibility that subject-produced responses may cause proactive or retroactive interference also requires independent examination, the present results being consistent with such a suggestion. Finally, these results cast doubt on the wisdom of a procedure whereby students are tested and the teacher subsequently "goes over" the test and provides the correct answers, on the implicit assumption that correction of student's answers will bring about a correction of his understanding that will prevent repetition of errors, but research studies more closely approximating classroom settings and procedure are needed to settle the issue.

REFERENCES

ALLPORT, G. W., & POSTMAN, L. *The psychology of rumor.* New York: Holt, 1947.

AUSUBEL, D. P. *Educational psychology: A cognitive view.* New York: Holt, Rinehart & Winston, 1968.

AUSUBEL, D. P., & BLAKE, E. Proactive inhibition in the forgetting of meaningful school material. *Journal of Educational Research,* 1958, **52,** 145–149.

AUSUBEL, D. P., ROBBINS, L. C., & BLAKE, E. Retroactive inhibition and facilitation in the learning of school materials. *Journal of Educational Psychology,* 1957, **48,** 334–343.

AUSUBEL, D. P., STAGER, M., & GAITE, A. J. H. Retroactive facilitation in meaningful verbal learning. *Journal of Educational Psychology,* 1968, **59,** 250–255.

AUSUBEL, D. P., STAGER, M., & GAITE, A. J. H. Proactive effects in meaningful verbal learning and retention. *Journal of Educational Psychology,* 1969, **60,** 59–64.

BARTLETT, F. C. *Remembering.* London: Cambridge University Press, 1932.

COFER, C. N. A comparison of logical and verbatim learning of prose passages of different lengths. *American Journal of Psychology,* 1941, **54,** 1–21.

KAY, H. Learning and retaining verbal material. *British Journal of Psychology,* 1955, **44,** 81–100.

MILLER, G. A. The magical number seven, plus or minus two: Some limits on our capacity for processing information. *Psychological Review,* 1956, **63,** 81–97.

SKINNER, B. F. Teaching machines. *Science,* 1958, **128,** 969–977.

TULVING, E. Subjective organization in free recall of "unrelated" words. *Psychological Review,* 1962, **69,** 344–354.

TULVING, E. Subjective organization and effects or repetition in multi-trial free recall learning. *Journal of Verbal Learning and Verbal Behavior,* 1966, **5,** 193–197.

J.D. Bransford, J.R. Barclay and J.J. Franks

Sentence memory: a constructive versus interpretive approach

Reprinted from *Cognitive Psychology* (1972)
3(2):193-209

The present studies investigated the adequacy of an interpretive linguistic approach to the description of the knowledge communicated by sentences by asking whether sentence retention was primarily a function of memory for the semantically interpreted deep structural relations underlying the input sentences or a function of memory for the overall semantic situations that such sentences described. Results were shown to be primarily a function of memory for the semantic situations. A constructive approach to sentence memory was outlined that dealt with memory for individual sentences as well as memory for sets of semantically related sentences contributing to the same overall idea.

Under normal circumstances a listener's memory for sentences may be inaccurate at the level of word-for-word recall but accurate at the level of semantic paraphrase (e.g., Sachs, 1967). A major task for psychology is to characterize the nature of the abstract semantic information that is retained. Most recent attempts to account for sentence memory have relied heavily on concepts developed within transformational linguistic theory. For example, the distinction between the deep and surface structures of sentences has had considerable influence in this regard. The surface structure of a sentence is said to characterize its phonological shape but its deep structure is considered necessary to characterize its meaning (Katz & Postal, 1964). A number of investigators have presented evidence for the importance of deep structural relations in characterizing what is retained (e.g., Blumenthal, 1967; Blumenthal & Boakes, 1967; Rohrman, 1968; Sachs, 1967).

It is important to note that the deep structural approach to linguistics generally assumes an *interpretive* approach to semantics. Katz and Postal (1964), for example, have proposed that the deep structure of a sentence represents the input to the semantic component of the grammar.

With few exceptions (see Katz & Fodor, 1963) the semantic interpretation assigned to a sentence is presumed to provide ". . . a full analysis of its cognitive meaning" (Katz & Postal, 1964, p. 12). Thus a semantically interpreted deep structure is assumed to provide a sufficient characterization of what is stored.

While the present authors heartily endorse the use of all available linguistic information in formulating a theory of sentence retention the purpose of this article is to demonstrate some of the possible pitfalls of the above-mentioned linguistic approach to sentence memory. It will be argued that a theory of sentence retention that restricts itself to a purely interpretive theory of semantics is not sufficient. An adequate deep structural analysis of input sentences may be necessary for a complete characterization of what one remembers, but it will not be sufficient to characterize what is retained.[1]

An alternative to the interpretive approach to sentence memory is one in which sentences are not viewed as linguistic objects to be remembered. Instead they are viewed as information which Ss can use to construct semantic descriptions of situations. These constructed descriptions may contain more information than is represented in the linguistic inputs, and hence a purely linguistic analysis of the input sentences will not adequately characterize the information available to the listener. The experiments to be outlined in the present paper represent an initial attempt to contrast the interpretive versus constructive approaches to sentence memory. Essentially these experiments ask whether sentence memory is primarily a function of the deep structural information underlying the input sentences or a function of the semantic descriptions that such inputs suggest.

Consider the following two sentences.

(1). Three turtles rested *beside* a floating log, and a fish swam beneath them.

(2). Three turtles rested *on* a floating log, and a fish swam beneath them.

These two sentences have identical deep structures that differ only in the specification of the lexical items *on* or *beside*, but the semantic situations suggested by the two sentences differ in at least one very important way. The description suggested by sentence (1) includes information about a fish swimming beneath the turtles. The description suggested by (2) also includes this information, but it includes something additional as well. Since the turtles were on the log and the fish swam beneath them, it follows that the fish swam beneath the log as well. This latter information (that the fish swam beneath the log) was

---

[1] On the question of the linguistic adequacy of deep structural characterizations of sentences see, for example, Fillmore, 1968; McCawley, 1968.

not supplied by the linguistic input, however, but had to come from one's general cognitive knowledge of the world (in this case, knowledge of spatial relations). Of course, one might construct a dynamic description of sentence (1) that also contained this latter information, but the probability of doing so is much lower than for sentence (2).

Sentences like (1) and (2) above can be used to compare the interpretive and constructive views of sentence memory. Assume, for example, that Ss hearing either sentence (1) or (2) are presented with a recognition sentence that merely changes the final pronoun specified in the input sentence, i.e., (3) Three turtles rested (beside/on) a floating log and a fish swam beneath *it*. The two theories make different predictions about the probability that Ss will think they actually heard this sentence before (i.e., the theories make different predictions about the probability of false positives). According to the interpretive theory Ss store only the linguistic information underlying the input sentence. Hence Ss hearing either sentence (1) or (2) above should be equally likely to detect the pronoun change in sentence (3). The constructive theory makes a different set of predictions, however. Ss are assumed to construct wholistic semantic descriptions of situations. If they forget the information underlying the input sentence they should not be reduced to guessing, but should base their recognition ratings on the complete semantic descriptions presumably acquired. Given this view, Ss hearing sentence (1) should still reject sentence (3) since it is neither consonant with the actual input sentence nor the complete semantic description constructed. Ss hearing sentence (2) should be quite likely to think they heard sentence (3), however, since the latter sentence is consonant with the complete semantic description presumably acquired. In short, the constructive theory predicts that one's ability to detect the pronoun change in sentence (3) depends on whether he originally heard sentence (1) or (2).

The first experiment was designed to contrast the interpretive and constructive theory by comparing recognition memory for sentences which have identical deep structures but differ in the semantic descriptions suggested. Two general types of sentences were used. The first type, exemplified by sentence (2) above suggested semantic descriptions that admitted a potential inference based on one's knowledge of spatial relations (i.e., that a fish swam beneath the log as well as the turtles). The second type, exemplified by (1) above did not suggest semantic descriptions that admitted the same inference. These two sentence types will be referred to as Potential Inference (PI), and Non-inference (NI) sentences, respectively. Of course, the term "Non-inference" is somewhat inaccurate, since the NI sentences used in the present study do offer bases for certain inferences. For example, from the fact that "Three turtles rested beside the floating log and a fish swam beneath it" (an NI sentence), one could infer that the fish did not swim under the turtles. The major differences between PI and NI sentences in the present study lay in the spontaneity and content of inferences they might provoke, and the sentences were intuitively chosen to exploit these differences. Thus, the convenient designation "Non-inference" is entirely relative to the present experimental situation.

EXPERIMENT I

Method

Subjects. The Ss were 18 female undergraduates enrolled in introductory psychology courses at the University of Minnesota. They were run in two groups, with 11 Ss in Group I, and 7 Ss in Group II.

Materials. Materials consisted of 14 sentence frames, such as *Three turtles rested (on/beside) a floating log and a fish swam beneath (it/them)*, and 7 filler (F) sentences. From each sentence frame it was possible to construct four different sentences. These differed among themselves in their PI vs NI status and/or in their final pronouns. One sentence from each frame was chosen for the acquisition list.

Each group of Ss received 21 acquisition sentences: 7 PI, 7 NI, and 7 F sentences. Sentence frame derivatives were counterbalanced across the two groups, such that each frame presented in PI form in one group was presented in NI form to the other group, and vice versa. For example, if sentence (1 above was presented to Group I, sentence (2) was presented to Group II. All PI and NI sentences dealt with relatively simple spatial relationships. Some additional examples are as follows: *Two robins crouched (on/beside) their nest as the hawk flew above (it/them); The raccoons (raced up/looked over towards) the tree and the dogs circled around (it/them)*.

For each group, 35 recognition sentences were also constructed. Fourteen of these were the PI and NI sentences presented during acquisition, and an additional 14 were their respective, alternative pronoun counterparts. For example, if a group heard sentence (1) above during acquisition, they heard both (1) and (3) during recognition. The remaining seven recognition sentences were Fillers. Three of these were presented in their original (acquisition) form; the other four were distortions of F sentences used during acquisition. As an example of the latter, during acquisition Ss heard *The contestant knew the quote but he couldn't remember where he had read it,* but during recognition they heard *The contestant knew the quote but he couldn't remember who had said it.* The distortions of F sentences were intuitively chosen to involve somewhat greater changes in meaning than the differences in meaning between the two versions of NI sentences.

Procedure

Acquisition. Ss were instructed to listen carefully to a set of sentences to be read to them because they would be asked questions about these sentences later in the experiment. Twenty-one sentences were read by the E with approximately 10 sec pause between sentences. Sentences were read in a random order, with the exception that a Filler sentence began and ended each acquisition list. After one completion of the list Ss were given a 3 min break.

Recognition. After the 3 min break Ss were told that they would be read a list of sentences, all of which would be closely related to the ones they had heard during acquisition. Their task was to indicate which exact sentences they had heard during acquisition, and which they had not. In addition, they were asked to rate their confidence in each response, using a 5-point confidence scale ranging from VERY HIGH to VERY LOW. Ss were told that some sentences might be read twice during recognition, but that they were to respond *only* on the basis of whether they had heard a sentence during acquisition or not. Actually, no sentences were read twice during recognition; the above instructions were meant to allay any confusion that might have arisen if Ss mistakenly thought that they were hearing repetitions of recognition sentences. Recognition sentences were read in random order with the exception that a Filler sentence began the recognition lists.

Results

Ss' confidence ratings were converted into numerical scores as follows. YES responses (indicating recognition of acquisition list sentences) received positive values, and NO responses received negative values. A VERY HIGH confidence rating received 5 points, a HIGH confidence rating received 4 points, and so on down to 1 point for VERY LOW confidence. Thus a 10-point rating scale emerged, ranging from $+5$ to -5 (excluding zero).

Each S's mean recognition rating was computed for each of the following six categories of sentences: (1) Potential inference sentences presented during acquisition (OLD-PI); (2) Potential inference sentences not presented during acquisition (NEW-PI); (3) Noninference sentences presented during acquisition (OLD-NI); (4) Noninference sentences not presented during acquisition (NEW-NI); (5) Filler sentences presented during acquisition (OLD-F); and (6) Filler sentences not presented during acquisition (NEW-F). Data were further analyzed in terms of these means across Ss. The overall mean ratings across Ss for the six categories were computed and are represented in Table 1.

The results are quite clear. A two factor analysis of variance with repeated measures on both factors produced a significant interaction

TABLE 1

Mean Recognition Scores for the Six Sentence Categories in Exp I

	OLDS	NEWS
PI	1.40	1.43
NI	2.22	−0.19
F	2.19	−4.15

between recognition status (OLD versus NEW), and sentence type ($F(2,34) = 40.54$, $p < .001$). Tests on simple main effects revealed that for both NI and F sentences, OLD's were rated higher than NEW's ($F(1,17) = 26.72$ and 186.73, respectively, $p < .001$ in both cases). For PI sentences the small OLD versus NEW difference was not significant ($F < 1.00$). Thus, for PI sentences alone, Ss could not distinguish those sentences they had heard before from those they had not.

A significant sentence type effect was found for NEW sentences ($F(2,34) = 90.59$, $p < .001$), but not for OLD sentences ($F(2,34) = 2.38$, $p > .10$). The difference between OLD PI's and NI's is probably meaningful, however, since OLD PI sentences were in effect surrounded by more difficult recognition foils. The Newman–Kuels test showed that among NEW sentences all differences were significant ($p < .01$). Thus, NEW PI sentences received significantly higher recognition ratings than NEW NI sentences, which in turn received higher ratings than NEW F sentences. NEW PI's received higher recognition ratings than NEW NI's for 10 of the 14 sentence frames used to construct the acquisition list. The difference between NEW NI and NEW F sentences agrees with one's intuitive expectation that increases in the semantic differences between an OLD sentence and its NEW counterpart will allow such sentences to become more distinguishable in a memory task, although such results for F sentences are also confounded with primacy and recency effects.

Discussion

Results indicate that PI and NI sentences were remembered differently in that Ss' inability to differentiate OLD from NEW sentences was generally confined to sentences in PI form. These results are consonant with the constructive approach to sentence memory, but additional controls are needed before one can rule out the purely linguistic approach. Specifically, it is possible that sentences in PI form are just *generally* more poorly comprehended. Perhaps the prepositions used to construct PI sentences (e.g., ON) cause all the semantic information in these sentences to be less easily remembered. If one forgets information about the turtles resting on the log, for example, he is likely to forget information about the appropriate pronoun as well, and hence he will not be able to differentiate OLDS from NEWS. Such a generalized memory decrement for PI sentences would not support the constructive hypothesis which, under the present circumstance, assumes that memory differences between PI and NI sentences are pronoun specific. For PI sentences, the constructive theory assumes that information about turtles resting on the log can be very well remembered. Ss should only be unsure of whether the input sentence indicated that the fish swam beneath *them* or *it*. It is possible to show that memory differences between PI and NI sentences *are* pronoun specific by the following procedure: Ss can be asked to recall the entire sentences heard during acquisition. If the PI form of a sentence causes it to be generally less poorly remembered, PI sentences should show a lower probability of recall than NI sentences even when one disregards the final pronoun that was remembered. If the memory differences between PI and NI sentences are pronoun specific, however, PI and NI sentences should be remembered with equal accuracy when one disregards the final pronoun that was recalled. Exp. II investigated memory differences between PI and NI sentences in a recall task.

EXPERIMENT II

Method

Subjects. The Ss were 17 undergraduates enrolled in introductory psychology courses at SUNY at Stony Brook. They were run in two groups with 9 Ss in Group I and 8 Ss in Group II.

Materials. Materials consisted of 14 sentence frames, and 7 fillers. Fillers were identical to those used in Exp. I. Since Exp. II included conditions that allowed a replication of Exp. I as well as conditions allowing a test of the pronoun-specificity of the memory differences between PI and NI sentences, a new sample of 14 sentence frames was chosen from a larger master list constructed after running the first experiment. Hence some sentences overlapped with those used in Exp. I, and some did not.

Each group received 21 acquisition sentences: 7 PI, 7 NI, and 7 F sentences. Sentence frame derivatives were counterbalanced across the two groups as in the first experiment. Acquisition sentences were randomized as in Exp. I. Recall prompts which consisted of the subject noun phrase of each sentence were constructed for the 7 PI and 7 NI sentences.

Procedure

Acquisition. The acquisition task was identical to Exp I.

Recall. During recall, Ss were read the sentence prompts (i.e., the subject noun phrases) for each PI and NI sentence. After hearing a prompt, Ss' task was to recall the rest of the sentence. Sentence prompts were randomized with respect to acquisition order and PI and NI sentences were equally distributed across both halves of the recall list.

Results

In order to pinpoint the locus of the memory differences between PI and NI sentences, data were analyzed in two ways. First, sentence recall scores were computed without regard for accuracy of recall of the final pronoun. Second, pronoun recall scores were computed for sentences which were otherwise correctly recalled.

The first analysis indicated that 34% of all sentences were paraphrased correctly (when accuracy of final pronouns was disregarded). Of these sentences 54% were PI sentences, and 46% were NI sentences. A randomization test for matched pairs indicated that recall scores were not significantly different $(p > .10)$. However, given correct recall of the rest of the sentence, the second analysis yielded pronoun accuracies consonant with those found in the preceeding experiment. Percent correct pronoun recall (given correct recall of the rest of the sentence) was 57%, and 76% for PI and NI sentences, respectively (by the randomization test, $p < .025$). For 10 of 14 sentence frames, PI sentences showed a lower probability of accurate pronoun recall than sentences in NI form. The less sensitive recall procedure thus replicated the results found for the first experiment, and in addition results showed that memory differences between PI and NI sentences were specific to memory for the particular pronoun forms.

Discussion

Results of Exp's I and II strongly support the constructive approach to sentence memory. Retention was primarily a function of the semantic descriptions generated by input sentences rather than a function of the actual information the latter contained. If Ss had merely stored linguistic information memory for pronouns in PI and NI sentences should have been roughly the same. Instead, pronoun memory was relatively good for NI sentences, but PI sentences produced very poor memory for those pronouns heard during the acquisition task. Memory differences were pronoun specific. When recall data were analyzed without regard for accuracy of the final pronoun, PI and NI sentences were recalled equally well.

The constructive approach to sentence retention can apply to memory for sets of semantically related sentences as well as memory for individual sentences. Various sentences can converge on a common semantic description, and knowledge of this wholistic description may be what is retained. Bransford and Franks (1970, 1971) have shown that Ss spontaneously integrated the information from semantically related acquisition sentences to construct wholistic semantic descriptions, and that these descriptions, rather than the exact sentences from which they were constructed, determined Ss' accuracy and response-confidence in a sentence recognition task. Bransford and Franks did not specifically investigate the construction of wholistic descriptions allowing extra-linguistic inferences, however. Some constructed descriptions should code more information that the whole set of acquisition sentences contained.

Consider the following description (Description A):

There is a tree with a box beside it, and a chair is on top of the box. The box is to the right of the tree. The tree is green and extremely tall.

One can treat this example as a set of linguistic entities or as information specifying a general semantic description, and these two different characterizations will make different claims about the nature of the information a listener may retain. Specifically, consider the sentence *The chair is to the right of the tree.* This information is not provided linguistically, but it is consonant with the description of the situation that most Ss would be likely to construct. Do Ss actually construct descriptions of situations that allow such "novel but appropriate sentences"? One can begin to answer this question by presenting Ss with the following 4 recognition sentences (Recognition Set A), and instructing them to pick which exact sentence they actually heard during acquisition. The interpretive and constructive theories make different predictions about the kinds of errors that Ss should make.

(a) The box is to the right of the tree.
(b) The chair is to the right of the tree.
(c) The box is to the left of the tree.
(d) The chair is to the left of the tree.

According to the constructive theory, comprehension of description A above should result in the construction of a wholistic description of the overall situation being communicated. Ss should generally remember something about the particular linguistic style through which the description was originally communicated, but given that they forget this they should not be reduced to total guessing. Instead they should tend to pick sentences consonant with the overall semantic descriptions constructed, even if such sentences were not heard during the acquisition task. Given the above set of recognition examples, for example, (Recognition Set A), Ss should thus be very likely to think they actually heard sentence (b). The interpretive linguistic approach postulates no overall wholistic description of the situation, however. Hence if one cannot remember which sentence he heard during acquisition he should be reduced to guessing or should tend to pick a sentence that is linguistically very similar to one heard during acquisition. Given those sentences in Recognition Set A above, Ss should thus be at least as likely to pick sentence (c) as (b), since (c) differs from the one actually heard at input only by the substitution of the word "left" for "right."

There exists an additional way one can use Description A above to compare the interpretive and constructive approaches to sentence memory. This involves the fact that there are many linguistically different ways to describe the same basic situation, and these linguistic forms can differ in deep structure as well as surface structure form. For example, the sentence *The tree is to the left of the chair.* is consonant with a description of the situation described by Description A above, but it is deep structurally very dissimilar to the input sentence actually heard (i.e., *The box is to the right of the tree*). One can present Ss with descriptions like A above, and then with the four recognition sentences below (Recognition Set B). If recognition is primarily a function of linguistic information Ss should be very confused with these items. If recognition can be based on an abstracted semantic description of the situation, however, Ss should show a strong tendency to make "situation-preserving" errors. That is, they should be likely to pick sentences like (a) and (b) below.

(a) The tree is to the left of the box.
(b) The tree is to the left of the chair.
(c) The tree is to the right of the box.
(d) The tree is to the right of the chair.

Exp II compared the interpretive and constructive approaches using descriptive paragraphs like A above, and recognition sets like examples A and B.

EXPERIMENT III

Method

Subjects. The Ss were 45 undergraduates enrolled in a course in Experimental Psychology at SUNY at Stony Brook. They were divided into 2 subgroups of 25 and 20 Ss with the 2 subgroups receiving a different form of the recognition test.

Materials. Materials consisted of 6 descriptive passages like example A presented above, and 4 filler passages. All passages consisted of 4 sentences. The 6 experimental passages suggested descriptions of situations which allowed inferences about the relations among objects: 3 used relations "to the right of," and three used relations "to the left of."

Two sets of recognition sheets were constructed that were analogous to Sets A and B presented above. First consider Recognition Set A. For each of the 6 experimental descriptions (plus two of the fillers) there was a block of 4 sentences: One was the old sentence actually heard during acquisition (OLD); one was a permissible inference (I); A third sentence (CHANGE R) merely changed the spatial relation described by the OLD sentence (e.g., change "right" to "left"), and a fourth sentence (CHANGE R and N) changed both the relation and the subject noun. These four sentence types are illustrated in Table 2.

Recognition Set B changed the linguistic format of all sentences, and hence there were no sentences that were actually OLD. Set B was identical to Set A except that the subject and object nouns were reversed as well as the spatial relations. Hence if an OLD for Set A was *The box was to the right of the tree* it would read as follows for Set B: *The tree was to the left of the box.* For Set B we shall refer to sentences like the latter as OLD′ since they preserve the semantic objects specified in the input string. Similarly, we thus have a NEW′, a CHANGE R′, and a CHANGE R and S′ which each correspond to the other 3 sentences in Recognition Set A. Examples are shown in Table 2. For both Sets A and B sentences were randomized within blocks, and order of blocks was randomized with respect to the order of passages in the acquisition list.

Procedure

Acquisition. All 45 Ss heard 10 acquisition passages: 6 experimental descriptions and 4 fillers. A filler appeared at the beginning and end of the acquisition list as well as in positions 4 and 7. Passages were read with normal intonation, and there was a 7-sec pause between each one. Ss were instructed to listen carefully to the passages and to attempt to comprehend them because they would later be asked some questions about their meanings. After reading each passage once there was a 3-min break.

Recognition. After the 3 min break Ss were told that they were to be given a recognition sheet with blocks of sentences typed on it, and they were to indicate which sentences from each block they had actually heard during the acquisition task. Recognition sheet A was given to 25 Ss and 20 Ss received recognition Sheet B.

TABLE 2
Examples of Recognition Sentences for Exp. III

	OLD	The box is to the right of the tree.
Recognition	I	The chair is to the right of the tree.
Set A	CHANGE R	The box is to the left of the tree.
	CHANGE R & S	The chair is to the left of the tree.
	OLD′	The tree is to the left of the box.
Recognition	I′	The tree is to the left of the chair.
Set B	CHANGE R′	The tree is to the right of the box.
	CHANGE S & R′	The tree is to the right of the chair.

Results

The response percentages for each type of sentence were computed separately for Recognition sets A and B. Results are presented in Table 3. First consider results for Recognition Set A. A difference T test showed OLDS to be recognized more often than I's ($T(24) = 1.81$, $p < .05$), indicating that Ss had some tendency to remember the linguistic form in which the information was originally expressed. However, given that Ss could not remember the actual form of the input (i.e., did not pick the OLD) they were most likely to pick an I sentence consonant with

TABLE 3
Percentage of Recognition Responses for the Sentence Categories Used in Exp. III

	Situation-preserving responses		Situation-distorting responses	
	OLD	I	CHANGE R	CHANGE S & R
Recognition Set A	42%	29%	16%	13%
Recognition Set B	OLD' 33%	I' 37%	CHANGE R' 22%	CHANGE S & R' 8%

the complete semantic descriptions presumably constructed. A difference T test showed I sentences to be picked more often than the next highest contender (i.e., CHANGE R sentences; $T(24) = 2.50$, $p < .01$). By combining ratings for both OLD and I sentences one can compute the number of responses consonant with the complete semantic descriptions suggested by the passages. For recognition set A this value is 71%.

Next consider recognition set B. A difference T test showed no difference between OLD' and I' ratings ($t(19) = -.60$, $p > .25$). This is to be expected, since no sentences are actually identical to those heard before. The results suggest that Ss were not simply responding by analogy to memory for the exact sentences heard during acquisition, however. If they were one would expect OLD' sentences to receive more recognition responses than I' sentences, since OLD' sentences preserve the content nouns of the OLDS. The I' sentences were picked significantly more often than the next highest contender (i.e., CHANGE R sentences), hence these results parallel those found for recognition set A ($t(19) = 2.83$, $p < .01$). A combination of ratings for OLD' and I' sentences indicated that 70% of all responses were situation preserving. A proportion test showed this value to be nonsignificantly different from the 71% found for recognition set A. These latter data provide especially strong evidence for the constructive approach to sentence memory. If Ss were simply storing information about which objects were described as "right of" or "left of" they should have been very confused by Recognition Set B, and hence should have picked many sentences that were not consonant with the wholistic descriptions acquired.

Overall Discussion

Results of Exp. III are congruent with those of the first two studies. Recognition was shown to be primarily a function of the complete semantic descriptions constructed rather than a function of just that information specified by the linguistic input strings. All three studies supported the constructive but not the interpretive theory. These results suggest that the contribution of an interpretive linguistic theory to psychological studies of sentence memory and comprehension should be more cautiously evaluated than has heretofore been the case. Although a linguistic description of sentences is invaluable in developing an adequate psycholinguistic theory it should be remember that a sentence (or set of sentences) is not merely a perceptual object which the listener may recall or recognize. If it were a linguistic description might sufficiently characterize it as such. Rather a sentence is also a source of information which the listener assimilates to his existing cognitive knowledge. In the present examples the descriptions Ss constructed contained more information than was directly represented in the linguistic input strings.

Note, incidentally, that it is generally more efficient to code descriptions of situations rather than descriptions of inputs. For example, suppose someone communicated the following situation: "There is a driveway on the right, a tree on the left and a baby sitting between the two." Now suppose another piece of information is added to this description; namely that "a dog sat directly to the right of the baby and licked the baby's face." This latter statement allows a considerable amount of information about the relation of the dog to other objects; namely that the dog is to the left of the driveway and to the right of the tree. These latter two propositions did not have to be provided linguistically, yet this information appears to spontaneously be "filled in." New information is assimilated into the existing structures one has in mind. Depending upon the context into which they are assimilated, sentences can have semantic implications that extend beyond the information they directly express.

So far we have said nothing about the nature of the semantic descriptions constructed by Ss except that they cannot be completely characterized from an interpretive linguistic viewpoint. One way to characterize the semantic descriptions presumably acquired in the present experiments is, of course, to assume that they represent images of the situations being communicated. The present experiments all used easily imaginable situations, and imagery has been shown to be an important variable in other linguistic memory tasks (e.g., Begg & Paivio, 1969;

Paivio; 1969, 1970). In addition, many Ss spontaneously noted that they constructed images of situations in the above experimental tasks. It is reasonable to suppose that imagery played an important role in the particular experiments outlined in the present paper, but it should be noted that the general constructive approach to sentence memory is not necessarily equivalent to a theory which states that concrete linguistic entities are stored in visual form. First, note that the emphasis of the constructive approach is not simply on concretizing the information specified in the *linguistic* input. Instead one is assumed to use linguistic information in conjunction with previous knowledge to construct semantic descriptions. It is this synthesis of present input and previous knowledge which determines the nature of the semantic descriptions one constructs. The semantic descriptions suggested by the sentences used in the present experiments may seem to be completely specified by the linguistic inputs, but this is only because one's previous knowledge of spatial relations is so strong and intuitive that it is easy to overlook the determining factor this previous knowledge plays in specifying the nature of the descriptions one will construct. To put it another way, someone with a different spatial system would construct different descriptions of what took place.

In a broader sense the constructive approach argues against the tacit assumption that sentences "carry meaning." People carry meanings, and linguistic inputs merely act as cues which people can use to recreate and modify their previous knowledge of the world. What is comprehended and remembered depends on an individual's general knowledge of his environment. If a few words or sentences are sufficient to allow a listener to construct a description of a whole situation he is doing much more than simply concretizing the linguistic inputs. Instead he now has considerably more information at his disposal than he actually heard. The constructive approach thus argues that the act of comprehension generally involves considerably more than merely recovering or even concretizing the information specified by the input string.

Finally it should be noted that the constructive approach to sentence memory does not assume that the complete semantic descriptions constructed by Ss can be adequately characterized by images, even if one assumes that such images code more information than the original input sentences directly expressed. First, images must somehow be "read" or "interpreted" (e.g., see Elkind, 1969; Reese, 1970), and the nature of such "readings" or "interpretations" must be included in any theory of what is retained. Second, the constructive approach does not deny the psychological reality of some level of linguistic representation in memory. One can remember linguistic representations as well as the more general semantic descriptions suggested by the linguistic inputs. The constructive approach merely denies that a specification of the linguistic representations constitutes a sufficient characterization of the information available to a listener.

It is the present authors' belief that the constructive approach will prove to be very important for characterizing the processes of communication and comprehension. Intuitively one knows that language can often be a very ineffective means of communication, whereas at other times it serves its purpose very well. In addition, the same inputs can be well comprehended by one individual, and be very poorly understood and remembered by someone else. Although lack of comprehension is due in part to lack of vocabulary (and perhaps lack of familiarity with some sentence structures) it seems clear that this constitutes only part of the problem. According to the constructive account efficient communication generally depends on shared knowledge which people can draw upon to construct descriptions of situations. Merely comprehending the information specified in the linguistic inputs is not sufficient to guarantee that a listener understands the implications that a speaker has in mind.

REFERENCES

BEGG, I. R., & PAIVIO, A. Concreteness and imagery in sentence meaning. *Journal of Verbal Learning and Verbal Behavior*, 1969, 8, 821–827.

BLUMENTHAL, A. Prompted recall of sentences. *Journal of Verbal Learning and Verbal Behavior*, 1967, 6, 203–206.

BLUMENTHAL, A., & BOAKES, R. Prompted recall of sentences: A further study. *Journal of Verbal Learning and Verbal Behavior*, 1967, 6, 674–675.

BRANSFORD, J. D., & FRANKS, J. J. Temporal integration in the acquisition of complex linguistic ideas. In J. J. Jenkins (Chm.), *Understanding Sentences*. Symposium presented at the Midwestern Psychological Association, Cincinnati, May, 1970

BRANSFORD, J. D., & FRANKS, J. J. The abstraction of linguistic ideas. *Cognitive Psychology*, in press.

CHOMSKY, N. *Aspects of the theory of syntax*, Cambridge: M.I.T. Press, 1965.

ELKIND, D. Developmental studies of figurative perception. In L. P. Lipsitt & H. H. Reese (Eds.), *Advances in child development and behavior*. Vol. 4 New York: Academic Press, 1970.

FILLMORE, C. J. The case for case. In E. Bach and R. T. Harms (Eds.), *Universals in Linguistic Theory*, New York: Holt, Rinehart and Winston, Inc., 1968.

HUMPHREY, G. *Thinking*, New York: John Wiley, 1963.

KATZ, J. J., & FODOR, J. A. The structure of semantic theory. *Language*, 1963, 39, 170–210.

KATZ, J. J., & POSTAL, P. M. *An integrated theory of linguistic descriptions*. Cambridge, M.I.T. Press, 1964.

MCCAWLEY, J. D. The role of semantics in a grammar. In E. Bach and R. T. Harms (Eds.), *Universals in Linguistic Theory*. New York: Holt, Rinehart, and Winston, 1968.

PAIVIO, A. Mental imagery in associative learning and memory. *Psychological Review*, 1969, 76, 241–263.

PAIVIO, A. On the functional significance of imagery. *Psychological Bulletin*, 1970, 73, 385–392.

POSTAL, P. M. Underlying and superficial linguistic structure. *Harvard Educational Review*, 1964, **34**, 246-266.

ROHRMAN, N. L. The role of syntactic structure in the recall of English nominalizations. *Journal of Verbal Learning and Verbal Behavior*, 1968, **7**, 904–912.

REESE, H. W. Imagery and contextual meaning. *Psychological Bulletin*, 1970, **73**, No. 6, 404–414.

SACHS, J. Recognition memory for syntactic and semantic aspects of connected discourse. *Perception and Psychophysics*, 1967, **2**, 437–442.

SAVIN, H. B., & PERCHONOK, E. Grammatical structure and the immediate recall of English sentences. *Journal of Verbal Learning and Verbal Behavior*, 1965, **4**, 348–353.

A.M. Collins and M.R. Quillian

Retrieval time from semantic memory

Reprinted from the *Journal of Verbal Learning and Verbal Behavior* (1969) **8**:240-71

To ascertain the truth of a sentence such as "A canary can fly," people utilize long-term memory. Consider two possible organizations of this memory. First, people might store with each kind of bird that flies (e.g., canary) the fact that it can fly. Then they could retrieve this fact directly to decide the sentence is true. An alternative organization would be to store only the generalization that *birds* can fly, and to infer that "A canary can fly" from the stored information that a canary is a bird and birds can fly. The latter organization is much more economical in terms of storage space but should require longer retrieval times when such inferences are necessary. The results of a true-false reaction-time task were found to support the latter hypothesis about memory organization.

Quillian (1967, 1969) has proposed a model for storing semantic information in a computer memory. In this model each word has stored with it a configuration of pointers to other words in the memory; this configuration represents the word's meaning. Figure 1 illustrates the organization of such a memory structure. If what is stored with canary is "a yellow bird that can sing" then there is a pointer to bird, which is the category name or *superset* of canary, and pointers to two *properties*, that a canary is yellow and that it can sing. Information true of birds in general (such as that they can fly, and that they have wings and feathers) need not be stored with the memory node for each separate kind of bird. Instead, the fact that a canary can fly can be inferred by retrieving that a canary is a bird and that birds can fly. Since an ostrich cannot fly, we assume this information is stored as a property with the node for ostrich, just as is done in a dictionary, to preclude the inference that an ostrich can fly. By organizing the memory in this way, the amount of space needed for storage is minimized.

If we take this as a model for the structure of human memory, it can lead to testable predictions about retrieving information. Suppose a person has only the information shown in Fig. 1 stored on each of the nodes. Then to decide "A canary can sing," the person need only start at the node canary and retrieve the properties stored there to find the statement is true. But, to decide that "A canary can fly," the person must move up one level to bird before he can retrieve the property about flying. Therefore, the person should require more *time* to decide that "A canary can fly" than he does to decide that "A canary can sing." Similarly, the person should require still longer to decide that "A canary has skin," since this fact is stored with his node for animal, which is yet another step removed from canary. More directly, sentences which themselves assert something about a node's supersets, such as "A canary is a bird," or "A canary is an animal," should also require

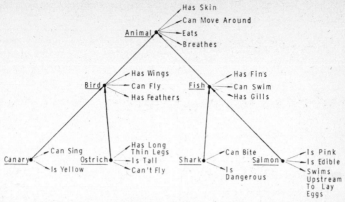

FIG. 1. Illustration of the hypothetical memory structure for a 3-level hierarchy.

decision times that vary directly with the number of levels separating the memory nodes they talk about.

A number of assumptions about the retrieval process must be made before predictions such as those above can be stated explicitly. First, we need to assume that both retrieving a property from a node and moving up a level in a hierarchy take a person time. Second, we shall assume that the times for these two processes are additive, whenever one step is dependent on completion of another step. This assumption is equivalent to Donders' assumption of additivity (Smith, 1968) for the following two cases: (a) When moving up a level is followed by moving up another level, and (b) when moving up a level is followed by retrieving a property at the higher level. Third, we assume that the time to retrieve a property from a node is independent of the level of the node, although different properties may take different times to retrieve from the same node. It also seems reasonable to assume that searching properties at a node and moving up to the next level occur in a parallel rather than a serial manner, and hence are not additive. However, this assumption is not essential, and our reasons for preferring it are made clear in the Discussion section.

We have labeled sentences that state property relations P sentences, and those that state superset relations S sentences. To these labels numbers are appended. These indicate

the number of levels the model predicts it would be necessary to move through to decide the sentence is true. Thus, "A canary can sing" would be a PO sentence, "A canary can fly" would be a P1 sentence, and "A canary has skin" would be a P2 sentence. Similarly, "A canary is a canary" would be an SO sentence, "A canary is a bird" would be an S1 sentence, and "A canary is an animal" would be an S2 sentence.

It follows from the assumptions above that the time differences predicted for PO, P1, and P2 sentences are entirely a result of moving from one level in the hierarchy to the next. Thus, the increase in time from SO to S1 should be the same as from PO to P1 since both increases are a result of moving from level O to level 1. Likewise, the time increase from S1 to S2 should equal the time increase from P1 to P2. In fact, if we assume that the time to move from one level to the next is not dependent on which levels are involved, all the time increases (from PO to P1, P1 to P2, SO to S1, and S1 to S2) should be equal.

Recently, reaction time (RT) has been used as a measure of the time it takes people to retrieve information from memory. By constructing a large number of true sentences of the six types discussed and interspersing these with equal numbers of false sentences, we can measure the reaction time for Ss to decide which sentences are true and which are false. Thus, this method can be used to test the prediction we have derived from the model and our assumptions about the retrieval process.

A caution is in order here: Dictionary definitions are not very orderly and we doubt that human memory, which is far richer, is even as orderly as a dictionary. One difficulty is that hierarchies are not always clearly ordered, as exemplified by dog, mammal, and animal. Subjects tend to categorize a dog as an animal, even though a stricter classification would interpose the category mammal between the two. A second difficulty is that people surely store certain properties at more than one level in the hierarchy. For example, having leaves is a general property of trees, but many people must have information stored about the maple leaf directly with maple, because of the distinctiveness of its leaf. In selecting examples, such hierarchies and instances were avoided. However, there will always be Ss for whom extensive familiarity will lead to the storing of many more properties (and sometimes supersets) than we have assumed. By averaging over different examples and different subjects, the effect of such individual idiosyncrasies of memory can be minimized.

METHOD

Three experiments were run, with eight Ss used in each experiment. The Ss were all employees of Bolt Beranek and Newman, Inc. who served voluntarily and had no knowledge of the nature of the experiment. Because of a faulty electrical connection, only three Ss gave usable data in Expt. 3. The same general method was used for all three experiments, except in the way the false sentences were constructed.

Apparatus. The sentences were displayed one at a time on the cathode ray tube (CRT) of a DEC PDP-1 computer.[1] The timing and recording of responses were under program control.[2] Each sentence was centered vertically on one line. The length of line varied from 10 to 34 characters (approximately 4–11° visual angle). The S sat directly in front of the CRT with his two index fingers resting on the two response

buttons. These each required a displacement of $\frac{1}{4}$ in to trigger a microswitch.

Procedure. The sentences were grouped in runs of 32 or 48, with a rest period of approximately 1 min between runs. Each sentence appeared on the CRT for 2 sec, and was followed by a blank screen for 2 sec before the next sentence. The S was instructed to press one button if the sentence was generally true, and the other button if it was generally false, and he was told to do so as accurately and as quickly as possible. The S could respond anytime within the 4 sec between sentences, but his response did not alter the timing of the sentences. Each S was given a practice run of 32 sentences similarly constructed.

Sentences. There were two kinds of semantic hierarchies used in constructing sentences for the experiments, 2-level and 3-level. In Fig. 1, a 2-level hierarchy might include bird, canary, and ostrich and their properties, whereas the whole diagram represents a 3-level hierarchy. A 2-level hierarchy included true P0, P1, S0 and S1 sentences; a 3-level hierarchy included true P2 and S2 sentences as well. Examples of sentence sets with 2-level and 3-level hierarchies are given in Table 1.[3] As illustrated in Table 1, equal numbers of true and false sentences were always present (but in random sequence) in the sentences an S read. Among both true and false sentences, there are the two general kinds: Property relations (P), and superset relations (S).

In Expt 1, each S read 128 two-level sentences followed by 96 three-level sentences. In Expt 2, each S read 128 two-level sentences, but different sentences from those used in Expt 1. In Expt 3, a different group of Ss read the same 96 three-level sentences used in Expt 1. Each run consisted of sentences from only four subject-matter hierarchies.

To generate the sentences we first picked a hierarchical group with a large set of what we shall call *instances* at the lowest level. For example, baseball, badminton, etc. are instances of the superset game. Different instances were used in each sentence, because repetition of a word is known to have substantial effects in reducing RT (Smith, 1967). In constructing S1 and S2 sentences, the choice of the category name or superset was in most cases obvious, though in a case such as the above 2-level example, sport might have been used as the superset rather than game. To assess how well our choices corresponded with the way most people categorize, two individuals who did not serve in any of the three experiments were asked to generate a category name for each S1 and S2

---

[1] Now at the University of Massachusetts, Amherst.
[2] The authors thank Ray Nickerson for the use of his program and for his help in modifying it to run on BBN's PDP-1.

[3] To obtain the entire set of true sentences for Expt 1 order NAPS Document NAPS-00265 from ASIS National Auxiliary Publications Service, c/o CCM Information Sciences, Inc., 22 West 34th Street, New York, New York 10001; remitting $1.00 for microfiche or $3.00 for photocopies.

TABLE 1

ILLUSTRATIVE SETS OF STIMULUS SENTENCES

Sentence type		True sentences	Sentence type[a]	False sentences
Expt 1, 2-level				
	PO	Baseball has innings	P	Checkers has pawns
	P1	Badminton has rules	P	Ping pong has baskets
	SO	Chess is chess	S	Hockey is a race
	S1	Tennis is a game	S	Football is a lottery
Expt 1, 3-level				
	PO	An oak has acorns	P	A hemlock has buckeyes
	P1	A spruce has branches	P	A poplar has thorns
	P2	A birch has seeds	P	A dogwood is lazy
	SO	A maple is a maple	S	A pine is barley
	S1	A cedar is a tree	S	A juniper is grain
	S2	An elm is a plant	S	A willow is grass
Expt 2, 2-level				
	PO	Seven-up is colorless	PO	Coca-cola is blue
	P1	Ginger ale is carbonated	P1	Lemonade is alcoholic
	SO	Pepsi-cola is Pepsi-cola	SO	Bitter lemon is orangeade
	S1	Root beer is a soft drink	S1	Club soda is wine

[a]There were no distinctions as to level made for false sentences in Expt 1.

sentence we used, e.g., "tennis is ————." These two individuals generated the category names we used in about 3/4 of their choices, and only in one case, "wine is a drink" instead of "liquid", was their choice clearly not synonymous.

In generating sentences that specified properties, only the verbs "is," "has," and "can" were used, where "is" was always followed by an adjective, "has" by a noun, and "can" by a verb. To produce the PO sentence one of the instances such as baseball was chosen that had a property (in this case innings) which was clearly identifiable with the instance and not the superset. To generate a P1 or P2 sentence, we took a salient property of the superset that could be expressed with the restriction to "is," "has," or "can." In the first example of Table 1, rules were felt to be a very salient property of games. Then an instance was chosen, in this case badminton, to which the P1 property seemed not particularly associated. Our assumption was that, if the model is correct, a typical S would decide whether badminton has rules or not by the path, badminton is a game and games have rules.

In Expt 1, false sentences were divided equally between supersets and properties. No systematic basis was used for constructing false sentences beyond an attempt to produce sentences that were not unreasonable or semantically anomalous, and that were always untrue rather than usually untrue. In Expt 2, additional restrictions were placed on the false sentences. The properties of the false PO sentences

were chosen so as to contradict a property of the instance itself. In example 3 of Table 1, "Coca-cola is blue" contradicts a property of Coca-cola, that it is brown or caramel-colored. In contrast, the properties of false P1 sentences were chosen so as to contradict a property of the superset. In the same example, alcoholic was chosen, because it is a contradiction of a property of soft drinks in general. The relation of elements in the false SO and S1 sentences can be illustrated by reference to Fig. 1. The false SO sentences were generated by stating that one instance of a category was equivalent to another, such as "A canary is an ostrich." The false S1 sentence was constructed by choosing a category one level up from the instance, but in a different branch of the structure, such as "A canary is a fish."

The sequence of sentences the S saw was randomly ordered, except for the restriction to four hierarchies in each run. The runs were counterbalanced over Ss with respect to the different sentence types, and each button was assigned true for half the Ss, and false for the other half.

RESULTS AND DISCUSSION

In analyzing the data from the three experiments, we have used the mean RT for each S's correct responses only. Error rates were on the average about 8% and tended to increase where RT increased.

Deciding a Sentence is True

The data from all three experiments have been averaged in Fig. 2. To evaluate the differences shown there for true sentences, two separate analyses of variance were performed: One for the 2-level runs and one answer the SO sentences, e.g., "A maple is a maple," by pattern matching. That they did so was substantiated by spontaneous reports from several Ss that on the SO sentences they often did not even think what the sentence said. Overall, the underlying model is supported by these data.

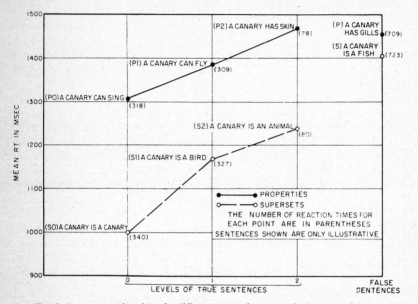

FIG. 2. Average reaction times for different types of sentences in three experiments.

for the 3-level runs. For the 2-level data the difference between P sentences and S sentences was significant, $F(1, 60) = 19.73, p < .01$, the difference between levels was significant $F(1, 60) = 7.74, p < .01$, but the interaction was not quite significant, $F(1, 60) = 2.06$. For the 3-level data, the difference between P and S sentences was significant, $F(1, 60) = 27.02$, $p < .01$, the difference between levels was significant, $F(2, 60) = 5.68, p < .01$, and the interaction was not significant, $F < 1$.

Our prediction was that the RT curves for PO, P1, and P2 sentences and for SO, S1, and S2 sentences should be two parallel straight lines. The results are certainly compatible with this prediction, except for the SO point, which is somewhat out of line. It was anticipated that presenting the entire sentence on the CRT at one time would permit the Ss to

It can also be concluded, if one accepts the model and disregards the SO point as distorted by pattern matching, that the time to move from a node to its superset is on the order of 75 msec, this figure being the average RT increase from PO to P1, P1 to P2, and S1 to S2. The differences between S1 and P1 and between S2 and P2, which average to about 225 msec, represent the time it takes to retrieve a property from the node at the level where we assume it is stored.

We have assumed that retrieval of properties at a node and moving up to the superset of the node are parallel processes, but this was not a necessary assumption. In actual fact the computer realization of the model completes the search for properties at a node *before* moving up one level to its superset. If the property search is assumed to be complete before moving up to the next level, then the 75 msec would have to be divided into two processes: (a) The time spent searching for properties, and (b) the time to move up to the superset. If such an assumption is made, then there is no clear prediction as to whether the increases for P sentences should parallel the increases for S sentences. If, given an S-type sentence, the S could dispense with process (a) above, then the slope of the curve for S sentences would be less than for P sentences; if he could not, then the prediction of two parallel lines would still hold. However, the fact that the time attributable to retrieving a property from a node is much longer than the time to move from one node to the next suggests that the processing is in fact parallel. It is unlikely that a search of all the properties at a node could be completed before moving up to the next level in less than 75 msec, if it takes some 225 msec actually to retrieve a property when it is found at a node. This might be reasonable if most of the 225 msec was spent in verification or some additional process necessary when the search at a node is successful, but attributing most of the 225 msec to such a process involves the unlikely assumption that this process takes much longer for P sentences than for S sentences. If it were the same for both sentence types, then it would not contribute to the difference (the 225 msec) between their RTs.

Since any other systematic differences between sentence types might affect RTs, we did three further checks. We computed the average number of letters for each sentence type and also weighted averages of the word-frequencies based on the Thorndike-Lorge (1944) general count. Then we asked four Ss to rate how important each property was for the relevant instance or superset, e.g., how important it is for birds that they can fly. In general, we found no effects that could account for the differences in Fig. 2 on the basis of sentence lengths, frequency counts, or subject ratings of importance. The only exception to this is that the higher frequency of superset words such as bird and animal in the predicates of S1 and S2 sentences may have lowered the averages for S1 and S2 sentences relative to those for P sentences.

Deciding a Sentence is False

There are a number of conceivable strategies or processes by which a person might decide a sentence is false. All of these involve a search of memory; they fall into two classes on the basis of how the search is assumed to terminate.

The Contradiction Hypothesis. Under this hypothesis, false responses involve finding a contradiction between information stored in memory and what the statement says. For example, if the sentence is "Coca-cola is blue," the S searches memory until he finds a property of Coca-cola (that it is brown or caramel colored) which contradicts the sentence.

The Contradiction Hypothesis was tested by the construction of false sentences for Expt 2. We predicted that the RT increase from PO to P1 found for true sentences might also be found for false sentences. The difference found was in the right direction, but it was negligibly small (7 msec). Similarly, it was thought that if Ss search for a contradiction, false SO sentences should produce faster times than the false S1 sentences since there is one less link in the path between the two nodes for an SO sentence. (This can be seen by comparing the path in Fig. 1 between canary and ostrich as in SO sentences to the path between canary and fish as in S1 sentences.) The difference turned out to be in the opposite direction by 59 msec on the average, $t(7) = 2.30$, $p < .1$. If anything, one should conclude from the false SO and S1 sentences in Expt 2 that the closer two nodes are in memory, the longer it takes to decide that they are not related in a stated manner.

The Unsuccessful Search Hypothesis. This is a generalization of what Sternberg (1966) calls the "self-terminating search," one of the two models he considered with regard to his RT studies of short-term memory search. Under this hypothesis an S would search for information to decide that a given sentence is true, and, when the search fails, as determined by some criterion, he would respond false. One possible variation, suggested by the longer RTs for false responses, would be that Ss search memory for a fixed period of time, responding true at any time information is found that confirms the statement is true, and responding false if nothing is found by the end of the time period. Such a hypothesis should lead to smaller standard deviations for false sentences than for true sentences, but the opposite was found for Expt 2, where it could be checked most easily.

The Search and Destroy Hypothesis. We developed another variation of the Unsuccessful Search Hypothesis after the Contradiction Hypothesis proved unsatisfactory and Ss had been interrogated as to what they thought they were doing on false sentences. Under this hypothesis we assume the S tries to find paths through his memory which connect the subject and predicate of the sentence (e.g., the path "canary → bird → animal → has skin" connects the two parts of "A canary has skin"). Whenever he finds such a path he must check to see if it agrees with what is stated in the sentence. When the S has checked to a certain number of levels or "depth" (Quillian, 1967), all connections found having been rejected, the S will then respond false. Under this hypothesis, the times for false sentences will be longer, in general, and highly variable depending upon how many connective paths the S has to check out before rejecting the statement. For instance, assuming people know Coca-cola comes in green bottles, a statement such as "Coca-cola is blue" would on the average take less time than "Coca-cola is green." This is because the S would have to spend time checking whether or not the above path between Coca-cola and green (i.e., that its bottles are green) corresponds to the relation stated in the sentence.

This hypothesis would explain the longer times in Expt 2 for sentences such as "A canary is an ostrich" as compared with "A canary is a fish" in terms of the greater number of connections between canary and ostrich that presumably would have to be checked out. This difference in the number of connections would derive from the greater number of properties that are common to two nodes close together in the network, such as canary and ostrich, than are common to nodes further apart and at different levels, such as canary and fish.

Finding contradictions can be included in this hypothesis, as is illustrated with "Gin is wet." Here the S might make a connection between gin and wet through the path "gin is dry and dry is the opposite of wet." Seeing the contradiction, he rejects this as a basis for responding true, but continues to search for an acceptable path. In this example, if he searches deep enough, he will find the path "gin is liquor, and liquor is liquid, and liquid

is wet" which is, in fact, what the sentence requires. The point we want to emphasize here is that even though a contradiction can be used to reject a path, it cannot be used to reject the truth of a statement.

There are certainly other possible hypotheses, and it is possible that a combination of this hypothesis with the Contradiction Hypothesis may be necessary to explain false judgments. Needless to say, the process by which a person decides that a statement is false does not seem to be very simple.

Conclusion

In a computer system designed for the storage of semantic information, it is more economical to store generalized information with superset nodes, rather than with all the individual nodes to which such a generalization might apply. But such a storage system incurs the cost of additional processing time in retrieving information. When the implications of such a model were tested for human Ss using well-ordered hierarchies that are part of the common culture, there was substantial agreement between the predictions and the data.

There is no clear picture that emerges as to how people decide a statement is false. Our current hypothesis, that people must spend time checking out any interpretations that are possible (see the discussion of the Search and Destroy Hypothesis), should be testable, but even corroborative evidence would not clear up many of the questions about such decisions.

The model also makes predictions for other RT tasks utilizing such hierarchies. For instance, if Ss are given the task of deciding what common category two instances belong to, then RT should reflect the number of supersets the S must move through to make the decision. (Consider fish and bird, vs. shark and bird, vs. shark and canary; see Fig. 1). Such RT differences should parallel those in our data. Furthermore, if utilizing a particular path in retrieval increases its accessibility temporarily, then we would expect prior exposure to "A canary is a bird" to have more effect in reducing RT to "A canary can fly" than to "A canary can sing." There are many similar experiments which would serve to pin down more precisely the structure and processing of human semantic memory.

REFERENCES

QUILLIAN, M. R. Word concepts: A theory and simulation of some basic semantic capabilities. *Behavioral Sci.*, 1967, **12**, 410–430.

QUILLIAN, M. R. The Teachable Language Comprehender: A simulation program and theory of language. *Communications Assn. Comp. Mach.*, 1969, (In press).

SMITH, E. E. Effects of familiarity on stimulus recognition and categorization. *J. exp. Psychol.*, 1967, **74**, 324–332.

SMITH, E. E. Choice reaction time: An analysis of the major theoretical positions. *Psychol. Bull.*, 1968, **69**, 77–110.

STERNBERG, S. High-speed scanning in human memory. *Science*, 1966, **153**, 652–654.

THORNDIKE, E. L. AND LORGE, I. *The teacher's word book of 30,000 words.* New York: Columbia Univ. Press, 1944.

B. Schaeffer and R. Wallace

The comparison of word meanings

Reprinted from the *Journal of Experimental Psychology* (1970) **86(2):**144-52

The present paper argues that data on two-word meaning comparisons reflect only the comparison process, not the retrieval from or the organization of semantic memory. A model of comparison is proposed which handles the available data without making assumptions about retrieval or organization. Experiment I supports the model by showing that semantic similarity interferes with the judgment that two words have different meanings, and disconfirms Collins and Quillian's major alternative model; Collins and Quillian's model assumes that the data on two-word comparisons reflect retrieval and organization. Experiments II–V demonstrate on important boundary condition for the proposed model: when Ss respond only to the names of words, formal semantic similarity has no effect on the judgment that two words have different meanings.

Recently, several investigators have begun to study the processes involved in the comparison of word meanings, Schaeffer and Wallace (1969) and Collins and Quillian (1969). They have asked Ss to judge whether two words have the "same" or "different" meanings and have used the data to test various models of the retrieval from and organization of semantic memory. It is possible to argue, however, that the data mirror only the comparison of meanings and not retrieval or organization. To strengthen this argument, the present paper (a) proposes a comparison model which handles the available data but says little about retrieval or organization and (b) describes the results of an experiment which support the model and disconfirm the major alternative model (Collins and Quillian, 1969). This alternative embodies strong assumptions about retrieval and organization, as well as comparison. In addition, the paper discusses and demonstrates the operation of an important boundary condition for the present model.

To contrast the two models and to place the experiment which distinguishes between them in perspective, the data available concerning meaning comparison will be presented and the two models' account of them will be outlined. The major finding that has emerged from studies in which the meanings of two words are compared is that semantic similarity facilitates the judgment that two words have the "same" meaning. Schaeffer and Wallace (1969) found that *lion* and *elephant* were more easily judged "same," both living, than were *lion* and *daisy*; *lion* and *elephant* are semantically similar in that both are animals. Collins and Quillian (1969) found *canary* and *bird* were more easily judged "same" than were *canary* and *animal*; *canary* and *bird* are semantically similar in that both fly, are feathered, are winged, lay eggs, etc.

The present model will be introduced by way of example because its basic terms are most easily understood in this context. The model explains Schaeffer and Wallace's

(1969) data, exemplified by the comparison between *lion* and *elephant* that determines that both are living things, as follows. The concept for lion may be partially denoted by *lion, animal, mammal, living, mane, carnivore,* etc., the concept for elephant by *elephant, animal, mammal, living, trunk, herbivore,* etc. According to the model, the concepts are compared in their entirety: the connection between the elements "living" in *lion* and "living" in *elephant,* the representations of the task decision criterion in both concepts, forms the decision unit from which information is sampled to decide whether *lion* and *elephant* are living things. The reason that it is easier to decide that *lion* and *elephant* are living things than that *lion* and *daisy* are living things is: the amount of information that must be sampled from the connection between "living" in *lion* and "living" in *elephant,* prior to a decision, is less than the amount that must be sampled from the connection between "living" in *lion* and "living" in *daisy;* i.e., the threshold for a "same" decision is lower for the former connection. Less information must be sampled because the overlap between the concepts lion and elephant is greater than that between the concepts lion and daisy; the concepts of lion and elephant both contain the elements animal and mammal; the concept of daisy does not. The idea that information is sampled from units of meaning for particular decisions, and that the amount sampled, the threshold of the unit, varies, forms the core of Morton's (1969) *logogen* model of word recognition.

Stated formally, the comparison model holds that: (*a*) when word meanings are compared, the concepts underlying the words are compared in their entirety; (*b*) concepts are composed of elements; (*c*) the connection between the elements of the concept which represent the task decision criterion forms the decision unit for the comparison; and (*d*) the amount of information that must be sampled from a decision unit, its threshold, is a function of the overlap between the concepts: the greater the overlap, the smaller the amount of information required for a "same" judgment, and the greater the

amount of information for a "different" judgment. The overlap effect follows from the assumption that concepts are compared in their entirety.

The basic terms are *concept, element, decision unit,* and *task decision criterion.* Concept refers to the net of information that constitutes the meaning of a word, and element refers to a component of a concept. The decision unit is a connection between elements from which information about element equivalence and element difference is sampled. The task decision criteria refer to the elements in decision units, which are determined by the experimental task. The model says little about the structure of concepts, arguing only that all the elements be activated when the concept is retrieved; neither the arrangement of the elements nor the organization of concepts is specified. The model does not argue for a particular form of retrieval, but only argues that the product of retrieval be a concept. This suggests that entire concepts are retrieved before comparison is begun, and that retrieval and comparison are independent steps in the processing sequence. In addition, the model does not demand that the information in concepts, the elements and their possible relationships, be represented in a particular form. The concept lion was represented in the examples discussed as *lion, animal, mammal, living, mane, carnivore,* etc.; the model does not insist, however, that the elements of concepts be ordered in any particular way or that they be word-like. In sum, the model argues that the data on meaning comparison reflect the comparison process, not retrieval or organization.

The major alternative model, Collins and Quillian (1969), embodies assumptions about retrieval and organization, as well as comparison. Collins and Quillian's model assumes that semantic memory is hierarchically organized and that comparison difficulty is directly proportional to distance that must be traveled in a hierarchically organized memory to complete a comparison. According to the model, it takes less time to judge that *lion* and *elephant* have the same meaning than that *lion* and *daisy* do, because the former requires a shorter journey in memory, from lion to animal to elephant than does the latter, from lion to animal to living to plant to daisy. The model thus assumes that the various meanings of *lion* are hierarchically organized, that meanings at successive levels are succesively retrieved. and that comparison is, after retrieval, just a simple yes–no decision.

Let us now consider Collins and Quillian's data (1969) exemplified by the finding that it takes less time to judge *canary* and *bird* as "same." than to judge *canary* and *animal* as "same." (Collins and Quillian call "same" judgments "true" and "different" judgments "false." The comparison model proposed here handles these data by the assumption that the concept for bird has a greater number of elements in common with the concept for canary than does the concept for animal. This assumption is not implausible, as a canary and a bird both *are winged, lay eggs, have feathers, fly, breathe, have protoplasm,* and *are living,* while an animal only *breathes, has protoplasm,* and *is living.* The greater overlap between *bird* and *canary* than between *bird* and *animal* facilitates the "same" judgment of the former pair. The comparison model thus incorporates the apparent hierarchic organization of semantic memory, not by assuming the use of branching tree structures, as does Collins and Quillian's model, but by assuming that the concepts at the upper levels of presumed hierarchies have fewer elements than do concepts at lower levels, and that this decrease in the number of elements decreases concept overlap.

Collins and Quillian's (1969) model would argue that it takes less time to judge *canary* and *bird* as "same," than to judge *canary* and *animal* as "same," because the journey from canary to bird is shorter than the journey from canary to bird to animal. In sum, both the present model and Collins and Quillian's model can account for the findings of Schaeffer and Wallace (1969) and Collins and Quillian that semantic similarity facilitates "same" judgments.

For "different" judgments, however, the two models make opposite predictions about the effects of semantic similarity. The present model predicts that semantic similarity will interfere with "different" judgments because it raises concept overlap; Collins and Quillian's (1969) model predicts that it will facilitate "different" judgments because it shortens the distance that must be traveled in memory. To explain by way of example, supose *S* sees word pairs composed of trees, flowers, birds, and mammals and that his task is to judge as "same" pairs containing two trees, two flowers, two birds, or two mammals, and as "different" all other pairs. In this situation, there are two types of "different" pairs: semantically similar ones, such as *hemlock* and *daisy,* both plants, and semantically dissimilar ones, such as *hemlock* and *parrot.*

The present model holds that concept overlap raises threshold for "different" judgments. Therefore, it predicts that *S*s will take longer to judge semantically similar pairs, such as *hemlock* and *daisy,* as "different" than to judge semantically dissimilar pairs, such as *hemlock* and *parrot,* as "different." According to the model, the decision unit for the *hemlock–daisy* comparison is formed by the connection between the element tree in *hemlock* and the element flower in *daisy,* the representations of the task decision criterion in both concepts; the decision unit for the *hemlock–parrot* comparison is formed by the connection between tree in *hemlock* and bird in *parrot.* The model predicts that the *hemlock–daisy* comparison will take more time than the *hemlock–parrot* comparison because the "different" threshold of the decision unit is raised by the overlap, the element plant, between the concepts underlying *hemlock* and *daisy.*

The Collins and Quillian (1969) model predicts that the *hemlock–daisy* comparison will take less time than the *hemlock–parrot* comparison because the journey from hemlock to tree to plant to flower to daisy is shorter than that from hemlock to tree to plant to living to animal to bird to parrot.

Experiment I tested these opposing predictions in the task described. Confirmation of the present model's prediction, that semantic similarity will interfere with "different" judgments, will (*a*) support the model, (*b*) disconfirm Collins and Quillian's model, and (*c*) argue that data on two-word comparisons reflect only the comparison process, not retrieval or organization. Confirmation of Collins and Quillian's model's prediction, that semantic similarity will facilitate "different" judgments, will (*i*) support Collins and Quillian's model, (*ii*) disconfirm the present model, and (*iii*) argue that data on two-word comparisons reflect retrieval and organization, not comparison.

The words of a pair were presented, one following the other, on two fields of a three-field tachistoscope so that long and short interword intervals could be used. The authors' bias in favor of the present model suggested that concepts might gain (or lose) elements over time, and thus that interword interval would affect overlap and, consequently, comparison.

Method

Subjects.—Eight students at the University of Oregon served individually as *S*s and were paid $1.50/hr for the experimental session.

Materials.—The *S*s were presented with pairs of words drawn from the following set of 32: *cedar, maple, poplar, walnut, cypress, hemlock, redwood,* and *willow; daisy, iris, lily, tulip, orchid, pansy, lilac,* and *violet; parrot, chicken, raven, sparrow, heron, pigeon, robin,* and *vulture; giraffe, donkey, leopard, tiger, camel, otter, rabbit,* and *weasel.* These items belong to the four superordinates tree, flower, bird, and mammal and are plants or animals.

The items were made with rub-on letters (Letraset USA, type Univers 67, 36 point), and arranged on two pasteboard disks so that they were aligned roughly as the spokes of a wheel. Capital letters were used to hold height constant. Since the items were to be presented in pairs, an item on one disk followed by an item on the other, 4 items belonging to each superordinate were placed on each disk. Thus, both disks had 16 items on them. In the above list, the first 4 items belonging to each superordinate were put on one disk, the second 4 on the other.

Each disk was fastened to the side of a tachistoscope (Scientific Prototype three-channel tachistoscope Model GB) with a screw which passed through the center of the disk. The disks could be rotated so that any item could be presented in one of the tachistoscope's fields.

The viewing distance of the words in the tachistoscope was about 49 in. The items subtended visual angles from 1° 24′ to 2° 20′ in a horizontal direction, and in the vertical direction, the letters subtended a visual angle of 26′. The illumination of the two fields was 1.50 (for the first channel) and 1.30 log₁₀ mL. Before each trial, all fields were dark.

The tachistoscope rested on cinder blocks, which, in turn, were set on a table. The *S* sat in a straight-backed chair in front of the tachistoscope. Before him, on the table, were two plastic response keys attached to a square of masonite inclined about 20°. The keys activated microswitches which recorded the responses.

Procedure.—The *S* was told that on each trial, he would see two items, one after the other, each belonging to one of the four superordinates, tree, flower, mammal, and bird. If both items belonged to the same superordinate, he was to press the left-hand key, marked "same;" if they did not, he was to press the right-hand key, marked "different." He was instructed to respond as quickly as he could while still keeping his errors to a minimum. Also, if he caught himself making an error, he was to signal this by calling out, "Mistake," or the like.

All 256 pairs of the items on the two disks were used. Two partially random orders were employed, which had the following restrictions: (*a*) no more than 4 successive trials in which the same response was required, (*b*) equal numbers of "same" and "different" responses in each set of 32 trials, and (*c*) in a set of 32 trials, there would be 4 Same pairs for each of the four superordinates; 8 Semantically Similar Different pairs, in which the items belonged to different superordinates but were both plants or both animals; and 8 Semantically Dissimilar Different pairs, where one item was a plant and one an animal. As a result of the third restriction, in one order, each of the 64 possible Same pairs appeared twice, each of the 64 possible Semantically Similar Different pairs appeared once, and only 64 of the 128 Semantically Dissimilar Different pairs were used. Therefore, the two orders contained different Semantically Dissimilar pairs, although every pair appeared in one of the orders.

The series of trials consisted of two sets of 8 practice trials, and then eight sets of 32 experimental trials. Between each set, there was a rest of about ½ min. On each trial, the first word was presented for .30 sec., the second for 2.00 sec. The interval between the words was either .01 sec. or 3.01 sec. A single interval was used for all of the trials in a set, and after each set, the interval was changed. Half of the *S*s began the series with one interval, half with the other; and half of each of these groups of *S*s responded to a given order.

Before each trial, *E* arranged the disk so that a particular pair of items would be shown. Then after *E* had said, "Ready," *S* began the trial by pressing a button on a foot pedal, which immediately turned on the first word. After *S* had responded, *E* recorded the response, which was signaled by one of two lights, and the time in milliseconds (recorded on a Hunter Klockounter) between the onset of the second item and the closing of the microswitch beneath the response key. The *E* then set the disks for the next trial, and so on. The intertrial interval was approximately 10 sec. During each rest between sets of trials, S was told the fastest and slowest reaction times of the set he had just completed, and the number of errors he had reported. The entire session lasted about 1½ hr.

Results

The mean error rate was 5.8%, low enough to consider correct reaction times a good measure of judgment difficulty, and errors increased as reaction time increased. Table 1 presents the mean reaction time in milliseconds for correct judgments.

As can be seen, Semantically Similar Different judgments were more difficult than Semantically Dissimilar Different judgments at both interword intervals. A repeated-measures analysis of variance showed that the average difference, 120 msec., was significant at the .001 level, $F (1, 21) = 64.11$. The same result was found when only the fastest two responses in each Different category were considered; average difference, 53 msec., was significant at the .001 level, $F (1, 14) = 23.93$. Clearly, semantic similarity interfered with "different" judgments.

Mean response time was longer at the longer intervals; average difference, 73 msec., was significant at the .05 level, $F (1, 7) = 9.47$. A similar trend was found for the fastest two responses in each Different category, but was not significant. This increase in response time appeared only to mean that Ss were distracted during the long interword intervals. There was no significant Overlap Effect × Interword Interval interaction, and hence no evidence concerning the gain or loss of concept elements over time.

Discussion

Experiment I demonstrated that semantic similarity interferes with "different" judgments and, taken together with Schaeffer and Wallace's (1969) and Collins and Quillian's (1969) finding that semantic similarity facilitates "same" judgments, supports the proposed comparison model, and argues that data on two-word comparisons reflect comparison, not retrieval or organization. In addition, the data clearly disconfirm the Collins and Quillian (1969) model. The Ss took longer to judge

TABLE 1

MEAN REACTION TIMES (IN MSEC.) FOR CORRECT JUDGMENTS IN EXPERIMENT I (ITEM–ITEM)

Data included	Semantically Similar Differents (cedar and daisy, parrot and giraffe, etc.)	Semantically Dissimilar Differents (cedar and parrot, daisy and giraffe, etc.)	Sames (cedar and maple, parrot and chicken, etc.)
All judgments .01-Sec. inter-word interval	787	687	677
3.01-Sec. inter-word interval	872	733	766
Fastest Two judgments .01-Sec. inter-word interval	591	538	
3.01-Sec. inter-word interval	617	564	

hemlock and daisy as "different" than to judge hemlock and parrot as "different," even though hemlock and daisy are hierarchically closer together than hemlock and parrot. The hierarchic paths read from hemlock to tree to plant to flower to daisy and from hemlock to tree to plant to living to animal to bird to parrot. Collins and Quillian's model, as it stands, cannot handle both Collins and Quillian's "same" data and the present "different" data.

But, one may ask, why should any model have to be capable of making both "same" and "different" judgments? The reason is that an S in a meaning comparison experiment does not know before a trial begins whether he will have to make a "same" judgment of a "different" judgment, and thus must use a comparison mechanism, such as the one the model proposed here envisions. which can make either judgment.

The present model holds that the concepts which comprise word meaning are compared in their entirety. The connection between the elements of concepts which represent the task decision criterion forms the decision unit from which information is sampled; the "same" and "different" thresholds of this decision unit vary over comparisons: the greater the overlap between the concepts being compared, the lower the threshold for a "same" decision, and the higher the threshold for a "different" decision. The finding of Exp. I that semantic similarity interfered with "different" judgments supports the model and argues that data on two-word comparisons reflect only the comparison process, not retrieval or organization.

Experiments II–V

An important boundary condition for the model arises from the ability of Ss to respond to a word on the basis of its name, not its underlying concept. That is, when a word's name represents the task decision criterion, Ss can respond to the name alone. Since it is concept overlap which affects comparison, when the name, not the concept, is responded to, no overlap effect can occur.

To explain, in Exp. I, Ss always judged pairs, such as *hemlock–daisy* and *hemlock–parrot*, in which the task decision criteria, here the superordinates, tree, flower, and bird, were represented in the underlying concepts. The Ss could not, therefore, respond on the basis of the words' names; they were forced to respond to the underlying concepts. And it was the concept overlap which affected "different" thresholds. Suppose Ss were asked to judge pairs one word of which was the superordinate representing the task decision criterion, pairs such as *hemlock–flower* and *hemlock–bird*. The Ss could judge these pairs by responding to the names of the superordinates, disregarding their underlying concepts, because the names of the superordinates represent the task decision criterion. Thus, although they would have to respond to the concept underlying the item *hemlock*, Ss could respond to the names of the superordinates flower and bird. There would in this situation be no necessary concept overlap to affect decision units, because the task decision criterion would be represented in the name of one of the words in each pair. The formal semantic similarity of pairs such as *hemlock–flower*, both plants, should not make these pairs any more difficult for Ss than formally dissimilar pairs such as *hemlock–bird*.

Experiments II–IV used item-superordinate pairs, such as those described above, to show that Ss can respond to the name of a word, disregarding the underlying concept. Long and short interword intervals were used to see whether over time the response to the name led involuntarily to a response to the concept, as evidenced by semantic similarity effects on "different" judgments.

TABLE 2

MEAN REACTION TIME (IN MSEC.) FOR CORRECT JUDGMENTS IN EXPERIMENT II (ITEM-SUPERORDINATE)

Data included	Semantically Similar Differents (*cedar* and *flower, parrot* and *mammal* etc.)	Semantically Dissimilar Differents (*cedar* and *bird, daisy,* and *mammal* etc.)	Sames (*cedar* and *tree, parrot* and *bird,* etc.)
All judgments .01-Sec. interword interval	601	588	536
3.01-Sec. interword interval	510	501	439
Fastest Two judgments .01-Sec. interword interval	453	455	
3.01-Sec. interword interval	364	370	

Method

In this experiment, the second field of the tachistoscope had on it the four superordinates, tree, flower, mammal, and bird. There were two instances of each superordinate so that the disk was moved before every trial. Two orders of word pairs were used; these were made by substituting the correct superordinate for the second item of each pair in the orders used in Exp. I. In all other ways the method was the same as that of Exp. I.

Results

The mean error rate was 6.2%, low enough to consider correct reaction times a good measure of judgment difficulty, and error rates increased as reaction time increased. Table 2 presents the mean reaction time in milliseconds for correct judgments.

As can be seen, Semantically Similar Different judgments and Semantically Dissimilar Different judgments were of nearly equal difficulty at both interword intervals. Clearly, Ss responded to the name of the superordinates; formal semantic similarity did not affect "different" judgments.

Mean response time was shorter at the longer interword interval; average difference, 92 msec., was significant at the .05 level, $F(1, 7) = 9.60$.

Experiment III

It might be argued that the absence of similarity effects in Exp. II, and their presence in Exp. I, was a result of the lower stimulus uncertainty in Exp. II, not a result of the superordinates replacing second-position items, i.e., the use of 4 second-position words in Exp. II and 16 in Exp. I, not the use of superordinates rather than items. To rule out this interpretation, a control study was run. Instead of four superordinates as second-position possibilities, four items (one for each superordinate) were used.

Method

The method was the same as that of Exp. II, except that the items *willow, violet, camel,* and *pigeon* were substituted for *tree, flower, mammal,* and *bird*.

Results

The mean error rate was 6.9%, low enough to consider correct reaction times a good measure of judgment difficulty, and error rates increased as reaction time increased. Table 3 presents the mean reaction time in milliseconds for correct judgments.

As can be seen, Semantically Similar Different judgments were more difficult than Semantically Dissimilar Different judgments at both interword intervals; average difference, 68 msec., was significant at the .01 level, $F(1, 21) = 11.41$. The same result was found for the fastest two responses in each Different category; average difference, 40 msec., was significant at the .05 level, $F(1, 14) = 8.00$. Semantic similarity raised

"different" thresholds despite the low stimulus uncertainty, as compared to that of Exp. I. Therefore, the lack of semantic similarity effect in Exp. II was not solely a function of low stimulus uncertainty.

EXPERIMENT IV

One might argue that the lack of semantic similarity effects in Exp. II depended on the item-superordinate order of presentation. To rule out this possibility, Exp. II was replicated with a superordinate-item order.

Method

The method was the same as in Exp. II, but the channels of the tachistoscope were reversed, so that the four superordinates on the second disk appeared initially for .30 sec., and the 16 items on the first disk appeared after, for 2.00 sec.

Results

The mean error rate was 7.3%, low enough to consider correct reaction times a good measure of judgment difficulty, and error rates increased as reaction time increased. Table 4 presents the mean reaction time in milliseconds for correct judgments.

As can be seen, Semantically Similar Different judgments and Semantically Dissimilar Different judgments were of nearly equal difficulty at both interword intervals. Semantic similarity did not raise "different" thresholds, and the lack of similarity effects was not a function of the item-superordinate or superordinate-item order of presentation.

TABLE 3

MEAN REACTION TIME (IN MSEC.) FOR CORRECT JUDGMENTS IN EXPERIMENT III (ITEM–ITEM)

Data included	Semantically Similar Differents	Semantically Dissimilar Differents	Sames
All judgments .01-Sec. inter- word interval	716	639	637
3.01-Sec. inter- word interval	659	601	588
Fastest two judgments .01-Sec. inter- word interval	507	460	
3.01-Sec. inter- word interval	465	433	

TABLE 4

MEAN REACTION TIME (IN MSEC.) FOR CORRECT JUDGMENTS IN EXPERIMENT IV (SUPERORDINATE–ITEM)

Data included	Semantically Similar Differents	Semantically Dissimilar Differents	Sames
All judgments .01-Sec. inter- word interval	570	555	500
3.01-Sec. inter- word interval	581	571	508
Fastest two judgments .01-Sec. inter- word interval	442	443	
3.01-Sec. inter- word interval	430	431	

Experiment V

It might be that the relative positional uncertainty, 4 first-position possibilities followed by 16 second-position possibilities, rather than the presence of a superordinate, determined the lack of similarity effects in the superordinate-item judgments of Exp. III. To rule out this interpretation, Exp. V used 4 first-position items and 16 second-position items. The occurrence of similarity effects in Exp. V, if found, will also discount relative positional uncertainty as the cause of similarity effects in Exp. III, where 4 second-position items followed 16 first-position items.

Method

The method was the same as in Exp. III, but as in Exp. IV, the channels of the tachistoscope were reversed.

Results

The mean error rate was 5.4%, low enough to consider reaction times a good measure of judgment difficulty, and error rates increased as reaction time increased. Table 5 presents the mean reaction time in milliseconds for correct judgments.

As can be seen, Semantically Similar Different judgments were more difficult than Semantically Dissimilar Different judgments at both interword intervals; average difference, 48 msec., was significant at the .001 level, $F (1, 21) = 20.58$. The effect was smaller and nonsignificant for the fastest two responses in each Different category.

TABLE 5

MEAN REACTION TIME (IN MSEC.) FOR CORRECT JUDGMENTS IN EXPERIMENT V (ITEM–ITEM)

Data included	Semantically Similar Differents	Semantically Dissimilar Differents	Sames
All judgments			
.01-Sec. interword interval	625	574	542
3.01-Sec. interword interval	641	597	563
Fastest two judgments			
.01-Sec. interword interval	469	448	
3.01-Sec. interword interval	444	434	

The effect of similarity is clearly not determined by relative positional uncertainty.

Discussion

Experiments II–IV showed that Ss can respond to the names of the superordinates such as tree, flower, bird, and mammal without responding to the underlying concepts; formal semantic similarity had no effect on item-superordinate or superordinate-item pairs. The experiments did not show that when no response to a concept is required, no similarity effects occur, as there is data which argue that task requirements alone do not determine whether the name, the concept, or both, will be responded to. Schaeffer and Wallace (1969) found that it was harder for Ss to signal that an orange was a fruit when they had to choose between *fruit* and *grain* than when they had to choose between *fruit* and *bird*. Clearly, the concept underlying *grain,* including the element plant, was responded to, even though the task did not require it.

A subsidiary finding emerged from Exp. II–IV. Item-superordinate judgments were affected by interword interval, while superordinate-item judgments were not. Table 6 shows the relevant data. Item-superordinate judgments at a 3.01-sec. interword interval took 92 msec. less than item-superordinate judgments at a .01-sec. interval. The difference may represent the time it takes to retrieve the concept.

In summary, the major point of the present paper is that the data on meaning comparison can be interpreted as reflecting only the comparison process, not retrieval or organization. To support this point, a model of meaning comparison was proposed which handles the data on comparisons without making assumptions about meaning retrieval and/or the organization of semantic memory. The model holds that: (a) the concepts which underlie words are compared in their entirety; (b) the connec-

TABLE 6

MEAN REACTION TIME (IN MSEC.) FOR CORRECT ITEM–SUPERORDINATE AND SUPERORDINATE–ITEM JUDGMENTS AT .01-SEC. AND 3.01-SEC. INTERWORD INTERVALS

Interword interval (in sec.)	Item-superordinate judgments	Superordinate-item judgments
.01	575	542
3.01	483	553

tion between the elements of the concepts which represent the task decision criterion forms the decision unit for the comparison; and (c) the amount of information that must be sampled from the decision unit varies as a function of the overlap between the concepts and the judgment required: less information must be sampled for a "same" judgment and more, for a "different" judgment, as overlap increases. The model suggests that retrieval precedes, and is independent of, comparison, but does not otherwise specify retrieval. Further, the model does not argue for a particular memory organization. Experiment I demonstrated that overlap raises the threshold for "different" judgments. This result supports the present model, disconfirms Collins and Quillian's (1969) retrieval-oriented model, and strengthens the argument that data on two-word comparisons reflect the comparison process, not the retrieval from or the organization of semantic memory.

The operation of an important boundary condition for the model was also demonstrated: Exp. II–V showed that when only the name of a word, and not the underlying concept, was responded to, formal semantic similarity did not affect "different" judgments.

REFERENCES

COLLINS, A. M., & QUILLIAN, M. R. Retrieval time from semantic memory. *Journal of Verbal Learning and Verbal Behavior,* 1969, **8**, 240–247.

MORTON, J. Interaction of information in word recognition. *Psychological Review,* 1969, **76**, 178–195.

SCHAEFFER, B., & WALLACE, R. Semantic similarity and the comparison of word meanings. *Journal of Experimental Psychology,* 1969, **82**, 343–346.

R. Brown and D. McNeill

The 'tip-of-the-tongue' phenomenon

Reprinted from the *Journal of Verbal Learning and Verbal Behavior* (1966) 5(4):325-37

The "tip of the tongue" (TOT) phenomenon is a state in which one cannot quite recall a familiar word but can recall words of similar form and meaning. Several hundred such states were precipitated by reading to Ss the definitions of English words of low frequency and asking them to try to recall the words. It was demonstrated that while in the TOT state, and before recall occurred, Ss had knowledge of some of the letters in the missing word, the number of syllables in it, and the location of the primary stress. The nearer S was to successful recall the more accurate the information he possessed. The recall of parts of words and attributes of words is termed "generic recall." The interpretation offered for generic recall involves the assumption that users of a language possess the mental equivalent of a dictionary. The features that figure in generic recall may be entered in the dictionary sooner than other features and so, perhaps, are wired into a more elaborate associative network. These more easily retrieved features of low-frequency words may be the features to which we chiefly attend in word-perception. The features favored by attention, especially the beginnings and endings of words, appear to carry more information than the features that are not favored, in particular the middles of words.

William James wrote, in 1893: "Suppose we try to recall a forgotten name. The state of our consciousness is peculiar. There is a gap therein; but no mere gap. It is a gap that is intensely active. A sort of wraith of the name is in it, beckoning us in a given direction, making us at moments tingle with the sense of our closeness and then letting us sink back without the longed-for term. If wrong names are proposed to us, this singularly definite gap acts immediately so as to negate them. They do not fit into its mould. And the gap of one word does not feel like the gap of another, all empty of content as both might seem necessarily to be when described as gaps" (p. 251).

The "tip of the tongue" (TOT) state involves a failure to recall a word of which one has knowledge. The evidence of knowledge is either an eventually successful recall or else an act of recognition that occurs, without additional training, when recall has failed. The class of cases defined by the conjunction of knowledge and a failure of recall is a large one. The TOT state, which James described, seems to be a small subclass in which recall is felt to be imminent.

For several months we watched for TOT states in ourselves. Unable to recall the name of the street on which a relative lives, one of us thought of *Congress* and *Corinth* and *Concord* and then looked up the address and learned that it was *Cornish*. The words that had come to mind have certain properties in common with the word that had been sought (the "target word"): all four begin with Co; all are two-syllable words; all put the primary stress on the first syllable. After this experience we began putting direct questions to ourselves when we fell into the TOT state, questions as to the number of syllables in the target word, its initial letter, etc.

Woodworth (1934), before us, made a record of data for naturally occurring TOT states and Wenzl (1932, 1936) did the same for German words. Their results are similar to those we obtained and consistent with the following preliminary characterization. When complete recall of a word is not presently possible but is felt to be imminent, one can often correctly recall the general type of the word; *generic* recall may succeed when particular recall fails. There seem to be two common varieties of generic recall. (a) Sometimes a part of the target word is recalled, a letter or two, a syllable, or affix. Partial recall is necessarily also *generic* since the class of words defined by the possession of any *part* of the target word will include words other than the target. (b) Sometimes the abstract form of the target is recalled, perhaps the fact that it was a two-syllable sequence with the primary stress on the first syllable. The whole word is represented in *abstract form recall* but not on the letter-by-letter level that constitutes its identity. The recall of an abstract form is also necessarily *generic*, since any such form defines a class of words extending beyond the target.

Wenzl and Woodworth had worked with small collections of data for naturally occurring TOT states. These data were, for the most part, provided by the investigators; were collected in an unsystematic fashion; and were analyzed in an impressionistic nonquantitative way. It seemed to us that such data left the facts of generic recall in doubt. An occasional correspondence between a retrieved word and a target word with respect to number of syllables, stress pattern or initial letter is, after all, to be expected by chance. Several months of "self-observation and asking-our-friends" yielded fewer than a dozen good cases and we realized that an improved method of data collection was essential.

We thought it might pay to "prospect" for TOT states by reading to S definitions of uncommon English words and asking him to supply the words. The procedure was given a preliminary test with nine Ss who were individually interviewed for 2 hrs each.[1] In 57 instances an S was, in fact, "seized" by a TOT state. The signs of it were unmistakable; he would appear to be in mild torment, something like the brink of a sneeze, and if he found the word his relief was considerable. While searching for the target S told us all the words that came to his mind. He volunteered the information that some of them resembled the target in sound but not in meaning; others he was sure were similar in meaning but not in sound. The E intruded on S's agony with two questions: (a) How many syllables has the target word? (b) What is its first letter? Answers to the first question were correct in 47% of all cases and answers to the second question were correct in 51% of the cases. These outcomes encouraged us to believe that generic recall was real and to devise a group procedure that would further speed up the rate of data collection.

METHOD

Subjects

Fifty-six Harvard and Radcliffe undergraduates participated in one of three evening sessions; each session was 2 hrs long. The Ss were volunteers from a large General Education Course and were paid for their time.

Word List. The list consisted of 49 words which, according to the Thorndike-Lorge *Word Book* (1952) occur at least once per four million words but not so often as once per one million words. The level is suggested by these examples: *apse, nepotism, cloaca, ambergris,* and *sampan.* We thought the words used were likely to be in the passive or recognition vocabularies of our Ss but not in their active recall vocabularies. There were 6 words of 1 syllable; 19 of 2 syllables; 20 of 3 syllables; 4 of 4 syllables. For each word we used

[1] We wish to thank Mr. Charles Hollen for doing the pretest interviews.

a definition from *The American College Dictionary* (Barnhart, 1948) edited so as to contain no words that closely resembled the one being defined.

Response Sheet. The response sheet was laid off in vertical columns headed as follows:

Intended word (+ *One I was thinking of*).
                    (− *Not*).

Number of syllables (*1-5*).
Initial letter.
Words of similar sound. (1. *Closest in sound*)
                          (2. *Middle*   )
                          (3. *Farthest in Sound*)
Words of similar meaning.
Word you had in mind if not intended word.

Procedure

We instructed Ss to the following effect.

In this experiment we are concerned with that state of mind in which a person is unable to think of a word that he is certain he knows, the state of mind in which a word seems to be on the tip of one's tongue. Our technique for pre-cipitating such states is, in general, to read defi-nitions of uncommon words and ask the subject to recall the word.

(1) We will first read the definition of a low-frequency word.

(2) If you should happen to know the word at once, or think you do, or, if you should simply not know it, then there is nothing further for you to do at the moment. Just wait.

(3) If you are unable to think of the word but feel sure that you know it and that it is on the verge of coming back to you then you are in a TOT state and should begin at once to fill in the columns of the response sheet.

(4) After reading each definition we will ask whether anyone is in the TOT state. Anyone who is in that state should raise his hand. The rest of us will then wait until those in the TOT state have written on the answer sheet all the informa-tion they are able to provide.

(5) When everyone who has been in the TOT state has signalled us to proceed, we will read the target word. At this time, everyone is to write the word in the leftmost column of the response sheet. Those of you who have known the word since first its definition was read are asked not to write it until this point. Those of you who simply did not know the word or who had thought of a different word will write now the word we read. For those of you who have been in the TOT state two eventualities are pos-sible. The word read may strike you as definitely the word you have been seeking. In that case please write '+' after the word, as the instruc-tions at the head of the column direct. The other possibility is that you will not be sure whether the word read is the one you have been seeking or, indeed, you may be sure that it is not. In this case you are asked to write the sign '−' after the word. Sometimes when the word read out is not the one you have been seeking your actual target may come to mind. In this case, in addi-tion to the minus sign in the leftmost column, please write the actual target word in the right-most column.

(6) Now we come to the column entries themselves. The first two entries, the guess as to the number of syllables and the initial letter, are required. The remaining entries should be filled out if possible. When you are in a TOT state, words that are related to the target word do almost always come to mind. List them as they come, but separate words which you think re-semble the target in sound from words which you think resemble the target in meaning.

(7) When you have finished all your entries, but before you signal us to read the intended target word, look again at the words you have listed as 'Words of similar sound.' If possible, rank these, as the instructions at the head of the column direct, in terms of the degree of their seeming resemblance to the target. This must be done without knowledge of what the target ac-tually is.

(8) The search procedure of a person in the TOT state will sometimes serve to retrieve the missing word before he has finished filling in the columns and before we read out the word. When this happens please mark the place where it happens with the words "Got it" and *do not provide any more data.*

Results

Classes of Data

There were 360 instances, across all words and all Ss, in which a TOT state was signalled. Of this total, 233 were positive TOTs. A positive TOT is one for which the target word is known and, consequently, one for which the data obtained can be scored as accurate or inaccurate. In those cases where the target was not the word intended but some other word which S finally recalled and wrote in the rightmost column his data were checked against that word, his effective target. A negative TOT is one for which the S judged the word read out not to have been his target and, in addition, one in which S proved unable to recall his own functional target.

The data provided by S while he searched for the target word are of two kinds: explicit guesses as to the number of syllables in the target and the initial letter of the target; words that came to mind while he searched for the target. The words that came to mind were classified by S into 224 words similar in sound to the target (hereafter called "SS" words) and 95 words similar in meaning to the target (hereafter called "SM" words). The S's information about the number of syllables in, and the initial letter of the target may be inferred from correspondences between the target and his SS words as well as directly discovered from his explicit guesses. For his knowledge of the stress pattern of the target and of letters in the target, other than the initial letter, we must rely on the SS words alone since explicit guesses were not required.

To convey a sense of the SS and SM words we offer the following examples. When the target was *sampan* the SS words (not all of them real words) included: *Saipan, Siam, Cheyenne, sarong, sanching,* and *sympoon*. The SM words were: *barge, houseboat,* and *junk*. When the target was *caduceus* the SS words included: *Casadesus, Aeschelus, cephalus,* and *leucosis*. The SM words were: *fasces, Hippocrates, lictor,* and *snake*. The spelling in all cases is S's own.

We will, in this report, use the SM words to provide baseline data against which to evaluate the accuracy of the explicit guesses and of the SS words. The SM words are words produced under the spell of the positive TOT state but judged by S to resemble the target in meaning rather than sound. We are quite sure that the SM words are somewhat more like the target than would be a collection of words produced by Ss with no knowledge of the target. However, the SM words make a better comparative baseline than any other data we collected.

General Problems of Analysis

The data present problems of analysis that are not common in psychology. To begin with, the words of the list did not reliably precipitate TOT states. Of the original 49 words, all but *zither* succeeded at least once; the range was from one success to nine. The Ss made actual targets of 51 words not on the original list and all but five of these were pursued by one S only. Clearly none of the 100 words came even close to precipitating a TOT state in all 56 Ss. Furthermore, the Ss varied in their susceptibility to TOT states. There are nine who experienced none at all in a 2-hr period; the largest number experienced in such a period by one S was eight. In out data, then, the entries for one word will not usually involve the same Ss or even the same number of Ss as the entries for another word. The entries for one S need not involve the

same words or even the same number of words as the entries for another S. Consequently for the tests we shall want to make there are no significance tests that we can be sure are appropriate.

In statistical theory our problem is called the "fragmentary data problem."[2] The best thing to do with fragmentary data is to report them very fully and analyze them in several different ways. Our detailed knowledge of these data suggests that the problems are not serious for, while there is some variation in the pull of words and the susceptibility of Ss there is not much variation in the quality of the data. The character of the material recalled is much the same from word to word and S to S.

Number of Syllables

As the main item of evidence that S in a TOT state can recall with significant success the number of syllables in a target word he has not yet found we offer Table 1. The entries on the diagonal are instances in which guesses were correct. The order of the means of the explicit guesses is the same as the order of the actual numbers of syllables in the target words. The rank order correlation between the two is 1.0 and such a correlation is significant with a $p < .001$ (one-tailed) even when only five items are correlated. The modes of the guesses correspond exactly with the actual numbers of syllables, for the values one through three; for words of four and five syllables the modes continue to be three.

When all TOTs are combined, the contributions to the total effects of individual Ss and of individual words are unequal. We have made an analysis in which each word counts but once. This was accomplished by calculating the mean of the guesses made by all Ss for whom a particular word precipitated a TOT state and taking that mean as the score for that word. The new means calculated with all words equally weighted were, in order: 1.62; 2.30; 2.80; 3.33; and 3.50. These values are close to those of Table 1 and *rho* with the actual numbers of syllables continues to be 1.0.

[2] We wish to thank Professor Frederick Mosteller for discussing the fragmentary data problem with us.

We also made an analysis in which each *S* counts but once. This was done by calculating the mean of an *S*'s guesses for all words of one syllable, the mean for all words of two syllables, etc. In comparing the means of guesses for words of different length one can only use those *S*s who made at least one guess for each actual length to be compared. In the present data only words of two syllables and three syllables precipitated enough TOTs to yield a substantial number of such matched scores. There were 21 *S*s who made guesses for both two-syllable and three-syllable words. The simplest way to evaluate the significance of the differences in these guesses is with the Sign Test. In only 6 of 21 matched scores was the mean guess for words of two syllables larger than the mean for words of three syllables. The difference is significant with a $p = .039$ (one-tailed). For actual words that were only one syllable apart in length, *S*s were able to make a significant distinction in the correct direction when the words themselves could not be called to mind.

The 224 SS words and the 95 SM words provide supporting evidence. Words of similar sound (SS) had the same number of syllables as the target in 48% of all cases. This value is close to the 57% that were correct for explicit guesses in the main experiment and still closer to the 47% correct already reported for the pretest. The SM words provide a clear contrast; only 20% matched the number of syllables in the target. We conclude that *S* in a positive TOT state has a significant ability to recall correctly the number of syllables in the word he is trying to retrieve.

In Table 1 it can be seen that the modes of guesses exactly correspond with the actual numbers of syllables in target words for the values one through three. For still longer target words (four and five syllables) the means of guesses continue to rise but the modes stay at the value three. Words of more than three syllables are rare in English and the generic entry for such words

TABLE 1

ACTUAL NUMBERS OF SYLLABLES AND GUESSED NUMBERS FOR ALL TOTs IN THE MAIN EXPERIMENT

		Guessed numbers				No		
	1	2	3	4	5	guess	Mode	Mean
Actual numbers 1	9	7	1	0	0	0	1	1.53
2	2	55	22	2	1	5	2	2.33
3	3	19	61	10	1	5	3	2.86
4	0	2	12	6	2	3	3	3.36
5	0	0	3	0	1	1	3	3.50

may be the same as for words of three syllables; something like "three or more" may be used for all long words.

Initial Letter

Over all positive TOTs, the initial letter of the word *S* was seeking was correctly guessed 57% of the time. The pretest result was 51% correct. The results from the main experiment were analyzed with each word counting just once by entering a word's score as "correct" whenever the most common guess or the only guess was in fact correct; 62% of words were, by this reckoning, correctly guessed. The SS words had initial letters matching the initial letters of the target words in 49% of all cases. We do not know the chance level of success for this performance but with 26 letters and many words that began with uncommon letters the level must be low. Probably the results for the SM words are better than chance and yet the outcome for these words was only 8% matches.

We did an analysis of the SS and SM words, with each *S* counting just once. There were 26 *S*s who had at least one such word. For each *S* we calculated the proportion of SS words matching the target in initial letter and the same proportion for SM words. For 21 *S*s the proportions were not tied and in all but 3 cases the larger value was that of the SS words. The difference is significant by Sign Test with $p = .001$ (one-tailed).

The evidence for significantly accurate generic recall of inital letters is even stronger than for syllables. The absolute levels of success are similar but the chance baseline must be much lower for letters than for syllables because the possibilities are more numerous.

Syllabic Stress

We did not ask S to guess the stress pattern of the target word but the SS words provide relevant data. The test was limited to the syllabic location of the primary or heaviest stress for which *The American College Dictionary* was our authority. The number of SS words that could be used was limited by three considerations. (a) Words of one syllable had to be excluded because there was no possibility of variation. (b) Stress locations could only be matched if the SS word had the same number of syllables as the target, and so only such matching words could be used. (c) Invented words and foreign words could not be used because they do not appear in the dictionary. Only 49 SS words remained.

As it happened all of the target words involved (whatever their length) placed the primary stress on either the first or the second syllable. It was possible, therefore, to make a 2×2 table for the 49 pairs of target and SS words which would reveal the correspondences and noncorrespondences. As can be seen in Table 2 the SS words tended to stress the same syllable as the target words. The χ^2 for this table is 10.96 and that value is significant with $p < .001$. However, the data do not meet the independence requirement, so we cannot be sure that the matching tendency is significant. There

were not enough data to permit any other analyses, and so we are left suspecting that S in a TOT state has knowledge of the stress pattern of the target, but we are not sure of it.

Letters in Various Positions

We did not require explicit guesses for letters in positions other than the first, but the SS words provide relevant data. The test was limited to the following positions: first, second, third, third-last, second-last, and last. A target word must have at least six letters in order to provide data on the six positions; it might have any number of letters larger than six and still provide data for the six (relatively defined) positions. Accordingly we included the data for all target words having six or more letters.

Figure 1 displays the percentages of letters in each of six positions of SS words which matched the letters in the same positions of the corresponding targets. For comparison purposes these data are also provided for SM words. The SS curve is at all points above the SM curve; the two are closest together at the third-last position. The values for the last three positions of the SS curve quite closely match the values for the first three positions. The values for the last three

TABLE 2

SYLLABLES RECEIVING PRIMARY STRESS IN TARGET WORDS AND SS WORDS

		Target words	
		1st syllable	2nd syllable
SS Words	1st syllable	25	6
	2nd syllable	6	12

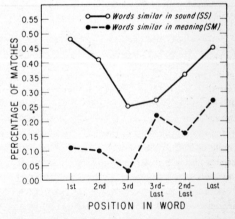

FIG. 1. Percentages of letter matches between target words and SS words for six serial positions.

positions of the SM curve, on the other hand, are well above the values for the first three positions. Consequently the *relative* superiority of the SS curve is greater in the first three positions.

The letter-position data were also analyzed in such a way as to count each target word just once, assigning each position in the target a single score representing the proportion of matches across all *S*s for that position in that word. The order of the SS and SM points is preserved in this finer analysis. We did Sign Tests comparing the SS and SM values for each of the six positions. As Fig. 1 would suggest the SS values for the first three positions all exceeded the SM values with *p*'s less than .01 (one-tailed). The SS values for the final two positions exceeded the SM values with *p*'s less than .05 (one-tailed). The SS values for the third-last position were greater than the SM values but not significantly so.

The cause of the upswing in the final three positions of the SM curve may be some difference in the distribution of information in early and late positions of English words. Probably there is less variety in the later positions. In any case the fact that the SS curve lies above the SM curve for the last three positions indicates that *S* in a TOT state has knowledge of the target in addition to his knowledge of English word structure.

Chunking of Suffixes

The request to *S* that he guess the initial letter of the target occasionally elicited a response of more than one letter; e.g., *ex* in the case of *extort* and *con* in the case of *convene*. This result suggested that some letter (or phoneme) sequences are stored as single entries having been "chunked" by long experience. We made only one test for chunking and that involved three-letter suffixes. It did not often happen that an *S* produced an SS word that matched the target with respect to all of its three last letters. The question asked of the data was whether

such three-letter matches occurred more often when the letters constituted an English suffix than when they did not. In order to determine which of the target words terminated in such a suffix, we entered *The American College Dictionary* with final trigrams. If there was an entry describing a suffix appropriate to the grammatical and semantic properties of the target we considered the trigram to be a suffix. There were 20 words that terminated in a suffix, including *fawning, unctuous,* and *philatelist.*

Of 93 SS words produced in response to a target terminating in a suffix, 30 matched the target in their final three letters. Of 130 SS words supplied in response to a target that did not terminate in a suffix only 5 matched the target in their final three letters. The data were also analyzed in a way that counts each *S* just once and uses only *S*s who produced SS words in response to both kinds of target. A Sign Test was made of the difference between matches of suffixes and matches of endings that were not suffixes; the former were more common with $p = .059$ (one-tailed). A comparable Sign Test for SM words was very far from significance. We conclude that suffix-chunking probably plays a role in generic recall.

Proximity to the Target and Quality of Information

There were three varieties of positive TOT states: (1) Cases in which *S recognized* the word read by *E* as the word he had been seeking; (2) Cases in which *S recalled* the intended word before it was read out; (3) Cases in which *S recalled* the word he had been seeking before *E* read the intended word and the recalled word was not the same as the word read. Since *S* in a TOT state of either type 2 or type 3 reached the target before the intended word was read and *S* in a TOT state of type 1 did not, the TOTs of the second and third types may be considered "nearer" the target than TOTs of the first type. We have no basis for ordering types 2 and 3 relative to one another. We predicted that Ss in the two kinds of TOT state that ended in recall (types 2 and 3) would produce more accurate information about the target than Ss in the TOT state that ended in recognition (type 1).

The prediction was tested on the explicit guesses of initial letters since these were the most complete and sensitive data. There were 138 guesses from Ss in a type 1 state and 58 of these, or 42%, were correct. There were 36 guesses from Ss in a type 2 state and, of these, 20, or 56%, were correct. There were 59 guesses from Ss in a type 3 state and of these 39, or 66%, were correct. We also analyzed the results in such a way as to count each word only once. The percentages correct were: for type 1, 50%; type 2, 62%; type 3, 63%. Finally, we performed an analysis counting each S just once but averaging together type 2 and type 3 results in order to bring a maximum number of Ss into the comparison. The combining action is justified since both type 2 and type 3 were states ending in recall. A Sign Test of the differences showed that guesses were more accurate in the states that ended in recall than in the states that ended in recognition; one-tailed $p < .01$. Supplementary analyses with SS and SM words confirmed these results. We conclude that when S is nearer his target his generic recall is more accurate than when he is farther from the target.

Special interest attaches to the results from type 2 TOTs. In the method of our experiment there is nothing to guarantee that when S said he recognized a word he had really done so. Perhaps when E read out a word, S could not help thinking that that was the word he had in mind. We ourselves do not believe anything of the sort happened. The single fact that most Ss claimed fewer than five positive TOTs in a 2-hr period argues against any such effect. Still it is reassuring to have the 36 type 2 cases in which S recalled the intended word *before* it was read. The fact that 56% of the guesses of initial letters made in type 2 states were correct is hard-core evidence of generic recall. It may be worth adding that 65% of the guesses of the number of syllables for type 2 cases were correct.

Judgments of the Proximity of SS Words

The several comparisons we have made of SS and SM words demonstrate that when recall is imminent S can distinguish among the words that come to mind those that resemble the target in form from those that do not resemble the target in form. There is a second kind of evidence which shows that S can tell when he is getting close (or "warm").

In 15 instances Ss rated two or more SS words for comparative similarity to the target. Our analysis contrasts those rated "most similar" (1) with those rated next most similar (2). Since there were very few words rated (3) we attempted no analysis of them. Similarity points were given for all the features of a word that have now been demonstrated to play a part in generic recall—with the single exception of stress. Stress had to be disregarded because some of the words were invented and their stress patterns were unknown.

The problem was to compare pairs of SS words, rated 1 and 2, for overall similarity to the target. We determined whether each member matched the target in number of syllables. If one did and the other did not, then a single similarity point was assigned the word that matched. For each word, we counted, beginning with the initial letter, the number of consecutive letters in common with the target. The word having the longer sequence that matched the target earned one similarity point. An exactly comparable procedure was followed for sequences starting from the final letter. In sum, each word in a pair could receive from zero to three similarity points.

We made Sign Tests comparing the total scores for words rated most like the target (1) and words rated next most like the target (2). This test was only slightly inappropriate since only two target words occurred twice in the set of 15 and only one S repeated in the set. Ten of 12 differences were in the predicted direction and the one-tailed $p = .019$. It is of some interest that similarity points awarded on the basis of letters in the middle of the words did not even go in the right direction. Figure 1 has already indicated that they also do not figure in Ss' judgments of the comparative similarity to the target of pairs of SS words. Our conclusion is that S at a given distance from the target can accurately judge which of two words that come to mind is more like the target and that he does so in terms of the features of words that appear in generic recall.

Conclusions

When complete recall of a word has not occurred but is felt to be imminent there is likely to be accurate generic recall. Generic recall of the *abstract form* variety is evidenced by S's knowledge of the number of syllables in the target and of the location of the primary stress. Generic recall of the *partial* variety is evidenced by S's knowledge of letters in the target word. This knowledge shows a bowed serial-position effect since it is better for the ends of a word than for the middle and somewhat better for beginning positions than for final positions. The accuracy of generic recall is greater when S is near the target (complete recall is imminent) than when S is far from the target. A person experiencing generic recall is able to judge the relative similarity to the target of words that occur to him and these judgments are based on the features of words that figure in partial and abstract form recall.

DISCUSSION

The facts of generic recall are relevant to theories of speech perception, reading, the understanding of sentences, and the organization of memory. We have not worked out all the implications. In this section we first attempt a model of the TOT process and then try to account for the existence of generic memory.

A Model of the Process

Let us suppose (with Katz and Fodor, 1963, and many others) that our long-term memory for words and definitions is organized into the functional equivalent of a dictionary. In real dictionaries, those that are books, entries are ordered alphabetically and bound in place. Such an arrangement is too simple and too inflexible to serve as a model for a mental dictionary. We will suppose that words are entered on keysort cards instead of pages and that the cards are punched for various features of the words entered. With real cards, paper ones, it is possible to retrieve from the total deck any subset punched for a common feature by putting a metal rod through the proper hole. We will suppose that there is in the mind some speedier equivalent of this retrieval technique.

The model will be described in terms of a single example. When the target word was *sextant*, Ss heard the definition: "A navigational instrument used in measuring angular distances, especially the altitude of sun, moon, and stars at sea." This definition precipitated a TOT state in 9 Ss of the total 56. The SM words included: *astrolabe, compass, dividers,* and *protractor.* The SS words included: *secant, sextet,* and *sexton.*

The problem begins with a definition rather than a word and so S must enter his dictionary backwards, or in a way that would be backwards and quite impossible for the dictionary that is a book. It is not impossible with keysort cards, providing we suppose that the cards are punched for some set of semantic features. Perhaps these are the semantic "markers" that Katz and Fodor (1963) postulate in their account of the comprehension of sentences. We will imagine that it is somehow possible to extract from the definition a set of markers and that these are, in the present case: "navigation, instrument, having to do with geometry." Metal rods thrust into the holes for each of these features might fish up such a collection of entries as: *astrolabe, compass, dividers,* and *protractor.* This first retrieval, which is in response to the definition, must be semantically based and it will not, therefore, account for the appearance of such SS words as *sextet* and *sexton.*

There are four major kinds of outcome of the

first retrieval and these outcomes correspond with the four main things that happen to Ss in the TOT experiment. We will assume that a definition of each word retrieved is entered on its card and that it is possible to check the input definition against those on the cards. The first possible outcome is that *sextant* is retrieved along with *compass* and *astrolabe* and the others and that the definitions are specific enough so that the one entered for *sextant* registers as matching the input and all the others as not-matching. This is the case of correct recall; S has found a word that matches the definition and it is the intended word. The second possibility is that *sextant* is not among the words retrieved and, in addition, the definitions entered for those retrieved are so imprecise that one of them (the definition for *compass*, for example) registers as matching the input. In this case S thinks he has found the target though he really has not. The third possibility is that *sextant* is not among the words retrieved, but the definitions entered for those retrieved are specific enough so that none of them will register a match with the input. In this case, S does not know the word and realizes the fact. The above three outcomes are the common ones and none of them represents a TOT state.

In the TOT case the first retrieval must include a card with the definition of *sextant* entered on it but with the word itself incompletely entered. The card might, for instance, have the following information about the word: two-syllables, initial s, final t. The entry would be a punchcard equivalent of S___T. Perhaps an incomplete entry of this sort is James's "singularly definite gap" and the basis for generic recall.

The S with a correct definition, matching the input, and an incomplete word entry will know that he knows the word, will feel that he almost has it, that it is on the tip of his tongue. If he is asked to guess the number of syllables and the initial letter he should, in the case we have imagined, be able to do so. He should also be able to produce SS words. The features that appear in the incomplete entry (two-syllables, initial s, and final t) can be used as the basis for a second retrieval. The subset of cards defined by the intersection of all three features would include cards for *secant* and *sextet*. If one feature were not used then *sexton* would be added to the set.

Which of the facts about the TOT state can now be accounted for? We know that Ss were able, when they had not recalled a target, to distinguish between words resembling the target in sound (SS words) and words resembling the target in meaning only (SM words). The basis for this distinction in the model would seem to be the distinction between the first and second retrievals. Membership in the

first subset retrieved defines SM words and membership in the second subset defines SS words.

We know that when S had produced several SS words but had not recalled the target he could sometimes accurately rank-order the SS words for similarity to the target. The model offers an account of this ranking performance. If the incomplete entry for *sextant* includes three features of the word then SS words having only one or two of these features (e.g., *sexton*) should be judged less similar to the target than SS words having all three of them (e.g., *secant*).

When an SS word has all of the features of the incomplete entry (as do *secant* and *sextet* in our example) what prevents its being mistaken for the target? Why did not the S who produced *sextet* think that the word was "right?" Because of the definitions. The forms meet all the requirements of the incomplete entry but the definitions do not match.

The TOT state often ended in recognition; i.e., S failed to recall the word but when E read out *sextant* S recognized it as the word he had been seeking. The model accounts for this outcome as follows. Suppose that there is only the incomplete entry S___T in memory, plus the definition. The E now says (in effect) that there exists a word *sextant* which has the definition in question. The word *sextant* then satisfies all the data points available to S; it has the right number of syllables, the right initial letter, the right final letter, and it is said to have the right definition. The result is recognition.

The proposed account has some testable implications. Suppose that E were to read out, when recall failed, not the correct word *sextant* but an invented word like *sekrant* or *saktint* which satisfies the incomplete entry as well as does *sextant* itself. If S had nothing but the incomplete entry and E's testimony to guide him then he should "recognize" the invented words just as he recognizes *sextant*.

The account we have given does not accord with intuition. Our intuitive notion of recognition is that the features which could not be called were actually in storage but less accessible than the features that were recalled. To stay with our example, intuition suggests that the features of *sextant* that could not be recalled, the letters between the first and the last, were entered on the card but were less "legible" than the recalled features. We might imagine them printed in small letters and faintly. When, however, the E reads out the word *sextant*, then S can make out the less legible parts of his entry and, since the total entry matches E's word, S recognizes it. This sort of recognition should be "tighter" than the one described previously. *Sekrant* and *saktint* would be rejected.

We did not try the effect of invented words and we do not know how they would have been received but among the outcomes of the actual experiment there is one that strongly favors the faint-entry theory. Subjects in a TOT state, after all, sometimes recalled the target word without any prompting. The incomplete entry theory does not admit of such a possibility. If we suppose that the entry is not S___T but something more like S*ex tan*T (with the italicized lower-case letters representing the faint-entry section) we must still explain how it happens that the faintly entered, and at first inaccessible, middle letters are made accessible in the case of recall.

Perhaps it works something like this. The features that are first recalled operate as we have suggested, to retrieve a set of SS words. Whenever an SS word (such as *secant*) includes middle letters that are matched in the faintly entered section of the target then those faintly entered letters become accessible. The match brings out the missing parts the way heat brings out anything written in lemon juice. In other words, when *secant* is retrieved the target entry grows from S*ex tan*T to SE*x t*ANT. The retrieval of *sextet* brings out the remaining letters and *S* recalls the complete word—*sextant*.

It is now possible to explain the one as yet unexplained outcome of the TOT experiment. Subjects whose state ended in recall had, before they found the target, more correct information about it than did *S*s whose state ended in recognition. More correct information means fewer features to be brought out by duplication in SS words and so should mean a greater likelihood that all essential features will be brought out in a short period of time.

All of the above assumes that each word is entered in memory just once, on a single card. There is another possibility. Suppose that there are entries for *sextant* on several different cards. They might all be incomplete, but at different points, or, some might be incomplete and one or more of them complete. The several cards would be punched for different semantic markers and perhaps for different associations so that the entry recovered would vary with the rule of retrieval. With this conception we do not require the notion of faint entry. The difference between features commonly recalled, such as the first and last letters, and features that are recalled with difficulty or perhaps only recognized, can be rendered in another way. The more accessible features are entered on more cards or else the cards on which they appear are punched for more markers; in effect, they are wired into a more extended associative net.

The Reason for Generic Recall

In adult minds words are stored in both visual and auditory terms and between the two there are complicated rules of translation. Generic recall involves letters (or phonemes), affixes, syllables, and stress location. In this section we will discuss only letters (legible forms) and will attempt to explain a single effect—the serial position effect in the recall of letters. It is not clear how far the explanation can be extended.

In brief overview this is the argument. The design of the English language is such that one word is usually distinguished from all others in a more-than-minimal way, i.e., by more than a single letter in a single position. It is consequently *possible* to recognize words when one has not stored the complete letter sequence. The evidence is that we do not store the complete sequence if we do not have to. We begin by attending chiefly to initial and final letters and storing these. The order of attention and of storage favors the ends of words because the ends carry more information than the middles. An incomplete entry will serve for recognition, but if words are to be produced (or recalled) they must be stored in full. For most words, then, it is eventually necessary to attend to the middle letters. Since end letters have been attended to from the first they should always be more clearly entered or more elaborately connected than middle letters. When recall is required, of words that are not very familiar to *S*, as it was in our experiment, the end letters should often be accessible when the middle are not.

In building pronounceable sequences the English language, like all other languages, utilizes only a small fraction of its combinatorial possibilities (Hockett, 1958). If a language used all possible sequences of phonemes (or letters) its words could be shorter, but they would be much more vulnerable to misconstruction. A change of any single letter would result in reception of a different word. As matters are actually arranged, most changes result in no word at all; for example: *textant, sixtant, sektant.* Our words are highly redundant and fairly indestructible.

Underwood (1963) has made a distinction for the learning of nonsense syllables between the "nominal" stimulus which is the syllable presented and the "functional" stimulus which is the set of characteristics of the syllable actually used to cue the response. Underwood reviews evidence showing that college students learning paired-associates do not learn any more of a stimulus trigram than they have to. If, for instance, each of a set of stimulus trigrams has a different initial letter, then *S*s are not likely to learn letters other than the first, since they do not need them.

Feigenbaum (1963) has written a computer program (EPAM) which simulates the selective-attention aspect of verbal learning as well as many other aspects. ". . . EPAM has a *noticing order for letters of syllables,* which prescribes at any moment a letter-scanning sequence for the matching process. Because it is observed that subjects generally consider end letters before middle letters, the noticing order is initialized as follows: first letter, third letter, second letter" (p. 304). We believe that the differential recall of letters in various positions, revealed in Fig. 1 of this paper, is to be explained by the operation in the perception of real words of a rule very much like Feigenbaum's.

Feigenbaum's EPAM is so written as to make it possible for the noticing rule to be changed by experience. If the middle position were consistently the position that differentiated syllables, the computer would learn to look there first. We suggest that the human tendency to look first at the beginning of a word, then at the end and finally the middle has "grown" in response to the distribution of information in words. Miller and Friedman (1957) asked English speakers to guess letters for various open positions in segments of English text that were 5, 7, or 11 characters long. The percentages of correct first guesses show a very clear serial position effect for segments of all three lengths. Success was lowest in the early positions, next lowest in the final positions, and at a maximum in the middle positions. Therefore, information was greatest at the start of a word, next greatest at the end, and least in the middle. Attention needs to be turned where information is, to the parts of the word that cannot be guessed. The Miller and Friedman segments did not necessarily break at word boundaries but their discovery that the middle positions of continuous text are more easily guessed than the ends applies to words.

Is there any evidence that speakers of English do attend first to the ends of English words? There is no evidence that the eye fixations of adult readers consistently favor particular parts of words (Woodworth and Schlosberg, 1954). However, it is not eye fixation that we have in mind. A considerable stretch of text can be taken in from a single fixation point. We are suggesting that there is selection within this stretch, selection accomplished centrally; perhaps by a mechanism like Broadbent's (1958) "biased filter."

Bruner and O'Dowd (1958) studied word perception with tachistoscopic exposures too brief to permit more than one fixation. In each word presented there was a single reversal of two letters and the *S* knew this. His task was to identify the *actual* English word responding as quickly as possible. When the *actual* word was AVIATION, *S*s were presented with one of the following: VAIATION, AVITAION, AVIATINO. Identification of the actual word as AVIATION was best when *S* saw AVITAION, next best when he saw AVIATINO, and most difficult when he saw VAIATION. In general, a reversal of the two initial letters made identification most difficult, reversal of the last two letters made it somewhat less difficult, reversal in the middle made least difficulty. This is what should happen if words are first scanned initially, then finally, then medially. But the scanning cannot be a matter of eye movements; it must be more central.

Selective attention to the ends of words should lead to the entry of these parts into the mental dictionary, in advance of the middle parts. However, we ordinarily need to know more than the ends of words. Underwood has pointed out (1963), in connection with paired-associate learning, that while partial knowledge may be enough for a stimulus syllable which need only be recognized it will not suffice for a response item which must be produced. The case is simi'ar for natural language. In order to speak one must know all of a word. However, the words of the present study were low-frequency words, words likely to be in the passive or recognition vocabularies of the college-student *S*s but not in their active vocabularies; stimulus items, in effect, rather than response items. If knowledge of the parts of new words begins at the ends and moves toward the middle we might expect a word like *numismatics,* which was on our list, to be still registered as NUM___ICS. Reduced entries of this sort would in many contexts serve to retrieve the definition.

The argument is reinforced by a well-known effect in spelling. Jensen (1962) has analyzed thousands of spelling errors for words of 7, 9, or 11 letters made by children in the eighth and tenth grades and by junior college freshmen. A striking serial position effect appears in all his sets of data such that errors are most common in the middle of the word, next most common at the end, and least common at the start. These results are as they should be if the order of attention and entry of information is first, last, and then, middle. Jensen's results show us what happens when children are forced to produce words that are still on the recognition level. His results remind us of those bluebooks in which students who are uncertain of the spelling of a word write the first and last letters with great clarity and fill in the middle with indecipherable squiggles. That is what should happen when a word that can be only partially recalled must be produced in its entirety. End letters and a stretch of squiggles may, however, be quite adequate for recognition purposes. In the TOT experiment we have perhaps placed adult *S*s in a situation comparable to that created for children by Jensen's spelling tests.

There are two points to clarify and the argument is finished. The *S*s in our experiment were college students, and so in order to obtain words on the margin of knowledge we had to use words that are very infrequent in English as a whole. It is not our thought, however, that the TOT phenomenon occurs only with rare words. The absolute location of the margin of word knowledge is a function of *S*'s age and education, and so with other *S*s we would expect to obtain TOT states for words more frequent in English. Finally the need to produce (or recall) a word is not the only factor that is likely to encourage registration of its middle letters. The amount of detail needed to specify a word uniquely must increase with the total number of words known, the number from which any one is to be distinguished. Consequently the growth of vocabulary, as well as the need to recall, should have some power to force attention into the middle of a word.

REFERENCES

BARNHART, C. L. (Ed.) *The American college dictionary.* New York: Harper, 1948.

BROADBENT, D. E. *Perception and communication.* New York: Macmillan, 1958.

BRUNER, J. S., AND O'DOWD, D. A note on the informativeness of words. *Language and Speech,* 1958, **1**, 98-101.

FEIGENBAUM, E. A. The simulation of verbal learning behavior. In E. A. Feigenbaum and J. Feldman (Eds.) *Computers and thought.* New York: McGraw-Hill, 1963. Pp. 297-309.

HOCKETT, C. F. *A course in modern linguistics.* New York: Macmillan, 1958.

JAMES, W. *The principles of psychology,* Vol. I. New York: Holt, 1893.

JENSEN, A. R. Spelling errors and the serial-position effect. *J. educ. Psychol.,* 1962, **53**, 105-109.

KATZ, J. J., AND FODOR, J. A. The structure of a semantic theory. *Language,* 1963, **39**, 170-210.

MILLER, G. A., AND FRIEDMAN, ELIZABETH A. The reconstruction of mutilated English texts. *Inform. Control,* 1957, **1**, 38-55.

THORNDIKE, E. L., AND LORGE, I. *The teacher's word book of 30,000 words.* New York: Columbia Univer., 1952.

UNDERWOOD, B. J. Stimulus selection in verbal learning. In C. N. Cofer and B. S. Musgrave (Eds.) *Verbal behavior and learning: problems and processes.* New York: McGraw-Hill, 1963. Pp. 33-48.

WENZL, A. Empirische und theoretische Beiträge zur Erinnerungsarbeit bei erschwerter Wortfindung. *Arch. ges. Psychol.,* 1932, **85**, 181-218.

WENZL, A. Empirische und theoretische Beiträge zur Erinnerungsarbeit bei erschwerter Wortfindung. *Arch. ges. Psychol.,* 1936, **97**, 294-318.

WOODWORTH, R. S. *Psychology.* (3rd ed.). New York: Holt, 1934.

WOODWORTH, R. S., AND SCHLOSBERG, H. *Experimental psychology.* (Rev. ed.). New York: Holt, 1954.

INDEX

acoustic similarity, 128
associationism, 1
association studies, 145
auditory registration, 29, 125
auditory-verbal-linguistic store,
  the, 25, 33-6
auditory versus visual presentation,
  117-22, 128
availability and accessibility,
  164-5, 194-5, 202

box models, 6
buffer mechanisms, 45-7

category names, 170, 174, 195 ff.
category recall, 185, 195, 202
category words, 98-100, 130 ff.,
  195 ff.
chunking strategies, 48-9
clustering, 98-9, 145, 155ff., 173
coding
  the concept of, 105
  representational, 107
  processes, 48
  and language, 186
  see also encoding
comparison of word meanings,
  234 ff.
concept overlap, 238 ff.
constructive approach to sentence
  memory, the, see sentence
  memory
continuous recognition, 145-6
control processes, 39-40, 41-9

decay
  of memory traces, 9
  rate of, 26
  of visual images, 28, 122-3

digit-span studies, 42-3
dimensional shifts, 133 ff.

encoding, 130 ff.
  and connotation, 133-5
  and consciousness, 141-2
  by grammatical class, 132-3
  multidimensional, 142-3
  phonemic, 85-7
  semantic, 85-7
  and word perception, 140
  see also under primary memory
encoding specificity, 106, 170
EPAM, 254-5
episodic memory, 186

false recognition, 151, 152
free recall
  and auditory presentation, 69,
    72
  and the serial position curve,
    58-66
  clustering in, 155, 173
  and distinctive items, 95-6
  immediate and final, 71, 72-3
  incidental tasks, 161-3
  input and response modes, 70-1
  learning, 189-90
  organization in, 154, 155
  and output position, 71-2, 73,
    94, 100
  and primary memory items,
    68-72
  rehearsal processes in, 6, 88-101
  effectiveness of, 193
  and shift effect, 138
  and trace storage, 173 ff.
  and two-store systems, 5-6

generic recall, 244, 251 ff.